ANNUAL EDITIONS

Human Development 09/10

2010 Update

Thirty-Eighth Edition

EDITOR

Karen L. Freiberg

University of Maryland, Baltimore County

Dr. Karen Freiberg has an interdisciplinary educational and employment background in nursing, education, and developmental psychology. She received her BS from the State University of New York at Plattsburgh, her MS from Cornell University, and her PhD from Syracuse University. Dr. Freiberg has worked as a school nurse, a pediatric nurse, a public health nurse for the Navajo Indians, an associate project director for a child development clinic, a researcher in several areas of child development, and a university professor. She is the author of an award-winning textbook, *Human Development: A Life-Span Approach,* which is now in its fourth edition. Dr. Freiberg is currently on the faculty at the University of Maryland, Baltimore County.

 **Higher Education**

Boston   Burr Ridge, IL   Dubuque, IA   New York   San Francisco   St. Louis
Bangkok   Bogotá   Caracas   Kuala Lumpur   Lisbon   London   Madrid   Mexico City
Milan   Montreal   New Delhi   Santiago   Seoul   Singapore   Sydney   Taipei   Toronto

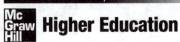

ANNUAL EDITIONS: HUMAN DEVELOPMENT (2010 UPDATE), THIRTY-EIGHTH EDITION

Published by McGraw-Hill, a business unit of The McGraw-Hill Companies, Inc., 1221 Avenue of the Americas, New York, NY 10020.

Some ancillaries, including electronic and print components, may not be available to customers outside the United States.

Annual Editions® is a registered trademark of The McGraw-Hill Companies, Inc.
Annual Editions is published by the **Contemporary Learning Series** group within the McGraw-Hill Higher Education division.

1 2 3 4 5 6 7 8 9 0 QPD/QPD 0 9

ISBN 978–0–07–812777–9
MHID 0–07–812777–7
ISSN 0278–4661

Managing Editor: *Larry Loeppke*
Senior Managing Editor: *Faye Schilling*
Developmental Editor: *Dave Welsh*
Editorial Assistant: *Nancy Meissner*
Production Service Assistant: *Rita Hingtgen*
Permissions Coordinator: *DeAnna Dausener*
Senior Marketing Manager: *Julie Keck*
Marketing Communications Specialist: *Mary Klein*
Marketing Coordinator: *Alice Link*
Project Manager: *Sandy Wille*
Design Specialist: *Tara McDermott*
Senior Production Supervisor: *Laura Fuller*
Cover Graphics: *Kristine Jubeck*

Compositor: Laserwords Private Limited
Cover Image: © Comstock/PunchStock/RF (inset); © Getty Images/RF (background)

Library in Congress Cataloging-in-Publication Data
Main entry under title: Annual Editions: Human Development, (2010 update). 2009/2010.
1. Human Development—Periodicals. I. Freiberg, Karen L., *comp*. II. Title: Human Development.
658'.05

www.mhhe.com

Editors/Advisory Board

Members of the Advisory Board are instrumental in the final selection of articles for each edition of ANNUAL EDITIONS. Their review of articles for content, level, currentness, and appropriateness provides critical direction to the editor and staff. We think that you will find their careful consideration well reflected in this volume.

Preface

In publishing ANNUAL EDITIONS we recognize the enormous role played by the magazines, newspapers, and journals of the public press in providing current, first-rate educational information in a broad spectrum of interest areas. Many of these articles are appropriate for students, researchers, and professionals seeking accurate, current material to help bridge the gap between principles and theories and the real world. These articles, however, become more useful for study when those of lasting value are carefully collected, organized, indexed, and reproduced in a low-cost format, which provides easy and permanent access when the material is needed. That is the role played by ANNUAL EDITIONS.

Science, technology, and education have dramatically altered the process of human development in the past millennium. Physical aging has been slowed, and the average survival age lengthened, by improved living conditions, health care, and nutrition. Emotional well-being, stress management, and conflict resolution are the focus of more attention. Social organizations include more tolerance of diversity. The borders separating cultures have blurred due to instant communications and rapid travel opportunities. Even our spiritual development has been transformed by more contemplation of the essence of life. The cognitive revolution of our time allows each of us greater perception of our humanity.

This compendium of articles about human development covers the life span, considering the physical, cognitive, psychosocial, and spiritual components. Development should be viewed as a circle of life. At conception a new human being is created, but each unique individual carries genetic materials from biological relatives alive and dead, and may pass them on to future generations.

Development through infancy proceeds from sensory and motor responses to verbal communication, thinking, conceptualizing, and learning from others. Childhood brings rapid physical growth, improved cognition, and social learning. Adolescence is when the individual begins to test out sexual maturity. Values and identity are questioned. Separation from parents begins. Under the influence of sex hormones, the brain undergoes multiple changes. Emotions may fluctuate rapidly.

Early adulthood usually establishes the individual as an independent person. Employment, further education, and the beginning of one's own family are all aspects of setting up a distinct life, with both its own characteristics and the characteristics and customs of previous generations.

During middle adulthood persons have new situations to face, new transitions to cope with. Children grow up and leave home. Signs of aging become apparent. Relationships change, roles shift. New abilities may be found and opportunities created.

Finally, during late adulthood, people assess what they've accomplished. Some are pleased. Some feel they could have done more or lived differently. In the best of instances, individuals accept who they are and are comfortable with themselves.

As you explore this anthology, you will discover that many articles ask questions that have no answers. As a student, I felt frustrated by such writing. I wanted answers, right answers, right away. However, over time I learned that lessons that are necessary to acquire maturity include accepting relativity and acknowledging extenuatory circumstances. Life frequently has no right or wrong answers, but rather various alternatives with multiple consequences. Instead of right versus wrong, a more helpful consideration is "What will bring about the greater good for the greater number?" Controversies, whether about terrorism or war, good or evil, stem cells or organ transplants, body-soul separate or unified, can promote healthy discussions. Different viewpoints should be weighed against societal standards. Different philosophies should be celebrated for what they offer in creating intellectual abilities in human beings to adapt to changing circumstances.

The Greek sophists were philosophers who specialized in argumentation, rhetoric (using language persuasively), and dialectics (finding synthesis or common ground between contradictory ideas). From their skilled thinking came the derogatory term "sophism," suggesting that some argumentation was deceptive or fallacious rather than wise. The term sophomore, which in this era means second-year student, comes from this variation of sophism, combining "sophos" (wise) with "moros" (dull or foolish). "Sophomoric" translates to exhibiting immaturity and lack of judgment, while "sophisticated" translates to having acquired knowledge. Educators strive to have their students move from knowing all the answers (sophomoric) to asking intelligent questions (sophisticated).

This anthology is dedicated to seekers of knowledge and searchers for what is true, right, or lasting. To this end, those articles have been selected that provide you with information that will stimulate discussion and give your thoughts direction, but not those that tell you what to think. May you be "seeking" learners all through your own years of human development. May each suggestive answer you discover open your mind to more erudite (instructive) learning, questioning, and sophistication.

Karen Freiberg

Karen Freiberg, PhD
Editor

Contents

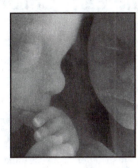

UNIT 1
Genetic and Prenatal Influences on Development

Part A. Genetic Influences

1. The Identity Dance, Gunjan Sinha, *Psychology Today,* March/April 2004

Identical twins are clones with the same *genetic profiles.* Life experience, therefore, must matter if identical twins develop unlike *emotions, health problems,* and *personalities.* This article reports scientific evidence that genes have the equivalent of molecular "switches" that can be turned on or off by *prenatal* and postnatal environmental factors. Several unlike identical twins are described.

2. The Power to Divide, Rick Weiss, *National Geographic,* July 2005

The United States under Bush limits federal funding of research on *stem cells.* Some states (e.g., California) and several countries (e.g., Singapore, Korea, U.K.) are making progress in therapeutic cloning of cells needed by diabetics, heart attack patients, and others. Some people with regenerated cells are already thriving. Will *ethicists* allow this research to continue? Should they?

Part B. Prenatal Influences

3. The Mystery of Fetal Life: Secrets of the Womb, John Pekkanen, *Washingtonian,* September 2001

Environment affects *prenatal development.* This article reviews known dangers (e.g., *alcohol and drug use,* viral infections) and recently discovered endocrine disrupters (e.g., chemicals in our air, food, and water). The author gives advice on *exercise, nutrition,* and *health maintenance* to optimize the *physical and cognitive status* of the offspring.

4. Fat, Carbs and the Science of Conception, Jorge E. Chavarro, Walter C. Willett, and Patrick J. Skerrett, *Newsweek,* December 10, 2007

Pregnancy is adversely affected by age, disease, *stress,* and environmental toxins. New research derived from computer *technology* using 32 years of data from Harvard's Nurses' Health Study shows that *nutrition* and *exercise* enhance it. This article explains how to choose high quality fats and carbs and optimally balance glycemic load.

5. The Hunt for Golden Eggs, Brooke Lea Foster, *Washingtonian,* July 2007

As explained in this article, thousands of infertile couples become *pregnant* each year with eggs donated by healthy young *women* with desirable *genetic* profiles. The *ethics* of donating ova for in vitro fertilization are being questioned for religious reasons, and for the prices paid. Tall, blonde, educated donors may earn the most. Donors say they want to help. There are no current regulations for donations in the United States.

The concepts in bold italics are developed in the article. For further expansion, please refer to the Topic Guide.

UNIT 2
Development During Infancy and Early Childhood

The concepts in bold italics are developed in the article. For further expansion, please refer to the Topic Guide.

UNIT 3
Development During Childhood: Cognition and Schooling

The concepts in bold italics are developed in the article. For further expansion, please refer to the Topic Guide.

UNIT 4
Development During Childhood: Family and Culture

The concepts in bold italics are developed in the article. For further expansion, please refer to the Topic Guide.

UNIT 5
Development During Adolescence and Young Adulthood

The concepts in bold italics are developed in the article. For further expansion, please refer to the Topic Guide.

UNIT 6
Development During Middle and Late Adulthood

The concepts in bold italics are developed in the article. For further expansion, please refer to the Topic Guide.

The concepts in bold italics are developed in the article. For further expansion, please refer to the Topic Guide.

Correlation Guide

The *Annual Editions* series provides students with convenient, inexpensive access to current, carefully selected articles from the public press. **Annual Editions: Human Development 09/10 (2010 Update)** is an easy-to-use reader that presents articles on important topics such as *genetics and prenatal development, school-age development, family and culture's roles in development, later-life development,* and many more. For more information on *Annual Editions* and other *McGraw-Hill Contemporary Learning Series* titles, visit www.mhcls.com.

This convenient guide matches the units in **Annual Editions: Human Development 09/10 (2010 Update)** with the corresponding chapters in three of our best-selling McGraw-Hill Human Development textbooks by Santrock and Dacey et al.

Annual Editions: Human Development 09/10 (2010 Update)	**A Topical Approach to Life-Span Development, 4/e by Santrock**	**Essentials of Life-Span Development by Santrock**	**Human Development Across the Lifespan, 7/e by Dacey et al.**
Unit 1: Genetic and Prenatal Influences on Development	**Chapter 2:** Biological Beginnings	**Chapter 2:** Biological Beginnings	**Chapter 3:** The Biological Basis of Development **Chapter 4:** Pregnancy and Birth
Unit 2: Development During Infancy and Early Childhood	**Chapter 2:** Biological Beginnings **Chapter 4:** Health **Chapter 5:** Motor, Sensory, and Perceptual Development **Chapter 7:** Information Processing **Chapter 8:** Intelligence **Chapter 9:** Language Development **Chapter 10:** Emotional Development **Chapter 12:** Gender and Sexuality **Chapter 15:** Peers and the Sociocultural World	**Chapter 3:** Physical and Cognitive Development in Infancy **Chapter 4:** Socioemotional Development in Infancy **Chapter 5:** Physical and Cognitive Development in Early Childhood **Chapter 6:** Socioemotional Development in Early Childhood	**Chapter 5:** Physical and Cognitive Development in Infancy **Chapter 6:** Psychosocial Development in Infancy **Chapter 7:** Physical and Cognitive Development in Early Childhood **Chapter 8:** Psychosocial Development in Early Childhood
Unit 3: Development During Childhood: Cognition and Schooling	**Chapter 3:** Physical Development and Biological Aging **Chapter 6:** Cognitive Developmental Approaches **Chapter 7:** Information Processing **Chapter 8:** Intelligence **Chapter 16:** Schools, Achievement, and Work	**Chapter 1:** Introduction **Chapter 5:** Physical and Cognitive Development in Early Childhood **Chapter 7:** Physical and Cognitive Development in Middle and Late Childhood	**Chapter 7:** Physical and Cognitive Development in Early Childhood **Chapter 9:** Physical and Cognitive Development in Middle Childhood **Chapter 10:** Psychosocial Development in Middle Childhood
Unit 4: Development During Childhood: Family and Culture	**Chapter 2:** Biological Beginnings **Chapter 3:** Physical Development and Biological Aging **Chapter 4:** Health **Chapter 9:** Language Development **Chapter 10:** Emotional Development **Chapter 12:** Gender and Sexuality **Chapter 16:** Schools, Achievement, and Work	**Chapter 4:** Socioemotional Development in Infancy **Chapter 6:** Socioemotional Development in Early Childhood **Chapter 8:** Socioemotional Development in Middle and Late Childhood	**Chapter 8:** Psychosocial Development in Early Childhood **Chapter 10:** Psychosocial Development in Middle Childhood
Unit 5: Development During Adolescence and Young Adulthood	**Chapter 3:** Physical Development and Biological Aging **Chapter 4:** Health **Chapter 7:** Information Processing **Chapter 8:** Intelligence **Chapter 9:** Language Development **Chapter 10:** Emotional Development **Chapter 12:** Gender and Sexuality **Chapter 14:** Families, Lifestyles, and Parenting **Chapter 15:** Peers and the Sociocultural World	**Chapter 9:** Physical and Cognitive Development in Adolescence **Chapter 10:** Socioemotional Development in Adolescence **Chapter 11:** Physical and Cognitive Development in Early Adulthood **Chapter 12:** Socioemotional Development in Early Adulthood	**Chapter 11:** Physical and Cognitive Development in Adolescence **Chapter 12:** Psychosocial Development in Adolescence **Chapter 13:** Physical and Cognitive Development in Early Adulthood **Chapter 14:** Psychosocial Development in Early Adulthood
Unit 6: Development During Middle and Late Adulthood	**Chapter 3:** Physical Development and Biological Aging **Chapter 4:** Health **Chapter 7:** Information Processing **Chapter 8:** Intelligence **Chapter 9:** Language Development **Chapter 10:** Emotional Development **Chapter 12:** Gender and Sexuality **Chapter 15:** Peers and the Sociocultural World **Chapter 17:** Death, Dying, and Grieving	**Chapter 13:** Physical and Cognitive Development in Middle Adulthood **Chapter 14:** Socioemotional Development in Middle Adulthood **Chapter 15:** Physical and Cognitive Development in Late Adulthood **Chapter 16:** Socioemotional Development in Late Adulthood	**Chapter 15:** Physical and Cognitive Development in Middle Adulthood **Chapter 16:** Psychosocial Development in Middle Adulthood **Chapter 17:** Physical and Cognitive Development in Late Adulthood **Chapter 18:** Psychosocial Development in Late Adulthood

Topic Guide

This topic guide suggests how the selections in this book relate to the subjects covered in your course. You may want to use the topics listed on these pages to search the Web more easily.

On the following pages a number of Web sites have been gathered specifically for this book. They are arranged to reflect the units of this Annual Editions reader. You can link to these sites by going to *http://www.mhcls.com*.

All the articles that relate to each topic are listed below the bold-faced term.

Internet References

The following Internet sites have been selected to support the articles found in this reader. These sites were available at the time of publication. However, because Web sites often change their structure and content, the information listed may no longer be available. We invite you to visit http://www.mhcls.com for easy access to these sites.

Annual Editions: Human Development 09/10 Update

General Sources

Association for Moral Education
http://www.amenetwork.org/

This association is dedicated to fostering communication, cooperation, training, curriculum development, and research that links moral theory to educational practices.

Behavior Analysis Resources
http://www.coedu.usf.edu/behavior/bares.htm

Dedicated to promoting the experimental, theoretical, and applied analysis of behavior, this site encompasses contemporary scientific and social issues, theoretical advances, and the dissemination of professional and public information.

Healthfinder
http://www.healthfinder.gov

Healthfinder is a consumer health site that contains the latest health news, prevention and care choices, and information about every phase of human development.

UNIT 1: Genetic and Prenatal Influences on Development

American Academy of Pediatrics (AAP)
http://www.aap.org

AAP provides data on optimal physical, mental, and social health for all children. The site links to professional educational sources and current research.

Basic Neural Processes
http://psych.hanover.edu/Krantz/neurotut.html

An extensive tutorial on brain structures is provided here.

Center for Evolutionary Psychology
http://www.psych.ucsb.edu/research/cep/

A link to an evolutionary psychology primer is available on this site. Extensive background information is included.

Conception
http://www.thefertilitydiet.com

The *Fertility Diet* guides couples toward diet and lifestyle choices that can make a real difference in fertility.

Genetics Education Center
http://www.kumc.edu/gec/

The University of Kansas Medical Center provides information on human genetics and the human genome project at this site. Included are a number of links to research areas.

MedlinePlus Health Information/Prenatal Care
http://www.nlm.nih.gov/medlineplus/prenatalcare.html

On this site of the National Library of Medicine and the National Institutes of Health, you'll find prenatal-related sections such as General Information, Diagnosis/Symptoms, Nutrition, Organizations, and more.

UNIT 2: Development During Infancy and Early Childhood

Autism
http://www.autism-society.org

ASA, the nation's leading grassroots autism organization, exists to improve the lives of all affected by autism. It has many excellent resources for those needing more information about autism.

BabyCenter
http://www.babycenter.com

This well-organized site offers quick access to practical information on a variety of baby-related topics that span the period from preconception to toddlerhood.

Children's Nutrition Research Center (CNRC)
http://www.kidsnutrition.org

CNRC is dedicated to defining the nutrient needs of healthy children, from conception through adolescence, and of pregnant and nursing mothers.

Early Childhood Care and Development
http://www.ecdgroup.com

Child development theory, programming and parenting data, and research can be found on this site of the Consultative Group. It is dedicated to the improvement of conditions of young children at risk.

Zero to Three: National Center for Infants, Toddlers, and Families
http://www.zerotothree.org

Zero to Three is dedicated solely to infants, toddlers, and their families. Organized by recognized experts in the field, it provides technical assistance to communities, states, and the federal government.

UNIT 3: Development During Childhood: Cognition and Schooling

Children Now
http://www.childrennow.org

Children Now focuses on improving conditions for children who are poor or at risk. Articles include information on education, the influence of media, health, and security.

Council for Exceptional Children
http://www.cec.sped.org

This is the home page of the Council for Exceptional Children, which is dedicated to improving education for exceptional children and the gifted child.

Educational Resources Information Center (ERIC)
http://www.eric.ed.gov/

Sponsored by the U.S. Department of Education, this site will lead to numerous documents related to elementary and early childhood education.

Internet References

Federation of Behavioral, Psychological, and Cognitive Science
http://www. thefederationonline.org

The federation's mission is fulfilled through legislative and regulatory advocacy, education, and information dissemination to the scientific community. Hotlink to the National Institutes of Health's Project on the Decade of the Brain.

The National Association for the Education of Young Children (NAEYC)
http://www.naeyc.org

NAEYC is the nation's largest organization of early childhood professionals. It is devoted to improving the quality of early childhood education programs for children from birth through the age of eight.

Project Zero
http://pzweb.harvard.edu

Following 30 years of research on the development of learning processes in children and adults, Project Zero is now helping to create communities of reflective, independent learners; to enhance deep understanding within disciplines; and to promote critical and creative thinking.

Teaching Technologies
http://www.inspiringteachers.com/bttindex.html

This is an excellent Web site for aspiring as well as experienced teachers.

UNIT 4: Development During Childhood: Family and Culture

Harborview Injury Prevention and Research Center
http://depts.washington.edu/hiprc/

Systematic reviews of childhood injury prevention and interventions on such diverse subjects as adolescent suicide, child abuse, accidental injuries, and youth violence are offered on this site.

Families and Work Institute
http://www.familiesandwork.org/index.html

The Families and Work Institute conducts policy research on issues related to the changing workforce, and it operates a national clearinghouse on work and family life.

iVillage Pregnancy and Parenting
http://parenting.ivillage.com

This resource focuses on issues concerning single parents and their children. The articles range from parenting children from infancy through adolescence.

Parentsplace.com: Single Parenting
http://www.parentsplace.com

This site provides links to resources valuable to parents, with topics ranging from pregnancy to teens.

UNIT 5: Development During Adolescence and Young Adulthood

Alcohol & Drug Addiction Resource Center
http://www.addict-help.com/

An online source for questions regarding alcohol and drug addiction.

ADOL: Adolescent Directory On-Line
http://site.educ.indiana.edu/aboutus/AdolescenceDirectoryonLine ADOL/tabid/4785/Default.aspx

The ADOL site contains a wide array of Web documents that address adolescent development. Specific content ranges from mental health issues to counselor resources.

AMA—Adolescent Health On-Line
http://www.ama-assn.org/ama/pub/category/1947.html

This AMA adolescent health initiative describes clinical preventive services that primary care physicians and other health professionals can provide to young people.

American Academy of Child and Adolescent Psychiatry
http://www.aacap.org/

Up-to-date data on a host of topics that include facts for families, public health, and clinical practice may be found here.

Depression
http://www.depression-primarycare.org

This site provides depression-related information for clinicians, organizations, and patients.

UNIT 6: Development During Middle and Late Adulthood

Alzheimer's Disease Research Center
http://alzheimer.wustl.edu/

ADRC facilitates advanced research on clinical, genetic, neuropathological, neuroanatomical, biomedical, neuropsychological, and psychosocial aspects of Alzheimer's disease and related brain disorders.

American Association of Retired Persons
http://www.aarp.org

Founded in 1958, AARP is a nonprofit, nonpartisan membership organization that helps people 50 and over improve the quality of their lives. AARP has 40 million members and has offices in all 50 states, the District of Columbia, Puerto Rico and the U.S. Virgin Islands.

Lifestyle Factors Affecting Late Adulthood
http://www.school-for-champions.com/health/lifestyle_elderly.htm

The way a person lives his or her life in the later years can affect the quality of life. Find here information to improve a senior's lifestyle plus a few relevant links.

National Aging Information and Referral Support Center
http://www.nausa.org/informationandreferral/index-ir.php

This service by the States United for Action in Aging is a central source of data on demographic, health, economic, and social status of older Americans.

Department of Health and Human Services—Aging
http://www.hhs.gov/aging/index.html

This is a complete site, with links and topics on aging.

UNIT 1

Genetic and Prenatal Influences on Development

Unit Selections

1. **The Identity Dance,** Gunjan Sinha
2. **The Power to Divide,** Rick Weiss
3. **The Mystery of Fetal Life: Secrets of the Womb,** John Pekkanen
4. **Fat, Carbs, and the Science of Conception,** Jorge E. Chavarro, Walter C. Willett, and Patrick J. Skerrett
5. **The Hunt for Golden Eggs,** Brooke Lea Foster
6. **The Curious Lives of Surrogates,** Lorraine Ali and Raina Kelley

Key Points to Consider

- Will genetic technology result in more attempts to alter genes than environmental factors in the 21st century? Will life experiences still conspire to switch new DNA sequences on and off?

- Will the United States become a laggard in body-part replacement research using stem cells? Why do many people oppose this life-saving technology?

- Does a specific period of prenatal development determine the cognitive abilities of the future human? Can, or should this time frame be manipulated?

- Describe the long-term effects of health status during pregnancy on the development of mental abilities in infants and children.

- How can diet affect conception?

- What are the ethical concerns about "selling" ova to help infertile couples have their own children?

- How prevalent is surrogate motherhood today? How do gestational carriers feel about surrogacy?

Student Web Site
www.mhcls.com

Internet References

American Academy of Pediatrics (AAP)
http://www.aap.org
Basic Neural Processes
http://psych.hanover.edu/Krantz/neurotut.html
Center for Evolutionary Psychology
http://www.psych.ucsb.edu/research/cep/
Conception
http://www.thefertilitydiet.com
Genetics Education Center
http://www.kumc.edu/gec/
Harvard Heart Letter
http://www.health.harvard.edu/newsweek
MedlinePlus Health Information/Prenatal Care
http://www.nlm.nih.gov/medlineplus/prenatalcare.html

The total human genome was mapped in 2003. This knowledge of the human complement of twenty-three pairs of chromosomes with their associated genes in the nucleus of every cell has the potential for allowing genetic manipulation. The use of stem cells (undifferentiated embryonic cells) in animal research has documented the possibility of morphing stem cells into any kind of human cells. Stem cells will turn into desired tissue cells when the gene sequences of cytosine, adenine, thymine, and guanine (CATG) of the desired tissues are expressed. Scientists may eventually use their knowledge of the human genome and embryonic stem cells to alter behavior or cure diseases. Cloning (complete reproduction) of a human already exists when one egg fertilized by one sperm separates into identical twins. Monozygotic twin research suggests that one's genetic CATG sequencing does not determine human behaviors, diseases, and traits without environmental input. Nature versus nurture is better phrased nature plus nurture. Genes appear to have mechanisms by which environmental factors can turn them on or leave them dormant.

Genetic precursors of human development and the use of stem cells, morphing, and cloning will be hot topics of the next several years as genetic manipulation becomes feasible. As DNA sequences associated with particular human traits (genetic markers) are uncovered, pressure will appear to alter these traits. Will the focus be on altering the CATG sequencing, or altering the environmental factors that will "operate" on the genes?

Human embryology (the study of the first through seventh weeks after conception) and human fetology (the study of the eighth week of pregnancy through birth) have given verification to the idea that behavior precedes birth. The genetic hardwiring of CATG directs much of this behavior. However, the developing embryo/fetus reacts to the internal and external environments provided by the mother as well. Substances diffuse through the placental barrier from the mother's body. The embryo reacts to toxins (viruses, antigens) that pass through the umbilical cord. The fetus reacts to an enormous number of other stimuli, such as the sounds from the mother's body (digestive rumblings, heartbeat) and the mother's movements, moods, and medicines. How the embryo/fetus reacts (weakly to strongly, positively to negatively) depends, in large part, on his or her genetic preprogramming. Genes and environment are so inextricably intertwined that the effect of each cannot be studied separately. Prenatal development always has strong environmental influences and vice versa.

The two articles in the genetic influences section of this unit are state-of-the-science expositions on how decoding of the human genome will affect our future views about human development. The information in them is central to many ongoing discussions of human development. The potentialities for altering structures and behaviors, by altering the CATG messages of DNA on chromosomes within cells or by cloning humans, are massive. We all need to understand what is happening. We need to make knowledgeable and well-thought-out choices for our futures.

The first article, "The Identity Dance," addresses the interplay of genes and environment. It presents research on identical twins suggesting that life factors conspire to switch genetic sequences of CATG on, or off, to create personality traits, diseases, and other human behaviors. What will we, the human race, choose to do with the technology in our hands: alter gene sequences or alter environment? The author poses several questions about human twins which should stimulate lively debates.

The second article, "The Power to Divide," explains how stem cell research could launch an era of body part replacement. Tissues and organs can be custom made for recipients. Will the political/moral movers of different countries allow this to take place? What are the objections to, and dangers of, creating new body parts for individuals with diseased tissues and/or organs? Which countries are moving ahead with this technology? Will the United States continue to be a cell-replacement laggard?

The third article, "The Mystery of Fetal Life: Secrets of the Womb," answers questions on fetal psychological development. Human behaviors such as intelligence and personality may be profoundly influenced by the environment of the mother's uterus.

Nurture occurs before and after birth. John Pekkanen addresses issues such as over-the-counter drugs, caffeine, infections, pets, and environmental pollutants. He reviews what is known about fetal memory, including the much misunderstood "Mozart effect."

The fourth article, "Fat, Carbs, and the Science of Conception," discusses how important good fats (unsaturated) and good carbs (complex) are to fertility. The famous longitudinal Nurses' Health Study in Harvard University has data to document the findings that trans fats and fast (easily digested) carbs in the diet are detrimental to conception.

The fifth article, "The Hunt for Golden Eggs," describes the use of donor eggs to help infertile couples have a ½ biological child (from sperm) and the experience of the pregnancy, child-birth, and raising of their own child. The United States does not regulate the amounts paid for donor eggs. Some religions object to the donations entirely.

The last selection, "The Curious Lives of Surrogates," discusses the use of surrogate mothers (gestational carriers) for prenatal incubation of babies for infertile couples. It explores the motivations and emotions of both the biological parents and the women they choose to sustain a pregnancy for them.

The Identity Dance

The battle between genes and the environment is over. As the dust settles, scientists piece together how DNA and life experience conspire to create personality.

GUNJAN SINHA

Sandra and Marisa Peña, 32-year-old identical twins, seem to be exactly the same. They have the same thick dark hair, the same high cheekbones, the same habit of delicately rubbing the tip of the nose in conversation. They had the same type of thyroid cyst at the same age (18) in the same place (right side). When San Diego is mentioned, they both say, simultaneously and with the same intonation, "Oh, I love San Diego!" They live together, work one floor away from each other at MTV, wear the same clothes, hang out with the same friends. They even have the same dreams.

The sisters are as alike as two people can be. At the same time, they are opposites. Sandra is outgoing and confident; Marisa is reserved. They have the same pretty face, but those cheekbones make shy Marisa look mysterious and brooding, while Sandra looks wholesome and sweet. Sandra tends to speak for her sister: "Marisa's always been more quiet, more subdued, an introvert"; Marisa nods her assent. They see themselves as a duo—but more like complementary photo negatives rather than duplicates of each other. "I think we balance each other out," says Sandra. "Definitely," Marisa chimes in. Sandra begins, "In every family photo, I'm smiling, she's—" "I'm not," Marisa says with a laugh.

When their father passed away ten years ago from pancreatic cancer and their mother died soon after, the deeper differences between the two became obvious. Their family had been very loving and protective, and the sisters were traumatized by the sudden loss. But as Marisa sank into a depression, Sandra picked up and changed her life. She left San Antonio for Germany to live with her boyfriend. Marisa stayed put, catatonic with sadness. It was the first time the two had ever been apart.

Then, after a few months in Germany, Sandra headed to New York City—the buzzing metropolis in which she had dreamed of living since she was a teenager. Marisa soon followed Sandra, but when she arrived in New York, "She just couldn't let go of [her sadness]," says Sandra. "I didn't know what to do with her."

In recent years, we've, come to believe that genes influence character and personality more than anything else does. It's not just about height and hair color—DNA seems to have its clutches on our very souls. But spend a few hours with identical twins, who have exactly the same set of genes, and you'll find that this simplistic belief crumbles before your eyes. If DNA dictates all, how can two people with identical genes—who are living, breathing clones of each other—be so different?

To answer such questions, scientists have begun to think more broadly about how genes and life experience combine to shape us. The rigid idea that genes determine identity has been replaced with a more flexible and complex view in which DNA and life experience conspire to mold our personalities. We now know that certain genes make people susceptible to traits like aggression and depression. But susceptibility is not inevitability. Gene expression is like putty: Genes are turned on and off, dialed up or down both by other genes and by the ups and downs of everyday life. A seminal study last year found that the ideal breeding ground for depression is a combination of specific genes *and* stressful triggers—simply having the gene will not send most people into despair. Such research promises to end the binary debate about nature vs. nurture—and usher in a revolution in understanding who we are.

We've come to believe genes influence character more than anything else—DNA seems to have its clutches on our souls.

"While scientists have been trying to tease apart environmental from genetic influences on diseases like cancer, this is the first study to show this effect [for a mental disorder]," says Thomas Insel, director of the National Institute of Mental Health. "This is really the science of the moment."

About ten years ago, technological advances made it possible to quickly identify human genes. That breakthrough launched a revolution in human biology—and in psychiatry. Not only were scientists rapidly discovering genes linked to illnesses such as cancer and birth defects like dwarfism, they also found genes associated with such traits as sexual preference and aggression as well as mental illnesses such as schizophrenia.

Genetic discoveries transformed the intellectual zeitgeist as well, marking a decisive shift from the idea that environment alone shapes human personality. Nurture-heavy theories about behavior dominated in the 1960s and 1970s, a reaction in part to the legacy of Nazi eugenics. By the 1990s, the genome was exalted as "the human blueprint," the ultimate dictator of our attributes. Behavioral geneticists offered refreshingly simple explanations for human identity—and for social problems. Bad parenting, poor neighborhoods or amoral television didn't cause bad behavior; genes did. No wonder all those welfare programs weren't working.

"People really believed that there must be something exclusively genetically wrong with people who are not successful. They were exhausted with these broken-hearted liberals saying that it's all social," says Andreas Heinz, professor of psychiatry at Humboldt and Freie University in Berlin, who has been studying the influence of genes and environment on behavior for years. The idea that violent behavior in particular might be genetically "set" was so accepted that in 1992, the director of the agency overseeing the National Institute of Mental Health compared urban African-American youth with "hyperaggressive" and "hypersexual" monkeys in a jungle.

Behavioral genetics had a simple argument: Bad parenting, poor neighborhoods or TV didn't cause bad behavior. Genes did.

Genetic explanations for behavior gained ground in part through great leaps in our understanding of mood disorders. In the early 1990s, research at the federal labs of Stephen Suomi and Dee Higley found that monkeys with low levels of serotonin—now known to be a major player in human anxiety and depression—were prone to alcoholism, anxiety and aggression. Around the same time, Klaus-Peter Lesch at the University of Würtzburg in Germany identified the serotonin transporter gene, which produces a protein that ferries serotonin between brain cells. Prozac and other drugs work by boosting levels of serotonin in the brain, so this gene seemed like an obvious target in the search for the genetic roots of depression.

Lesch, who was working on the connection between this gene and psychiatric disorders, later found that people who had at least one copy of the short version of this gene were much more likely to have an anxiety disorder. Short and long versions of genes function much like synonymous words: Different lengths, or "spellings," generate subtle but critical differences in biology.

Genetics couldn't explain why some people bounce back from terrible trauma that shatters others, or why some people are ruthlessly ambitious and others laid-back.

Despite these groundbreaking insights, it quickly became clear that complex human behaviors couldn't be reduced to pure genetics. Apart from a few exceptions, scientists couldn't find a gene that directly caused depression or schizophrenia or any other major mental of mood disorder. The new research also failed to answer a lot of common-sense questions: If identical twins are genetically indistinguishable, how could just one end up schizophrenic or homosexual? And it couldn't address subtler questions about character and behavior. Why do some people bounce back from terrible trauma that shatters others? Why are some people ruthlessly ambitious and others laid-back?

Thanks to misfit monkeys like George, a rhesus macaque living in a lab in Maryland, researchers have clues to the missing element. In most ways, George is a typical male monkey. He's covered in sandy fur and has a rubbery, almost maniacal grin. But a couple of things set George apart. After he was born, Higley and Suomi's team separated George from his mother, raising him instead in a nursery with other macaque infants his own age. George has another strike against him: a short version of the serotonin transporter gene (monkeys, like people, can have either a short form or a long form of the gene).

But the most notable thing about George is that he is an alcoholic. Each day, George and his simian chums have happy hour, with alcohol freely available in their cage for one hour. Unlike his buddies, George drinks like the resident barroom lush—he sways and wobbles and can't walk a straight line.

And his problems go beyond the bottle. He's reluctant to explore new objects, and he is shy around strangers. He always seems to be on edge and tends to get aggressive and impulsive quickly. In short, he's a completely different animal from his cousin Jim, who also has the short version of the transporter gene but was raised by his biological mom. Jim's "normal" upbringing seems to have protected him from the gene: This monkey is laid-back and prefers sugar water to booze.

After studying 36 family-raised monkeys and 79 nursery-raised animals, the team found that the long version of the gene seems to help the animals shrug off stress. The short form of the gene, by contrast, doesn't directly *cause* alcoholism: Monkeys with the short gene and a normal family upbringing have few personality problems. But the short version of the gene definitely puts the animals at a disadvantage when life gets tough. Raised without the care and support of their mothers, their predisposition toward anxiety and alcoholism comes to the fore.

"Maternal nurturing and discipline seem to buffer the effect of the serotonin gene," says Suomi. "If they don't have good mothers, then the [troubled] behavior comes out loud and clear."

The implications of this research are tantalizing, since people also carry long and short versions of the transporter gene. These variants, unlike those that have been identified as making people susceptible to diseases like breast cancer or Alzheimer's, are very common: Among Caucasians, about one-fifth of the population has two copies of the short gene (everyone gets one copy from Mom and the other from Dad), and another third have two copies of the long gene. The rest have one of each. (The gene has not yet been studied in other populations.) The evidence indicated that this gene was related to resilience and depression in humans. Why, then, had researchers thus far failed to find a convincing correlation between the gene and the risk of depression?

Terrie Moffitt and Avshalom Caspi, a husband-and-wife team of psychologists at King's College in London, had the insight that environmental influences might be the missing part of the puzzle. Moffitt and Caspi turned to a long-term study of almost 900 New Zealanders, identified these subjects' transporter genes and interviewed the subjects about traumatic experiences in early adulthood—like a major breakup, death in the family or serious injury—to see if the difficulties brought out an underlying genetic tendency toward depression.

The results were striking: 43 percent of subjects who had the short genes and who had experienced four or more tumultuous events became clinically depressed. By contrast, only 17 percent of the long-gene people who had endured four or more stressful events wound up depressed—no more than the rate of depression in the general population. People with the short gene who experienced no stressful events fared pretty well too—they also became depressed at the average rate. Clearly, it was the combination of hard knocks and short genes that more than doubled the risk of depression.

Caspi and Moffitt's study, published last summer, was one of the first to examine the combined effects of genetic predisposition and experience on a specific trait. Psychiatrists were delighted. "It's just a wonderful story," says Insel. "It changed the way we think about genes and psychiatric disorders."

Moffitt and Caspi have found a similar relationship between another gene and antisocial behavior. Abused and neglected children with a gene responsible for low levels of monoamine oxidase in the brain were nine times more likely to engage in violent of other antisocial behavior as adults than were people with the same gene who were not mistreated. Finnish scientists have since found similar effects on genes for novelty seeking—a trait associated with attention deficit hyperactivity disorder. Children who had the genes and who were also raised by strict, emotionally distant parents were much more likely to engage in risky behavior and make impulsive decisions as adults than children with the same genes who were raised in more tolerant and accepting environments.

While scientists don't exactly know how genes are influenced by environment at the molecular level, there are clues that genes have the equivalent of molecular "switches" and can be programmed—turned on or off, up or down—very early. Both Lesch and Suomi have shown that the level of biochemicals such as the serotonin transporter molecule can be "set" as early as in the womb, at least in mice and monkeys.

Mothers of multiples will tell you their babies were distinct the moment they were born.

The prenatal environment also has a major influence on differences between identical twins. Mothers of multiples will tell you that their babies were distinct the moment they were born, and research backs them up. Twins experience different environments even in the womb, as they compete with each other for nutrients. One can beat out the other, which is why they often have different birth weights: Marisa Pena is a bit taller and heavier than her sister.

Prenatal experiences are just the first in a lifetime of differentiating factors. Only about 50 percent of the characteristics twins have in common are due to genes alone. Researchers now believe that an illness suffered by only one twin, or different amounts of attention from peers or parents, can set the stage for personality differences. This makes it easier to understand why the Pena sisters reacted as they did: By the time their parents died, "these twins had had a lifetime of experiences which might have made them react differently," says Moffitt. "In addition, some pairs of identical twins individuate themselves in early childhood. They seem to take on the roles of 'the shy one' and 'the outgoing one' and then live up to those roles." in other words, they customize their environment, and the world treats them accordingly.

The new science of nature *and* nurture isn't as straightforward as the DNA-is-destiny mantra, but it is more accurate. "People have a really hard time understanding the probabilistic nature of how genes impact traits like depression," says Kenneth Kendler, director of the Virginia Institute for Psychiatric and Behavioral Genetics at Virginia Commonwealth University, who heads a major twin registry. "They think that if something is heritable, then it can't be modified by the environment." The knowledge that the traits we inherit are also contingent on what the world does to us promises more insight into why people act and feel differently—even when they look exactly the same.

GUNJAN SINHA is an award-winning science writer based in Frankfurt, Germany.

Additional reporting by Jeff Grossman.

The Power to Divide

Stem cells could launch a new era of medicine, curing deadly diseases with custom-made tissues and organs. But science may take a backseat to politics in deciding if—and where—that hope will be realized.

RICK WEISS

In the beginning, one cell becomes two, and two become four. Being fruitful, they multiply into a ball of many cells, a shimmering sphere of human potential. Scientists have long dreamed of plucking those naive cells from a young human embryo and coaxing them to perform, in sterile isolation, the everyday miracle they perform in wombs: transforming into all the 200 or so kinds of cells that constitute a human body. Liver cells. Brain cells. Skin, bone, and nerve.

The dream is to launch a medical revolution in which ailing organs and tissues might be repaired—not with crude mechanical devices like insulin pumps and titanium joints but with living, homegrown replacements. It would be the dawn of a new era of regenerative medicine, one of the holy grails of modern biology.

Revolutions, alas, are almost always messy. So when James Thomson, a soft-spoken scientist at the University of Wisconsin in Madison, reported in November 1998 that he had succeeded in removing cells from spare embryos at fertility clinics and establishing the world's first human embryonic stem cell line, he and other scientists got a lot more than they bargained for. It was the kind of discovery that under most circumstances would have blossomed into a major federal research enterprise. Instead the discovery was quickly engulfed in the turbulent waters of religion and politics. In church pews, congressional hearing rooms, and finally the Oval Office, people wanted to know: Where were the needed embryos going to come from, and how many would have to be destroyed to treat the millions of patients who might be helped? Before long, countries around the world were embroiled in the debate.

Most alarmed have been people who see embryos as fully vested, vulnerable members of society, and who decry the harvesting of cells from embryos as akin to cannibalism. They warn of a brave new world of "embryo farms" and "cloning mills" for the cultivation of human spare parts. And they argue that scientists can achieve the same results using adult stem cells—immature cells found in bone marrow and other organs in adult human beings, as well as in umbilical cords normally discarded at birth.

Advocates counter that adult stem cells, useful as they may be for some diseases, have thus far proved incapable of producing the full range of cell types that embryonic stem cells can. They point out that fertility clinic freezers worldwide are bulging with thousands of unwanted embryos slated for disposal. Those embryos are each smaller than the period at the end of this sentence. They have no identifying features or hints of a nervous system. If parents agree to donate them, supporters say, it would be unethical not to do so in the quest to cure people of disease.

Immature and full of potential, stem cells haven't yet differentiated into the specialized cells that form body parts, like the museum specimens stacked in the Berlin lab of pathologist Rudolf Virchow. He pioneered the idea, in the 1800s, that disease begins at the cellular level.

Few question the medical promise of embryonic stem cells. Consider the biggest United States killer of all: heart disease. Embryonic stem cells can be trained to grow into heart muscle cells that, even in a laboratory dish, clump together and pulse in spooky unison. And when those heart cells have been injected into mice and pigs with heart disease, they've filled in for injured or dead cells and sped recovery. Similar studies have suggested stem cells' potential for conditions such as diabetes and spinal cord injury.

Critics point to worrisome animal research showing that embryonic stem cells sometimes grow into tumors or morph into unwanted kinds of tissues—possibly forming, for example, dangerous bits of bone in those hearts they are supposedly repairing. But supporters respond that such problems are rare and a lot has recently been learned about how to prevent them.

The arguments go back and forth, but policymakers and governments aren't waiting for answers. Some countries, such as Germany, worried about a slippery slope toward unethical human experimentation, have already prohibited some types of stem cell research. Others, like the U.S., have imposed severe limits on government funding but have left the private sector to do what it wants. Still others, such as the U.K., China, Korea, and Singapore, have set out to become the epicenters of stem cell research, providing money as well as ethical oversight to encourage the field within carefully drawn bounds.

In such varied political climates, scientists around the globe are racing to see which techniques will produce treatments soonest. Their approaches vary, but on one point, all seem to agree: How humanity handles its control over the mysteries of embryo development will say a lot about who we are and what we're becoming.

For more than half of his seven years, Cedric Seldon has been fighting leukemia. Now having run out of options, he is about to become a biomedical pioneer—one of about 600 Americans last year to be treated with an umbilical cord blood transplant.

Cord blood transplants—considered an adult stem cell therapy because the cells come from infants, not embryos—have been performed since 1988. Like bone marrow, which doctors have been transplanting since 1968, cord blood is richly endowed with a kind of stem cell that gives rise to oxygen-carrying red blood cells, disease-fighting white blood cells, and other parts of the blood and immune systems. Unlike a simple blood transfusion, which provides a batch of cells destined to die in a few months, the stem cells found in bone marrow and cord blood can—if all goes well—burrow into a person's bones, settle there for good, and generate fresh blood and immune cells for a lifetime.

Propped on a hospital bed at Duke University Medical Center, Cedric works his thumbs furiously against a pair of joysticks that control a careening vehicle in a Starsky and Hutch video game. "Hang on, Hutch!" older brother Daniel shouts from the bedside, as a nurse, ignoring the screeching tires and gunshots, sorts through a jumble of tubes and hangs a bag of cord blood cells from a chrome pole. Just an hour ago I watched those cells being thawed and spun in a centrifuge—awakening them for the first time since 2001, when they were extracted from the umbilical cord of a newborn and donated by her parents to a cell bank at Duke. The time has come for those cells to prove their reputed mettle.

For days Cedric has endured walloping doses of chemotherapy and radiation in a last-ditch effort to kill every cancer cell in his body. Such powerful therapy has the dangerous side-effect of destroying patients' blood-making stem cells, and so is never applied unless replacement stem cells are available. A search of every bone marrow bank in the country had found no match for Cedric's genetic profile, and it was beginning to look as if he'd run out of time. Then a computer search turned up the frozen cord blood cells at Duke—not a perfect match, but close enough to justify trying.

"Ready?" the nurse asks. Mom and dad, who have spent hours in prayer, nod yes, and a line of crimson wends its way down the tube, bringing the first of about 600 million cells into the boy's body. The video game's sound effects seem to fade behind a muffling curtain of suspense. Although Cedric's balloon-laden room is buoyant with optimism, success is far from certain.

"Grow, cells, grow," Cedric's dad whispers.

His mom's eyes are misty. I ask what she sees when she looks at the cells trickling into her son.

"Life," she says. "It's his rebirth."

It will be a month before tests reveal whether Cedric's new cells have taken root, but in a way he's lucky. All he needs is a new blood supply and immune system, which are relatively easy to re-create. Countless other patients are desperate to regenerate more than that. Diabetics need new insulin-producing cells. Heart attack victims could benefit from new cardiac cells. Paraplegics might even walk again if the nerves in their spinal cords could regrow.

In a brightly lit laboratory halfway across the country from Cedric's hospital room, three teams of scientists at the University of Wisconsin in Madison are learning how to grow the embryonic stem cells that might make such cures possible. Unlike adult stem cells, which appear to have limited repertoires, embryonic stem cells are pluripotent—they can become virtually every kind of human cell. The cells being nurtured here are direct descendants of the ones James Thomson isolated seven years ago.

For years Thomson and his colleagues have been expanding some of those original stem cells into what are called stem cell lines—colonies of millions of pluripotent cells that keep proliferating without differentiating into specific cell types. The scientists have repeatedly moved each cell's offspring to less crowded laboratory dishes, allowing them to divide again and again. And while they worked, the nation struggled to get a handle on the morality of what they were doing.

It took almost two years for President Bill Clinton's administration to devise ethics guidelines and a system for funding the new field. George W. Bush's ascension prevented that plan from going into effect, and all eyes turned to the conservative Texan to see what he would do. On August 9, 2001, Bush announced that federal funds could be used to study embryonic stem cells. But to prevent taxpayers from becoming complicit in the destruction of human embryos, that money could be used only to study the stem cell lines already in the works as of that date—a number that, for practical reasons, has resulted in about two dozen usable lines. Those wishing to work with any of the more than a hundred stem cell lines created after that date can do so only with private funding.

Every month scientists from around the world arrive in Madison to take a three-day course in how to grow those approved cells. To watch what they must go through to keep the cells happy is to appreciate why many feel hobbled by the Bush doctrine. For one thing—and for reasons not fully understood—the surest way to keep these cells alive is to place them on a layer of other cells taken from mouse embryos, a time-consuming requirement. Hunched over lab benches, deftly handling forceps and pipettes with blue latex gloves, each scientist in Madison spends the better half of a day dissecting a pregnant mouse, removing its uterus, and prying loose a string of embryos that look like little red peas in a pod. They then wash them, mash them, tease apart their cells, and get them growing in lab dishes. The result is a hormone-rich carpet of mouse cells upon which a few human embryonic stem cells are finally placed. There they live like pampered pashas.

If their scientist-servants don't feed them fresh liquid nutrients at least once a day, the cells die of starvation. If each colony is not split in half each week, it dies from overcrowding. And if a new layer of mouse cells is not prepared and provided every two weeks, the stem cells grow into weird and useless masses that finally die. By contrast, scientists working with private money have been developing embryonic stem cell lines that are hardier, less demanding, and not dependent on mouse cells. Bypassing the use of mouse cells is not only easier, but it also eliminates the risk that therapeutic stem cells might carry rodent viruses, thereby potentially speeding their approval for testing in humans.

Here in the Madison lab, scientists grumble about how fragile the precious colonies are. "They're hard to get to know," concedes Leann Crandall, one of the course's instructors and a co-author of the 85-page manual on their care and feeding. "But once you get to know them, you love them. You can't help it. They're so great. I see so many good things coming from them."

A few American scientists are finding it is easier to indulge their enthusiasm for stem cells overseas. Scores of new embryonic stem cell lines have now been created outside the U.S., and many countries are aggressively seeking to spur the development of therapies using these cells, raising a delicate question: Can the nation in which embryonic stem cells were discovered maintain its initial research lead?

"I know a lot of people back in the U.S. who would like to move into embryonic stem cell work but who won't because of the political uncertainties," says Stephen Minger, director of the Stem Cell Biology Laboratory at King's College in London, speaking to me in his cramped and cluttered office. "I think the United States is in real danger of being left behind."

Minger could be right. He is one of at least two high-profile stem cell scientists to move from the U.S. to England in the past few years, something less than a brain drain but a signal, perhaps, of bubbling discontent.

The research climate is good here, says Minger. In 2003 his team became the first in the U.K. to grow colonies of human embryonic stem cells, and his nine-person staff is poised to nearly double. He's developing new growth culture systems that won't rely on potentially infectious mouse cells. He's also figuring out how to make stem cells morph into cardiac, neural, pancreatic, and retinal cells and preparing to test those cells in animals. And in stark contrast to how things are done in the U.S., Minger says, he's doing all this with government support—and oversight.

The Human Fertilisation and Embryology Authority (HFEA), the government agency that has long overseen U.K. fertility clinics, is now also regulating the country's embryonic stem cell research. In closed-door meetings a committee of 18 people appointed by the National Health Service considers all requests to conduct research using embryos. The committee includes scientists, ethicists, lawyers, and clergy, but the majority are lay people representing the public.

To an American accustomed to high security and protesters at venues dealing regularly with embryo research, the most striking thing about the HFEA's headquarters in downtown London is its ordinariness. The office, a standard-issue warren of cubicles and metal filing cabinets, is on the second floor of a building that also houses the agency that deals with bankruptcy. I ask Ross Thacker, a research officer at the authority, whether the HFEA is regularly in need of yellow police tape to keep protesters at bay.

"Now that you mention it," he says, "there was a placard holder outside this morning . . ."

Aha!

". . . but he was protesting something about the insolvency office."

Thacker politely refrains from criticizing U.S. policy on embryo research, but he clearly takes pride in the orderliness of the British system. The committee has approved about a dozen requests to create stem cell lines in the past 18 months, increasing the number of projects to 35. Most were relatively routine—until a strong-willed fertility doctor named Alison Murdoch decided to ask for permission to do something nobody had done before: create cloned human embryos as sources of stem cells.

As controversial as embryonic stem cell research can be, cloning embryos to produce those stem cells is even thornier. Much of the world became familiar with cloning in 1997, when scientists announced they'd cloned a sheep named Dolly. The process involves creating an animal not from egg and sperm but by placing the nucleus of a cell inside an egg that's had its nucleus removed. It's since been used to replicate mice, rabbits, cats, and cattle, among others.

How Many Lines Exist?

Since President Bush banned U.S. government funding for the study of embryonic stem cell lines created after August 9, 2001, the number of lines worldwide has doubled, though reliable data are hard to come by. Biologist Douglas Melton of Harvard says many lines approved for federal dollars "are old fuddy-duddies that have lost potential" because of how they were cultured. "That's why we need new lines," he says.

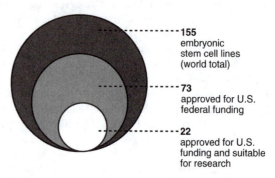

155 embryonic stem cell lines (world total)

73 approved for U.S. federal funding

22 approved for U.S. funding and suitable for research

International Society for Stem Cell Research. (published data only)

As in many other countries and a few U.S. states, it's illegal in the U.K. to create cloned human babies (called reproductive cloning), because of concerns that clones may be biologically abnormal and because of ethical issues surrounding the creation of children who would be genetic replicas of their one-and-only "parent."

In 2001 the British Parliament made it legal to create cloned human embryos—as opposed to babies—for use in medical research (called therapeutic cloning). Still, no one on the HFEA was completely comfortable with the idea. The fear was that some rogue scientist would take the work a step further, gestate the embryo in a woman's womb, and make the birth announcement that no one wanted to hear.

But Murdoch, of the University of Newcastle upon Tyne, made a compelling case. If replacement tissues grown from stem cells bore the patient's exact genetic fingerprint, they would be less likely to be rejected by a patient's immune system, she told the committee. And what better way to get such a match than to derive the cells from an embryo cloned from the patient's own DNA? Disease research could also benefit, she said. Imagine an embryo—and its stem cells—cloned from a person with Lou Gehrig's disease, a fatal genetic disorder that affects nerves and muscles. Scientists might learn quite a bit, she argued, by watching how the disease damages nerve and muscle cells grown from those stem cells, and then testing various drugs on them. It's the kind of experiment that could never be done in a person with the disease.

The HFEA deliberated for five months before giving Murdoch permission to make human embryo clones in her lab at the Centre for Life in Newcastle, a sprawling neon-illuminated complex of buildings that strikes a decidedly modern note in the aging industrial hub. But there was a catch: It takes an egg to make a clone. And under the terms of HFEA approval, Murdoch is allowed to use only those eggs being disposed of by the center's fertility clinic after they failed to fertilize when mixed with sperm.

It's not a perfect arrangement, Murdoch says. After all, eggs that have failed to fertilize are almost by definition of poor quality. "They're not brilliant," she says of the eggs. "But the U.K. has decided at the moment that these are the most ethical sort to use. So that's really all we can work with." As of April the group hadn't managed to clone any embryos, despite numerous attempts.

No such obstacle faced Woo-Suk Hwang and his colleagues at Seoul National University in February 2004 when they became the world's first to clone human embryos and extract stem cells from them. The South Korean government allows research on human embryos made from healthy eggs—in this case, donated by 16 women who took egg-ripening hormones.

Cloning is an arduous process that requires great patience and almost always ends in failure as cells burst, tear, or suffer damage to their DNA, but the Koreans are expert cloners, their skills sharpened in the country's state-funded livestock-cloning enterprise. In Hwang's lab alone, technicians produce more than 700 cloned pig or cattle embryos every day, seven days a week, in a quest to produce livestock with precise genetic traits. "There is no holiday in our lab," Hwang told me with a smile.

But there is something else that gives Koreans an edge over other would-be cloners, Hwang says. "As you know, Asian countries use chopsticks, but only the Koreans use steel chopsticks," he explains. "The steel ones are the most difficult to use. Very slippery." I look at him, trying to tell if he's kidding. A lifetime of using steel chop sticks makes Koreans better at manipulating tiny eggs? "This is not simply a joke," he says.

Time will tell whether such skill will be enough to keep Korea in the lead as other countries turn to cloning as a source of stem cells. The competition will be tough. China has pioneered a potentially groundbreaking technique that produces cloned human embryos by mixing human skin cells with the eggs of rabbits, which are more easily obtained than human eggs. A few privately funded researchers in the U.S. are also pursuing therapeutic cloning.

Yet the biggest competition in the international race to develop stem cell therapies may ultimately come from one of the smallest of countries—a tiny nation committed to becoming a stem cell superpower. To find that place, one need only track the migration patterns of top scientists who've been wooed there from the U.S., Australia, even the U.K. Where they've been landing, it turns out, is Singapore.

Amid the scores of small, botanically rich but barely inhabited islands in the South China Sea, Singapore stands out like a post-modern mirage. The towering laboratory buildings of its Biopolis were created in 2001 to jump-start Singapore's biotechnology industry. Like a scene from a science fiction story, it features futuristic glass-and-metal buildings with names like Matrix, Proteos, and Chromos, connected by skywalks that facilitate exchanges among researchers.

Academic grants, corporate development money, laws that ban reproductive cloning but allow therapeutic cloning, and a science-savvy workforce are among the lures attracting stem cell researchers and entrepreneurs. Even Alan Colman—the renowned cloning expert who was part of the team that created Dolly, the cloned sheep—has taken leave of his home in the U.K. and become the chief executive of ES Cell International, one of a handful of major stem cell research companies blossoming in Singapore's fertile environs.

"You don't have to fly from New York to San Diego to see what's going on in other labs," says Robert Klupacs, the firm's previous CEO. "You just walk across the street. Because Singapore is small, things can happen quickly. And you don't have to go to Congress at every turn."

The company's team of 36, with 15 nationalities represented, has taken advantage of that milieu. It already owns six stem cell lines made from conventional, noncloned embryos that are approved for U.S. federal funding. Now it is perfecting methods of turning those cells into the kind of pancreatic islet cells that diabetics need, as well as into heart muscle cells that could help heart attack patients. The company is developing new, mouse-free culture systems and sterile production facilities to satisfy regulators such as the U.S. Food and Drug Administration. It hopes to begin clinical tests in humans by 2007.

Despite its research-friendly ethos—and its emphasis on entre-preneurial aspects of stem cell science—Singapore doesn't want to be known as the world's "Wild West" of stem cell research. A panel of scientific and humanitarian representatives spent two years devising ethical guidelines, stresses Hwai-Loong Kong, executive director of Singapore's Biomedical Research Council. Even the public was invited to participate, Kong says—an unusual degree of democratic input for the authoritarian island nation. The country's policies represent a "judicious balance," he says, that has earned widespread public support.

Widespread, perhaps, but not universal. After my conversation with Kong, a government official offered me a ride to my next destination. As we approached her parked car, she saw the surprise on my face as I read the bumper sticker on her left rear window: "Embryos—Let Them Live. You Were Once an Embryo Too!"

"I guess this is not completely settled," I said. "No," she replied, choosing not to elaborate.

That bumper sticker made me feel strangely at home. I am an American, after all. And no country has struggled more with the moral implications of embryonic stem cell research than the U.S., with its high church attendance rates and pockets of skepticism for many things scientific. That struggle promises to grow in the months and years ahead. Many in Congress want to ban the cloning of human embryos, even in those states where it is currently legal and being pursued with private funding. Some states have already passed legislation banning various kinds of embryo research. And federally backed scientists are sure to become increasingly frustrated as the handful of cell colonies they're allowed to work with becomes an ever smaller fraction of what's available.

Yet one thing I've noticed while talking to stem cell experts around the world: Whenever I ask who is the best in the field, the answers are inevitably weighted with the names of Americans. The work of U.S. researchers still fills the pages of the best scientific journals. And while federal policy continues to frustrate them, they are finding some support. Following the lead of California, which has committed 300 million dollars a year for embryonic stem cell research for the next decade, several states are pushing initiatives to fund research, bypassing the federal restrictions in hopes of generating well-paying jobs to boost their economies. Moves like those prompt some observers to predict that when all is said and done, it will be an American team that wins the race to create the first FDA-approved embryonic stem cell therapy.

Tom Okarma certainly believes so, and he intends to be that winner. Okarma is president of Geron, the company in Menlo Park, California, that has been at the center of the embryonic stem cell revolution from the beginning. Geron financed James Thomson's discovery of the cells in Wisconsin and has since developed more than a dozen new colonies. It holds key patents on stem cell processes and products. And now it's laying the groundwork for what the company hopes will be the first controlled clinical trials of treatments derived from embryonic stem cells. Moreover, while others look to stem cells from cloned embryos or newer colonies that haven't come into contact with mouse cells, Okarma is looking no further than the very first colonies of human embryonic stem cells ever grown: the ones Thomson nurtured back in 1998. That may seem surprising, he acknowledges, but after all these years, he knows those cells inside out.

"We've shown they're free of human, pig, cow, and mouse viruses, so they're qualified for use in humans," Okarma says at the company's headquarters. Most important, Geron has perfected a system for growing uniform batches of daughter cells from a master batch that resides, like a precious gem, in a locked freezer. The ability to produce a consistent product, batch after batch, just as drug companies do with their pills is what the FDA wants—and it will be the key to success in the emerging marketplace of stem cell therapies, Okarma says. "Why do you think San Francisco sourdough bread is so successful?" he asks. "They've got a reliable sourdough culture, and they stick with it."

Geron scientists can now make eight different cell types from their embryonic lines, Okarma says, including nerve cells, heart cells, pancreatic islet cells, liver cells, and the kind of brain cells that are lost in Parkinson's disease. But what Geron wants most at this point is to develop a treatment for spinal cord injuries.

Okarma clicks on a laptop and shows me a movie of white rats in a cage. "Pay attention to the tail and the two hind legs," he says. Two months before, the rats were subjected to spinal cord procedures that left their rear legs unable to support their weight and their tails dragging along the floor. "That's a permanent injury," he says. He flips to a different movie: white rats again, also two months after injury. But these rats received injections of a specialized nervous system cell grown from human embryonic stem cells. They have only the slightest shuffle in their gait. They hold their tails high. One even stands upright on its rear legs for a few moments.

"It's not perfect," Okarma says. "It's not like we've made a brand new spinal cord." But tests show the nerves are regrowing, he says. He hopes to get FDA permission to start testing the cells in people with spinal cord injuries in 2006.

Those experiments will surely be followed by many others around the world, as teams in China, the U.K., Singapore, and other nations gain greater control over the remarkable energy of stem cells. With any luck the political and ethical issues may even settle down. Many suspect that with a little more looking, new kinds of stem cells may be found in adults that are as versatile as those in embryos.

Where Are They?

The U.S. still leads in the number of embryonic stem cell lines, despite the restrictions on federal funding; states such as California are investing in research to create new and better lines. But the U.K. and rising Asian economies, such as South Korea and Singapore, are pouring funds into their research labs in an effort to catch up—with government oversight and financial support.

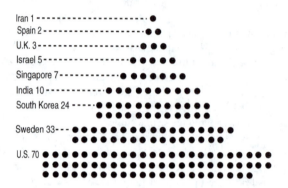

International Society for Stem Cell Research.
(published data only)

At least two candidates have already emerged. Catherine Verfaillie, a blood disease specialist at the University of Minnesota, has discovered a strange new kind of bone marrow cell that seems able to do many, and perhaps even all, the same things human embryonic stem cells can do. Researchers at Tufts University announced in February that they had found similar cells. While some scientists have expressed doubts that either kind of cell will prove as useful as embryonic ones, the discoveries have given birth to new hopes that scientists may yet find the perfect adult stem cell hiding in plain sight.

Maybe Cedric Seldon himself will discover them. The stem cells he got in his cord blood transplant did the trick, it turns out. They took root in his marrow faster than in anyone his doctors have seen. "Everyone's saying, 'Oh my God, you're doing so well'" his mother says.

That makes Cedric part of the world's first generation of regenerated people, a seamless blend of old and new—and, oddly enough, of male and female. His stem cells, remember, came from a girl, and they've been diligently churning out blood cells with two X chromosomes ever since. It's a detail that will not affect his sexual development, which is under the control of his hormones, not his blood. But it's a quirk that could save him, his mother jokes, if he ever commits a crime and leaves a bit of blood behind. The DNA results would be unambiguous, she notes correctly. "They'll be looking for a girl."

The Mystery of Fetal Life: Secrets of the Womb

John Pekkanen

In the dim light of an ultrasound room, a wand slides over the abdomen of a young woman. As it emits sound waves, it allows us to see into her womb. The video screen brightens with a grainy image of a 20-week-old fetus. It floats in its amniotic sac, like an astronaut free of gravity.

The fetal face stares upward, then turns toward us, as if to mug for the camera. The sound waves strike different tissues with different densities, and their echoes form different images. These images are computer-enhanced, so although the fetus weighs only 14 ounces and is no longer than my hand, we can see its elfin features.

Close up, we peek into the fetal brain. In the seconds we observe, a quarter million new brain cells are born. This happens constantly. By the end of the nine months, the baby's brain will hold 100 billion brain cells.

The sound waves focus on the chest, rendering images of a vibrating four-chambered heart no bigger than the tip of my little finger. The monitor tells us it is moving at 163 beats a minute. It sounds like a frightened bird fluttering in its cage.

We watch the rib cage move. Although the fetus lives in an airless environment, it "breathes" intermittently inside the womb by swallowing amniotic fluid. Some researchers speculate that the fetus is exercising its chest and diaphragm as its way of preparing for life outside the womb.

The clarity of ultrasound pictures is now so good that subtle abnormalities can be detected. The shape of the skull, brain, and spinal cord, along with the heart and other vital organs, can be seen in breathtaking detail.

In this ultrasound exam, there are no hints to suggest that anything is abnormal. The husband squeezes his wife's hand. They both smile.

The fetus we have just watched is at the midpoint of its 40-week gestation. At conception 20 weeks earlier, it began as a single cell that carried in its nucleus the genetic code for the human it will become.

After dividing and redividing for a week, it grew to 32 cells. Like the initial cell, these offspring cells carry 40,000 or so genes, located on 23 pairs of chromosomes inherited from the mother and father. Smaller than the head of a pin, this clump of cells began a slow journey down the fallopian tube and attached itself to the spongy wall of the uterus.

Once settled, some embryonic cells began to form a placenta to supply the embryo with food, water, and nutrients from the mother's bloodstream. The placenta also filtered out harmful substances in the mother's bloodstream. The embryo and mother exchange chemical information to ensure that they work together toward their common goal.

Instructed by their genes, the cells continued to divide but didn't always produce exact replicas. In a process still not well understood, the cells began to differentiate to seek out their own destinies. Some helped build internal organs, others bones, muscles, and brain.

At 19 days postconception, the earliest brain tissues began to form. They developed at the top end of the neural tube, a sheath of cells that ran nearly the entire length of the embryo.

The human brain requires virtually the entire pregnancy to emerge fully, longer than the other organ systems. Even in the earliest stage of development, the fetus knows to protect its brain. The brain gets the most highly oxygenated blood, and should there be any shortage, the fetus will send the available blood to the brain.

Extending downward from the brain, the neural tube began to form the spinal cord. At four weeks, a rudimentary heart started to beat, and four limbs began sprouting. By eight weeks, the two-inch-long embryo took human form and was more properly called a fetus. At 10 to 12 weeks, it began moving its arms and legs, opened its jaws, swallowed, and yawned. Mostly it slept.

"We are never more clever than we are as a fetus," says Dr. Peter Nathanielsz, a fetal researcher, obstetrician, and professor of reproductive medicine at Cornell University. "We pass far more biological milestones before we are born than we'll ever pass after we're born."

Not long ago, the process of fetal development was shrouded in mystery. But through the power of scanning techniques, biotechnology, and fetal and animal studies, much of the mystery of fetal life has been unveiled.

We now know that as the fetus matures it experiences a broad range of sensory stimulation. It hears, sees, tastes, smells, feels, and has rapid eye movement (REM) sleep, the sleep stage we associate with dreaming. From observation of its sleep and wake cycles, the fetus appears to know night from day. It learns and remembers, and it may cry. It seems to do everything in utero that it will do after it is born. In the words of one researcher, "Fetal life is us."

Studies now show that it's the fetus, not the mother, who sends the hormonal signals that determine when a baby will be born. And we've found out that its health in the womb depends in part on its mother's health when she was in the womb.

Finally, we've discovered that the prenatal environment is not as benign, or as neutral, as once thought. It is sensitive to the mother's health, emotions, and behavior.

The fetus is strongly affected by the mother's eating habits. If the mother exercises more than usual, the fetus may become temporarily short of oxygen. If she takes a hot bath, the fetus feels the heat. If she smokes, so does the fetus. One study has found that pregnant women exposed to more sunlight had more outgoing children.

We now know that our genes do not encode a complete design for us, that our "genetic destiny" is not hard-wired at the time of conception. Instead, our development involves an interplay between genes and the environment, including that of the uterus. Because genes take "cues" from their environment, an expectant mother's physical and psychological health influences her unborn child's genetic well-being.

Factors such as low prenatal oxygen levels, stress, infections, and poor maternal nutrition may determine whether certain genes are switched on or off. Some researchers believe that our time in the womb is the single most important period of our life.

"Because of genetics, we once thought that we would unfold in the womb like a blueprint, but now we know it's not that simple," says Janet DiPietro, an associate professor of maternal and child health at the Johns Hopkins School of Public Health and one of a handful of fetal-behavior specialists. "The mother and the uterine environment she creates have a major impact on many aspects of fetal development, and a number of things laid down during that time remain with you throughout your life."

The impact of the womb on our intelligence, personality, and emotional and physical health is beginning to be understood. There's also an emerging understanding of something called fetal programming, which says that the effects of our life in the womb may be not felt until decades after we're born, and in ways that are more powerful than previously imagined.

Says Dr. Nathanielsz, whose book *Life in the Womb* details the emerging science of fetal development: "It's an area of great scientific importance that until recently remained largely unknown."

I'm pregnant. Is it okay to have a glass of wine? Can I take my Prozac? What about a Diet Coke?

Years ago, before she knew she was pregnant, a friend of mine had a glass of wine with dinner. When she discovered she was pregnant, she worried all through her pregnancy and beyond.

She feels some guilt to this day, even though the son she bore turned out very well.

Many mothers have experienced the same tangled emotions. "There's no evidence that a glass of wine a day during pregnancy has a negative impact on the developing fetus," says Dr. John Larsen, professor and chair of obstetrics and gynecology at George Washington University. Larsen says that at one time doctors gave alcohol by IV to pregnant women who were experiencing preterm labor; it relaxed the muscles and quelled contractions.

Larsen now sometimes recommends a little wine to women who experience mild contractions after a puncture from an amniocentesis needle, and some studies suggest that moderate alcohol intake in pregnancy may prevent preterm delivery in some women.

Even though most experts agree with Larsen, the alcohol message that most women hear calls for total abstinence. Experts worry that declaring moderate alcohol intake to be safe in pregnancy may encourage some pregnant women to drink immoderately. They say that pregnant women who have an occasional drink should not think they've placed their baby at risk.

What is safe? Some studies show children born to mothers who consumed three drinks a day in pregnancy averaged seven points lower on IQ tests than unexposed children. There is evidence that six drinks a day during pregnancy puts babies at risk of fetal alcohol syndrome (FAS), a constellation of serious birth defects that includes mental retardation. The higher the alcohol intake, the higher the FAS risk.

Are there drugs and drug combinations that women should avoid or take with caution during pregnancy? Accutane (isotretinoin), a prescription drug for acne and psoriasis, is known to cause birth defects. So too are some anticonvulsant drugs, including Epitol, Tegretol, and Valproate. Tetracycline, a widely prescribed antibiotic, can cause bone-growth delays and permanent teeth problems for a baby if a mother takes it during pregnancy.

Most over-the-counter drugs are considered safe in pregnancy, but some of them carry risks. Heavy doses of aspirin and other nonsteroidal anti-inflammatory drugs such as ibuprofen can delay the start of labor. They are also linked to a life-threatening disorder of newborns called persistent pulmonary hypertension (PPHN), which diverts airflow away from the baby's lungs, causing oxygen depletion. The March issue of the journal *Pediatrics* published a study linking these nonprescription painkillers to PPHN, which results in the death of 15 percent of the infants who have it.

OTC Drugs

In 1998, researchers at the University of Nebraska Medical Center reported dextromethorphan, a cough suppressant found in 40 or more OTC drugs including Nyquil, Tylenol Cold, Dayquil, Robitussin Maximum Strength, and Dimetapp DM, caused congenital malformations in chick embryos. The research was published in *Pediatric Research* and supported by the National Institutes of Health.

Although no connection between dextromethorphan and human birth defects has been shown, the Nebraska researchers noted that similar genes regulate early development in virtually all species. For this reason, the researchers predicted that dextromethorphan, which acts on the brain to suppress coughing, would have the same harmful effect on a human fetus.

Many women worry about antidepressants. Some need them during pregnancy or took them before they knew they were pregnant. A study published in the *New England Journal of Medicine* found no association between fetal exposure to antidepressants and brain damage. The study compared the IQ, temperament, activity level, and distractibility of more than 125 children whose mothers took antidepressants in pregnancy with 84 children whose mothers took no drugs known to harm the fetus.

The two groups of children, between 16 months and eight years old when tested, were comparable in every way. The antidepressants taken by the mothers included both tricyclates such as Elavil and Tofranil and selective serotonin reuptake inhibitors such as Prozac.

Not all mood-altering drugs may be safe. There is some evidence that minor tranquilizers taken for anxiety may cause developmental problems if taken in the first trimester, but there is no hard proof of this. Evidence of fetal damage caused by illegal drugs such as cocaine is widely accepted, as is the case against cigarette smoking. A 1998 survey found that 13 percent of all mothers who gave birth smoked. Evidence is striking that cigarette smoking in pregnancy lowers birth weight and increases the risks of premature birth, attention deficit hyperactive disorder, and diminished IQ.

A long-running study based on information from the National Collaborative Perinatal Project found that years after they were born, children were more apt to become addicted to certain drugs if their mother took them during delivery.

"We found drug-dependent individuals were five times more likely to have exposure to high doses of painkillers and anesthesia during their delivery than their nonaddicted siblings," says Stephen Buka of the Harvard School of Public Health. Buka suspects this is caused by a modification in the infant's brain receptors as the drugs pass from mother to child during an especially sensitive time.

Caffeine

Coffee consumption has worried mothers because there have been hints that caffeine may be harmful to the fetus. Like most things in life, moderation is the key. There's no evidence that 300 milligrams of caffeine a day (about three cups of coffee, or four or five cups of most regular teas, or five to six cola drinks) harms a developing baby. Higher caffeine consumption has been weakly linked to miscarriage and difficulty in conceiving.

Expectant mothers concerned about weight gain should be careful of how much of the artificial sweetener aspartame they consume. Marketed under brand names such as NutraSweet and Equal, it's found in diet soft drinks and foods.

The concern is this: In the body, aspartame converts into phenylalanine, a naturally occurring amino acid we ingest when we eat protein. At high levels, phenylalanine can be toxic to brain cells.

When we consume phenylalanine in protein, we also consume a number of other amino acids that neutralize any ill effects. When we consume it in aspartame, we get none of the neutralizing amino acids to dampen phenylalanine's impact. And as it crosses the placenta, phenylalanine's concentrations are magnified in the fetal brain.

If a fetal brain is exposed to high levels of phenylalanine because its mother consumes a lot of aspartame, will it be harmed? One study found average IQ declines of ten points in children born to mothers with a fivefold increase of phenylalanine blood levels in pregnancy. That's a lot of aspartame, and it doesn't mean an expectant mother who drinks moderate amounts of diet soda need worry.

Researchers say consuming up to three servings of aspartame a day—in either diet soda or low-calorie foods—appears to be safe for the fetus. However, a pregnant woman of average weight who eats ten or more servings a day may put her unborn baby at risk. In testimony before Congress, Dr. William Pardridge, a neuroscience researcher at UCLA, said it's likely that the effect of high phenylalanine levels in the fetal brain "will be very subtle" and many not manifest until years later.

One wild card concerns the 10 to 20 million Americans who unknowingly carry a gene linked to a genetic disease called phenylketonuria (PKU), which can lead to severe mental retardation. Most carriers don't know it, because PKU is a recessive genetic disorder, and both mother and father must carry the defective gene to pass PKU on to their child. A carrier feels no ill effects. According to researchers, a pregnant woman who unknowingly carries the PKU gene might place her unborn child at risk if she consumes even relatively moderate amounts of aspartame. There is no hard evidence that this will happen, but it remains a serious concern. PKU can be detected in the fetus by amniocentesis; a restrictive diet can prevent the worst effects of PKU on the child.

How does a mother's getting an infection affect her unborn baby? And should she be careful of cats?

Many experts think pregnant women should be more concerned about infections and household pets than a glass of wine or can of diet drink. There's overwhelming evidence of the potential harm of infections during pregnancy. We've known for a long time that rubella (German measles), a viral infection, can cause devastating birth defects.

More worrisome are recent studies showing that exposure to one of the most common of winter's ills—influenza—may put an unborn child at risk of cognitive and emotional problems. If flu strikes in the second trimester, it may increase the unborn baby's risk of developing schizophrenia later in life. While the flu may be a trigger, it's likely that a genetic susceptibility is also needed for schizophrenia to develop.

Some evidence exists that maternal flu may also lead to dyslexia, and suspicions persist that a first-trimester flu may cause fetal neural-tube defects resulting in spina bifida. The common cold, sometimes confused with the flu, has not been linked to any adverse outcomes for the baby.

"Infections are probably the most important thing for a pregnant woman to protect herself against," says Lise Eliot, a developmental neurobiologist at the Chicago Medical School. "She should always practice good hygiene, like washing her hands frequently, avoiding crowds, and never drinking from someone else's cup." She adds that the flu vaccine has been approved for use during pregnancy.

Some researchers recommend that pregnant women avoid close contact with cats. Toxoplasmosis, a parasitic infection, can travel from a cat to a woman to her unborn child.

Most humans become infected through cat litter boxes. An infected woman might experience only mild symptoms, if any, so the illness usually goes undetected. If she is diagnosed with the infection, antiparasitic drugs are helpful, but they don't completely eliminate the disease. The infection is relatively rare, and the odds of passing it from mother to child are only one in five during the first two trimesters, when the fetal harm is most serious. The bad news is that a fetus infected by toxoplasmosis can suffer severe brain damage, including mental retardation and epilepsy. Some researchers also suspect it may be a latent trigger for serious mental illness as the child grows older.

Cerebral Palsy

An expectant mother may not realize she has potentially harmful infections. The prime suspects are infections in the reproductive tract. Researchers suspect most cerebral-palsy cases are not caused by delivery problems, as has been widely assumed. There's strong evidence that some cases of cerebral-palsy may be linked to placental infections that occur during uterine life. Other cerebral-palsy cases may be triggered by oxygen deprivation in early development, but very few appear to be caused by oxygen deprivation during delivery. It's now estimated that only 10 percent of cerebral-palsy cases are related to delivery problems.

Maternal urinary-tract infections have been linked to lower IQs in children. Another infection, cytomegalovirus (CMV), has been linked to congenital deafness. Sexually transmitted diseases such as chlamydia are suspected to be a trigger for preterm birth. Despite the serious threat posed to developing babies, infections during pregnancy remain poorly understood.

"We just don't know right now when or how the uterine infections that really make a difference to the fetus are transmitted in pregnancy," says Dr. Karin Nelson, a child neurologist and acting chief of the neuro-epidemiology branch of the National Institute of Neurologic Disorders and Stroke at NIH. "Nor do we know all the potential problems they may cause."

Because of this, researchers offer little in the way of recommendations other than clean living and careful sex. They recommend that any woman contemplating pregnancy get in her best physical condition, because a number of studies have found that a woman's general health before she becomes pregnant is vital to fetal health. They also recommend a thorough gynecological exam because it may detect a treatable infection that could harm the fetus.

Rachel Carson was right about pesticides. So if you're pregnant, how careful should you be about what you eat?

In her book *Silent Spring,* author Rachel Carson noted that when pregnant mammals were exposed to synthetic pesticides, including DDT and methoxychlor, the pesticides caused developmental abnormalities in offspring. Carson, a scientist, noted that some pesticides mimicked the female hormone estrogen and caused the male offspring to be feminized.

About the time of Carson's 1962 book, another story was emerging about diethylstilbestrol (DES), a man-made female hormone administered in the 1940s and '50s to prevent miscarriages. In the 1960s it became clear that many young daughters of DES mothers were turning up reproductive malformations and vaginal cancers. Sons born to DES mothers suffered reproductive problems, including undescended testicles and abnormal sperm counts.

Endocrine Disrupters

Over the years, suspicion grew from both animal and human studies that something in the environment was disrupting fetal development. In the 1990s it was given a name—endocrine disruption. The theory was that DES and the pesticides cited by Carson caused defects in offspring because they disrupted the normal endocrine process. They did this by mimicking hormones inside the human body.

It's now clear that DDT and DES are the tip of the iceberg. Today more than 90,000 synthetic chemicals are used, most made after World War II. New chemicals are produced every week. They are used in everything from pesticides to plastics.

How many of these man-made chemicals might act as endocrine disrupters? More than 50 have been identified, and hundreds more are suspects.

To understand the threat from endocrine disrupters, it helps to understand what human hormones do. Secreted by endocrine glands, these tiny molecules circulate through the bloodstream to the organs. They include estrogen, adrenalin, thyroid, melatonin, and testosterone. Each is designed to fit only into a specific receptor on a cell, like a key that fits only one lock. When a hormone connects with the cell receptor, it enters the cell's nucleus. Once there, the hormone acts as a signaling agent to direct the cell's DNA to produce specific proteins.

During fetal life, the right type and concentration of hormones must be available at the right time for normal fetal development to occur. Produced by both mother and fetus, hormones are involved in cell division and differentiation, the development of the brain and reproductive organs, and virtually everything else needed to produce a baby.

"We know from animal experiments and wildlife observations that periods in development are very sensitive to alterations in the hormone levels," says Robert Kavlock, director of reproductive toxicology for the Environmental Protection Agency.

The damage is done when chemical mimickers get into cells at the wrong time, or at the wrong strength, or both. When this happens, something in the fetus will not develop as it should.

After years of witnessing the harmful impact on wildlife, we now know that humans are not immune to endocrine disrupters. More troubling, because of the pervasiveness of these chemicals, is that we can't escape them. We get them in the food we eat, the water we drink, the products we buy.

One of the most dramatic examples came to light in the 1970s when researchers wanted to find out why so many babies born in the Great Lakes region suffered serious neurological defects. They found the answer in polychlorinated biphenyls (PCBs), organic chemicals once used in electrical insulation and adhesives. Heavy PCB contamination of Great Lakes fish eaten by the mothers turned out to be the cause.

It is not clear how PCBs cause fetal brain damage, but it's believed to happen when they disrupt thyroid hormones. Severe thyroid deficiency in pregnancy is known to cause mental retardation. Another study found reduced penis size in boys born to mothers exposed to high levels of PCBs.

The U.S. manufacture of PCBs ended in 1977. PCB levels found in the mothers and the fish they ate suggested at the time that only very high exposure caused a problem for developing babies. Now we know this isn't true.

Because PCBs don't break down, they've remained a toxin that continues to enter our bodies through the food we eat. They have leached into soil and water and are found in shellfish and freshwater fish and to a smaller degree in ocean fish. Bottom-feeding freshwater fish, such as catfish and carp, have the highest PCB concentrations.

PCBs store in fat tissue and are found in dairy products and meats. Fatty meats, especially processed meats like cold cuts, sausages, and hot dogs, are usually heaviest in PCBs. They get into these products because farm animals graze on PCB-contaminated land. However, eating fish from PCB-contaminated water remains the primary way we get these chemicals into our systems. In pregnant women, PCBs easily cross the placenta and circulate in the fetus.

PCBs are ubiquitous. They've been detected in the Antarctic snow. If you had detection equipment sensitive enough, you'd find them in the milk at the supermarket.

What concerns experts are findings from studies in the Netherlands and upstate New York that found even low maternal PCB exposures pose risk to a fetus.

The Dutch study followed 418 children from birth into early childhood. In the final month of pregnancy, researchers measured the maternal PCB blood levels, and at birth they measured PCB levels in the umbilical cord. None of the mothers was a heavy fish eater or had any history of high PCB exposure, and none of their PCB levels was considered high by safety standards.

At 3½ years of age, the children's cognitive abilities were assessed with tests. After adjusting for other variables, the researchers found that maternal and cord blood PCB levels correlated with the children's cognitive abilities. As the PCB blood levels went up, the children suffered more attention problems and their cognitive abilities went down. It should be noted that the brain damage in these Dutch children was not devastating. They were not retarded or autistic. But on a relative scale, they had suffered measurable harm.

The Dutch researchers concluded that the in utero PCB exposure, and not any postnatal exposure, caused the children's brain damage. The study also revealed that these children had depressed immune function.

"All we can say now," says Deborah Rice, a toxicologist at the EPA's National Center for Environmental Assessment in Washington, "is we have strong evidence that PCB levels commonly found among women living in industrialized society can cause subtle neurological damage in their offspring." But one of the difficulties, according to Rice, is that we really don't yet know what an unsafe maternal PCB level might be.

"I think the bottom line is that women should be aware of PCBs and aware of what they're putting in their mouth," adds Rice.

The Dutch study is a warning not only about the potential impact of low levels of PCBs but about the potential harm from low levels of other endocrine disrupters.

More news arrived in March when the results from the federal government's on-going Fourth National Health and Nutrition Examination Survey (NHANES) became public. The survey of 38,000 people revealed that most of us have at least trace levels of pesticides, heavy metals, and plastics in our body tissues. In all, NHANES tested for 27 elements.

The survey found widespread exposure to phthalates, synthetic chemicals used as softeners in plastics and other products. Phthalates are one of the most heavily produced chemicals and have been linked in animal studies to endocrine disruption and birth defects. The likely sources of human exposure are foods and personal-care products such as shampoos, lotions, soaps, and perfumes; phthalates are absorbed through the skin.

Dr. Ted Schettler, a member of the Greater Boston Physicians for Social Responsibility, suspects endocrine disrupters may be linked to increases in the three hormone-driven cancers—breast, prostate, and testicular. The rate of testicular cancer among young men has nearly doubled in recent years, and the rates of learning disabilities and infertility also have increased.

"We can't blame all that is happening on toxic chemicals," says Schettler, who coauthored *In Harm's Way,* a report on how chemical contaminants affect human health. "But we need to ask ourselves if we're seeing patterns that suggest these chemicals are having a major impact on fetal development and human populations. We also need to ask what level of evidence we're going to need before we take public-health measures. That's a political question."

The EPA's Kavlock says, "We don't know the safe or unsafe levels for many of these chemicals." Nor do we know how many of the thousands of man-made chemicals in the environment will turn out to be endocrine disrupters or cause human harm. The EPA received a mandate from Congress in 1996 to find the answers, but it will be a long wait.

"If we devoted all the toxicology testing capacity in the entire world to look for endocrine-disrupting chemicals, we couldn't do all the chemicals. There's just not enough capacity," Kavlock says. "So we are focusing on 500 to 1,000 chemicals that are the major suspects. It will take many years and a lot of money just to understand how they interact with hormonal-system and fetal development."

What is all this bad stuff we can get from eating fish or from microwaving food in plastics? Do vitamins help?

Methylmercury is a heavy metal that can cause fetal brain damage. NHANES revealed that 10 percent of American women of child-bearing age—a representative sample of all American women—had methylmercury blood and hair levels close to "potentially hazardous levels." The EPA and some non-government experts consider these existing methylmercury levels already above what is safe.

Dr. Jill Stein, an adolescent-medicine specialist and instructor at Harvard Medical School, has studied methylmercury's toxicity. She says the acceptable levels of methylmercury in the NHANES report were too high and that many more women are in the danger zone. "The NHANES data tells me that more than 10 percent of American women today are carrying around enough mercury to put their future children at risk for learning and behavior problems," she says.

Like PCBs and other toxic chemicals, mercury is hard to avoid because it is abundant in our environment. It comes from natural and man-made sources, chiefly coal-fired power plants and municipal waste treatment. Each year an estimated 160 tons of mercury is released into the nation's environment. In water, mercury combines with natural bacteria to form methylmercury, a toxic form of the metal. It is easily absorbed by fish. When a pregnant woman consumes the contaminated fish, methylmercury crosses the placenta and the fetal blood-brain barrier.

The world became aware of methylmercury's potential for harm more than 40 years ago in the fishing village of Minamata in Japan. People there were exposed to high levels of the heavy metal from industrial dumping of mercury compounds into Minamata Bay. The villagers, who ate a diet heavy in fish caught in the bay, experienced devastating effects. The hardest hit were the unborn. Women gave birth to babies with cerebral-palsy-like symptoms. Many were retarded.

Mercury

Fish are the major source of mercury for humans. The Food and Drug Administration recommends that pregnant women not eat swordfish, king mackerel, shark, and tilefish. These fish are singled out because large oceangoing fish contain more methylmercury. Smaller ocean fish, especially cod, haddock, and pollock, generally have low methylmercury levels. A whitefish found off the coast of Alaska, pollock is commonly found in fish sticks and fast-food fish. Salmon have low methylmercury levels, but they are a fatty fish and apt to carry higher levels of PCBs.

Like the Dutch PCB studies, recent studies of maternal methylmercury exposure have turned up trouble. They've shown that the so-called "safe" maternal levels of the metal can cause brain damage during fetal development.

One study was carried out in the 1990s by a Danish research team that studied 917 children in the Faroe Islands, where seafood is a big part of the diet. Children were grouped into categories depending on their level of maternal methylmercury exposure; they were assessed up to age seven by neurological tests. None of the children's methylmercury exposure levels was considered high, yet many of the children had evidence of brain damage, including memory, attention, and learning problems.

"Subtle effects on brain function therefore seem to be detectable at prenatal methylmercury exposure levels currently considered safe," the study concluded. In a follow-up report published in a 1999 issue of the *Journal of the American Medical Association,* the authors said the blood concentrations of methylmercury found in the umbilical cord corresponded with the severity of the neurological damage suffered by the children.

In a study of 237 children, New Zealand researchers found similar neurological harm, including IQ impairment and attention problems, in children whose mothers' exposure to methylmercury came from fish they ate during pregnancy.

"The children in these studies were not bathed in methylmercury," notes Rita Schoeny, a toxicologist in the EPA's Office of Water. "Can people in the U.S. be exposed to the same levels of mercury in the course of their dietary practice? We think so."

Jill Stein and other experts worry that the more scientific studies we do, the more we'll realize that in fetal development there may be no such thing as a "safe" maternal level for methylmercury, PCBs, and scores of other synthetic chemicals.

"We keep learning from studies that these chemicals are harmful to fetal development at lower and lower doses," Stein says. "It's what we call the declining threshold of harm."

What about canned tuna? It has been assumed to contain low methylmercury levels because most of it comes from smaller fish. The FDA offers no advisories about it. But according to EPA researchers, a recent State of Florida survey of more than 100 samples of canned tuna found high levels of methylmercury. The more-expensive canned tuna, such as albacore and solid white tuna, usually carried higher methylmercury levels, according to the survey. This apparently is because more expensive canned tuna comes from larger tuna. In some of the canned tuna, the methylmercury levels were high enough to prevent their export to several countries, including Canada.

Some of the methylmercury levels were "worrisomely high," according to Kathryn Mahaffey, a toxicologist and director of the division of exposure assessment at the EPA. They were high enough to cause concern for pregnant women.

"A big problem is the tremendous variability out there in the tuna supply," adds Stein. "You have no idea when you're eating a can of tuna how much methylmercury you're getting."

"Even if you ate just a small serving of some of these canned tunas each day," says Mahaffey, "you'd be substantially above a level we would consider safe."

Mahaffey and Stein agree that an expectant mother who ate even a few servings a week with methylmercury levels found in some of the canned tuna would put her developing baby at risk of brain and other neurological damage.

Now that we know a developing fetus is sensitive to even low levels of toxic chemicals, women can exercise some basic precautions to help protect their developing babies.

Don't microwave food that is wrapped in plastic or is still in plastic containers. "There are endocrine-disrupting chemicals in these plastics," Schettler says, "that leach right into the food when it's microwaved. This has been well documented and measured." Studies suggest that even at very low levels these chemicals can have an adverse effect on the fetus's hormonal system.

The EPA's Kavlock considers the fruits and vegetables you buy at the supermarket to be safe in pregnancy, but Schettler says you should try to eat organic foods to avoid even trace amounts of pesticides. Wash fruits and vegetables before eating them. Avoid pesticides or insecticide use around the house during pregnancy as well as the use of chemical solvents for painting or remodeling.

Herbicides and pesticides have leached into reservoirs that supply home drinking water, and filtration plants can't remove them all. Some are known to be endocrine disrupters. Home water filters can reduce contaminants; the best ones use active charcoal as a filtering agent.

Experts agree that a pregnant woman, or a woman who may get pregnant, can eat fish but should be careful about the kind she eats and how much of it. EPA's Rice cautions any woman who is pregnant or thinking of becoming pregnant to avoid eating any sport fish caught in a lake or river.

Vegetable Fats

Rice adds that the PCB risk with fish can be reduced. "Trim the fish of fat and skin, and broil or grill it," see says. "That way you cook off fat and minimize your PCB exposure." There is not much you can do to reduce the methylmercury levels in fish because it binds to protein.

"Fat is important for a baby's neurological development before and after birth, so pregnant women should consider vegetable fats like olive oil and flaxseed oil as a source," Rice adds. She says low fat dairy and meat products carry fewer PCBs than higher-fat ones.

The EPA has issued a PCB advisory for the Potomac River in the District, Virginia, and Maryland, citing in particular catfish and carp. You can go to www.epa.gov/ost/fish/epafish.pdf for EPA advisories on PCB and methylmercury environmental contamination. From there you can connect to state Web sites for advisories on local waters and specific fish.

Women can help prevent neurological and other birth defects by taking vitamin supplements before pregnancy. A daily dose of 400 micrograms of folic acid can reduce the risk of such problems as spina bifida by more than 70 percent as well as prevent brain defects and cleft lip and palate. Indirect evidence from a study published last year in the *New England Journal of Medicine* suggests that folic acid may also help prevent congenital heart defects.

To be effective, folic acid should be taken before pregnancy to prevent developmental defects. Folic acid comes in multivitamins and prenatal vitamins and is found naturally in legumes, whole-wheat bread, citrus fruits, fortified breakfast cereal, and leafy green vegetables. Despite the proven value of folic acid, a recent March of Dimes survey found that only 32 percent of American women of childbearing age—including pregnant women—took folic-acid supplements.

What can a fetus learn in the womb? And does playing Mozart make a baby lots smarter?

Developmental psychologist Anthony DeCasper wanted to answer two questions: What does a fetus know, and when does it know it?

DeCasper's aim was to find out if a fetus could learn in utero and remember what it learned after it was born. He enlisted the help of 33 healthy expectant mothers and asked each to tape-record herself reading passages from Dr. Seuss's *The Cat in the Hat* or from another children's book, *The King, the Mice, and the Cheese*. The mothers were randomly assigned to play one of these readings, each of which lasted two or three minutes, to their unborn children three times a day during the final three weeks of their pregnancies.

DeCasper, a professor of developmental psychology at the University of North Carolina at Greensboro, could do the experiment because it was known that fetuses could hear by the third trimester and probably earlier. DeCasper had shown earlier that at birth, babies preferred their mother's voice to all other voices. Studies in the early 1990s found that fetuses could be soothed by lullabies and sometimes moved in rhythm to their mother's voice. Fetuses hear their mother's voice from the outside, just as they can hear any other voice, but they hear the mother's voice clearer and stronger through bone conduction as it resonates inside her.

A little more than two days after birth, each of the newborns in DeCasper's study was given a specially devised nipple. The device worked by utilizing the baby's sucking reflex. When the baby sucked on the nipple, it would hear its mother's voice. But if it paused for too long a time between sucks, it would hear another woman's voice. This gave the baby control over whose voice it would hear by controlling the length of its pause between sucks.

DeCasper also placed small earphones over the infant's ears through which it could hear its mother's voice read from the books.

"Now two days or so after it was born, the baby gets to choose between two stories read by its own mother," DeCasper said. "One was the story she'd recited three times a day for the last three weeks of pregnancy, and the other is one the baby's never heard before, except for the one day his mother recorded it. So the big question was: Would the babies prefer the story they'd heard in the womb, or wouldn't they? The answer was a clear yes—the babies preferred to hear the familiar story."

DeCasper did a second experiment by having women who were not the baby's mothers recite the same two stories. The babies again showed a strong preference for the story they'd heard in the womb.

"These studies not only tell us something about the fidelity with which the fetal ear can hear," DeCasper says, "but they also show that during those two or three weeks in the womb, fetal learning and memory are occurring."

British researchers observed expectant mothers who watched a TV soap opera. The researchers placed monitors on the mother's abdomens to listen in on fetal movements when the program aired. By the 37th week of pregnancy, the babies responded to the show's theme music by increasing their movements, an indication they remembered it.

Soon after the babies were born, the researchers replayed the theme music to them. This time, instead of moving more, the babies appeared to calm down and pay attention to the music. The researchers considered this a response to familiar music.

Fetal Memory

"The fact that we find evidence of fetal memory doesn't mean fetuses carry conscious memories, like we remember what we ate for breakfast," explains Lise Eliot, author of *What's Going On in There?*, a book on early brain development. "But we now know there is a tremendous continuity from prenatal to postnatal life, and the prenatal experience begins to shape a child's interaction with the world it will confront after birth. Babies go through the same activity patterns and behavioral states before and after birth. Well before it is born, the baby is primed to gravitate to its mother and its mother's voice."

Some researchers speculate a baby's ability to remember in the womb may be a way of easing its transition from prenatal life to postnatal life. A baby already accustomed to and comforted by its mother's voice may be reassured as it enters a new world of bright lights, needle pricks, curious faces, and loud noises.

The question arises: Can the uterine environment affect a baby's intelligence? Twins studies have shown that genes exert an all-powerful influence on IQ. The role of environment in IQ has traditionally meant the nurturance and stimulation the baby receives after birth.

Bernie Devlin, a biostatistician and assistant professor of psychiatry at the University of Pittsburgh, did an analysis of 212 twins studies on intelligence. In a paper published in *Nature,* he concluded that the accepted figure of 60 to 80 percent for IQ heritability is too high. It should be closer to 50 percent, he says, which leaves more room for environmental factors. Devlin says the one environmental factor that's been missing in understanding human intelligence is time in the womb.

"I'm surprised that the impact of fetal life on a child's intelligence had not been accounted for in these IQ studies," Devlin says. "I know it's very complicated, but it's surprising that people who study the heritability of intelligence really haven't considered this factor."

What is the impact of life in the womb on intelligence? Devlin thinks it's equal to if not greater than the impact of a child's upbringing. In other words, it's possible a mother may have more influence over her child's intelligence before birth than after.

As the brain develops in utero, we know it undergoes changes that affect its ultimate capacity. Nutritional and hormonal influences from the mother have a big impact. And twins studies show that the heavier twin at birth most often has the higher IQ.

A number of studies from the United States and Latin America also found that a range of vitamins, as well as sufficient protein in the mother's prenatal diet, had an impact on the child's intelligence.

Links between specific vitamins and intelligence have been borne out in two studies. An animal study conducted at the University of North Carolina and published in the March issue of *Developmental Brain Research* found that rats with a choline deficiency during pregnancy gave birth to offspring with severe brain impairments. Choline, a B-complex vitamin involved in nerve transmission, is found in eggs, meat, peanuts, and dietary supplements.

The August 1999 issue of the *New England Journal of Medicine* reported that expectant mothers with low thyroid function gave birth to children with markedly diminished IQs as well as motor and attention deficits. The study said one cause of hypothyroidism—present in 2 to 3 percent of American women—is a lack of iodine in the American diet. Women whose hypothyroidism was detected and treated before pregnancy had children with normal test scores. Hypothyroidism can be detected with a blood test, but expectant mothers who receive little or late prenatal care often go undiagnosed or are diagnosed too late to help their child.

Although most American women get the nutrition they need through diet and prenatal vitamins, not all do. According to a National Center for Health Statistics survey, more than one in four expectant mothers in the U.S. received inadequate prenatal care.

Devlin's *Nature* article took a parting shot at the conclusions reached in the 1994 book *The Bell Curve,* in which Richard J. Herrnstein and Charles Murray argued that different social classes are a result of genetically determined, and therefore unalterable, IQ levels. The lower the IQ, the argument goes, the lower the social class.

Not only does the data show IQ to be far less heritable than that book alleges, Devlin says, but he suspects improvements in the health status of mostly poor expectant mothers would see measurable increases in the IQs of their offspring.

Devlin's argument is supported by Randy Thornhill, a biologist at the University of New Mexico. Thornhill's research suggests that IQ differences are due in part to what he calls "heritable vulnerabilities to environmental sources of developmental stress." In other words, vulnerable genes interact with environmental insults in utero resulting in gene mutations that affect fetal development. Thornhill says environmental insults may include viruses, maternal drug abuse, or poor nutrition.

"The developmental instability that results," Thornhill says, "is most readily seen in the body's asymmetry when one side of the body differs from the other. For example, on average an individual's index fingers will differ in length by about two millimeters. Some people have much more asymmetries than others."

But the asymmetries we see on the outside also occur in the nervous system. When this happens, neurons are harmed and memory and intelligence are impaired. Thornhill says the more physical asymmetries you have, the more neurological impairment you have. He calculates that these factors can account for as much as 50 percent of the differences we find in IQ.

Thornhill adds that a fetus that carries these genetic vulnerabilities, but develops in an ideal uterine environment, will not experience any serious problems because the worrisome mutations will not occur.

"The practical implications for this are tremendous," Thornhill says. "If we can understand what environmental factors most disrupt fetal development of the nervous system, then we'll be in a position to remove them and have many more intelligent people born."

Studies on fetal IQ development suggest that the current emphasis on nurturance and stimulation for young children be rethought. The philosophy behind initiatives such as Zero to Three and Early Head Start makes sense. The programs are based on evidence that the first three years are very important for brain development and that early stimulation can effect positive changes in a child's life. But Devlin and Thornhill's research suggests a stronger public-health emphasis on a baby's prenatal life if we are to equalize the opportunities for children.

Does that mean unborn babies need to hear more Mozart? Companies are offering kits so expectant mothers can play music or different sounds to their developing babies—the prenatal "Mozart effect." One kit promises this stimulation will lead to "longer new-born attention span, better sleep patterns,

accelerated development, expanded cognitive powers, enhanced social awareness and extraordinary language abilities." Will acceptance to Harvard come next?

"The number of bogus and dangerous devices available to expectant parents to make their babies smarter constantly shocks me," says DiPietro. "All these claims are made without a shred of evidence to support them."

Adds DeCasper: "I think it is dangerous to stimulate the baby in the womb. If you play Mozart and it remembers Mozart, is it going to be a smarter baby? I haven't got a clue. Could it hurt the baby? Yes, I think it could. If you started this stimulation too early and played it too loud, there is evidence from animal studies that you can destroy the ear's ability to hear sounds in a particular range. That's an established fact. Would I take a risk with my fetus? No!"

DeCasper and other researches emphasize that no devices or tricks can enhance the brainpower of a developing baby. Their advice to the expectant mother: Take the best possible care of yourself.

"The womb is a quiet, protective place for a reason," DiPietro concludes. "Nature didn't design megaphones to be placed on the abdomen. The fetus gets all the stimulation it needs for its brain to develop."

Mr. John Pekkanen is a contributing editor to *The Washingtonian*. From "Secrets of the Womb," by John Pekkanen, *The Washingtonian*, August 2001, pages 44–51, 126–135.

Fat, Carbs and the Science of Conception

In a groundbreaking new book, Harvard researchers look at the role of diet, exercise and weight control in fertility. Guarantee: you will be surprised.

JORGE E. CHAVARRO, M.D., WALTER C. WILLETT, M.D., AND PATRICK J. SKERRETT

Every new life starts with two seemingly simple events. First, an active sperm burrows into a perfectly mature egg. Then the resulting fertilized egg nestles into the specially prepared lining of the uterus and begins to grow. The key phrase in that description is "seemingly simple." Dozens of steps influenced by a cascade of carefully timed hormones are needed to make and mature eggs and sperm. Their union is both a mad dash and a complex dance, choreographed by hormones, physiology and environmental cues.

A constellation of other factors can come into play. Many couples delay having a baby until they are financially ready or have established themselves in their professions. Waiting, though, decreases the odds of conceiving and increases the chances of having a miscarriage. Fewer than 10 percent of women in their early 20s have issues with infertility, compared with nearly 30 percent of those in their early 40s. Sexually transmitted diseases such as chlamydia and gonorrhea, which are on the upswing, can cause or contribute to infertility. The linked epidemics of obesity and diabetes sweeping the country have reproductive repercussions. Environmental contaminants known as endocrine disruptors, such as some pesticides and emissions from burning plastics, appear to affect fertility in women and men. Stress and anxiety, both in general and about fertility, can also interfere with getting pregnant. Add all these to the complexity of conception and it's no wonder that infertility is a common problem, besetting an estimated 6 million American couples.

It's almost become a cliché that diet, exercise and lifestyle choices affect how long you'll live, the health of your heart, the odds you'll develop cancer and a host of other health-related issues. Is fertility on this list? The answer to that question has long been a qualified "maybe," based on old wives' tales, conventional wisdom—and almost no science. Farmers, ranchers and animal scientists know more about how nutrition affects fertility in cows, pigs and other commercially important animals than fertility experts know about how it affects reproduction in humans. There are small hints scattered across medical journals, but few systematic studies of this crucial connection in people.

We set out to change this critical information gap with the help of more than 18,000 women taking part in the Nurses' Health Study, a long-term research project looking at the effects of diet and other factors on the development of chronic conditions such as heart disease, cancer and other diseases. Each of these women said she was trying to have a baby. Over eight years of follow-up, most of them did. About one in six women, though, had some trouble getting pregnant, including hundreds who experienced ovulatory infertility—a problem related to the maturation or release of a mature egg each month. When we compared their diets, exercise habits and other lifestyle choices with those of women who readily got pregnant, several key differences emerged. We have translated these differences into fertility-boosting strategies.

At least for now, these recommendations are aimed at preventing and reversing ovulatory infertility, which accounts for one quarter or more of all cases of infertility. They won't work for infertility due to physical impediments like blocked fallopian tubes. They may work for other types of infertility, but we don't yet have enough data to explore connections between nutrition and infertility due to other causes. And since the Nurses' Health Study doesn't include information on the participants' partners, we weren't able to explore how nutrition affects male infertility. From what we have gleaned from the limited research in this area, some of our strategies might improve fertility in men, too. The plan described in The Fertility Diet doesn't guarantee a pregnancy any more than do in vitro fertilization or other forms of assisted reproduction. But it's virtually free, available to everyone, has no side effects, sets the stage for a healthy pregnancy, and forms the foundation of a healthy eating strategy for motherhood and beyond. That's a winning combination no matter how you look at it.

Slow Carbs, Not No Carbs

Once upon a time, and not that long ago, carbohydrates were the go-to gang for taste, comfort, convenience and energy. Bread, pasta, rice, potatoes—these were the highly recommended, base-of-the-food-pyramid foods that supplied us with half or more of our calories. Then in rumbled the Atkins and South Beach diets. In a scene out of George Orwell's "1984," good became bad almost overnight as the two weight-loss juggernauts turned carbohydrates into dietary demons, vilifying them as the source of big bellies and jiggling thighs. Following the no-carb gospel, millions of Americans spurned carbohydrates in hopes of shedding pounds. Then, like all diet fads great and small, the no-carb craze lost its luster and faded from prominence.

It had a silver lining, though, and not just for those selling low-carb advice and products. All the attention made scientists and the rest of us more aware of carbohydrates and their role in a healthy diet. It spurred several solid head-to-head comparisons of low-carb and low-fat diets that have given us a better understanding of how carbohydrates affect weight and weight loss. The new work supports the growing realization that carbohydrate choices have a major impact—for better and for worse—on the risk for heart disease, stroke, type 2 diabetes and digestive health.

New research from the Nurses' Health Study shows that carbohydrate choices also influence fertility. Eating lots of easily digested carbohydrates (fast carbs), such as white bread, potatoes and sugared sodas, increases the odds that you'll find yourself struggling with ovulatory infertility. Choosing slowly digested carbohydrates that are rich in fiber can improve fertility. This lines up nicely with work showing that a diet rich in these slow carbs and fiber before pregnancy helps prevent gestational diabetes, a common and worrisome problem for pregnant women and their babies. What do carbohydrates have to do with ovulation and pregnancy?

More than any other nutrient, carbohydrates determine your blood-sugar and insulin levels. When these rise too high, as they do in millions of individuals with insulin resistance, they disrupt the finely tuned balance of hormones needed for reproduction. The ensuing hormonal changes throw ovulation off-kilter.

Knowing that diet can strongly influence blood sugar and insulin, we wondered if carbohydrate choices could influence fertility in average, relatively healthy women. The answer from the Nurses' Health Study was yes. We started by grouping the study participants from low daily carbohydrate intake to high. One of the first things we noticed was a connection between high carbohydrate intake and healthy lifestyles.

Women in the high-carb group, who got nearly 60 percent of their calories from carbs, ate less fat and animal protein, drank less alcohol and coffee, and consumed more plant protein and fiber than those in the low-carb group, who got 42 percent of calories from carbohydrates. Women in the top group also weighed less, weren't as likely to smoke and were more physically active. This is a good sign that carbohydrates can be just fine for health, especially if you choose good ones.

The *total* amount of carbohydrate in the diet wasn't connected with ovulatory infertility. Women in the low-carb and high-carb groups were equally likely to have had fertility problems. That wasn't a complete surprise. As we described earlier, different carbohydrate sources can have different effects on blood sugar, insulin and long-term health.

Evaluating total carbohydrate intake can hide some important differences. So we looked at something called the glycemic load. This relatively new measure conveys information about both the amount of carbohydrate in the diet and how quickly it is turned to blood sugar. The more fast carbs in the diet, the higher the glycemic load. (For more on glycemic load, go to health.harvard.edu/ newsweek.) Women in the highest glycemic-load category were 92 percent more likely to have had ovulatory infertility than women in the lowest category, after accounting for age, smoking, how much animal and vegetable protein they ate, and other factors that can also influence fertility. In other words, eating a lot of easily digested carbohydrates increases the odds of ovulatory infertility, while eating more slow carbs decreases the odds.

Because the participants of the Nurses' Health Study complete reports every few years detailing their average daily diets, we were able to see if certain foods contributed to ovulatory infertility more than others. In general, cold breakfast cereals, white rice and potatoes were linked with a higher risk of ovulatory infertility. Slow carbs, such as brown rice, pasta and dark bread, were linked with greater success getting pregnant.

Computer models of the nurses' diets were also revealing. We electronically replaced different nutrients with carbohydrates. Most of these substitutions didn't make a difference. One, though, did. Adding more carbohydrates at the expense of naturally occurring fats predicted a decrease in fertility. This could very well mean that natural fats, especially unsaturated fats, improve ovulation when they replace easily digested carbohydrates.

In a nutshell, results from the Nurses' Health Study indicate that the *amount* of carbohydrates in the diet doesn't affect fertility, but the *quality* of those carbohydrates does. Eating a lot of rapidly digested carbohydrates that continually boost your blood-sugar and insulin levels higher can lower your chances of getting pregnant. This is especially true if you are eating carbohydrates in place of healthful unsaturated fats. On the other hand, eating whole grains, beans, vegetables and whole fruits—all of which are good sources of slowly digested carbohydrates—can improve ovulation and your chances of getting pregnant.

Eating whole grains, beans, vegetables and whole fruits—all sources of 'slow carbs'— can improve ovulation and chances of pregnancy.

Balancing Fats

In 2003, the government of Denmark made a bold decision that is helping protect its citizens from heart disease: it essentially banned trans fats in fast food, baked goods and other commercially prepared foods. That move may have an unexpected effect—more little Danes. Exciting findings from the Nurses' Health Study indicate that trans fats are a powerful deterrent to ovulation and conception. Eating less of this artificial fat can improve fertility, and simultaneously adding in healthful unsaturated fats whenever possible can boost it even further.

Women, their midwives and doctors, and fertility researchers have known for ages that body fat and energy stores affect reproduction. Women who don't have enough stored energy to sustain a pregnancy often have trouble ovulating or stop menstruating altogether. Women who have too much stored energy often have difficulty conceiving for other reasons, many of which affect ovulation. These include insensitivity to the hormone insulin, an excess of male sex hormones and overproduction of leptin, a hormone that helps the body keep tabs on body fat.

A related issue is whether *dietary* fats influence ovulation and reproduction. We were shocked to discover that this was largely uncharted territory. Until now, only a few studies have explored this connection. They focused mainly on the relationship between fat intake and characteristics of the menstrual cycle, such as cycle length and the duration of different phases of the cycle. In general, these studies suggest that more fat in the diet, and in some cases more saturated fat, improves the menstrual cycle. Most of these studies were very small and didn't account for total calories, physical activity or other factors that also influence reproduction. None of them examined the effect of dietary fat on fertility.

The dearth of research in this area has been a gaping hole in nutrition research. If there is a link between fats in the diet and reproduction, then simple changes in food choices could offer delicious, easy and inexpensive ways to improve fertility. The Nurses' Health Study research team looked for connections between dietary fats and fertility from a number of different angles. Among the 18,555 women in the study, the total amount of fat in the diet wasn't connected with ovulatory infertility once weight, exercise, smoking and other factors that can influence reproduction had been accounted for. The same was true for cholesterol, saturated fat and monounsaturated fat—none were linked with fertility or infertility. A high intake of polyunsaturated fat appeared to provide some protection against ovulatory infertility in women who also had high intakes of iron, but the effect wasn't strong enough to be sure exactly what role this healthy fat plays in fertility and infertility.

Trans fats were a different story. Across the board, the more trans fat in the diet, the greater the likelihood of developing ovulatory infertility. We saw an effect even at daily trans fat intakes of about four grams a day. That's less than the amount the average American gets each day.

Eating more trans fat usually means eating less of another type of fat or carbohydrates. Computer models of the nurses' diet patterns indicated that eating a modest amount of trans fat (2 percent of calories) in place of other, more healthful nutrients like polyunsaturated fat, monounsaturated fat or carbohydrate would dramatically increase the risk of infertility. To put this into perspective, for someone who eats 2,000 calories a day, 2 percent of calories translates into about four grams of trans fat. That's the amount in two tablespoons of stick margarine, one medium order of fast-food french fries or one doughnut.

Fats aren't merely inert carriers of calories or building blocks for hormones or cellular machinery. They sometimes have powerful biological effects, such as turning genes on or off, revving up or calming inflammation and influencing cell function. Unsaturated fats do things to improve fertility—increase insulin sensitivity and cool inflammation—that are the opposite of what trans fats do. That is probably why the largest decline in fertility among the nurses was seen when trans fats were eaten instead of monounsaturated fats.

The Protein Factor

At the center of most dinner plates sits, to put it bluntly, a hunk of protein. Beef, chicken and pork are Americans' favorites, trailed by fish. Beans lag far, far behind. That's too bad. Beans are an excellent source of protein and other needed nutrients, like fiber and many minerals. And by promoting the lowly bean from side dish to center stage and becoming more inventive with protein-rich nuts, you might find yourself eating for two. Findings from the Nurses' Health Study indicate that getting more protein from plants and less from animals is another big step toward walking away from ovulatory infertility.

Scattered hints in the medical literature that protein in the diet may influence blood sugar, sensitivity to insulin and the production of insulin-like growth factor-1—all of which play important roles in ovulation—prompted us to look at protein's impact on ovulatory infertility in the Nurses' Health Study.

We grouped the participants by their average daily protein intake. The lowest-protein group took in an average of 77 grams a day; the highest, an average of 115 grams. After factoring in smoking, fat intake, weight and other things that can affect fertility, we found that women in the highest-protein group were 41 percent more likely to have reported problems with ovulatory infertility than women in the lowest-protein group.

When we looked at animal protein intake separately from plant protein, an interesting distinction appeared. Ovulatory infertility was 39 percent more likely in women with the highest intake of animal protein than in those with the lowest. The reverse was true for women with the highest intake of plant protein, who were substantially less likely to have had ovulatory infertility than women with the lowest plant protein intake.

That's the big picture. Computer models helped refine these relationships and put them in perspective. When total calories were kept constant, adding one serving a day of red meat, chicken or turkey predicted nearly a one-third increase in the risk of ovulatory infertility. And while adding one serving a day of fish or eggs didn't influence ovulatory infertility, adding one serving a day of beans, peas, tofu or soybeans, peanuts or other nuts predicted modest protection against ovulatory infertility.

Eating more of one thing means eating less of another, if you want to keep your weight stable. We modeled the effect that juggling the proportions of protein and carbohydrate would have on fertility. Adding animal protein instead of carbohydrate was related to a greater risk of ovulatory infertility. Swapping 25 grams of animal protein for 25 grams of carbohydrates upped the risk by nearly 20 percent. Adding plant protein instead of carbohydrates was related to a lower risk of ovulatory infertility. Swapping 25 grams of plant protein for 25 grams of carbohydrates shrank the risk by 43 percent. Adding plant protein instead of animal protein was even more effective. Replacing 25 grams of animal protein with 25 grams of plant protein was related to a 50 percent lower risk of ovulatory infertility.

These results point the way to another strategy for overcoming ovulatory infertility—eating more protein from plants and less from animals. They also add to the small but growing body of evidence that plant protein is somehow different from animal protein.

Milk and Ice Cream

Consider the classic sundae: a scoop of creamy vanilla ice cream crisscrossed by rivulets of chocolate sauce, sprinkled with walnuts and topped with a spritz of whipped cream. If you are having trouble getting pregnant, and ovulatory infertility is suspected, think of it as temporary health food. OK, maybe that's going a bit too far. But a fascinating finding from the Nurses' Health Study is that a daily serving or two of whole milk and foods made from whole milk—full-fat yogurt, cottage cheese, and, yes, even ice cream—seem to offer some protection against ovulatory infertility, while skim and low-fat milk do the opposite.

The results fly in the face of current standard nutrition advice. But they make sense when you consider what skim and low-fat milk do, and don't, contain. Removing fat from milk radically changes its balance of sex hormones in a way that could tip the scales against ovulation and conception. Proteins added to make skim and low-fat milk look and taste "creamier" push it even farther away.

It would be an overstatement to say that there is a handful of research into possible links between consumption of dairy products and fertility. The vanishingly small body of work in this area is interesting, to say the least, given our fondness for milk, ice cream and other dairy foods. The average American woman has about two servings of dairy products a day, short of the three servings a day the government's dietary guidelines would like her to have.

The depth and detail of the Nurses' Health Study database allowed us to see which foods had the biggest effects. The most potent fertility food from the dairy case was, by far, whole milk, followed by ice cream. Sherbet and frozen yogurt, followed by low-fat yogurt, topped the list as the biggest contributors to ovulatory infertility. The more low-fat dairy products in a woman's diet, the more likely she was to have had trouble getting pregnant. The more full-fat dairy products in a woman's diet, the less likely she was to have had problems getting pregnant.

Our advice on milk and dairy products might be criticized as breaking the rules. The "rules," though, aren't based on solid science and may even conflict with the evidence. And for solving the problem of ovulatory infertility, the rules may need tweaking. Think about switching to full-fat milk or dairy products as a temporary nutrition therapy designed to improve your chances of becoming pregnant. If your efforts pay off, or if you stop trying to have a baby, then you may want to rethink dairy—especially whole milk and other full-fat dairy foods—altogether. Over the long haul, eating a lot of these isn't great for your heart, your blood vessels or the rest of your body.

Before you sit down to a nightly carton of Häagen-Dazs ("*The Fertility Diet* said I needed ice cream, honey"), keep in mind that it doesn't take much in the way of full-fat dairy foods to measurably affect fertility. Among the women in the Nurses' Health Study, having just one serving a day of a full-fat dairy food, particularly milk, decreased the chances of having ovulatory infertility. The impact of ice cream was seen at two half-cup servings a week. If you eat ice cream at that rate, a pint should last about two weeks.

Equally important, you'll need to do some dietary readjusting to keep your calorie count and your waistline from expanding. Whole milk has nearly double the calories of skim milk. If you have been following the U.S. government's poorly-thought-out recommendation and are drinking three glasses of milk a day, trading skim milk for whole means an extra 189 calories a day. That could translate into a weight gain of 15 to 20 pounds over a year if you don't cut back somewhere else. Those extra pounds can edge aside any fertility benefits you might get from dairy foods. There's also the saturated fat to consider, an extra 13 grams in three glasses of whole milk compared with skim, which would put you close to the healthy daily limit.

Aim for one to two servings of dairy products a day, both of them full fat. This can be as easy as having your breakfast cereal with whole milk and a slice of cheese at lunch or a cup of whole-milk yogurt for lunch and a half-cup of ice cream for dessert. Easy targets for cutting back on calories and saturated fat are red and processed meats, along with foods made with fully or partially hydrogenated vegetable oils.

Once you become pregnant, or if you decide to stop trying, going back to low-fat dairy products makes sense as a way to keep a lid on your intake of saturated fat and calories. You could also try some of the nondairy strategies for getting calcium and protecting your bones. If you don't like milk or other dairy products, or they don't agree with your digestive system, don't force yourself to have them. There are many other things you can do to fight ovulatory infertility. This one is like dessert—enjoyable but optional.

The Role of Body Weight

Weighing too much or too little can interrupt normal menstrual cycles, throw off ovulation or stop it altogether. Excess weight lowers the odds that in vitro fertilization or other assisted reproductive technologies will succeed. It increases the chances of miscarriage, puts a mother at risk during pregnancy of developing high blood pressure (pre-eclampsia) or diabetes, and elevates her chances of needing a Cesarean section. The dangers of being overweight or underweight extend to a woman's baby as well.

Weight is one bit of information that the participants of the Nurses' Health Study report every other year. By linking this information with their accounts of pregnancy, birth, miscarriage and difficulty getting pregnant, we were able to see a strong connection between weight and fertility. Women with the lowest and highest Body Mass Indexes (BMI) were more likely to have had trouble with ovulatory infertility than women in the middle. Infertility was least common among women with BMIs of 20 to 24, with an ideal around 21.

Keep in mind that this is a statistical model of probabilities that links weight and fertility. It doesn't mean you'll get pregnant only if you have a BMI between 20 and 24. Women with higher and lower BMIs than this get pregnant all the time without delay or any medical help. But it supports the idea that weighing too much or too little for your frame can get in the way of having a baby.

We call the range of BMIs from 20 to 24 the fertility zone. It isn't magic—nothing is for fertility—but having a weight in that range seems to be best for getting pregnant. If you aren't in or near the zone, don't despair. Working to move your BMI in that direction by gaining or losing some weight is almost as good. Relatively small changes are often enough to have the desired effects of healthy ovulation and improved fertility. If you are too lean, gaining five or 10 pounds can sometimes be enough to restart ovulation and menstrual periods. If you are overweight, losing 5 percent to 10 percent of your current weight is often enough to improve ovulation.

Being at a healthy weight or aiming toward one is great for ovulatory function and your chances of getting pregnant. The "side effects" aren't so bad, either. Working to achieve a healthy weight can improve your sensitivity to insulin, your cholesterol, your blood pressure and your kidney function. It can give you more energy and make you look and feel better.

While dietary and lifestyle contributions to fertility and infertility in men have received short shrift, weight is one area in which there has been some research. A few small studies indicate that overweight men aren't as fertile as their healthy-weight counterparts. Excess weight can lower testosterone levels, throw off the ratio of testosterone to estrogen (men make some estrogen, just as women make some testosterone) and hinder the production of sperm cells that are good swimmers. A study published in 2006 of more than 2,000 American farmers and their wives showed that as BMI went up, fertility declined. In men, the connection between increasing weight and decreasing fertility can't yet be classified as rock solid. But it is good enough to warrant action, mainly because from a health perspective there aren't any downsides to losing weight if you are overweight. We can't define a fertility zone for weight in men, nor can anyone else. In lieu of that, we can say to men who are carrying too many pounds that shedding some could be good for fertility and will be good for overall health.

The Importance of Exercise

Baby, we were born to run. That isn't just the tagline of Bruce Springsteen's anthem to young love and leavin' town. It's also a perfect motto for getting pregnant and for living a long, healthy life. Inactivity deprives muscles of the constant push and pull they need to stay healthy. It also saps their ability to respond to insulin and to efficiently absorb blood sugar. When that leads to too much blood sugar and insulin in the bloodstream, it endangers ovulation, conception and pregnancy. Physical activity and exercise are recommended and even prescribed for almost everyone—except women who are having trouble getting pregnant. Forty-year-old findings that too much exercise can turn off menstruation and ovulation make some women shy away from exercise and nudge some doctors to recommend avoiding exercise altogether, at least temporarily. That's clearly the right approach for women who exercise hard for many hours a week and who are extremely lean. But taking it easy isn't likely to help women who aren't active or those whose weights are normal or above where they should be. In other words, the vast majority of women.

Some exciting results from the Nurses' Health Study and a handful of small studies show that exercise can be a boon for fertility. These important findings are establishing a vital link between activity and getting pregnant. Much as we would like to offer a single prescription for conception-boosting exercise, however, we can't. Some women need more exercise than others, for their weight or moods, and others are active just because they enjoy it. Some who need to be active aren't, while a small number of others may be too active.

Instead of focusing on an absolute number, try aiming for the fertility zone. This is a range of exercise that offers the biggest window of opportunity for fertility. Being in the fertility zone means you aren't overdoing or underdoing exercise. For most women, this means getting at least 30 minutes of exercise every day. But if you are carrying more pounds than is considered healthy for your frame (i.e., a BMI above 25), you may need to exercise for an hour or more. If you are quite lean (i.e., your BMI is 19 or below), aim for the middle of the exercise window for a few months. Keep in mind that the fertility zone is an ideal, not an absolute. Hospital delivery rooms are full of women who rarely, or never, exercise. Not everyone is so lucky. If you are having trouble getting pregnant, then maybe the zone is the right place for you.

Whether you classify yourself as a couch potato or an exercise aficionado, your fertility zone should include four types of activity: aerobic exercise, strength training, stretching and the activities of daily living. This quartet works together to control weight, guard against high blood sugar and insulin, and keep your muscles limber and strong. They are also natural stress relievers, something almost everyone coping with or worrying about infertility can use.

Exercise has gotten a bad rap when it comes to fertility. While the pioneering studies of Dr. Rose Frisch and her colleagues convincingly show that too much exercise coupled with too little stored energy can throw off or turn off ovulation in elite athletes, their work says nothing about the impact of usual exercise in normal-weight or overweight women. Common sense says that it can't be a big deterrent to conception. If it were, many of us wouldn't be here. Our ancestors worked hard to hunt, forage, clear fields and travel from place to place. Early *Homo sapiens* burned twice as many calories each day as the average American does today and were fertile despite it—or because of it.

Results from the Nurses' Health Study support this evolutionary perspective and show that exercise, particularly vigorous exercise, actually improves fertility. Exercising for at least 30 minutes on most days of the week is a great place to start. It doesn't really matter how you exercise, as long as you find something other than your true love that moves you and gets your heart beating faster.

JORGE E. CHAVARRO and WALTER C. WILLETT are in the Department of Nutrition at the Harvard School of Public Health. PATRICK J. SKERRETT is editor of the Harvard Heart Letter. For more information, go to health.harvard.edu/newsweek or thefertilitydiet.com.

Acknowledgements—Adapted from THE FERTILITY DIET by Forge E. Chavarro, M.D., Sc. D., Walter C. Willett, M.D., Dr. P.H., and Patrick F. Skerrett. Adapted by permission from The McGraw Hill Companies, Inc. Copyright © 2008 by the President and Fellows of Harvard College.

The Hunt for Golden Eggs

Young women who donate their eggs say they're driven by a desire to help couples who are trying to have a baby. In an age of widespread infertility, they're also paid well.

BROOKE LEA FOSTER

Melissa says she's again ready to put her eggs up for sale. She keeps long hours as an attorney, making it hard to commit to the infertility clinic where she last donated. But she's finally found the time.

Melissa, 29, is tall with long blond hair and blue eyes. She arrives at Fairfax's Genetics and IVF Institute in a sleek pantsuit, carrying a designer Ferragamo purse. "I love all things Italian," she says.

After graduating from law school two years ago, Melissa left the Midwest and moved to DC to launch a career in public policy. She was sorting through her mail one afternoon when a flyer caught her eye: EGG DONORS WANTED.

The ad tugged at her heart strings. Her eggs could help a couple have a child—and she could make several thousand dollars. Even though Melissa earned a good salary, she had student-loan payments. Plus, she knew she didn't want kids of her own. Her eggs might help someone.

She researched egg donation online. She talked to her parents, who'd had infertility troubles before having Melissa. They thought it was wonderful that she was willing to help a couple have a baby. She didn't have a boyfriend. If she did, she would have sought his approval, too.

As soon as Melissa was accepted into the program at Genetics and IVF, she became Donor 811. Her profile and childhood photographs were put online so shopping parents could get to know her. They could hear audio clips of her answering questions like "Who's your hero?" and "How would friends describe you?" Couples could learn nearly everything about her, from her family's health background to her SAT scores.

Donor 811 is one of Genetics and IVF's most popular egg donors. "She's the girl next door," says a staffer. Four couples have bought her eggs over the last two years, earning Melissa $28,000. Melissa says she'll donate as many times as the clinic will allow her to: "I was surprised by how easy it was."

Conception used to be easy: Man and woman went into the bedroom. Woman got pregnant. But with more women putting pregnancy on hold to further their careers, couples in their thirties and forties are facing fertility troubles. As women age, so does the vitality of their eggs.

"We make it possible for a 50-year-old woman to have 21-year-old eggs," says Michael Levy, a doctor at Shady Grove Fertility Center in Rockville.

Decades ago, women past their reproductive prime began relying on costly in vitro fertilization (IVF) treatments—fertilization of the woman's egg with her husband's sperm outside the body. If that failed, they adopted children or had no children at all.

IVF with a donor egg, first used in the early 1980s to help women with premature ovarian failure get pregnant, has introduced a third option. If a husband's sperm is healthy, couples can still have a child that is "half" their own.

It's often the treatment of last resort. Women struggle with the idea that they'll be carrying a baby that doesn't share their genetic makeup; the child will merge the genes of an egg donor and the woman's husband. But they often choose this method over adoption because it satisfies a primordial urge to give birth. Some women believe the baby will feel more like their own if they carry the child in their womb.

Egg donors are typically between the ages of 20 and 32, with most in their midtwenties. Many are college students and young professionals. Some are moms. Most egg donors say they feel surprisingly little for the child conceived using their genetic makeup. They don't allow themselves to see the procedure as more than an organ donation. Most believe, as fertility clinics are quick to point out, that it's nurture that makes a parent, not nature.

In exchange for a substantial payment, donors go through a monthlong process requiring injections and invasive doctor's appointments. "It's like getting a pap smear over and over again," says one donor. "It's not pleasant, but it's not horrible."

Women typically produce one mature egg a month. Donors are pumped full of drugs so they will artificially stimulate and create 15 to 20 eggs.

On egg-retrieval day, doctors use a vaginal probe to explore a donor's ovaries, removing her microscopic eggs with a small needle. Those eggs are fertilized with the would-be father's sperm to create embryos. Within a few days, one or two of those embryos will be implanted into the would-be mother's uterus.

Most local clinics pay donors $6,000 to $8,000. Couples wanting a highly educated donor pay more.

At Shady Grove Fertility Clinic, donors go home with $6,000 to $6,500—the money is paid throughout the process—and a box of chocolates.

An IVF patient at Shady Grove using her own eggs has a 47-percent chance of getting pregnant. If she uses a donor egg, her chances move to 55 percent.

Says Trina Leonard of Genetics and IVF: "Egg donors are the unsung heroes of infertility."

Sarah decided to donate her eggs last year after seeing an ad in *Washington Parent* newspaper. The money drew her. She could start a college fund for her two-year-old son, Shawn. But the decision was also driven by emotion. Sarah, 32, couldn't imagine not having her little boy. "It's a fantastic thing to be able to do this for someone," says Sarah, who lives in Woodbridge.

Sarah had dozens of friends who'd suffered from infertility. She'd watched several go through in vitro and others adopt. She knew infertility could destroy a marriage. "I felt a little awkward the first time I went to the clinic," she says, "because my husband and I got pregnant right away."

Shady Grove matched Sarah with a couple in July 2005. The clinic required that Sarah's husband meet with a social worker. Clinics like to make sure that husbands are okay with the idea that their children could potentially have a half-sibling somewhere. Sarah's husband was. She'd reassured him that it was an anonymous donation. It's not like they'd have any responsibility for the conceived child. Later, Sarah and her husband would find out that the intended mother had survived Hodgkin's disease, but chemotherapy treatments had rendered her eggs useless. Sarah was so touched that she cried.

For the first two weeks, Sarah took a daily injection of Lupron, often used in the treatment of endometriosis, so doctors could control her ovulation cycle. Then she began mixing and injecting a cocktail of medications into her belly fat to stimulate the production of eggs. Her ovaries grew from the size of a walnut to the size of a tennis ball. "You're packed with eggs," Sarah says. "The only way to describe it is that you feel really, really full."

Donors inject themselves morning and night for 18 to 22 days, depending on how quickly they produce. They can't have sex during the injection period and for about a month after the last one. Not only will their ovaries be sore after the retrieval,

making intercourse painful, but they run the risk of getting pregnant with twins or triplets. Doctors may not locate every egg their ovaries produce.

Almost immediately after starting the injections, Sarah fell ill. She had a high fever and was throwing up.

"They didn't realize how active my ovaries would be," she says. Doctors had overstimulated her, so they scaled back her medication, and she felt better. After that, she got very hormonal. She describes it as really bad PMS.

Donors often say that they're driven to donate because of a desire to help people. Many women have a friend or a family member struggling with infertility. They believe that they are doing the ultimate good deed.

But Julia Derek, author of the 2004 book *Confessions of a Serial Egg Donor,* says women tell themselves they're helping others because they feel like they're selling themselves. "The bottom line is that if they weren't getting paid, they wouldn't be doing it," she says. "The clinics know that—it's why the compensation keeps going up."

England passed egg-donation laws in 2005 forbidding the sale of eggs as a commodity. Donors can only "volunteer" their eggs. So many women stopped donating that infertile English couples today face a five-year waiting list for a donor egg.

Julia Derek was a broke college student at George Mason University when she saw an ad in the *Washington Post:* "Infertile couple searching for tall (5'8" minimum), athletic, green eyes, brunette egg donor between the ages of 18–30. Preferably from Northern or Eastern Europe. Very discreet. Compensation: $3,500." She could live off that money for an entire semester, Julia thought. So she met the couple for coffee. Meetings between donors and couples is forbidden in many clinics; this couple wanted to find a donor before approaching a clinic. Ultimately, they didn't choose her.

But a few months later, Derek, a five-foot-eight Swede with model-good looks, moved to Los Angeles, where she was recruited by an "egg broker" who sold her eggs for top dollar. Derek donated 12 times over the next four years, earning about $50,000.

That was several years ago. Today she could earn double that.

Most local clinics pay donors $6,000 to $8,000 per retrieval. If a couple is looking for a highly educated or particularly attractive donor or a specific religion or ethnicity, they pay more. The American Society for Reproductive Medicine has said that any payment over $10,000 isn't "appropriate," but that doesn't keep some agencies from paying more. In 2002, the *Chronicle of Higher Education* reported that a couple had paid $500,000 for the eggs of an Ivy League egg donor who was five-foot-ten or taller and scored over 1400 on her SATs.

Prices are driven by demand—in 2005, the most recent year of recorded statistics, upward of 6,500 babies were born in the United States because of egg donation. Some estimates run as high as 10,000.

The global egg trade is driving prices, too, according to Debora Spar, a professor at Harvard Business School and author of *The Baby Business: How Markets Are Changing the Future of Birth.* Many area clinics work with couples from countries with strict donor egg laws like England and France. These couples have no other choice but to look abroad. Some fly to cities like Washington to buy donor eggs.

Joe was a single physician who wanted a baby of his own. He planned to use a surrogate to carry the child, and he wanted to buy the eggs of someone who was his intellectual equal.

"Whatever the going rate is—double it," he told Diane Hinson, founder of Chevy Chase–based Creative Family Connections, an agency that works with donors and surrogates.

Hinson reassured her client that she could find a great donor for no more than her standard rate. She doesn't believe in "overpaying" for eggs. Whether you went to Maryland or to Harvard, says Hinson, "we pay you $7,500 for your eggs."

If a client has a type of donor in mind, Hinson's agency offers "a specialized search." Most agencies give couples a book filled with donor profiles; depending on the agency or the clinic, there may be two donors to choose from or a hundred. Hinson will search for someone specific, down to a donor's height and ethnicity.

Hinson placed an ad for her physician client in student newspapers at Princeton, Columbia, and New York University. She was hoping for a graduate student. But the ad didn't generate much response.

Then she found a copy of NYU's paper. Says Hinson: "The ad above ours was offering $20,000."

Competition to find good egg donors is fierce. There are ads on such radio stations as 107.3 FM and in such newspapers as the *Washington Post's Express.* Some couples are beginning to post their own ads on sites from Craigslist.org to Myspace.com.

James Shrybman, a reproduction lawyer in Burtonsville, Maryland, has been connecting couples with egg donors for several years. His most reliable source—universities.

Because of religious traditions, Georgetown University and Catholic University forbid such ads. So Shrybman advertises in papers like University of Maryland's *Diamondback* and George Washington University's *Hatchet.* He typically gets about 20 calls after his ad comes out; one local clinic says it gets as many as 600 within a few weeks of advertising. Shrybman trolls for women on campus because "the younger the person is, the better the chance that she'll produce a lot of eggs in one retrieval."

Hinson's agency and at least two other area clinics don't like to recruit undergraduates; they find them unreliable. "I had a few drop off the face of the earth in the middle of the process," Hinson says. Instead, she targets young professionals. Young mothers are sought after, too—they have a track record of fertility. "And they empathize more," says Kelly Rugola, egg-donor recruiter at Shady Grove Fertility Center.

Julia Derek was 25 when she first donated her eggs. She says the younger you are, the less emotionally mature you are. "It's so seductive," Derek says. "You're making money. You're spreading your genes. You feel wanted. It's an ego boost. For me, it became easier and easier."

After Derek donated five times, she asked her egg broker if it was safe to continue. The broker used to be the egg-donor coordinator at the clinic where Derek had been donating. But she'd lured Derek away when she started her own donor agency. "Trust me," the broker said. "I'm a professional. You'll be fine." Derek believed her. She knew someone who'd donated for the broker 16 times, and she'd seemed okay.

Derek's egg broker called her every day and played mom to her—until Derek's health waned. With a body pumped full of hormones for four straight years, Derek grew depressed. Sometimes she didn't want to get out of bed. She asked for help, but the broker stopped returning her phone calls. Months later, the broker finally did call back. She said she'd get Derek some estrogen to help her feel better. Now her broker wanted to play doctor.

It's so seductive. You're making money. You're spreading your genes. You feel wanted. It's an ego boost.

"These clinics have a bottom line," says Derek. "You're not the patient. The couple is the patient. You're the product that's going to keep the patient happy."

Derek doesn't know how many children were born as a result of her donations. "It makes it too concrete to know that," she says. "I prefer to think of it in the abstract."

There isn't a watchdog group that looks out for egg donors. Recent FDA regulations require only that donated genetic material is tested for infectious diseases.

The closest thing the industry has to rules are the "suggestions" released by the American Society for Reproductive Medicine, which recommends that women donate their eggs no more than six times. But there's no national registry to track donors. A woman could donate six times at Genetics and IVF, six times at Shady Grove, and again at Dominion Fertility.

Area clinics are upfront with donors about the risks associated with the procedure: They may experience some mild cramping. Doctors could nick an ovary when they go in to retrieve the eggs. A donor's ovaries could "hyperstimulate," a condition that at its most extreme causes fluid to build in the abdomen and can cause kidney failure or even death.

Shady Grove's Levy says such dangerous complications from hyperstimulation occur in 1 to 3 percent of the population or less. "We've had about 1,000 donors over the years," he says; fewer than five required hospitalization.

What's less certain are the long-term effects of the drugs used to stimulate the ovaries. In an August 2006 *Nature* article, authors cite several studies that say it's unclear whether reproductive drugs can stimulate the growth of cancers. Some have speculated that fertility treatments Elizabeth Edwards used to have her two youngest children may have contributed to her recent breast-cancer recurrence.

But several studies show no link between fertility drugs and the disease. At NIH's National Cancer Institute, Louise Brinton collected medical records of more than 12,000 women who received ovulation-stimulating drugs between 1965 and 1988. There weren't any statistically significant increases in breast and ovarian cancer, but Brinton did find that such women were about 80 percent more likely to develop uterine cancer.

It's uncertain whether scarier statistics will emerge. Most women Brinton studied took a different kind of drug than the drugs introduced for IVF in the 1980s—the same drugs that are used on egg donors today.

On the fourth floor of Shady Grove Fertility Clinic is the embryology lab. It's like a photographer's darkroom, lit only by dim yellow fluorescent lights. Lab techs in scrubs, masks, and plastic gloves move about holding vials and petri dishes. They disappear into cubicles and hover over microscopes.

At one end of the hall is a large closet filled with what look like 25 giant thermoses. When the top of one is unscrewed, a white fog of liquid nitrogen comes out. Inside are dozens of test tubes holding hundreds of embryos.

At the other end of the lab is a steel door leading to the operating room. A dry-erase board hangs on the door with the name of the next donor coming in for a retrieval. The lab may do a dozen retrievals in a day, says Jim Graham, its head.

Graham, who hangs pictures of funny-shaped embryos on a bulletin board, explains that two hours before the donor's eggs are collected, the recipient husband goes to another floor to "produce." The clinic says it's careful to schedule the donor and husband appointments far apart so there's no chance they'll run into each other. But both need to come in on the same day. "Fresh sperm is best," Graham says.

The sperm is then brought up to embryology, where Graham's techs will sift through it, eliminating any weak ones and storing the rest in an incubator until the donor's eggs are retrieved. The fertilization happens within a few hours.

Many women who donate at fertility clinics don't have any say over what happens to their eggs. "As soon as the eggs are retrieved," says Shady Grove donor-program coordinator Kara Weaver, "they become the recipient's."

One retrieval of 15 to 20 eggs can produce two or three children. Even though all mature eggs are fertilized, only about half will produce strong embryos. A would-be mother will have one or two of the best implanted in her uterus; she and her husband can freeze the rest for later use, which costs about $360 a year. Sometimes they want a second child to have a genetic sibling.

A donor's eggs may be shared with up to three families in some fertility clinics' "shared cost" program—meaning three different families may have babies from one batch of a woman's eggs. The donor is not told if this happens.

Some outside agencies require that couples pay for their egg donors to consult a lawyer. One of the biggest issues that comes up in the contract is what happens to the leftover frozen embryos. Unless it's stipulated in the contract, a couple can donate the embryos to another couple or to science.

A donor will never know if any of the leftover embryos are donated to a place like the Snowflake Embryo Adoption Program, an agency in California heralded by President Bush, which matches frozen embryos with parents unable to produce embryos of their own. A decision to donate embryos is often steeped in religion. Some believe that life begins with an embryo and that destroying one is like killing a child.

One egg donor says she was floored when her attorney said that the embryos she helped create for a couple could be sold by that couple to another. She made sure that her contract was clear. If the couple didn't use the embryos, they were to be destroyed: "I didn't want all of these kids with my genes running around."

Inside the operating room, a 27-year-old egg donor named Heidi is under anesthesia and attached to an IV. A vaginal probe—outfitted with ultrasound and a needle—is inserted, and her ovaries come into view on a monitor beside her. The doctor sees a few large black sacs on the screen. They're follicles, which may hold an egg. Doctors never know until retrieval.

The tip of a needle comes into view on screen, and one by one the black sacs begin to collapse. They're being drained.

A lab tech pours the fluid from a vial into a petri dish and begins searching for eggs through a microscope. An untrained eye would never see the eggs. They look like cloudy masses, almost like the whites of a chicken egg. "Four, five," she yells. She's handed another vial. "Six." The lab tech holds the petri dish sideways under the microscope, trying to glimpse some that she may have missed.

Ultimately, they'll collect seven eggs from Heidi that morning—hardly the harvest of 15 to 20 they're accustomed to. Says Graham: "It's like panning for gold."

Jessica, 28, ran into her coworker's office the minute she found out that the couple to whom she'd donated her eggs had gotten pregnant. "It's just so cool," she said. Even after Jessica got home from work, she couldn't stop thinking about the news. She sent an e-mail to her agency, Creative Family Connections, one of those that will inform a woman about the outcome of her donation: "This is one of the most amazing things I've ever done."

The first time that Jessica went to a fertility clinic to donate her eggs, she left uneasy. The doctor there made "me feel like my organs were nothing to them but a business transaction." She'd nearly walked away from egg donation.

Then she got an e-mail from a friend who knew she'd been thinking about donating her eggs. Her friend's aunt worked at Creative Family Connections, and it just so happened that Jessica looked exactly like one of its clients who was searching for an egg donor. The agency e-mailed her: "Will you consider it?"

The couple sent Jessica a letter about their quest to have a child. They'd tried everything; egg donation was their last resort. Their last egg donor had dropped out midcycle. They were desperate.

Jessica thought of her mother. She and her stepfather had struggled with infertility for years—and her mom never again got pregnant. Imagine that someone like me could have helped them, Jessica thought.

Jessica filled out a 15-page application and began the donor "screening" process, which includes the collection of a medical history and personality test. The clinic drew blood and checked her hormone levels and her ovaries.

Then officials sent her to a social worker to gauge how attached she was to her eggs. If she seemed too emotionally vested, clinics say, she'd be disqualified. The social worker asked whether her family was supportive. Many agencies strongly recommend that younger donors talk the decision over with their families. "We don't want them to drop out later because their mom finds out and gets upset," says Creative Family Connections attorney Linda ReVeal.

The social worker asked Jessica how she viewed her role in the donation. It was a way to help someone, she said. Jessica was asked about her circle of friends and her job—there's fear that loner or depressed women might focus too much on the resulting child.

"Are you going to feel resentful if you can't have your own children several years from now?" a therapist asked.

Jessica shook her head: "It would give me hope because I'd know that this process was out there."

About 20 percent of applicants at area clinics will ultimately become donors.

Donors at Genetics and IVF have to be college-educated. The clinic checks their college transcripts and asks for their SAT scores. Donors in its "doctoral" program, who have advanced degrees, earn $1,000 more than the others.

The most popular donors? Sometimes it's those who show lots of personality on their audiotape. Parents loved a donor at a local clinic who told a story about how she was singing on stage once—and fell off midsong. They liked that she stood up and kept singing.

Many parents want a donor who looks like the intended mother. But a very attractive donor is almost always swooped up; some donors have a waiting list. All donor programs dismiss anyone who is overweight. People like tall donors. "Short donors aren't picked as quickly," says Shrybman. In the Washington area, blondes are in demand.

As are donors from specific ethnic groups. It's hard for area clinics to recruit Asian or Indian donors. Muslim donors are more rare than Jewish ones; there are several agencies that specialize in Jewish donors. Sometimes couples have only one donor to choose from, and it's only after a long search. For some, it takes years to find an ethnic match.

My whole life I'm going to wonder and theorize about these children. I can't help but be curious.

Levy says that cultural and religious reasons keep some women from donating. One local Vietnamese couple searched for a year before finding a donor in California. They flew her to Washington for the procedure.

Some area agencies post fliers in ethnic marketplaces. If they find one Asian donor, they might ask her to ask her friends. Still, some Indians and Asians may resist; there's a desire to keep bloodlines pure, particularly among immigrant groups trying to remain true to their heritage. "We tried advertising in an Asian newspaper," says Michele Purcell, a nurse at Shady Grove. "No response."

Most local egg-donation programs are anonymous. A couple may know everything about their donor except identifying information like her full name or address. Donors don't know anything about the couple they're providing eggs to. Both could live in Bethesda and stand next to each other at Chipotle but never know it. One donor and recipient mother were so curious about each other that they sent notes back and forth through their nurse.

"I don't want to know who they are," says Sarah. "Then I'd think about the child." And it would make the process more personal, the way it is for a surrogate, she says. Sarah thinks she'd analyze what kind of parents the couple might be. She'd wonder if they were going to raise the child the way she would. "That's not my place once I hand over the eggs," she says. "I just tell myself that anyone who'd work this hard to have a child will treasure it."

Most local clinics don't tell donors if their eggs result in a pregnancy. Those details might cause the donor to grow attached. Clinics sometimes refer to the eggs as "genetic material" to keep donors from thinking the newborn has anything to do with them.

Most donors like that kind of language. They say they don't want to have anything to do with the child that's created. A few say they don't care much about having children themselves. "I might as well let somebody use my eggs if I'm not going to," says one 27-year-old donor.

Says Sarah: "I see it as a blood donation. I don't walk around wondering who got my blood. I'm just happy I did it."

When you've donated eggs successfully, there's someone related to you in a biological sense walking the earth, says Jessica. That reality hit her when she found out that both her donations resulted in successful pregnancies. "My whole life I'm going to wonder and theorize about these children," she says. "I can't help but be curious."

She and her boyfriend are planning to get engaged this year. She wants to have her own kids soon after. When her future child starts kindergarten, she says, she'll think about the two donor children. She's quick to say it's not an attachment she feels to them. "I used to work for a daycare center," she says. "I wonder about those kids, too."

Jessica believes that nurture makes a parent, not nature. Her own father disappeared from her life when she was toddler. "He's like a sperm donor to me," she says. "My stepfather is my dad."

Donors can indicate on an application whether they're open to donating an organ or bone marrow to the child if he or she falls ill. Jessica checked yes.

Donors can also indicate how they feel about being contacted by the resulting child years from now. Says Jessica: "If they show up on my doorstep in 20 years, I'd be thrilled."

Senior writer **BROOKE LEA FOSTER** wrote about Condoleezza Rice in the March issue.

The Curious Lives of Surrogates

Thousands of largely invisible American women have given birth to other people's babies. Many are married to men in the military.

LORRAINE ALI AND RAINA KELLEY

Jennifer Cantor, a 34-year-old surgical nurse from Huntsville, Ala., loves being pregnant. Not *having* children, necessarily—she has one, an 8-year-old daughter named Dahlia, and has no plans for another—but just the experience of growing a human being beneath her heart. She was fascinated with the idea of it when she was a child, spending an entire two-week vacation, at the age of 11, with a pillow stuffed under her shirt. She's built perfectly for it: six feet tall, fit and slender but broad-hipped. Which is why she found herself two weeks ago in a birthing room in a hospital in Huntsville, swollen with two six-pound boys she had been carrying for eight months. Also in the room was Kerry Smith and his wife, Lisa, running her hands over the little lumps beneath the taut skin of Cantor's belly. "That's an elbow," said Cantor, who knew how the babies were lying in her womb. "Here's a foot." Lisa smiled proudly at her husband. She is, after all, the twins' mother.

Transatlantic carrier: Dawne Dill is carrying twins for a couple from Europe. The money she earns as a surrogate will go toward care for her autistic son.

It is an act of love, but also a financial transaction, that brings people together like this. For Kerry and for Lisa—who had a hysterectomy at the age of 20 and could never bear her own children—the benefits are obvious: Ethan and Jonathan, healthy six-pound, 12-ounce boys born by C-section on March 20. But what about Cantor? She was paid, of course; the Smiths declined to discuss the exact amount, but typically, surrogacy agreements in the United States involve payments of $20,000 to $25,000 to the woman who bears the child. She enjoyed the somewhat naughty pleasure of telling strangers who asked about her pregnancy, "Oh, they aren't mine," which invariably invoked the question, "Did you have sex with the father?" (In case anyone is wondering, Lisa's eggs were fertilized in vitro with Kerry's sperm before they were implanted on about day five.)

Surrogacy is as old as civilization, but the concept still challenges our most basic ideas about motherhood.

But what kind of woman would carry a child to term, only to hand him over moments after birth? Surrogates challenge our most basic ideas about motherhood, and call into question what we've always thought of as an unbreakable bond between mother and child. It's no wonder many conservative Christians decry the practice as tampering with the miracle of life, while far-left feminists liken gestational carriers to prostitutes who degrade themselves by renting out their bodies. Some medical ethicists describe the process of arranging surrogacy as "baby brokering," while rumors circulate that self-obsessed, shallow New Yorkers have their babies by surrogate to avoid stretch marks. Much of Europe bans the practice, and 12 states, including New York, New Jersey and Michigan, refuse to recognize surrogacy contracts. But in the past five years, four—states Texas, Illinois, Utah and Florida—have passed laws legalizing surrogacy, and Minnesota is considering doing the same. More than a dozen states, including Pennsylvania, Massachusetts and, most notably, California, specifically legalize and regulate the practice.

Today, a greater acceptance of the practice, and advances in science, find more women than ever before having babies for those who cannot. In the course of reporting this story, we discovered that many of these women are military wives who have taken on surrogacy to supplement the family income, some while their husbands are serving overseas. Several agencies reported a significant increase in the number of wives of soldiers and naval personnel applying to be surrogates since the invasion of Iraq in 2003. At the high end, industry experts estimate there were about 1,000 surrogate births in the United States last year, while the Society for Assisted Reproductive Technology (SART)—the only organization that makes an effort to track surrogate births—counted about 260 in 2006, a 30 percent increase over three years. But the number is surely much higher than this—in just five of the agencies NEWSWEEK spoke to, there were 400 surrogate births in 2007. The numbers vary because at least 15 percent of clinics—and there are dozens of them across the United States don't report numbers to SART. Private agreements made outside an agency aren't counted, and the figures do not factor in pregnancies in which one of the intended parents does not provide the egg—for example, where the baby will be raised by a gay male couple. Even though the cost to the intended parents, including medical and legal bills, runs from $40,000 to $120,000, the demand for qualified surrogates is well ahead of supply.

A few good women: Despite family objections and children of her own, Gernisha Myers was set on being a surrogate. She is now carrying white twins for a German couple.

Another reason for the rise in surrogacies is that technology has made them safer and more likely to succeed. Clinics such as Genetics & IVF Institute in Virginia, where Cantor and the Smiths underwent their IVF cycles, now boast a 70 to 90 percent pregnancy success rate—up 40 percent in the past decade. Rather than just putting an egg into a petri dish with thousands of sperm and hoping for a match, embryologists can inject a single sperm directly into the egg. The great majority of clinics can now test embryos for genetic diseases before implantation. It's revolutionizing the way clinics treat patients. Ric Ross, lab director at La Jolla IVF in San Diego, says these advances have helped "drop IVF miscarriage rates by 85 percent."

IVF has been around only since the 1970s, but the idea of one woman bearing a baby for another is as old as civilization. Surrogacy was regulated in the Code of Hammurabi, dating from 1800 B.C., and appears several times in the Hebrew Bible. In the 16th chapter of Genesis, the infertile Sarah gives her servant, Hagar, to her husband, Abraham, to bear a child for them. Later, Jacob fathers children by the maids of his wives Leah and Rachel, who raise them as their own. It is also possible to view the story of Jesus' birth as a case of surrogacy, mediated not by a lawyer but an angel, though in that instance the birth mother did raise the baby.

The most celebrated case of late, though, resulted in the legal and ethical morass known as the "Baby M" affair. Mary Beth Whitehead, age 29 in 1986, gave birth to a girl she had agreed to carry for an infertile couple. But Whitehead was also the baby's biological mother and tried to keep her after the birth, leading to a two-year custody battle. (In the end, she was denied custody but awarded visitation rights.) As a result, surrogacy agreements now almost always stipulate that the woman who carries the baby cannot also donate the egg.

But even as surrogacy is becoming less of a "Jerry Springer" spectacle and more of a viable family option for those who can afford it, the culture still stereotypes surrogates as either hicks or opportunists whose ethics could use some

fine-tuning. Even pop culture has bought into the caricature. In the upcoming feature film "Baby Mama," a single businesswoman (Tina Fey) is told by a doctor she is infertile. She hires a working-class gal (Amy Poehler) to be her surrogate. The client is a savvy, smart and well-to-do health-store-chain exec while Poehler is an unemployed, deceitful wild child who wants easy money.

When Fey's character refers to her surrogate as "white trash," we're supposed to laugh. "I just don't understand how they can think that," says surrogate Gina Scanlon of the stereotypes that influenced the film. Scanlon, 40, is a married mother of three who lives in Pittsburgh. Scanlon is also a working artist and illustrator who gave birth to twin girls for a gay New Jersey couple 18 months ago. The couple—a college professor and a certified public accountant—chose Scanlon because she was emotionally stable, with a husband and children of her own. Unlike egg donors, who are usually in their 20s, healthy women as old as 40 can serve as surrogates; Scanlon two weeks ago underwent an embryo transfer and is now pregnant again for a new set of intended parents. "Poor or desperate women wouldn't qualify [with surrogacy agencies]," she says. As for the implication that surrogates are in it only for the money, she notes that there are many easier jobs than carrying a baby 24 hours a day, seven days a week. (And most jobs don't run the risk of making you throw up for weeks at a time, or keep you from drinking if you feel like it.) "If you broke it down by the hour," Scanlon says wryly, "it would barely be minimum wage. I mean, have [these detractors] ever met a gestational carrier?" And even if they have, how would they know?

Very little is understood about the world of the surrogate. That's why we talked to dozens of women across America who are, or have been, gestational carriers. What we found is surprising and defies stereotyping. The experiences of this vast group of women—including a single mom from Murrietta, Calif., a military spouse from Glen Burnie, Md., and a small-business owner from Dallas—range from the wonderful and life-affirming to the heart-rending. One surrogate, Scanlon, is the godmother of the twins she bore, while another still struggles because she has little contact with the baby she once carried. Some resent being told what to eat or drink; others feel more responsible bearing someone else's child than they did with their own. Their motivations are varied: one upper-middle-class carrier in California said that as a child she watched a family member suffer with infertility and wished she could help. A working-class surrogate from Idaho said it was the only way her family could afford things they never could before, like a $6,000 trip to Disney World. But all were agreed that the grueling IVF treatments, morning sickness, bed rest, C-sections and stretch marks were worth it once they saw their intended parent hold the child, or children (multiples are common with IVF), for the first time. "Being a surrogate is like giving an organ transplant to someone," says Jennifer Cantor, "only before you die, and you actually get to see their joy."

That sense of empowerment and self-worth is one of the greatest rewards surrogate mothers experience. "I felt like, 'What else am I going to do with my life that means so much?'" says Amber Boersma, 30, of Wausau, Wis.

She is blond, outgoing and six months pregnant with twins for a couple on the East Coast who could not bear children on their own due to a hysterectomy. Boersma, married to a pharmaceutical rep, is a stay-at-home mom with a 6-year-old girl and 4-year-old boy, and a college graduate with a communications degree. "Some people can be successful in a major career, but I thought I do not want to go through this life meaning nothing, and I want to do something substantial for someone else. I want to make a difference."

Then there's the money. Military wife Gernisha Myers, 24, says she was looking through the local San Diego PennySaver circular for a job when she saw the listing: "Surrogate Mothers Wanted! Up to $20,000 Compensation!" The full-time mother of two thought it would be a great way to make money from home, and it would give her that sense of purpose she'd lacked since she left her job as an X-ray technician in Phoenix. In 2004, Myers and her husband, Tim, a petty officer third class in the Navy, were transferred from Arizona to California. Ever since, she missed bringing home a paycheck, helping other people—and being pregnant. She loved the feel of her belly with a baby inside, and the natural high that comes from "all those rushing hormones." So last fall she signed with one of the many surrogacy agencies near the 32nd Street Naval Station, where her husband is assigned. Her grandmother was not pleased with Myers's decision. "She said, 'Gernisha! We just do not do that in this family'," recalls Myers. "My uncle even said he was disgusted. But you know what? I'm OK with it because I know I am doing something good for somebody else. I am giving another couple what they could never have on their own—a family."

Like Myers, military wives are largely young stay-at-home moms who've completed their own families before they hit 28. IVF clinics and surrogate agencies in Texas and California say military spouses make up 50 percent of their carriers. "In the military, we have that mentality of going to extremes, fighting for your country, risking your life," says Jennifer Hansen, 25, a paralegal who's married to Army Sgt. Chase Hansen. They live in Lincoln, Neb., and have two young kids, and Chase has been deployed to Iraq for two of the past five years. "I think that being married to someone in the military embeds those values in you. I feel I'm taking a risk now, in less of a way than he is, but still a risk with my life and body to help someone." Surrogate agencies target the population by dropping leaflets in the mailboxes of military housing complexes, such as those around San Diego's Camp Pendleton, and placing ads in on-base publications such as the Military Times and Military Spouse. Now surrogate agencies say they are solicited by ad reps from these publications. Military wives who do decide to become surrogates can earn more with one pregnancy than their husbands' annual base pay (which ranges for new enlistees from $16,080 to $28,900). "Military wives can't sink their teeth into a career because they have to move around so much," says Melissa Brisman of New Jersey, a lawyer who specializes in reproductive and family issues, and heads the largest surrogacy firm on the East Coast. "But they still want to contribute, do something positive. And being a carrier only takes a year—that gives them enough time between postings."

Dawne Dill, 32, was a high-school English teacher before she married her husband, Travis, a Navy chief, and settled in Maryland. She's now a full-time mother with two boys of her own, and is carrying twins for a European couple who prefer to remain anonymous. Dill is due in May. The attraction of surrogacy for her, apart from wanting to feel useful, was that the money could help pay for an occupational-therapy gym for her older son, who is autistic. "We're thinking of building the gym in our basement so he can get to it whenever he needs," says Dill. She worried that having an autistic child might disqualify her as a surrogate, but fortunately the agency was unconcerned. "They said because I was not genetically related to the twins, that it was just not an issue, and my IPs [intended parents] never brought it up to me personally. I assume they're OK with it, but maybe think it's too touchy of a subject to discuss openly with me," says Dill. As a prepartum gift, the couple sent Dawne and her husband to the Super Bowl.

Military wives are attractive candidates because of their health insurance, Tricare, which is provided by three different companies—Humana, TriWest and Health Net Federal Services—and has some of the most comprehensive coverage for surrogates in the industry. Fertility agencies know this, and may offer a potential surrogate with this health plan an extra $5,000. Last year military officials asked for a provision in the 2008 defense authorization bill to cut off coverage for any medical procedures related to surrogate pregnancy. They were unsuccessful—there are no real data on how much the government spends on these cases. Tricare suggests that surrogate mothers who receive payment for their pregnancy should declare the amount they're receiving, which can then be deducted from their coverage. But since paid carriers have no incentive to say anything, most don't. "I was told by multiple people—congressional staff, doctors and even ordinary taxpayers—that they overheard conversations of women bragging about how easy it was to use Tricare coverage to finance surrogacy and delivery costs and make money on the side," says Navy Capt. Patricia Buss, who recently left the Defense Department and now holds a senior position with Health Net Federal Services. The subject of Tricare surrogacy coverage is becoming a hot topic throughout the military world; on Web sites such as militarySOS.com, bloggers with sign-on names such as "Ms. Ordinance" and "ProudArmyWife" fiercely debate the subject.

Surrogacy is not just an American debate—it is global. Thanks to reproductive science, Gernisha Myers, who is African-American, is now 18 weeks pregnant with the twins of Karin and Lars, a white couple who live in Germany. They are one of many international couples who turned to America to solve their infertility issues because surrogacy is not allowed in their own country. Couples have come to the United States from many countries, including Iceland, Canada, France, Japan, Saudi Arabia, Israel, Australia, Spain and Dubai in recent years. Although some couples are now turning to India for cheaper fertility solutions—yes, even surrogacy is being outsourced at a tenth of the price—the trend has yet to diminish America's draw as a baby mecca.

Karin and Lars picked Myers after they read her agency profile. Myers says that the psychological screening is one of the most grueling, invasive and odd parts of the process. The "[questionnaire] asked some weird questions, like 'Do you think about killing people sometimes?' Or 'Would you want to be a mountain ranger if you could?' Or 'Do you find yourself happier than most?' But when they asked 'Are you afraid you're going to get attached to the babies?' I said, 'In a way, yes, even though I know they're not mine.' They said, 'Believe it or not, some GCs [gestational carriers] never feel any kind of bond.' I found that hard to believe back then, but now I know what they're talking about. I don't feel that motherly bond. I feel more like a caring babysitter."

Myers's psychological detachment has a lot to do with the fact that, like most carriers today, she's in no way biologically related to the baby inside her—the legacy of the "Baby M" case. The most recent significant case involving a surrogacy dispute, *Johnson v. Calvert* in 1993, was resolved in favor of the intended parents, and against a surrogate who wanted to keep the baby. John Weltman, president of Circle Surrogacy in Boston, says that parents who work with a reputable agency have a "99 percent chance of getting a baby and a 100 percent chance of keeping it." But up until just about two years ago, Weltman says every single intended parent asked, "Will she [the carrier] try and keep the baby?" Now, he says, a third of his clients don't even mention it.

Scanlon felt like a celebrity when she was pregnant. After it was over, no one called. She felt guilty and egotistical.

That doesn't mean that it's gotten any easier for the surrogate to give up the baby. Most gestational carriers say it is still the hardest part of the job, and some have a rougher time than others. Gina Scanlon recalls the days after the birth of her first pair of surrogate twins: "When you go home it's so quiet," she says. "The crash comes. It's not the baby blues. It's not postpartum depression. It's that the performance is over. I was practically a celebrity during the pregnancy—someone was always asking me questions. After I had them, no one was calling. Now nobody cares. You're out. You're done. It's the most vain thing. I felt guilty and selfish and egotistical."

The few, the proud: Christina and Joseph Slason in San Diego, Calif. Last year she carried for a gay couple from Mexico. Now she's matched with partners from Los Angeles.

Stephanie Scott also found that life after surrogacy was not what she expected, especially since everything hummed along so nicely when she was pregnant. Seven and a half months in,

she was feeling great—all except for those damn nesting urges. The stay-at-home mom tried to stay out of the baby stores and avoid those sweet pink onesies and baby booties shaped like tiny ballet slippers—but it was near impossible to resist. Her mind-set should have served as a warning. Although she knew the baby in her swollen belly belonged to a couple on the East Coast, she hadn't prepared herself for that biological surge that keeps stores like Babies "R" Us in business. "I showed up to the delivery room with six months' worth of baby clothes," admits Scott, 28. "They ended up being my gift to the baby's intended parents. Sort of like a baby shower in reverse. I know, it's weird." But that was nothing compared to the childbirth: "When she was born, they handed her to me for a second," she says. "I couldn't look, so I closed my eyes tight, counted 10 fingers and 10 toes, then gave her away. I cried for a month straight. I was devastated."

The baby Scott gave birth to is now 3, and photos of the toddler come twice a year, on the child's birthday and Christmas. Scott says she thinks things would have been different had she been counseled more by the agency on attachment issues, but it was a small and less than professional operation (and there are plenty of those in the unregulated world of surrogacy agencies). It's one of the reasons Scott opened her own business in Dallas, Simple Surrogacy. "I would never just throw a girl out there like that. Surrogates need to know what lies ahead."

Any comprehensive road map of surrogacy should include not just potential attachment but an entire pull-down sheet on the second most difficult area of terrain: the relationship between surrogate and intended parent. The intentions and expectations of both parties are supposed to be ironed out ahead of time through a series of agency questionnaires and meetings. What kind of bond do they seek with one another—distant, friendly, close? Do they agree on difficult moral issues, like abortion and selective termination? And what requests do the IPs have of potential carriers? The parties are then matched by the agency, just as singles would be through a dating service. And the intended parents—or parent are—as diverse as the surrogates: gay, straight, single, married, young and old. Much of the time it works, even though it does often resemble an experiment in cross-cultural studies. "In what other world would you find a conservative military wife forming a close bond with a gay couple from Paris?" says Hilary Hanafin, chief psychologist for the oldest agency in the country, Center for Surrogate Parenting. And a good match doesn't necessarily equal a tight connection like that of Jennifer Cantor's and Lisa Smith's. Christina Slason, 29, who delivered a boy in January for same-sex partners from Mexico City, felt as the couple did—that a close relationship was not necessary. "We agreed that we would keep in touch, but neither of us felt the need to really bond," says Slason, a mother of three who lives in San Diego with her husband, Joseph, a Navy corpsman. "We were there to have a baby, nothing more. We were all clear on that."

But things are not always that clear. For Joseph, a single father from Massachusetts who asked to be identified only by his first name for privacy reasons, the process of finding a suitable surrogate on his own was frustrating, particularly when the first match got cold feet and pulled out. Intended parents Tamara and Joe Bove were troubled when the carrier for their triplets refused to go on bed rest even when a doctor advised her the babies' lives would be at risk if she did not: "She had delivered monstrously large twins vaginally before, even though one of them was breech. So she was kind of surprised that this could happen to her and just wouldn't cooperate." Tamara was plagued with worry. "Our plan was to keep in touch even after the babies were born, but then she stopped listening to the doctors. But you still have to keep acting like everything is fine because she's in control until the babies are born." (Despite Tamara's worries, the triplets were born healthy at 31 weeks via a C-section.)

Intended parents have little control over the surrogate's behavior and lifestyle choices during pregnancy.

Control, not surprisingly, is a sore point. A favorite pastime among surrogates—most of whom join support groups at the request of their agencies—is sharing stories of the most bizarre IP requests they've heard. One military surrogate was told if her husband was deployed anywhere in Asia, she was not to have sex with him when he returned for fear that he was unfaithful and carrying an STD.

Jennifer Hansen, the surrogate from Nebraska, says she had a few requests from her intended parents that were odd to her "as a Midwestern girl." Hansen says she's been asked not to pump her own gas. "They believe it leads to miscarriage," she says. "I've also been asked to change my cleaning supplies to all green, natural products. I'm a Clorox girl, and have no idea where to even buy these products. So they just box them up and send them to me from California." What most surrogates don't realize, according to Margaret Little, a professor of philosophy at Georgetown University and fellow at the Kennedy School of Ethics, is that the contracts governing their conduct during the pregnancy are not enforceable. She does have to surrender the baby once he's born, but cannot be forced to have (or not have) an abortion, or to obey restrictions on what she can eat, drink or do. The intended parents' only recourse is to withhold payment; they cannot police her conduct. "Surrogacy raises important red flags," Little says, "because you are selling use of the body, and historically when that's happened, that hasn't been good for women."

On the other hand, other agencies reported that some concerned surrogates have pumped and shipped their breast milk to the intended parents weeks after the birth out of fear that the newborn will not build a strong immune system without it.

As for Jennifer Cantor, resting at home last week after delivering Jonathan and Ethan, she intends to stay in touch with the family whose lives are now inextricably bound up with hers. Before returning to their home in Georgia, Lisa and Kerry brought the twins for a visit with the stranger who bore them, and with Cantor's daughter, Dahlia, whose relationship to them doesn't even have a word in the language yet. Lisa described her babies as the true meaning of life . . . absolutely perfect. Next time they're hoping for girls. They're also hoping to find someone like Cantor—who, however, does not plan to be a surrogate again, much as she enjoyed it. She is relieved that she can sit normally and put her arms around Dahlia again, without a big belly in between them. She was happy that she had been able to fulfill her dream of bearing a child for someone else. "It was exactly," she said last week, "the experience I imagined it would be."

With Jeneen Interlandi and Daniel Stone

UNIT 2

Development During Infancy and Early Childhood

Unit Selections

Key Points to Consider

- If mothers' milk is the best milk for babies, why are fewer mothers choosing to breastfeed?

- How much do babies understand at birth? What emotions do they feel? Are there social and emotional "milestones" to help caregivers trace progress?

- Are there inexpensive and easy ways to boost a baby's brain power? Can any caregiver incorporate them into daily activities?

- Should the United States provide preschooling to every child? What would be the advantages of this expensive undertaking?

- Should preschools focus on pre-reading and pre-math skills? If so, how much? What else should good preschools provide for their charges?

- Do autism and the other autistic spectrum disorders have their origins long before vaccinations? What are the early signs of ASDs?

Student Web Site
www.mhcls.com

Internet References

Autism
   http://www.autism-society.org
BabyCenter
   http://www.babycenter.com
Children's Nutrition Research Center (CNRC)
   http://www.kidsnutrition.org
Early Childhood Care and Development
   http://www.ecdgroup.com
Zero to Three: National Center for Infants, Toddlers, and Families
   http://www.zerotothree.org

Development during infancy and early childhood is more rapid than in any other life stage, excluding the prenatal period. Newborns are quite well developed in some areas, and incredibly deficient in others. Babies' cerebral hemispheres already have their full complement of neurons (worker cells). The neuroglia (supportive cells) are almost completely developed and will reach their final numbers by age one. In contrast, babies' legs and feet are tiny, weak, and barely functional. Look at newborns from another perspective, however, and their brains seem somewhat less superior. The neurons and neuroglia present at birth must be protected. We may discover ways to make more cerebral neurons in the future, but such knowledge now is in its infancy and does not go very far. By contrast, the cells of the baby's legs and feet (skin, fat, muscles, bones, blood vessels) are able to replace themselves by mitosis indefinitely. Their numbers will continue to grow through early adulthood; then their quantity and quality can be regenerated through advanced old age.

The developing brain in infancy is a truly fascinating organ. At birth it is poorly organized. The lower (primitive) brain parts (brain stem, pons, medulla, cerebellum) are developed enough to allow the infant to live. The lower brain directs vital organ systems (heart, lungs, kidneys, etc.). The higher (advanced) brain parts (cerebral hemispheres) have allocated neurons, but the nerve cells and cell processes (axons, dendrites) are small, underdeveloped, and unorganized. During infancy, these higher (cerebral) nerve cells (that allow the baby to think, reason, and remember) grow at astronomical rates. They migrate to permanent locations in the hemispheres, develop myelin sheathing (insulation), and conduct messages. Many 20th century researchers, including Jean Piaget, the father of cognitive psychology, believed that all brain activities in the newborn were reflexive, based on instincts for survival. They were wrong. New research has documented that fetuses can learn, and newborns can think as well as learn.

The role played by electrical and chemical activity of neurons in actively shaping the physical structure of the brain is particularly awe-inspiring. The neurons are produced prenatally. After birth, the flood of sensory inputs from the environment (sights, sounds, smells, tastes, touch, balance, and kinesthetic sensations) drives the neurons to form circuits and become wired to each other. Trillions of connections are established in a baby's brain. During childhood, the connections that are seldom or never used are eliminated or pruned. The first three years are critical for establishing these connections. Environments that provide both good nutrition and lots of sensory stimulation actually produce richer, more connected brains.

The first selection on infancy asks and partially answers the question, "Why are fewer mothers in the United States choosing to breastfeed today, when the nutritional benefits of human milk far outweigh formula milk?" Data clearly demonstrate that human

© Digital Vision/Getty Images

milk for human infants is associated with fewer gastrointestinal disturbances and protection against many infections, including all diseases for which the mother has developed antibodies. The rates of otitis media (ear infections) are much lower in breastfed babies, as is the incidence of SIDS. Breast milk is associated with long-term reduced risk for diabetes, asthma, leukemia, and obesity. The partial answer in this article is that the formula industry blocks the public from realizing all these benefits in order to sell more formula.

The second selection on infancy, "Reading Your Baby's Mind," addresses a concern of many parents: "How much does this baby understand?" With electroencephalography and laser eye tracking, scientists are providing surprising answers. In short, a lot! They feel empathy when others are stressed, as well as fear and contentment from birth onwards. This article explains how infant minds develop, the role of the environment, and gives milestones of progress in the first 18 months of life.

To complete the infancy section, Alice Honig suggests "20 Ways to Boost Your Baby's Brain Power." These ideas are easily put into practice without a great deal of time or money. They really work, too!

The first early childhood article addresses "Long-Term Studies of Preschool: Lasting Benefits Far Outweigh Costs." Many industrialized nations subsidize high-quality early childhood education. The United States does not. Long-term studies of three excellent preschool programs in the United States have documented long-lasting benefits. While national preschool funding would be an expensive investment, the authors argue that it would be worth the costs.

Deborah Stipek, in the second early childhood article, "Accountability Comes to Preschool: Can We Make It Work for Young Children?," gives sketches of what a good preschool can do, and what will happen if the nonacademic aspects of preschools are dropped in favor of a narrow set of reading and math skills. Young children, advises Stipek, need preschool programs that emphasize social skills, emotional well-being, and health habits, as well as an enthusiasm for learning. Preschools should not evolve into the kindergartens or first grades of yesteryear.

HHS Toned Down Breast-Feeding Ads
Formula Industry Urged Softer Campaign

MARC KAUFMAN AND CHRISTOPHER LEE

In an attempt to raise the nation's historically low rate of breast-feeding, federal health officials commissioned an attention-grabbing advertising campaign a few years ago to convince mothers that their babies faced real health risks if they did not breast-feed. It featured striking photos of insulin syringes and asthma inhalers topped with rubber nipples.

Plans to run these blunt ads infuriated the politically powerful infant formula industry, which hired a former chairman of the Republican National Committee and a former top regulatory official to lobby the Health and Human Services Department. Not long afterward, department political appointees toned down the campaign.

The ads ran instead with more friendly images of dandelions and cherry-topped ice cream scoops, to dramatize how breast-feeding could help avert respiratory problems and obesity. In a February 2004 letter (pdf), the lobbyists told then-HHS Secretary Tommy G. Thompson they were "grateful" for his staff's intervention to stop health officials from "scaring expectant mothers into breast-feeding," and asked for help in scaling back more of the ads.

The formula industry's intervention—which did not block the ads but helped change their content—is being scrutinized by Congress in the wake of last month's testimony by former surgeon general Richard H. Carmona that the Bush administration repeatedly allowed political considerations to interfere with his efforts to promote public health.

Rep. Henry A. Waxman's Committee on Oversight and Government Reform is investigating allegations from former officials that Carmona was blocked from participating in the breast-feeding advocacy effort and that those designing the ad campaign were overruled by superiors at the formula industry's insistence.

"This is a credible allegation of political interference that might have had serious public health consequences," said Waxman, a California Democrat.

The milder campaign HHS eventually used had no discernible impact on the nation's breast-feeding rate, which lags behind the rate in many European countries.

Some senior HHS officials involved in the deliberations over the ad campaign defended the outcome, saying the final ads raised the profile of breast-feeding while following the scientific evidence available then—which they say did not fully support the claims of the original ad campaign.

But other current and former HHS officials say the muting of the ads was not the only episode in which HHS missed a chance to try to raise the breast-feeding rate. In April, according to officials and documents, the department chose not to promote a comprehensive analysis by its own Agency for Healthcare Research and Quality (AHRQ) of multiple studies on breast-feeding, which generally found it was associated with fewer ear and gastrointestinal infections, as well as lower rates of diabetes, leukemia, obesity, asthma and sudden infant death syndrome.

The report did not assert a direct cause and effect, because doing so would require studies in which some women are told not to breast-feed their infants—a request considered unethical, given the obvious health benefits of the practice.

A top HHS official said that at the time, Suzanne Haynes, an epidemiologist and senior science adviser for the department's Office on Women's Health, argued strongly in favor of promoting the new conclusions in the media and among medical professionals. But her office, which commissioned the report, was specifically instructed by political appointees not to disseminate a news release.

Wanda K. Jones, director of the women's health office, said agency media officials have "all been hammering me" about getting Haynes to stop trying to draw attention to the AHRQ report. HHS press officer Rebecca Ayer emphatically told Haynes and others in mid-July that there should be "no media outreach to anyone" on that topic, current and former officials said.

Both HHS and AHRQ ultimately sent out a few e-mail notices, but the report was generally ignored. Requests to speak with Haynes were turned down by other HHS officials.

Regarding the changes made to the earlier HHS ad campaign, Kevin Keane, then HHS assistant secretary for public affairs and now a spokesman for the American Beverage Association, said formula companies lobbied hard, as did breast-feeding advocates.

"We took heat from the formula industry, who didn't want to see a campaign like this. And we took some heat from the advocates who didn't think it was strong enough," Keane said. "At the end of the day, we had a ground-breaking campaign that goes further than any other administration ever went."

But the campaign HHS used did not simply drop the disputed statistics in the draft ads. The initial idea was to startle women with images starkly warning that babies could become ill. Instead, the final ads cited how breast-feeding benefits babies—an approach that the ad company hired by HHS had advised would be ineffective. The department also pulled back on several related promotional efforts.

After the 2003–05 period in which the HHS ads were aired, the proportion of mothers who breast-fed in the hospital after their babies were born dropped, from 70 percent in 2002 to 63.6 percent in 2006, according to statistics collected in Abbott Nutrition's Ross Mothers Survey, an industry-backed effort that has been measuring breast-feeding rates for more than 30 years. In 2002, 33.2 percent of women were doing any breast-feeding at six months; by 2006, that rate had declined to 30 percent.

The World Health Organization recommends that, if at all possible, women breast-feed their infants exclusively for at least six months.

The breast-feeding ad campaign originated in a formal "Blueprint for Action on Breastfeeding" released in 2000 by David Satcher, who had been appointed surgeon general by President Bill Clinton. The Office on Women's Health convinced the nonprofit Ad Council to donate $30 million in media time, and it hired an ad agency to work alongside scientists from the National Institutes of Health, the Centers for Disease Control and Prevention, and elsewhere.

Officials met with dozens of focus groups before concluding that the best way to influence mothers was to delineate in graphic terms the risks of not breast-feeding, an approach in keeping with edgy Ad Council campaigns on smoking, seat belts and drunken driving. For example, an ad portraying a nipple-tipped insulin bottle said, "Babies who aren't breastfed are 40% more likely to suffer Type 1 diabetes."

Gina Ciagne, the office's public affairs specialist for the campaign, said, "We were ready to go with our risk-based campaign—making breast-feeding a real public health issue—when the formula companies learned about it and came in to complain. Before long, we were told we had to water things down, get rid of the hard-hitting ads and generally make sure we didn't somehow offend."

Ciagne and others involved in the campaign said the pushback coincided with a high-level lobbying campaign by formula makers, which are mostly divisions of large pharmaceutical companies that are among the most generous campaign donors in the nation.

The campaign the industry mounted was a Washington classic—a full-court press to reach top political appointees at HHS, using influential former government officials, now working for the industry, to act as go-betweens.

Two of the those involved were Clayton Yeutter, an agriculture secretary under President George H.W. Bush and a former chairman of the Republican National Committee, and Joseph A. Levitt, who four months earlier directed the Food and Drug Administration's Center for Food Safety and Applied Nutrition food safety center, which regulates infant formula. A spokesman for the International Formula Council said both were paid by a formula manufacturer to arrange meetings at HHS.

In a Feb. 17, 2004, letter to Thompson (pdf), Yeutter began "Dear Tommy" and explained that the council wished to meet with him because the draft ad campaign was inappropriately "implying that mothers who use infant formula are placing their babies at risk," and could give rise to class-action lawsuits.

Yeutter acknowledged that the ad agency "may well be correct" in asserting that a softer approach would garner less attention, but he said many women cannot breast-feed or choose not to for legitimate reasons, which may give them "guilty feelings." He asked, "Does the U.S. government really want to engage in an ad campaign that will magnify that guilt?"

He also praised Keane, the HHS public affairs official, for making "helpful changes" and removing "egregious statements," but asked that more be done. Two months later, Yeutter wrote Thompson to thank him for meeting with a group that included Levitt and an official of the council. The group members supported breast-feeding, he said, but they wanted HHS to use "positive visual images."

The formula companies also approached Carden Johnston, then president of the American Academy of Pediatrics. Afterward, Johnston wrote a letter to Thompson advising him that "we have some concerns about this negative approach and how it will be received by the general public."

The letter made a strong impression at HHS, former and current officials said. But it angered many of the medical group's members and the head of its section on breast-feeding, Lawrence M. Gartner, a Chicago physician. Gartner told Thompson in a letter that the 800 members of the breast-feeding section did not share Johnston's concerns and had not known of his letter.

"This campaign needed to be much stronger than it was," Gartner said, adding that in his view, the original ads were backed by solid scientific evidence.

According to former and current HHS officials, Cristina V. Beato, then an acting assistant secretary at HHS, played a key role—in addition to that of Keane—in toning down the ads. They said she stressed to associates that it was essential to "be fair" to the formula companies.

Beato was then serving in an acting capacity because lawmakers refused to vote on her confirmation because of complaints that she had padded her official resume. In a 2004 interview with the ABC newsmagazine "20/20," which described some of the industry's efforts to change the breast-feeding ad campaign, Beato confirmed that she "met with the industry, because they kept calling my office, every two weeks." She said in a telephone interview that their complaints played no role in her decisions.

"I brought together our top public health people to examine the health claims, and they examined the science and concluded what should be in and what should be out," Beato said.

Duane Alexander, head of the government's National Institute of Child Health and Human Development, was among the officials contacted by the industry who later supported eliminating some of the ads.

Staff researcher Madonna Lebling contributed to this report.

Reading Your Baby's Mind

**New research on infants finally begins to answer
the question: what's going on in there?**

PAT WINGERT AND MARTHA BRANT

Little Victoria Bateman is blond and blue-eyed and as cute a baby as there ever was. At 6 months, she is also trusting and unsuspecting, which is a good thing, because otherwise she'd never go along with what's about to happen. It's a blistering June afternoon in Lubbock, Texas, and inside the Human Sciences lab at Texas Tech University, Victoria's mother is settling her daughter into a high chair, where she is the latest subject in an ongoing experiment aimed at understanding the way babies think. Sybil Hart, an associate professor of human development and leader of the study, trains video cameras on mother and daughter. Everything is set. Hart hands Cheryl Bateman a children's book, "Elmo Pops In," and instructs her to engross herself in its pages. "Just have a conversation with me about the book," Hart tells her. "The most important thing is, do not look at [Victoria.]" As the two women chat, Victoria looks around the room, impassive and a little bored.

After a few minutes, Hart leaves the room and returns cradling a lifelike baby doll. Dramatically, Hart places it in Cheryl Bateman's arms, and tells her to cuddle the doll while continuing to ignore Victoria. "That's OK, little baby," Bateman coos, hugging and rocking the doll. Victoria is not bored anymore. At first, she cracks her best smile, showcasing a lone stubby tooth. When that doesn't work, she begins kicking. But her mom pays her no mind. That's when Victoria loses it. Soon she's beet red and crying so hard it looks like she might spit up. Hart rushes in. "OK, we're done," she says, and takes back the doll. Cheryl Bateman goes to comfort her daughter. "I've never seen her react like that to anything," she says. Over the last 10 months, Hart has repeated the scenario hundreds of times. It's the same in nearly every case: tiny babies, overwhelmed with jealousy. Even Hart was stunned to find that infants could experience an emotion, which, until recently, was thought to be way beyond their grasp.

And that's just for starters. The helpless, seemingly clueless infant staring up at you from his crib, limbs flailing, drool oozing, has a lot more going on inside his head than you ever imagined. A wealth of new research is leading pediatricians and child psychologists to rethink their long-held beliefs about the emotional and intellectual abilities of even very young babies.

In 1890, psychologist William James famously described an infant's view of the world as "one great blooming, buzzing confusion." It was a notion that held for nearly a century: infants were simple-minded creatures who merely mimicked those around them and grasped only the most basic emotions—happy, sad, angry. Science is now giving us a much different picture of what goes on inside their hearts and heads. Long before they form their first words or attempt the feat of sitting up, they are already mastering complex emotions—jealousy, empathy, frustration—that were once thought to be learned much later in toddlerhood.

They are also far more sophisticated intellectually than we once believed. Babies as young as 4 months have advanced powers of deduction and an ability to decipher intricate patterns. They have a strikingly nuanced visual palette, which enables them to notice small differences, especially in faces, that adults and older children lose the ability to see. Until a baby is 3 months old, he can recognize a scrambled photograph of his mother just as quickly as a photo in which everything is in the right place. And big brothers and sisters beware: your sib has a long memory—and she can hold a grudge.

**Babies yet to utter an INTELLIGENT
SYLLABLE are now known to feel a range
of COMPLEX EMOTIONS like envy
and empathy.**

The new research is sure to enthrall new parents—See, Junior *is* a genius!—but it's more than just an academic exercise. Armed with the new information, pediatricians are starting to change the way they evaluate their youngest patients. In addition to tracking physical development, they are now focusing much more deeply on emotional advancement. The research shows how powerful emotional well-being is to a child's future health. A baby who fails to meet certain key "emotional milestones" may have trouble learning to speak, read and, later, do well in school. By reading emotional responses, doctors have begun to discover ways to tell if a baby as young as 3 months is showing early signs of possible psychological disorders, including depression, anxiety, learning disabilities and perhaps autism. "Instead of just asking if they're crawling or sitting, we're asking more questions about how they share their world with their caregivers," says Dr. Chet Johnson, chairman of the American Academy of Pediatrics' early-childhood committee. "Do they point to things? When they see a new person, how do they react? How children do on social and emotional and language skills are better predictors of success in adulthood than motor skills are." The goal: in the not-too-distant future, researchers hope doctors will routinely identify at-risk kids years earlier than they do now—giving parents crucial extra time to turn things around.

One of the earliest emotions that even tiny babies display is, admirably enough, empathy. In fact, concern for others may be hard-wired into babies' brains. Plop a newborn down next to another crying infant, and chances are, both babies will soon be wailing away. "People have always known that babies cry when they hear other babies cry," says Martin Hoffman, a psychology professor at New York University who did the first studies on infant empathy in the 1970s. "The question was, why are they crying?" Does it mean that the baby is truly concerned for his fellow human, or just annoyed by the racket? A recent study conducted in Italy, which built on Hoffman's own work, has largely settled the question. Researchers played infants tapes of other babies crying. As predicted, that was enough to start the tears flowing. But when researchers played babies recordings of their own cries, they rarely began crying themselves. The verdict: "There is some rudimentary empathy in place, right from birth," Hoffman says. The intensity of the emotion tends to fade over time. Babies older than 6 months no longer cry but grimace at the discomfort of others. By 13 to 15 months, babies tend to take matters into their own hands. They'll try to comfort a crying playmate. "What I find most charming is when, even if the two mothers are present, they'll bring their own mother over to help," Hoffman says.

Part of that empathy may come from another early-baby skill that's now better understood, the ability to discern emotions from the facial expressions of the people around them. "Most textbooks still say that babies younger than 6 months don't recognize emotions," says Diane Montague, assistant professor of psychology at LaSalle University in Philadelphia. To put that belief to the test, Montague came up with a twist on every infant's favorite game, peekaboo, and recruited dozens of 4-month-olds to play along. She began by peeking around a cloth with a big smile on her face. Predictably, the babies were delighted, and stared at her intently—the time-tested way to tell if a baby is interested. On the fourth peek, though, Montague emerged with a sad look on her face. This time, the response was much different. "They not only looked away," she says, but wouldn't look back even when she began smiling again. Refusing to make eye contact is a classic baby sign of distress. An angry face got their attention once again, but their faces showed no pleasure. "They seemed primed to be alert, even vigilant," Montague says. "I realize that's speculative in regard

to infants . . . I think it shows that babies younger than 6 months find meaning in expressions."

This might be a good place to pause for a word about the challenges and perils of baby research. Since the subjects can't speak for themselves, figuring out what's going on inside their heads is often a matter of reading their faces and body language. If this seems speculative, it's not. Over decades of trial and error, researchers have fine-tuned their observation skills and zeroed in on numerous consistent baby responses to various stimuli: how long they stare at an object, what they reach out for and what makes them recoil in fear or disgust can often tell experienced researchers everything they need to know. More recently, scientists have added EEGs and laser eye tracking, which allow more precise readings. Coming soon: advanced MRI scans that will allow a deeper view inside the brain.

When infants near their first birthdays, they become increasingly sophisticated social learners. They begin to infer what others are thinking by following the gaze of those around them. "By understanding others' gaze, babies come to understand others' minds," says Andrew Meltzoff, a professor of psychology at the University of Washington who has studied the "gaze following" of thousands of babies. "You can tell a lot about people, what they're interested in and what they intend to do next, by watching their eyes. It appears that even babies know that . . . This is how they learn to become expert members of our culture."

Meltzoff and colleague Rechele Brooks have found that this skill first appears at 10 to 11 months, and is not only an important marker of a baby's emotional and social growth, but can predict later language development. In their study, babies who weren't proficient at gaze-following by their first birthday had much less advanced-language skills at 2. Meltzoff says this helps explain why language occurs more slowly in blind children, as well as children of depressed mothers, who tend not to interact as much with their babies.

In fact, at just a few months, infants begin to develop superpowers when it comes to observation. Infants can easily tell the difference between human faces. But at the University of Minnesota, neuroscientist Charles Nelson (now of Harvard) wanted to test how discerning infants really are. He showed a group of 6-month-old babies a photo of a chimpanzee, and gave them time to stare at it until they lost interest. They were then shown another chimp. The babies perked up and stared at the new photo. The infants easily recognized each chimp as an individual—they were fascinated by each new face. Now unless you spend a good chunk of your day hanging around the local zoo, chances are you couldn't tell the difference between a roomful of chimps at a glance. As it turned out, neither could babies just a few months older. By 9 months, those kids had lost the ability to tell chimps apart; but at the same time, they had increased their powers of observation when it came to human faces.

Nelson has now taken his experiment a step further, to see how early babies can detect subtle differences in facial expressions, a key building block of social development. He designed a new study that is attempting to get deep inside babies' heads by measuring brain-wave activity. Nelson sent out letters to the parents of nearly every newborn in the area, inviting them to participate. Earlier this summer it was Dagny Winberg's turn. The 7-month-old was all smiles as her mother, Armaiti, carried her into the lab, where she was fitted with a snug cap wired with 64 sponge sensors. Nelson's assistant, grad student Meg Moulson, began flashing photographs on a screen of a woman. In each photo, the woman had a slightly different expression—many different shades of happiness and fear. Dagny was given time to look at each photo until she became bored and looked away. The whole time, a computer was closely tracking her brain activity, measuring her mind's minutest responses to the different photos. Eventually, after she'd run through 60 photos, Dagny had had enough of the game and began whimpering and fidgeting. That ended the session. The point of the experiment is to see if baby brain scans look like those of adults. "We want to see if babies categorize emotions in the ways that adults do," Moulson says. "An adult can see a slight smile and categorize it as happy. We want to know if babies can do the same." They don't have the answer yet, but Nelson believes that infants who display early signs of emotional disorders, such as autism, may be helped if they can develop these critical powers of observation and emotional engagement.

Halfway across the country, researchers are working to dispel another baby cliché: out of sight, out of mind. It was long believed that babies under 9 months didn't grasp the idea of "object permanence"—the ability to know, for instance, that when Mom leaves the room, she isn't gone forever. New research by psychologist Su-hua Wang at the University of California, Santa Cruz, is showing that babies understand the concept as early as 10 weeks. Working with 2- and 3-month-olds, she performs a little puppet show. Each baby sees a duck on a stage. Wang covers the duck, moves it across the stage and lifts the cover. Sometimes the duck is there. Other times, the duck disappears beneath a trapdoor. When they see the duck has gone missing, the babies stare intently at the empty stage, searching for it. "At 2½ months," she says, "they already have the idea that the object continues to exist."

A strong, well-developed ability to connect with the world—and with parents in particular—is especially important when babies begin making their first efforts at learning to speak. Baby talk is much more than mimickry. Michael Goldstein, a psychologist at Cornell University, gathered two groups of 8-month-olds and decked them out in overalls rigged up with wireless microphones and transmitters. One group of mothers was told to react immediately when their babies cooed or babbled, giving them big smiles and loving pats. The other group of parents was also told to smile at their kids, but randomly, unconnected to the babies' sounds. It came as no surprise that the babies who received immediate feedback babbled more and advanced quicker than those who didn't. But what interested Goldstein was the way in which the parents, without realizing it, raised the "babble bar" with their kids. "The kinds of simple sounds that get parents' attention at 4 months don't get the same reaction at 8 months," he says. "That motivates babies to experiment with different sound combinations until they find new ones that get noticed."

A decade ago Patricia Kuhl, a professor of speech and hearing at the University of Washington and a leading authority on early language, proved that tiny babies have a unique ability to learn a foreign language. As a result of her well-publicized findings, parents ran out to buy foreign-language tapes, hoping their little Einsteins would pick up Russian or French before they left their cribs. It didn't work, and Kuhl's new research shows why. Kuhl put American 9-month-olds in a room with Mandarin-speaking adults, who showed them toys while talking to them. After 12 sessions, the babies had learned to detect subtle Mandarin phonetic sounds that couldn't be heard by a separate group of babies who were exposed only to English. Kuhl then repeated the experiment, but this time played the identical Mandarin lessons to babies on video- and audiotape. That group of babies failed to learn any Mandarin. Kuhl says that without the emotional connection, the babies considered the tape recording just another background noise, like a vacuum cleaner. "We were genuinely surprised by the outcome," she says. "We all assumed that when infants stare at a television, and look engaged, that they are learning from it." Kuhl says there's plenty of work to be done to explain why that isn't true. "But at first blush one thinks that people—at least babies—need people to learn."

So there you have it. That kid over there with one sock missing and smashed peas all over his face is actually a formidable presence, in possession of keen powers of observation, acute emotional sensitivity and an impressive arsenal of deductive powers. "For the last 15 years, we've been focused on babies' abilities—what they know and when they knew it," says the University of Washington's Meltzoff. "But now we want to know what all this predicts about later development. What does all this mean for the child?"

Some of these questions are now finding answers. Take shyness, for instance. It's long been known that 15 to 20 percent of children are shy and anxious by nature. But doctors didn't know why some seemed simply to grow out of it, while for others it became a debilitating condition. Recent studies conducted by Nathan Fox of the University of Maryland show that shyness is initially driven by biology. He proved it by wiring dozens of 9-month-olds to EEG machines and conducting a simple experiment. When greeted by a stranger, "behaviorally inhibited" infants tensed up, and showed more activity in the parts of the brain associated with anxiety and fear. Babies with outgoing personalities reached out to the stranger. Their EEG scans showed heightened activity in the parts of the brain that govern positive emotions like pleasure.

Just because your baby is MORE PERCEPTIVE than you thought doesn't mean she'll be DAMAGED if she cries for a minute.

But Fox, who has followed some of these children for 15 years, says that parenting style has a big impact on which kind of adult a child will turn out to be. Children of overprotective parents, or those whose parents didn't encourage them to overcome shyness and childhood anxiety, often remain shy and anxious as adults. But kids born to confident and sensitive parents who gently help them to take emotional risks and coax them out of their shells can often overcome early awkwardness. That's an important finding, since behaviorally inhibited kids are also at higher risk for other problems.

Stanley Greenspan, clinical professor of psychiatry and pediatrics at George Washington University Medical School, is one of the leaders in developing diagnostic tools to help doctors identify babies who may be at risk for language and learning problems, autism and a whole range of other problems. He recently completed a checklist of social and emotional "milestones" that babies should reach by specific ages. "I'd like to see doctors screen babies for these milestones and tell parents exactly what to do if their babies are not mastering them. One of our biggest problems now is that parents may sense intuitively that something is not right," but by the time they are able to get their child evaluated, "that family has missed a critical time to, maybe, get that baby back on track."

So what should parents do with all this new information? First thing: relax. Just because your baby is more perceptive than you might have thought doesn't mean she's going to be damaged for life if she cries in her crib for a minute while you answer the phone. Or that he'll wind up quitting school and stealing cars if he witnesses an occasional argument between his parents. Children crave—and thrive on—interaction, one-on-one time and lots of eye contact. That doesn't mean filling the baby's room with "educational" toys and posters. A child's social, emotional, and academic life begins with the earliest conversations between parent and child: the first time the baby locks eyes with you; the quiet smile you give your infant and the smile she gives you back. Your child is speaking to you all the time. It's just a matter of knowing how to listen.

With T. Trent Gegax, Margaret Nelson, Karen Breslau, Nadine Joseph and Ben Whitford

20 Ways to Boost Your Baby's Brain Power

ALICE STERLING HONIG, PhD

At birth, your baby's brain contains 100 billion neurons (as many as there are stars in the Milky Way)! During his first years, he will grow trillions of brain-cell connections, called neural synapses.

The rule for brain wiring is "use it or lose it." Synapses that are not "wired together" through stimulation are pruned and lost during a child's school years. Although an infant's brain does have some neurological hard wiring (such as the ability to learn any language), it is more pliable and more vulnerable than an adult's brain. And, amazingly, a toddler's brain has twice as many neural connections as an adult's.

When you provide loving, language-enriched experiences for your baby, you are giving his brain's neural connections and pathways more chances to become wired together. In turn, he will acquire rich language, reasoning, and planning skills.

1. **Give your baby a physically healthy start before he is born.** Stay healthy while you are pregnant, and be aware that certain drugs can be destructive to your baby's brain in utero. Many children who were drug-abused in the womb struggle with severe learning problems and suddenly act with unprovoked aggressive behaviors. Studies have also revealed that cigarette smoking during pregnancy causes lower fourth-grade reading scores.

2. **Have meaningful conversations.** Respond to infant coos with delighted vocalizations. Slowly draw out your syllables in a high-pitched voice as you exclaim, "Pretty baby!" This talk is called "parentese." The areas in the brain for understanding speech and producing language need your rich input.

3. **Play games that involve the hands** (Patty-cake, Peekaboo, This Little Piggy). Babies respond well to learning simple sequential games.

4. **Be attentive.** When your baby points, be sure to follow with your gaze and remark on items or events of interest to her. This "joint attention" confirms for your baby how important her interests and observations are to you.

5. **Foster an early passion for books.** Choose books with large and colorful pictures, and share your baby's delight in pointing and making noises—say, the animal sounds to go along with farm pictures. Modulate the tone of your voice; simplify or elaborate on story lines; encourage toddlers to talk about books. Remember that building your baby's "receptive" language (understanding spoken words) is more important than developing his "expressive" language (speaking) in infancy.

6. **Use diaper time to build your baby's emotional feelings** of having a "lovable body." Stroke your baby's tummy and hair. Studies have shown that babies who are not often touched have brains that are smaller than normal for their age. Also, when diapering your baby, you are at the ideal 12 to 18 inches from her eyes to attract attention to your speech.

7. **Choose developmentally appropriate toys** that allow babies to explore and interact. Toys such as a windup jack-in-the-box or stackable blocks help your baby learn cause-and-effect relationships and "if-then" reasoning. If a baby stacks a big block on a smaller one, the top block falls off. If he successfully stacks a small block on a bigger one, he "wires in" the information.

8. **Respond promptly when your baby cries.** Soothe, nurture, cuddle, and reassure him so that you build positive brain circuitry in the limbic area of the brain, which relates to emotions. Your calm holding and cuddling, and your day-to-day intimate engagement with your baby, signal emotional security to the brain.

9. **Build trust by being attentive and focused.** Babies who are securely attached to you emotionally will be able to invest more life energy in the pleasures of exploration, learning, and discovery.

10. **Use body massage** to decrease your infant's stress and enhance her feelings of well-being and emotional security. Loving touches promote growth in young babies. Research has shown that premature babies who are massaged three times daily are ready to leave the hospital days earlier than babies who do not receive massages.

11. **Enlist help from your toddler at clean-up times**—a good way to practice categorization. Toddlers learn that stuffed animals have one place to go for "night-night"

time; cars, trucks, and other vehicles also have their special storage place. Children need to learn about sorting into categories and seriation (placing things in order; for example, from littlest to biggest) as part of their cognitive advancement in preschool.

12. **Set up a safe environment** for your crawling baby or toddler. Spatial learning is important, and your mobile child will begin to understand parameters such as under, over, near, and far. He will be able to establish mental maps of his environment and a comfortable relationship with the world in which he lives.

13. **Sing songs** such as "Itsy Bitsy Spider" and "Ring-Around-the-Rosy." The body motions and finger play will help your baby integrate sounds with large and small motor actions. Songs also enhance your child's learning of rhythms, rhymes, and language patterns.

14. **Match your tempo to your child's temperament.** Some children adjust easily to strange situations, some are bold and impulsive, and some are quite shy. Go with the flow as you try to increase a shy child's courage and comfort level. Help a highly active child safely use his wonderful energy while learning impulse control. Your acceptance will give him the comfort he needs to experiment and learn freely.

15. **Make meals and rest times positive.** Say the names of foods out loud as your baby eats. Express pleasure as she learns to feed herself, no matter how messy the initial attempts may be. This will wire in good associations with mealtime and eating. Battles and nagging about food can lead to negative emotional brain patterns.

16. **Provide clear responses to your baby's actions.** A young, developing brain learns to make sense of the world if you respond to your child's behavior in predictable, reassuring, and appropriate ways. Be consistent.

17. **Use positive discipline.** Create clear consequences without frightening or causing shame to your child. If your toddler acts inappropriately, such as by hitting another child, get down to his eye level, use a low, serious tone of voice, and clearly restate the rule. Keep rules simple, consistent, and reasonable for your child's age. Expecting a toddling baby not to touch a glass vase on a coffee table is not reasonable. Expecting a toddler to keep sand in the sandbox and not throw it is reasonable!

18. **Model empathic feelings** for others. Use "teachable moments" when someone seems sad or upset to help your toddler learn about feelings, caring, sharing, and kindness. The more brain connections you create for empathic responses and gentle courtesies, the more these brain circuits will be wired in. This helps not only with language and cognitive learning, but with positive emotional skills, too!

19. **Arrange supervised play** with messy materials, such as water, sand, and even mud. This will teach your toddler about the physics and properties of mixtures and textures, liquids and solids. During bath time, the brain wires in knowledge about water, slippery soap, and terry towel textures. Sensory experiences are grist for the learning brain.

20. **Express joy and interest in your baby.** Let your body language, your shining eyes, your attentiveness to babbling and baby activities, and your gentle caresses and smiles validate the deeply lovable nature of your little one.

ALICE STERLING HONIG, PhD, professor emerita at Syracuse University, is the author, with H. Brophy, of *Talking With Your Baby: Family as the First School.*

Long-Term Studies of Preschool: Lasting Benefits Far Outweigh Costs

Mr. Bracey and Mr. Stellar summarize the findings of three studies that provide strong evidence of long-term positive outcomes for high-quality preschool programs. All that remains now, they argue, is for the U.S. to make a commitment to universal, free preschool.

GERALD W. BRACEY AND ARTHUR STELLAR

The November 2001 issue of the *Kappan* contained a special section offering a cross-national perspective on early childhood education and day care. Day-care programs in England, Italy, and Sweden were described and contrasted with day care in the U.S. The other countries, especially Sweden, have coherent, comprehensive programs based on a set of assumptions about the positive outcomes of early education. In the U.S., by contrast, there is a "nonsystem." Sharon Lynn Kagan and Linda Hallmark wrote that, in the U.S., "not only has early childhood never been a national priority, but decades of episodic, on-again, off-again efforts have yielded a set of uncoordinated programs and insufficient investment in the infrastructure. Often, the most important components of high-quality education and care—financing, curriculum development, and teacher education—are neglected."[1]

According to Kagan and Hallmark, the U.S. has historically resisted major government intrusions into the early years of education because such intervention would signal a failure on the part of the family. This resistance has produced a vicious circle: parents resist government intervention in the education of young children on ideological grounds; the government, for its part, doesn't produce high-quality day care; parental resistance to government day care solidifies because of the low quality of the care. Today, the ideology that seeks to keep government out of family matters is still very much alive. David Salisbury of the Cato Institute put it this way: "The key to producing intelligent, healthy children does not lie in putting more of them in taxpayer-funded preschools. . . . Instead of forcing mothers into the workplace through heavy taxation, the government should reduce the tax burden on families and, thereby, allow child care to remain in the capable hands of parents."[2]

This view of day care is most unfortunate, as evidence is now strong that high-quality day care produces long-term positive outcomes. Three studies of specific programs provide the evidence.

The "granddaddy" of these three studies is known as the High/Scope Perry Preschool Project.[3] In the mid-1960s, African American children whose parents had applied to a preschool program in Ypsilanti, Michigan, were randomly assigned to receive the program or not. Those who tested the children, interviewed the parents, or were the children's teachers once they reached school age did not know to which group the children had been assigned. Random assignment eliminates any systematic bias between the groups, although it cannot *guarantee* that they will be the same. By keeping the information on group assignment confidential, the experimenters sought to minimize any kind of Pygmalion effects stemming from expectations about the children who had been in preschool and those who had not. Few preschool programs existed at the time, and children in the control group remained at home.

Parents of the preschool children had completed an average of 9.4 years of school. Only 20% of the parents had high school diplomas, compared to 33% of all African American adults at the time of the study. The children attended preschool for a half day for eight months. The first group of children, entering in 1962, received one year of the preschool program; later groups received two. The program also included weekly, 90-minute home visits by members of the project staff.

The vision of childhood underlying the High/Scope Program was shaped by Piaget and other theorists who viewed children as active learners. Teachers asked questions that allowed children to generate conversations with them. Those who developed the program isolated 10 categories of preschool experience that they deemed important for developing children: creative representation, language and literacy, social relations and personal initiative, movement, music, classification, seriation (creating series and patterns), number, space, and time. Children participated in individual, small-and large-group activities. The curriculum and instruction flowed from both constructivist and cognitive/developmental approaches.[4]

Teachers rarely assessed the children's specific knowledge. This approach stood in marked contrast to another preschool curriculum, Direct Instruction (DI). DI attempts to impart specific bits of knowledge through rapid-fire drill and highly programmed scripts.

A study of the Perry preschoolers and controls at age 40 is in progress. Other studies took place when the subjects reached ages 19 and 27. At age 19, the preschoolers had higher graduation rates and were less likely to have been in special education. The graduation rate effect, though, was limited to females. The preschoolers also had higher scores on the Adult Performance Level Survey, a test from the American College Testing Program that simulates real-life problem situations.

By the time the two groups turned 27, 71% of the preschool group had earned high school diplomas or GEDs, compared to 54% of the control group. The preschoolers also earned more, were more likely to own their own homes, and had longer and more stable marriages. Members of the control group were arrested twice as often, and five times as many members of the control group (35%) had been arrested five or more times.

The second study is called the Abecedarian Project and has been run out of the University of North Carolina, Chapel Hill, since 1972.[5] The study identified children at birth and provided them full-day care, 50 weeks a year, from birth until they entered school. Adults would talk to the children, show them toys or pictures, and offer them opportunities to react to sights and sounds in the environment. As the children grew, these adult/child interactions became more concept and skill oriented. For older preschoolers, they also became more group oriented. Some children continued in the program until age 8, while another group of children began to receive an enrichment program after they started school.

Although the children were randomly assigned, it is important to note that children in the "control" group were not without assistance. To reduce the chances that any differences might come from nutritional deficiencies affecting brain growth, the researchers supplied an enriched baby formula. Social work and crisis intervention services were also available to families in the control group. If the researchers' assessments indicated that the children were lagging developmentally, the families were referred to a relevant social agency. As a consequence of these policies and services, four of the children in the control group were moved to the head of the waiting list for what the researchers called "scarce slots in other quality community child centers."

In the decade following the start of the Perry Project, early childhood education became more prevalent, especially in university areas like Chapel Hill. Thus some of the families in the control group sent their children to other preschool programs. It seems likely, therefore, that some children in the control group received benefits similar to those provided to the children in the experimental group. These benefits would tend to reduce the differences seen between experimental and control groups.

A 1988 follow-up study of the subjects at age 21 found that young adults who had taken part in the Abecedarian Project completed more years of schooling than the controls (12.2 versus 11.6). As with the Perry Project, this difference was most evident among the females in the study. More members of the experimental group were still in school (42% versus 20%), and more had enrolled in four-year colleges (35.9% versus 13.7%). Forty-seven percent of the experimental group worked at skilled jobs, such as electrician, compared to just 27% of the control group. The subjects who had attended the Abecedarian preschool were less likely to smoke or to use marijuana, but they were no less likely to use alcohol or to indulge in binge drinking.

The researchers administered reading and math tests at ages 8, 12, 15, and 21. Subjects who had been in the program for eight years showed much better reading skills than those in the control group. The "effect sizes" obtained for reading ranged from 1.04 at age 8 to .79 at age 21. Effect sizes for math ranged from .64 at age 8 to .42 at age 21. Judgment must be used in interpreting effect sizes, but all researchers would consider these to be large, with the possible exception of the .42 for math at age 21, which might be considered "medium."

For subjects who had terminated the program when they entered school, the reading effect sizes ran from .75 at age 8 to .28 at age 21. The impact of math for the same group actually grew over time, from .27 at age 8 to .73 at age 21. In general, it appears that participants who continued with the Abecedarian program into the elementary grades were affected more than those who stopped at the end of preschool.

Subjects who received the school-only program showed smaller effect sizes. For reading, the effect size was .28 at age 8 and dwindled to just .11 at age 21. Once again, math showed increased impact over time, from .11 at age 8 to .26 at age 21.

The third major long-term study of preschool outcomes is known as the Chicago Child-Parent Center Program (CPC).[6] It was a much larger study than the Perry or Abecedarian project, but the children were not randomly assigned to experimental and control groups. The CPC was also much more diffuse than the other projects, taking place in some 20 centers, and initially teachers had more latitude over what kinds of materials were incorporated. Later, all centers adopted a program developed through the Chicago Board of Education that emphasized three major areas: body image and gross motor skills, perceptual/motor and arithmetic skills, and language.

As with the other projects, extensive parent involvement was emphasized. Project staff members visited the homes of participants, and parents often accompanied children on field trips. In a 2000 follow-up study, subjects at age 21 who had taken part in the project had lower crime rates, higher high school completion rates, and fewer retentions in grade.

Quality Concerns

There is now some evidence to suggest that even diffuse programs that are broad in scope, such as Head Start, produce increases in high school graduation rates and in college attendance.[7] It seems clear, though, that high-quality programs are more effective. As laid out by Steven Barnett of Rutgers University, to be high quality, programs should have the following characteristics:

- low child/teacher ratios,
- highly qualified and well-paid teachers,
- intellectually rich and broad curricula,
- parents engaged as active partners with the program, and
- starting dates at or before the child reaches age 3.[8]

According to Kagan and Hallmark, many programs in the U.S. do not meet these criteria. Samuel Meisels of the Erikson Institute posits that the proposed "national reporting system" for Head Start will not bring such qualities to Head Start, either.[9] Indeed, Meisels worries that the system might reduce the quality of Head Start and psychologically damage children.

Costs and Benefits

The three preschool programs discussed here cost money, substantially more money than Head Start and even more than most preschools provided by private companies. The question arises as to whether the benefits from the programs are worth these costs. Cost-benefit analyses on all three conclude that they are.

A recent analysis of the Abecedarian Project by Leonard Masse and Steven Barnett of Rutgers University concluded that the benefit/cost ratio for the program was 4 to 1.[10] That is, society received four dollars in return for every dollar invested. This is not as high as analyses suggested for the Perry and Chicago projects. These yielded benefit/cost ratios on the order of 7 to 1. As we noted, though, a number of children in the Abecedarian project control groups attended some other preschools, and this could have reduced the differences between the groups.

Masse and Barnett estimated that children who took part in the program would earn $143,000 more over their lifetimes than those who did not. Their mothers would earn $133,000 more. The latter figure might surprise readers at first, but Masse and Barnett cite other studies finding that given stable, continuous child care, mothers are able to effectively reallocate their time to allow them to establish better, longer-term, and more productive relationships with employers.

Masse and Barnett also infer that the children of the children who participated in high-quality preschool programs will earn more as a consequence. Although it is difficult to quantify such projected earnings increases, they estimate a lifetime increase of $48,000 for the children of the participants. Although clearly conjectural, the logic is straightforward: the children who participated will experience outcomes, such as higher educational attainment, that are associated with higher earnings for future generations.

The cost-benefit analysts warn that these programs can be expensive. They estimated the cost of the Perry Project at $9,200 per child, per year, while the Abecedarian cost figure comes in at $13,900 (both estimates in constant 2002 dollars). This compares to $7,000 for Head Start. They worry that governments might experience "sticker shock" if they try to replicate these projects on a large-scale basis, but they caution that "costs alone offer little guidance. The costs of a program must

be compared against the benefits that the program generates. Benefit/cost ratios that are greater than one indicate that a program is worthy of consideration regardless of the absolute level of program costs."[11]

The programs described in this article all involved children living in poverty. Little if any research exists on long-term benefits for middle-class children. Masse and Barnett argue that, if we limit the programs to children under age 5 and assume that 20% of those children live in poverty, the annual cost for high-quality preschool for those 20% would be $53 billion per year.

Governments, however, appear to be looking at absolute costs. The Education Commission of the States reports that eight states have cut back on funds available for preschool in 2002–03. Moreover, today, in early 2003, state government budgets are in their worst shape since World War II. Still, sentiment for universal preschool is growing. After reviewing the evidence on the impact of early childhood education, the Committee for Economic Development led off a monograph as follows:

> The Committee for Economic Development (CED) calls on the federal and state governments to undertake a new national compact to make early education available to all children age 3 and over. To ensure that all children have the opportunity to enter school ready to learn, the nation needs to reform its current, haphazard, piecemeal, and underfunded approach to early learning by linking programs and providers to coherent state-based systems. The goal should be universal access to free, high-quality prekindergarten classes, offered by a variety of providers for all children whose parents want them to participate.[12]

Such a program makes much more sense to us than a program that tests all children in reading, math, and science in grades 3 through 8. Alas, Chris Dreibelbis of the CED reports that, while the CED monograph has been well received in both the education and business communities, there is little movement that might make its proposal a reality.[13]

Notes

1. Sharon L. Kagan and Linda G. Hallmark, "Early Care and Education Policies in Sweden: Implications for the United States," *Phi Delta Kappan*, November 2001, p. 241.

2. David Salisbury, "Preschool Is Overhyped," *USA Today*, 18 September 2002.

3. John R. Berrueta-Clement et al., *Changed Lives: The Effects of the Perry Preschool Program on Youths Through Age 19* (Ypsilanti, Mich.: High/ Scope Press, 1984); and Lawrence J. Schweinhart, Helen V. Barnes, and David P. Weikart, *Significant Benefits: The High/Scope Perry Preschool Study Through Age 27* (Ypsilanti, Mich.: High/Scope Press, 1993).

4. Mary Hohmann and David P. Weikart, *Educating Young Children: Active Learning Practices for Preschool and Child Care Programs* (Ypsilanti, Mich.: High/Scope Press, 1995).

5. Frances A. Campbell et al., "Early Childhood Education: Young Adult Outcomes for the Abecedarian Project," *Applied Developmental Science*, vol. 6, 2002, pp. 42–57; and

Frances A. Campbell, "The Development of Cognitive and Academic Abilities: Growth Curves from an Early Childhood Experiment," *Developmental Psychology*, vol. 37, 2001, pp. 231–42.

6. Arthur J. Reynolds et al., "Age 21 Benefit-Cost Analysis of the Chicago Child-Parent Center Program," paper presented to the Society for Prevention Research, Madison, Wis., 21 May–2 June 2001; and idem, "Long-Term Effects of an Early Childhood Intervention on Educational Achievement and Juvenile Arrest," *Journal of the American Medical Association*, 9 May 2001.

7. Eliana Garces, Duncan Thomas, and Janet Currie, "Longer Term Effects of Head Start," Working Paper No. 8054, National Bureau of Economic Research, December 2000, available at www.nber.org/papers/w8054; and Janet Currie and Duncan Thomas, "School Quality and the Longer-Term Effects of Head Start," *Journal of Human Resources*, Fall 2000, pp. 755–74.

8. W. Steven Barnett, "Early Childhood Education," in Alex Molnar, ed., *School Reform Proposals: The Research Evidence* (Greenwich, Conn.: Information Age Publishing, 2002),

available at www.asu.edu/educ/epsl. Click on Education Policy Research Unit, then, under "archives," click on "research and writing."

9. Samuel J. Meisels, "Can Head Start Pass the Test?," *Education Week*, 19 March 2003, p. 44.

10. Leonard N. Masse and W. Steven Barnett, *Benefit Cost Analysis of the Abecedarian Early Childhood Intervention Project* (New Brunswick, N.J.: National Institute for Early Childhood Research, Rutgers University, 2002).

11. Ibid., p. 14.

12. *Preschool for All: Investing in a Productive and Just Society* (New York: Committee for Economic Development, 2002), p. 1.

13. Personal communication, 3 February 2003.

GERALD W. BRACEY is an associate for the High/Scope Educational Research Foundation, Ypsilanti, Mich., and an associate professor at George Mason University, Fairfax, Va. He lives in the Washington, D.C., area. **ARTHUR STELLAR** is president and CEO, High/Scope Educational Research Foundation, Ypsilanti, Mich.

Accountability Comes to Preschool
Can We Make It Work for Young Children?

Early childhood educators are justifiably concerned that demands for academic standards in preschool will result in developmentally inappropriate instruction that focuses on a narrow set of isolated skills. But Ms. Stipek believes that teaching preschoolers basic skills can give them a good foundation for their school careers, and she shows that it is possible to do this in ways that are both effective and enjoyable.

DEBORAH STIPEK

P ressures to raise academic achievement and to close the achievement gap have taken a firm hold on elementary and secondary schools. Now, preschools are beginning to feel the heat. Testing for No Child Left Behind isn't required until third grade. But as elementary schools ratchet up demands on children in the early grades and as kindergarten becomes more academic, children entering school without basic literacy and math skills are at an increasingly significant disadvantage.

Accountability is also beginning to enter the preschool arena. Both the House and Senate versions of the Head Start reauthorization bill require the development of educational performance standards based on recommendations of a National Academy of Sciences panel. Head Start programs would then be held accountable for making progress toward meeting these goals, and their funding would be withdrawn after some period of time if they failed. States and districts are likely to follow with initiatives designed to ensure that children in publicly funded early childhood education programs are being prepared academically to succeed in school.

There are good reasons for the increased attention to academic skills in preschool, especially in programs serving economically disadvantaged children. Children from low-income families enter kindergarten on average a year to a year and a half behind their middle-class peers in terms of school readiness. And the relatively poor cognitive skills of low-income children at school entry predict poor achievement in the long term. Meredith Phillips, James Crouse, and John Ralph estimated in a meta-analysis that about half of the total black/white gap in math and reading achievement at the end of high school is explained by the gap between blacks and whites at school entry.[1] Preschool education can give children from economically disadvantaged homes a better chance of succeeding in school by contributing to their cognitive skills. Moreover, all young children are capable of learning far more than is typically believed, and they enjoy the process.

Until recently, kindergarten was a time for children to *prepare* for school. Today, it *is* school.

This new focus on academic preparation will undoubtedly have significant implications for the nature of preschool programs, and it could have negative consequences. Until recently, kindergarten was a time for children to *prepare* for school. Today, it *is* school—in most places as focused on academic skill as first grade used to be. Will the same thing happen to preschool? We need to think hard about how we will balance the pressure to prepare young children academically with their social/emotional needs. How will we increase young children's academic skills without undermining their enthusiasm for learning or reducing the attention we give to the many other domains of development that are important for their success?

The early childhood education community has resisted a focus on academic skills primarily because experts are worried that it will come in the form of whole-group instruction, rigid pacing, and repetitive, decontextualized tasks—the kind of "drill and kill" that is becoming commonplace in the early elementary grades and that is well known to suffocate young children's natural enthusiasm for learning. My own recent observations in preschools suggest that these concerns are well founded.

I am seeing children in preschool classrooms counting by rote to 10 or 20 in a chorus. When I interview the children, many have no idea what an 8 or a 10 is. They can't tell me, for example, how many cookies they would have if they started with 7 and I gave them one more, or whether 8 is more or less than 9. I am seeing children recite the alphabet, call out letters shown on flashcards, and identify letter/sound connections on worksheets (e.g., by drawing a line from a *b* to a picture of a ball). Some can read the word *mop* but have no idea that they are referring to a tool for cleaning floors, and they are not able to retell in their own words a simple story that had been read to them.[2] I am seeing young children recite by rote the days of the week and the months of the year while the teacher points to the words written on the board—without any understanding of what a week or a month is and without even a clear understanding that the written words the teacher points to are connected to the words they are saying. In these classrooms every child in the class gets the same task or is involved in the same activity, despite huge variability in their current skill levels. Some children are bored because they already know what is being taught; others are clueless.

Alternatives to Drill and Kill

The good news is that young children can be taught basic skills in ways that engage rather than undermine their motivation to learn. Motivating instruction must be child-centered—adapted to the varying skills and interests of children.

Good teachers embed instruction in activities that make sense to young children. They teach vocabulary, for example, by systematically using and reinforcing the meaning of new words in the context of everyday activities. When children are blowing bubbles, the teacher might introduce different descriptive terms (e.g., "shimmer") or names of shapes (e.g., "oval" versus "round"). Teachers promote oral language by reading stories, encouraging story making, joining in role play, asking children to explain how things work, giving children opportunities to share experiences, helping them to expand what they say, and introducing and reinforcing more complex sentence structures. Comprehension and analytic skills can be developed by reading to children and asking them to predict what will happen next and to identify patterns and draw conclusions. Print awareness is promoted by creating a book area, having materials and other things in the classroom labeled, and pointing out features of books being read to children. Phonics can be taught through songs, rhyming games, and language play. Early writing skills can be encouraged and developed in the context of pretend play (e.g., running a restaurant or post office) and by having children dictate stories or feelings to an adult and gradually begin to write some of the words themselves.

Good teachers are busy asking questions, focusing children's attention, helping them document and interpret what they see, and providing scaffolds and suggestions.

Young children develop basic number concepts best by actively manipulating objects, not by rote counting.[3] Mathematics, like literacy, can be learned in the context of playful activities. A pretend restaurant can provide many opportunities for learning math. Children can match one straw for each glass for each person, count out amounts to pay for menu items (five poker chips for a plastic pizza,

four chips for a glass of apple juice, and so on), tally the number of people who visit the restaurant, or split the pizza between two customers. Questions about relative quantities (less and more, bigger and smaller) can be embedded in restaurant activities and conversations. (Who has *fewer* crackers or *more* juice left in her glass?) Children can categorize and sort objects (e.g., put all the large plates on this shelf and the tall glasses on the shelf below). Measurement of weight and even a basic notion of fractions can be learned by cooking for the restaurant (a half cup of milk, a quarter cup of sugar); volume can be learned by pouring water from measuring cups into larger containers.

Effective teaching of young children cannot be delivered through a one-size-fits-all or scripted instructional program, in part because teachers need to be responsive to children's individual skills and interests. Good teachers know well what each child knows and understands, and they use that knowledge to plan appropriate and varied learning opportunities. For example, whereas one child may dictate a few sentences to the teacher for his journal each day, another might actually write some of the words herself. While some children are asked to count beans by ones, others are asked to count them by twos or by fives.

Teaching in the kinds of playful contexts mentioned above can be direct and explicit. Young children are not left to their own devices—to explore aimlessly or to invent while the teacher observes. To the contrary, effective and motivating teaching requires a great deal of active teacher involvement. Teachers need to have clear learning goals, plan activities carefully to achieve those goals, assess children's learning regularly, and make modifications when activities are not helping children learn.

Good teachers are busy asking questions, focusing children's attention, helping them document and interpret what they see, and providing scaffolds and suggestions. Which object do you think will float, the small metal ball or the block of wood? Why do you think the wood floated and the ball didn't, even though the wood block is bigger? On the paper, let's put an "F" for float after the pictures of the objects that float and an "S" after the pictures of the objects that sink. Then we can look at our summary of findings to figure out how the floating objects and the sinking objects are different from each other. Teachers need to assess children's understanding and skill levels both informally—as they listen to children's replies and comments during classroom activities—and more formally—interacting with each child individually for a few minutes every few weeks. And teachers need to use what they learn from their assessments to plan instructional interventions that will move *each child* from where he or she is to the next step.

Effective teachers also maintain children's enthusiasm for learning by being vigilant and seizing opportunities to use children's interests to teach. I once observed a brilliant teacher turn a child's comment about new shoes (which most teachers would have found distracting) into a multidisciplinary lesson. She asked the students to take off one shoe and use it to measure the length of their leg, from their waist to their ankle. Some had to learn how to find their waist and ankle to accomplish the task (physiology and vocabulary). They also had to count each time they turned the shoe and keep track of where they ended up (math). The teacher then led a conversation about who had the longest and the shortest leg (comparisons). Then they measured arms and talked about whether arms were shorter or longer than legs and by how much (introduction to subtraction and idea of averages). The conversation finally turned to other objects that could be used as measuring instruments.

This teacher didn't always rely on spontaneous teaching opportunities. She had a very well-planned instructional program. But she also took good advantage of children's interests and seized opportunities to build academic lessons out of them.

Beyond Academic Skills

Ironically, to achieve high academic standards, we need to be more, not less, concerned about the nonacademic aspects of children's development. Children's social skills and dispositions toward learning, as well as their emotional and physical well-being, directly affect their academic learning.

Fortunately, efforts to promote development on important nonacademic dimensions need not reduce the amount of time children spend learning academic skills. As I describe below, efforts to support positive social, emotional, and physical development can be embedded in the academic instructional program and the social climate of the classroom.

Social skills. Children who have good social skills—who are empathic, attentive to others' needs, helpful, respectful, and able to engage in sustained social interactions—achieve academically at a higher level than children who lack social skills or are aggressive.[4] The higher achievement results in part because children who are socially adept develop positive relationships with teachers and peers. They are motivated to work hard to please their teachers, and they feel more comfortable and secure in the classroom. Aggressive and disruptive children develop conflictual relationships with teachers and peers and spend more time being disciplined (and thus less time engaged in academic tasks).

Social skills can be taught in the context of classroom routines and activities designed to teach academic skills. Lessons about appropriate social behavior can be provided as stories that are read to children and discussed. Opportunities to develop skills in collaboration can be built into tasks and activities designed to teach literacy and math skills. Teachers can encourage children to develop social problem-solving skills when interpersonal conflicts arise by helping them solve the problem themselves—"Is there another way you could have let Sam know that you wanted to play with the airplane?"—rather than solving the problem for them—"Sam, give the airplane to Jim. It's his turn."

A program called "Cool Tools," designed to promote social and academic skills, begins with preschoolers at the UCLA laboratory elementary school—the Corinne A. Seeds University Elementary School. Children create an alphabet that decorates the walls of their classroom: "S" is for "share," "K" is for "kindness," "H" is for "help," "C" is for "cooperation." Teachers also take advantage of events in the world and in the community. Following the tsunamis in Southeast Asia, the children made lists of what survivors might need. They donated the coins they had collected for their study of money in mathematics to a fund for survivors, and they made muffins and granola and sold them to parents and friends to raise additional funds. Thus literacy and math instruction, and a little geography, were embedded in activities designed to promote feelings of responsibility and generosity.

Dispositions toward learning. Children's beliefs about their ability to learn also affect their learning. Children who develop perceptions of themselves as academically incompetent and expect to fail don't exert much effort on school tasks, and they give up as soon as they encounter difficulty. Engagement in academic tasks is also affected by students' sense of personal control. Children enjoy schoolwork less and are less engaged when they feel they are working only because they have to, not because they want to.[5]

Luckily, much is known about practices that foster feelings of competence and expectations for success. These beliefs are not "taught" directly. Rather, they are influenced by the nature and difficulty level of the tasks children are asked to complete and by the kind of evaluation used and the nature of the feedback they receive. Children's self-confidence is maintained by working on tasks that require some effort (so that when they complete them they have a sense of satisfaction and achievement). However, the tasks must not be so difficult that the children cannot complete them even if they try. The huge variability in children's skill levels is why rigidly paced instruction is inappropriate; if all children are asked to do the same task, it will invariably be too easy (and thus boring) for some students or too difficult (and thus discouraging) for others.

Classroom climate is also important. Self-confidence is engendered better in classrooms in which all children's academic achievements are celebrated than in classrooms in which only the best performance is praised, rewarded, or displayed on bulletin boards. Effective teachers encourage and praise children for taking on challenges and persisting when they run into difficulty, and they invoke no negative consequences for failure. ("You didn't get it this time, but I bet if you keep working on these kinds of problems, by lunch, you'll have figured out how to do them.")

The nature of evaluation also matters. Evaluation that tells children what they have learned and mastered and what they need to do next, rather than how their performance compares to that of other children, fosters self-confidence and high expectations. ("You are really good at consonants, but it looks like you need to practice vowels a little more.") All children can learn and will stay motivated if they see their skills developing, but only a few can perform better than their peers, and many will become discouraged if they need to compete for rewards.

We also know how to foster a feeling of autonomy. Clearly children cannot be given carte blanche to engage in any activity they want and be expected to master a set of skills and understandings adults believe to be important. But children can be given choices in what they do and how and when they do it, within a constrained set of alternatives. Even modest choices (whether to use beans or chips for a counting activity; which puzzle to work on) promote interest and engagement in learning.[6]

Emotional well-being and mental health. Children's emotional well-being and mental health (a clear and positive sense of the self; a positive, optimistic mood; the ability to cope with novel and challenging situations) have an enormous impact on how well they learn. Students who are depressed, anxious, or angry are not effective learners. Feeling disrespected, disliked, or disconnected from the social context can also promote disengagement—from academic work in the short term and, eventually for many students, from school altogether. Paying close attention to the social and emotional needs of students and creating a socially supportive environment can go a long way toward promoting social/emotional and mental well-being. It can also reduce the need for special services.

Substantial research suggests that the school social climate is also critical to mental health. A respectful and caring social context that ensures close, personal relationships with adults, that is orderly and predictable, and that promotes feelings of self-determination and autonomy in students can contribute substantially to students' emotional well-being. Peers affect the social context as much as teachers, and thus they have to be taught the effects of their behavior on other children. The "Cool Tools" program, for example, teaches 4-year-olds about "put-ups" and "put-downs," noting that it takes five put-ups to repair one put-down. Children also play games that illustrate how the same comment can be heard differently, depending on the volume and tone of voice and body posture.

Physical development. Lack of exercise and consumption of too much sugar are two behaviors that have immediate negative effects on children's ability to focus on academic work. We need to provide children with opportunities—such as outdoor play time and healthy snacks—to engage in positive behavior while they are at school. And we need to help them develop healthy habits—such as brushing teeth, washing hands, and exercising—that will contribute to their well-being.

Teachers can talk to children about how exercise affects their bodies in the context of a science lesson on physiology. (Why do we need a heart? How are muscles different from fat?) And compelling and visible messages can be given through science experiments, such as observing what happens to two pieces of bread several days after one piece was touched with a dirty hand and the other with a clean one.

Programs serving children from low-income families should also make an effort to work with community agencies to ensure access to dentists and physicians. Even a trip to the doctor or dentist can be used to promote academic skills. Children can develop communication skills by being asked to describe their experience, they can learn vocabulary, and they can develop the cultural knowledge that we now know is necessary for becoming a proficient reader. (It's hard to make sense of a sentence with the word "stethoscope" in it if you've never seen one used.)

Educating Children

Educational leaders need to take seriously the accountability demands made on them. By paying more attention to academic skills in preschool, we can help close the achievement gap, and we can give all children a chance to expand their intellectual skills. But we need to avoid teaching strategies that take all the joy out of learning. This will not, in the end, help students achieve the high standards being set for them.

We also need to resist pressures to prepare children only to perform on tests that assess a very narrow set of academic outcomes. Attention to other domains of development is also important if we want children to be effective learners as well as effective citizens and human beings. Policy makers should demand that if assessments for accountability are to be used in early childhood programs, they measure genuine understanding and the nonacademic skills and dispositions that we want teachers to promote. We have learned from No Child Left Behind that, if the tools used for accountability focus on a narrow set of skills, so will the educational program.

Finally, teaching young children effectively takes a great deal of skill. If we want teachers to promote students' learning and motivation, we need to invest in their training. States vary considerably in their credentialing requirements for early childhood education teachers. Few require a sufficient level of training. On-the-job opportunities for collegial interactions focused on teaching and learning and professional development are also critical. Preschools that are good learning environments for adults are likely to be good learning environments for children.

An investment in preschool education could help us achieve the high academic standards to which we aspire. Let's make sure we provide it in a way that does more good than harm.

Notes

1. Meredith Phillips, James Crouse, and John Ralph, "Does the Black-White Test Score Gap Widen After Children Enter School?," in Christopher Jencks and Meredith Phillips, eds., *The Black-White Test Score Gap* (Washington, D.C.: Brookings Institution Press, 1998), pp. 229–72.

2. A story recounted to me by a researcher who was assessing a young child's reading skill illustrates what can happen if decoding is overemphasized. The child read a brief passage flawlessly but was unable to answer a simple question about what he had read. He complained to the researcher that he had asked him to read the passage, not to understand it. Clearly this child had learned that reading was synonymous with decoding sounds.

3. See, for example, Barbara Bowman, M. Suzanne Donovan, and M. Susan Burns, eds., *Eager to Learn: Educating Our Preschoolers* (Washington, D.C.: National Academy Press, 2001); and Douglas Clements, Julie Sarama, and Ann-Marie DiBiase, *Engaging Young Children in Mathematics: Standards for Early Childhood Mathematics Education* (Mahwah, N.J.: Erlbaum, 2003).

4. See, for example, David Arnold, "Co-Occurrence of Externalizing Behavior Problems and Emergent Academic Difficulties in Young High-Risk Boys: A Preliminary Evaluation of Patterns and Mechanisms," *Journal of Applied Developmental Psychology,* vol. 18, 1997, pp. 317–30; Nancy Eisenberg and Richard A. Fabes, "Prosocial Development," in William Damon and Nancy Eisenberg, eds., *Handbook of Child Psychology,* 5th ed., vol. 3 (New York: Wiley, 1997), pp. 701–78.

5. For a review, see Deborah Stipek, *Motivation to Learn: Integrating Theory and Practice,* 4th ed. (Needham Heights, Mass.: Allyn & Bacon, 2002).

6. See, for example, Leslie Gutman and Elizabeth Sulzby, "The Role of Autonomy-Support Versus Control in the Emergent Writing Behaviors of African-American Kindergarten Children," *Reading Research & Instruction,* vol. 39, 2000, pp. 170–83; and Richard Ryan and Jennifer La Guardia, "Achievement Motivation Within a Pressured Society: Intrinsic and Extrinsic Motivations to Learn and the Politics of School Reform," in Timothy Urdan, ed., *Advances in Motivation and Achievement: A Research Annual,* vol. II (Greenwich, Conn.: JAI Press, 1999), pp. 45–85.

DEBORAH STIPEK is a professor of education and dean of the School of Education at Stanford University, Stanford, Calif.

From *Phi Delta Kappan,* June 2006, pp. 740–744, 747. Copyright © 2006 by Phi Delta Kappan. Reprinted by permission of *Phi Delta Kappan* and Deborah Stipek.

UNIT 3

Development During Childhood: Cognition and Schooling

Unit Selections

Key Points to Consider

- Should children with attention deficit disorders be given stimulation medications? Why or why not?

- Why should foreign language instruction be emphasized in American education before high school?

- Are achievement tests necessary to make sure first graders acquire sufficient reading and math skills? Should 5- and 6-year-old children be given homework? Should they be tutored if they fall behind their peers? What impact will this have?

- What has the No Child Left Behind (NCLB) legislation done for American education? What are its weaknesses? How can it be improved?

- Should school teachers emphasize students' strengths instead of weaknesses? What might be the consequences of such a practice?

- Should teachers encourage perfectionistic students to modify their attitudes toward learning? How?

Student Web Site

www.mhcls.com

Internet References

Children Now
http://www.childrennow.org
Council for Exceptional Children
http://www.cec.sped.org
Educational Resources Information Center (ERIC)
http://www.eric.ed.gov/
Federation of Behavioral, Psychological, and Cognitive Science
http://federation.apa.org
The National Association for the Education of Young Children (NAEYC)
http://www.naeyc.org
Project Zero
http://pzweb.harvard.edu
Teaching Technologies
http://www.inspiringteachers.com/bttindex.html

New research in 2007 suggested that human brain stem cells may make new neurons as they migrate to the olfactory bulb. While the outcome of these new brain cells for human cognition is yet to be learned, the smell-sensing mechanism can help children learn and adapt in some areas (e.g., safe smells, dangerous odors).

The mental process of knowing—cognition—includes aspects such as sensing, understanding, associating, and discriminating. Cognitive research has been hampered by the limitations of trying to understand what is happening inside the minds of living persons without doing harm. It has also been challenged by the problem of defining concepts such as intuition, unconsciousness, unawareness, implicit learning, incomprehension, and all the aspects of knowing present behind our sensations and perceptions (metacognition). Many kinds of achievement that require cognitive processes (awareness, perception, reasoning, judgment) cannot be measured with intelligence tests or with achievement tests.

Intelligence is the capacity to acquire and apply knowledge. It is usually assumed that intelligence can be measured. The ratio of tested mental age to chronological age is expressed as intelligence quotient (IQ). For years, schoolchildren have been classified by IQ scores. The links between IQ scores and school achievement are positive, but no significant correlations exist between IQ scores and life success. Consider, for example, the motor coordination and kinesthetic abilities of Hall of Fame baseball player Cal Ripken, Jr. He had a use of his body that surpassed the capacity of most other athletes and nonathletes. Is knowledge of kinesthetics a form of intelligence? Many people believe it is.

Some psychologists have suggested that uncovering more about how the brain processes various types of intelligences will soon be translated into new educational practices. Today's tests of intelligence only measure abilities in the logical/mathematical, spatial, and linguistic areas of intelligence, which is what schools now teach. Jean Piaget, the Swiss founder of cognitive psychology, was involved in the creation of the world's first intelligence test, the Binet-Simon Scale. He became disillusioned with trying to quantify how much children knew at different chronological ages. He was much more intrigued with what they did not know, what they knew incorrectly, and how they came to know the world as they did. He started the Centre for Genetic Epistemology in Geneva, Switzerland, where he began to study the nature, extent, and validity of children's knowledge. He discovered qualitative, rather than quantitative, differences in cognitive processes over the life span. Infants know the world through their senses and their motor responses. After language develops, toddlers and preschoolers know the world through their language/symbolic perspective. Piaget likened early childhood cognitive processes to bad thought, or thought akin to daydreams. By school age, children know things in concrete terms, which allows them to number, seriate, classify, conserve, think backward and forward, and think about their own thinking (metacognition). However, Piaget believed that children do not acquire the cognitive processes necessary to think abstractly and to use clear, consistent, logical patterns of thought until early adolescence. Their moral sense and personal philosophies of behavior are not completed until adulthood.

The first article in this unit, "Informing the ADHD Debate," gives a comprehensive commentary on the many issues surrounding attention deficit hyperactivity disorder. The authors make clear that ADHD has biological causes. They

© Banana Stock/PunchStock

review new research, which documents that brain differences exist in children with ADHD, as observed using imaging technology. While ADHD has roots in genetic and prenatal development, the environment in childhood also plays a role in ADHD. The use of medication is explained in terms of how and why it helps. The use of behavioral therapy is also strongly recommended.

The second article, "Why We Need 'The Year of Languages,'" opens the door for discussing early emphasis on second-language learning in contemporary schooling. Are American children linguistically ignorant? What effect will this have in the global economy? Why are languages acquired more rapidly before puberty? Why do females acquire languages more rapidly than males? Should our American schoolchildren be taught languages important in global economy such as Chinese or Arabic?

The third article of this unit address "The New First Grade: Too Much Too Soon?" Pressure to succeed academically is very high for first-grade students some parents are propelling the movement for more education at earlier ages and other parents are resisting the pressures. Many experts worry that the stress on achievement can lead to frustration and eventual emotional-behavioral disorders.

"Ten Big Effects of the No Child Left Behind Act on Public Schools" explains the findings of a four-year, comprehensive review of the implementation of NCLB. The ten effects are broad generalizations drawn from all 50 states. While test scores are rising and low-performing schools are being restructured across the United States, there are problems. Many of these relate to rising costs, staffing, quality teaching, high-stakes testing, and accountability requirements for children with exceptionalities.

The fifth article in the schooling section of this unit addresses the power of teaching based on the strengths of the students. Gloria Henderson discusses her conscious efforts to change her teaching style from remediation to abilities guidance. Students achieved at higher levels when they were led to improve their preexisting skills.

The sixth and final article in this unit, "A 'Perfect' Case Study," discusses students who try too hard to be perfect. Their behaviors create unnecessary anxiety about underachievement. Jill Adelson describes five types of perfectionists and suggests ways to support healthy learning behaviors.

Informing the ADHD Debate

The latest neurological research has injected much needed objectivity into the disagreement over how best to treat children with attention-deficit disorders.

ARIBERT ROTHENBERGER AND TOBIAS BANASCHEWSKI

From the moment Julia entered first grade, she appeared to spend most of her time daydreaming. She needed more time to complete assignments than the other children did. As she moved through elementary school, her test scores deteriorated. She felt increasingly unable to do her homework or follow the teacher's instructions in class. She made few real friends and said her teachers got on her nerves. She complained that her parents pressured her all day long and that nothing she did was right.

Julia was actually very friendly and talkative, but a lack of self-control made others feel uneasy around her. By age 14, she found that concentrating on assignments seemed impossible. She constantly lost her belongings. Neuropsychological exams showed Julia was of average intelligence but repeatedly interrupted the tests. She was easily distracted and seemed to expect failure in everything she did. So she just gave up. Ultimately Julia was diagnosed with attention-deficit hyperactivity disorder (ADHD) and was treated with methylphenidate, one of the standard drugs for her condition. The medication helped Julia organize her life and tackle her schoolwork more readily. She says she now feels better and is much more self-confident.

Julia's symptoms constitute just one profile of a child with ADHD. Other girls and boys exhibit similar yet varied traits, and whereas medication has helped in many cases, for just as many it provides no relief. With the number of cases increasing every year, debate over basic questions has heightened: Is ADHD overdiagnosed? Do drugs offer better treatment than behavior modification? Recent progress in understanding how brain activity differs in ADHD children is suggesting answers.

What Causes ADHD?

ADHD is diagnosed in 2 to 5 percent of children between the ages of six and 16; approximately 80 percent are boys. The typical symptoms of distractibility, hyperactivity and agitation occur at all ages, even in adults who have the condition, but with considerable disparity. Children often seem forgetful or impatient, tend to disturb others and have a hard time observing limits. Poor impulse control manifests itself in rash decision making, silly antics and rapid mood swings. The child acts before thinking. And yet ADHD children often behave perfectly

normally in new situations, particularly those of short duration that involve direct contact with individuals or are pleasurable or exciting, like watching TV or playing games.

Precursor behaviors such as a difficult temperament or sleep and appetite disorders have often been found in children younger than three who were later diagnosed with ADHD, but no definitive diagnosis can be made in those first three years. Physical restlessness often diminishes in teenagers, but attention failure continues and can often become associated with aggressive or antisocial behavior and emotional problems, as well as a tendency toward drug abuse. Symptoms persist into adulthood in 30 to 50 percent of cases.

Longitudinal epidemiological studies demonstrate that ADHD is no more common today than in the past. The apparent statistical rise in the number of cases may be explained by increased public awareness and improved diagnosis. The condition can now be reliably identified according to a set of characteristics that differentiate it from age-appropriate behavior. Nevertheless, debates about overdiagnosis, as well as preferred treatments, are sharper than ever.

Neurologists are making headway in informing these debates. For starters, researchers using state-of-the-art imaging techniques have found differences in several brain regions of ADHD and non-ADHD children of similar ages. On average, both the frontal lobe and the cerebellum are smaller in ADHD brains, as are the parietal and temporal lobes. ADHD seems to be the result of abnormal information processing in these brain regions, which are responsible for emotions and control over impulses and movements.

Yet these variations do not indicate any basic mental deficiency. Currently physicians see the disorder as an extreme within the natural variability of human behavior. On neuropsychological tests such as letter-sequence recognition on a computer, ADHD children have varied but frequently slower reaction times. The reason, experts now believe, is that neural information processing—the foundation of experience and behavior—may break down, especially when many competing demands suddenly flood the brain. In this circumstance or when faced with tasks requiring speed, thoroughness or endurance, the performance of ADHD brains decreases dramatically compared with the brains of other children. A lack of stimulation, on the other hand, quickly leads to boredom.

The attention deficit is particularly evident whenever children are asked to control their behavior—stopping an impulsive action or maintaining a high level of performance in a given task. The problem is not so much a lack of attention per se but a rapid drop in the ability to continually pay attention.

A different phenomenon, however, gives hyperactive children the uncontrollable urge to move. Together with the cerebellum, which coordinates movement, various control systems within and underneath the cerebral cortex are responsible for motor functions. This region is where the neurons of the motor cortex, the basal ganglia and the thalamus come together. The motor cortex represents the final stage of neural processing, after which motor impulses are sent to muscles. When activity in these regions is not balanced, children have difficulty preparing for, selecting and executing movements because they cannot adequately control or inhibit their motor system. Complex movements that require precise sequencing are initiated too early and then overshoot their target. Hyperactivity also often goes hand in hand with deficits in fine-motor coordination and an inability of children to stop speech from bursting forth uncontrollably.

In general, the underlying trait of impulsivity is linked to the development of the brain's so-called executive function: the ability to plan and to monitor working memory. Executive function develops over time as the brain matures. In children with ADHD, however, it tends to remain rudimentary. Anatomically, the executive function stems from neural networks in the prefrontal cortex—the so-called anterior attentional system. Together with the posterior attentional system, located largely in the parietal lobes, it tracks and regulates behavior.

While trying to navigate life without a strong ability to monitor and plan, ADHD children are often in constant battle with their emotions. They are barely able to control their feelings, and they do not endure frustration well. They easily become excited and impatient and tend toward hostility. They also find it hard to motivate themselves for certain tasks. And they are apt to grasp at the first reward that comes their way, no matter how small, rather than wait for a larger, more attractive payoff.

Dopamine plays an important role in the limbic system, which addresses emotional challenges, and ADHD children typically have low levels of this neurotransmitter. Normally, for example, dopamine release strengthens the neural connections that lead to a desired behavior when a reward stimulus is presented. But when dopamine is absent, rewards that are minor or presented at the wrong time have no effect.

Genes or Environment

One question that arises from all these findings is why specific brain regions are smaller than others and why certain brain functions are weak or unbalanced. Genes may play a considerable role. Comprehensive metastudies of parents and children and identical and fraternal twins, such as those conducted by Anita Thapar, then at the University of Manchester in England, in 1999, Philip Asherson of King's College in London in 2001, and Susan Sprich of Massachusetts General Hospital in 2001, show that heredity

greatly influences the occurrence of ADHD. For example, children of parents who have had ADHD are far more likely to suffer similar symptoms. The studies indicate that approximately 80 percent of ADHD cases can be traced to genetic factors.

As a result, researchers have been busily trying to identify which genes might be different in ADHD children. High on the suspect list are genes involved in transferring information between neurons. This group includes genes for proteins that influence the circulation of dopamine at the synapses between neurons—for example, proteins that clear away old messenger molecules so new ones can come through. So far researchers have found that receptor mediation of the dopamine signal is too weak in some patients, and dopamine reuptake is too rapid in others.

The genetics work seems to indicate that behavior problems are associated with insufficient regulation of dopamine metabolism, which derails neural information processing. The neurotransmitter norepinephrine may play a role, too. Although the genetic links between norepinephrine and its receptors and transporters are not as clearly understood as those for dopamine, medications such as atomoxetine that inhibit norepinephrine reuptake by neurons do improve symptoms.

When coupled, the neurotransmitter and brain-imaging evidence imply that the brains of ADHD children may be organized and function differently from an early age. These organic disparities may actually be the cause of behavioral changes and not a consequence of them, as has sometimes been suggested. Another piece of evidence is that in some cases, as children mature, certain physiological peculiarities—such as the size of the corpus striatum—become normal, and ADHD fades.

Still, ADHD cannot yet be tied neatly to known physical, genetic factors. Experts believe that the gene loci discovered to date explain at most 5 percent of problematic behaviors. If more fundamental gene variations are at fault, they have not yet been found. The probability of developing a hyperactivity disorder depends on a combination of many different genes.

Furthermore, there is wide variability in the degree to which these genetic factors are expressed. That means environmental influences must certainly play a role. For example, alcohol and nicotine consumption by a mother during pregnancy tend to increase the risk of ADHD in offspring, much the same way they contribute to extreme prematurity, low birth weight and food allergies.

On the other hand, it is also true that mothers with a genetic predisposition to ADHD have a propensity to smoke and drink during pregnancy. They tend to make basic child-rearing errors, too, such as failing to establish clear rules and effective limits. A chaotic household can strengthen biological ADHD tendencies, leading to a vicious cycle.

Other psychosocial factors, including a non-supportive school environment, marital crises or psychological problems arising between parents, and poor parent-child attachment can also transform a latent tendency into a full-blown disorder.

Medication Dispute

Recent findings about deficits in brain function and neurotransmitters make it clear why certain drugs are likely treatments. And yet the role of environment suggests that behavioral therapy can also be effective. Today uncertainty surrounds both options, and the increasing use of medication has proved divisive. Opinion runs from euphoric endorsement to outright rejection.

The body of evidence suggests that neurotransmitter systems need to be targeted. Psycho-stimulants such as amphetamine sulfates and methylphenidate, marketed under such names as Ritalin, have had widespread success. Numerous clinical studies show that these medications can decrease or eliminate behavioral disorders in 70 to 90 percent of patients.

Administering stimulants to hyperactive children might seem counterintuitive. Yet these substances fix the genetically based dopamine imbalance in the parts of the brain responsible for self-regulation, impulse control and perception. In effect, they prevent the overly rapid reuptake of dopamine at synapses. Other substances with similar modes of action, such as the norepinephrine reuptake inhibitor atomoxetine, work equally well.

Many parents are understandably nervous about subjecting their children to a long-term regimen of medication. News that Ritalin use may be implicated in Parkinson's disease, a dopamine deficiency illness, has added to the worry. Such a connection was suspected because rats that received methylphenidate before sexual maturity exhibited fewer than normal dopamine transporters in their striatum. But to date, not a single case of Parkinson's has been attributed to the use of Ritalin during childhood, and on average Parkinson's patients do not have a history of taking psychostimulants more frequently than other people. Nevertheless, many parents may fear that long-term treatment with psychoactive drugs could leave their child vulnerable to drug or medication abuse in the future.

In 2003, however, Timothy E. Wilens and his colleagues at Harvard Medical School laid these concerns to rest with a large-scale metastudy. It turns out that the use of psychostimulants significantly reduces the risk of future abuse. In comparing ADHD adults with comparable symptoms, those who had not received ADHD medications as children were three times more likely to succumb to drug addiction later in life than those who had received medication.

Drugs Plus Behavior

This does not mean that physicians should prescribe drugs lightly. And under no circumstances should doctors, parents or patients rely exclusively on medication. Studies show that adding behavioral therapy greatly enhances improvements. It also can teach children how to overcome any kind of problematic behavior that might arise in their lifetime. Children learn how to observe and control themselves. Unless ADHD erupts in its most extreme form, behavioral therapy should be the initial treatment of choice. If a child shows no significant signs of improvement after several months, a drug regimen can then be considered.

For the youngest children—those of preschool age—psychostimulants should generally be avoided. Parents should instead try to work daily with their children on their behavior. They would also do well to draw on the expertise of preschool teachers, who see many different children with a wide range of challenges.

A comprehensive examination conducted in 2000 by the National Institute of Mental Health rated the effectiveness of medical and behavioral treatments of ADHD. Conducted over two years, the Multimodal Treatment Study of Children with ADHD included 579 ADHD children at six different university medical centers. The principal investigators divided the test subjects, all of whom were between the ages of seven and nine, into four groups that had different treatment plans. The results strongly suggest that a combination of drug and behavioral therapies leads to the highest success:

- Routine daily treatment with prescribed medication normalized behavior in 25 percent of children treated.
- Intensive behavioral therapy without medication ended with 34 percent of patients exhibiting no further remarkable symptoms.
- Carefully tailored medical treatment with accompanying counseling for the child and parents helped 56 percent of the children.
- A combination of medication and behavioral therapy resulted in a success rate of 68 percent.

Always Count to 10

These findings allow us to draw concrete conclusions about how parents and educators might best help ADHD children. With or without drugs, it is imperative that children be taught how to handle tasks with more organization and less impulsivity. One common tool, for example, is teaching them to count to 10 before carrying out an impulse, such as jumping up from a table at school. Wall posters or cards shaped like stop signs can remind children to use the various devices they have learned in the heat of a moment. Older children and teenagers can learn how to make detailed plans and how to follow through when complicated tasks threaten to shut them down—for example, when they must straighten a messy bedroom.

Parents also need aids for dealing with trying situations. They can receive guidance in parent training programs that focus on their child-rearing skills as well as their child's interactions within the family. One common recommendation is to set up written schedules with children so that getting ready for school, for example, does not turn into a contest every morning. Clear rules, specific expectations and known consequences as well as reward points for desired behaviors can all be effective. Particularly with teenagers, parents and even siblings should be included in family therapy.

As neuroscience progresses, therapists continue to try to refine which mixes of drugs and behavioral therapy are best for which types of ADHD. More work is needed. Little is known, for example, about what occurs in the brains of ADHD children between birth and the time they enter school. One conclusion has become increasingly clear, however: the varying combinations of behaviors cannot be grouped into a picture of a single disorder. Researchers are now trying to define subgroups that are more coherent in terms of symptoms and neurological causes. To this end, they are looking at other disturbances

Latest Leap

Neurofeedback is the newest treatment alternative that therapists are exploring to combat ADHD. It is based on the finding that the electrical brain activity of ADHD children often differs from that of their peers. In this scheme, children play special computer games to learn how to consciously influence their brain waves—and therefore their behavior. For example, they can make themselves calmer and more attentive by strengthening certain electrical activity and decreasing other activity. Sounds, music or movie clips reward them when they can elicit a desired change.

In one game (photograph), a child wearing electrodes watches a cartoon of a pole-vaulting mouse. The mouse can only clear the bar when the pole turns red. This feat occurs when the child concentrates, but the pole turns blue when the child does not.

Children in neurofeedback therapy usually undergo three or four 30- to 40-minute sessions a week for six to 10 weeks. Attention, concentration, impulsivity and mild forms of hyperactivity frequently improve. A child's feelings of self-esteem also improve because he sees that he can control his own behavior. Many succeed in transferring the concentration skills they develop to their schoolwork.

—A.R. and T.B.

that are often associated with attention deficit or hyperactivity; approximately 80 percent of ADHD children suffer from at least one other challenge, such as nervous tics, antisocial behavior, anxiety, or reading and spelling problems.

In the meantime, as parents and teachers do the best they can, they must remember that ADHD children possess many positive traits. They tend to be free-spirited, inquisitive, energetic and funny, as well as intelligent and creative. Their behavior is often spontaneous, helpful and sensitive. Many ADHD children are talented multitaskers, last-minute specialists and improvisationalists. Parents and educators should encourage these strengths and let their children know whenever possible that these qualities are highly valued. That will help them feel less under attack, a relief that all by itself can help them begin to turn the corner.

Further Readings

Driven to Distraction: Recognizing and Coping with Attention Deficit Disorder from Childhood through Adulthood. Reprint edition. Edward M. Hallowell and John J. Ratey. Touchstone, 1995.

Does Stimulant Therapy of Attention-Deficit/Hyperactivity Disorder Beget Later Substance Abuse? A Meta-Analytic Review of the Literature. T. E. Wilens, S. V. Faraone, J. Biederman and S. Gunawardene in *Pediatrics,* Vol. 111, pages 179–185; January 2003.

ARIBERT ROTHENBERGER and **TOBIAS BANASCHEWSKI** are both in the clinic for child and *adolescent* psychiatry at the University of Goettingen in Germany. Rothenberger is a professor and director of the clinic. Banaschewski is the clinic's chief physician.

Why We Need "The Year of Languages"

"2005: The Year of Languages" will focus on educating the U.S. public about the benefits of learning another language.

Sandy Cutshall

Q: What do you call a person who speaks three languages?
A: Trilingual.
Q: What do you call a person who speaks two languages?
A: Bilingual.
Q: What do you call a person who speaks one language?
A: An American.

The late Paul Simon, senator from Illinois and a champion of foreign language learning, once called the United States "linguistically malnourished" compared with other nations (Simon, 1980). People from different cultural and linguistic backgrounds have always come together to season the American melting pot, yet we have nevertheless held monolingualism in English as the gold standard of U.S. citizenship for immigrants, often at the expense of heritage languages.

Sadly, a chronic case of *xenoglossophobia*—the fear of foreign languages—has marked U.S. history. Only a few generations back, 22 states had restrictions prohibiting the teaching of foreign languages; it was not until 1923 that the U.S. Supreme Court overturned those laws. In 1954, only 14.2 percent of U.S. high school students were enrolled in foreign language classes; most public high schools (56 percent) offered no foreign language instruction at all (Clifford, 2004).

Studies have frequently reported on this area of national weakness. In 1979, the President's Commission on Foreign Language and International Studies noted that "Americans' incompetence in foreign languages is nothing short of scandalous, and it is becoming worse" (Clifford, 2004). Two decades later, a senior Department of Defense official said that the United States' greatest national challenge was its "general apathy toward learning foreign languages" (Clifford, 2004). In August 2001—one month before the September 11 terrorist attacks against the United States—the National Foreign Language Center at the University of Maryland noted that the country faced "a critical shortage of linguistically competent professionals across federal agencies and departments responsible for national security" (Simon, 2001).

This apathy plays out in the education landscape as well. Fewer than 1 in 10 students at U.S. colleges major in foreign languages, and most of those language majors choose French, German, Italian, or Spanish. Only 9 percent learn Arabic, Chinese, Japanese, Russian, or Indonesian—languages that are spoken by the majority of the planet's people (Strauss, 2002).

The current lack of accurate U.S. intelligence has heightened awareness of our lack of foreign language prowess. Many are hoping that the United States will finally change its priorities and find new and better ways to encourage and support language learning. Multilingualism carries many benefits. Individuals who speak, read, and understand more than one language can communicate with more people, read more literature, and benefit more fully from travel to other countries. Further, people who can communicate in at least two languages are a great asset to the communities in which they live and work. Jobs today are increasingly requiring workers who can interact with those who speak languages other than English and who can adapt to a wide range of cultural backgrounds. Every year, more than 200,000 Americans lose out on jobs because they do not know another language (Simon, 1980).

Allen Over Geld

So are we putting our money where our "tongues" are? Total federal funding for foreign language education was approximately $85 million for 2003, which represents less than one-sixth of 1 percent of the overall Department of Education budget. This means that for every $100 spent by the Department of Education in 2003, approximately $0.15 went to foreign language education (Keatley, 2004).

According to Thomas Keith Cothrun, president of the American Council on the Teaching of Foreign Languages (ACTFL), there is clearly a disconnect in the government: On one hand, the military and intelligence communities decry the lack of language experts; on the other hand, the Department of Education underemphasizes the importance of language learning. A recent study by the Council for Basic Education (CBE) indicates that the No Child Left Behind Act (NCLB) has forced a narrow focus on reading, math, and science at the expense of languages. Instruction time in foreign languages has decreased—particularly in schools serving minority populations—as a direct result of NCLB (CBE, 2004). The National Association of State Boards of Education (NASBE) also recently reported that both arts and foreign language education are increasingly at risk of being eliminated from the core curriculum (NASBE, 2003).

Non è Facile

Foreign language learning is not something that happens overnight; it takes a commitment of time and money. U.S. schools compound the problem by waiting too long to start foreign language instruction. According to ACTFL Professional Programs Director Elvira Swender, U.S. students often start learning foreign languages at puberty, "an age at which their brains are least receptive to language learning." Swender also notes the relative unimportance that schools assign to languages. "It doesn't occur to anyone that we should wait to teach students math," she points out, "so why do we wait with foreign languages?"

ACTFL recommends that elementary school language programs include classes three to five days a week for 30 to 40 minutes; middle schools should hold classes daily for 40 to 50 minutes. Few public schools do this even in Spanish and French, the most commonly taught languages (Strauss, 2002).

Further, some of the languages that are most crucial for Americans to learn are the most challenging for English speakers, thus requiring the greatest commitment of time and effort. Research estimates that it takes between 2,400 and 2,760 hours of instruction for someone with a superior aptitude for languages to attain the highest level of achievement in Arabic, for example (Strauss, 2002).

Quel est le Problème?

It's not that people in the United States don't want to learn languages; rather, they often believe that they are unable to do so or that they simply don't need to. As ACTFL Executive Director Bret Lovejoy points out,

> This perception that languages are too difficult to learn can often be traced to the fact that a person didn't start early enough, didn't have enough time devoted to the language, or had a difficult time in a language course in the past. (Personal communication, April 7, 2004)

People in the United States may travel hundreds of miles in their own nation and never hear a language other than English spoken, a decidedly different situation from that of European countries, whose citizens live in a much more multilingual world. In addition, the widespread perception of English as the international language of business has contributed to a pervasive belief in the United States that everyone should learn English and that Americans simply don't need to learn another language. In fact, the international language of business is always the language of the client or customer. If businesses in the United States don't speak the language of their customers, those businesses end up at a competitive disadvantage.

Beginning language learning at an early age is crucial to increasing our language capabilities. A primary difference between the United States and nations that boast greater language strengths is the latter countries' emphasis on learning languages at younger ages. The Center for Applied Linguistics (CAL) issued a report on approaches to language learning that compared the United States with 22 other nations. Seven countries—Australia, Austria, Germany, Italy, Luxembourg, Spain, and Thailand—had widespread or compulsory education in additional languages by age 8, and another eight—Canada, the Czech Republic, Denmark, Finland, Israel, Kazakhstan, Morocco, and the Netherlands—introduced a foreign language in the upper elementary grades. In many cases, a *second* foreign language was offered or required in the elementary grade.

In stark contrast, the majority of students in the United States do not start studying foreign language until age 14 (Pufahl, Rhodes, & Christian, 2000). Most foreign language study in the United States takes place in grades 9–12, during which time more than one-third (39 percent) of students study a foreign language. Only 6 percent of U.S. students study a foreign language in grades 1–6.

The shortage of language teachers in the United States is yet another challenge. Because early language learning has not been part of the traditional U.S. education model and most communities don't have access to foreign languages in elementary schools, there is a lack of well-trained language teachers at these levels.

People who can communicate in at least two languages are a great asset to the communities in which they live and work.

El Año de Lenguas

Language learning is a complex, long-term issue. In a culture unfortunately known for its short attention span, we need to do something dramatic to draw sustained attention to this issue.

Enter "2005: The Year of Languages," a national public awareness campaign that may be our best hope to put language learning in the spotlight and engage in a fruitful national conversation about the relationship between Americans and foreign language learning. Under the guidance and stewardship of ACTFL, 2005: The Year of Languages advances the concept that every person in the United States should develop proficiency in at least one language in addition to English. Each month of the yearlong endeavor will focus on a different area—such as language policy, higher education, language advocacy, heritage languages, and early language learning—with specific events reflecting the monthly focus.

For example, in February—the month that will tackle international engagement—a panel of Fulbright Exchange participants and representatives from other international programs will discuss the importance of study-abroad programs. There are currently more than 3,000 study-abroad programs for U.S. students to choose from. Although the number of U.S. students studying abroad for credit doubled in the past decade to more than 150,000 in the 2000–2001 school year, this number represents only 1 percent of college enrollments (Institute of International Education, 2003). Many students lack access to study-abroad programs through their institutions.

July's focus will be on languages and communities; during that month, the annual Folk Life Festival sponsored by the Smithsonian Institution will feature communities within and outside the United States and their respective languages and cultures. October will emphasize the benefits of early language learning: Activities cosponsored by the National Council of PTAs will provide parents with information on the benefits of learning languages at an early age and will feature K-12 programs that highlight language learning.

Language teachers in a school or district may choose to meet as a group to brainstorm ideas for promoting foreign language awareness, using the official Year of Languages Calendar of Events as a starting point. The calendar (available at www.yearoflanguages.org) may be used as a guide in planning local school events. ACTFL state and regional organizations have also coordinated plans for 2005: The Year of Languages and can serve as a local resource for schools to get involved with activities planned in their areas.

Alle Sind Optimistisch

There is great hope that the 2005: The Year of Languages campaign will not only draw U.S. attention to the important issue of foreign language learning but also inspire actions like those that resulted from a similar European effort in 2001, such as an ongoing annual National Language Day/Week, a national language agenda, and an official language policy.

With so much at stake—international relations, global competitiveness, support for internal diversity, and national security—it may well be time for everyone involved in education to think about what they can personally do to make this a successful Year of Languages.

References

Clifford, R. (2004, Jan. 16). Remarks at *National briefing on language and national security*, National Press Club, Washington, DC. Available: www.ndu.edu/nsep/january 16_briefing.htm

Council for Basic Education. (2004). *Academic atrophy: The condition of the liberal arts in America's public schools.* Washington, DC: Author.

Institute of International Education. (2003). *Open doors 2003: Report on international educational exchange.* New York: Author.

Keatley, C. (2004, March). Who is paying the bills? The federal budget and foreign language education in U.S. schools and universities. *The Language Resource Newsletter.* Available: www.nclrc.org/caidlr82.htm#no2

National Association of State Boards of Education. (2003). *The complete curriculum: Ensuring a place for the arts and foreign languages in America's schools.* Alexandria, VA: Author.

Pufahl, I., Rhodes, N., & Christian, D. (2000, December). *Foreign language teaching: What the United States can learn from other countries.* Washington, DC: Center for Applied Linguistics. Available: www.cal.org/resources/countries.html

Simon, P. (1980). *The tongue-tied American: Confronting the foreign language crisis.* New York: Continuum.

Strauss, V. (2002, May 28). Mastering Arabic's nuances no easy mission. *The Washington Post,* p. A9.

SANDY CUTSHALL is Managing Editor of *Foreign Language Annals*, the quarterly journal of the American Council on the Teaching of Foreign Languages, and a teacher of English as a second language to adults in Mountain View, California.

Author's note—Thomas Keith Cothrun, Bret Lovejoy, Mary Louise Pratt, Nancy Rhodes, and Elvira Swender contributed to this article. For more information about 2005: The Year of Languages, visit www.yearoflanguages.org or contact the American Council on the Teaching of Foreign Languages (ACTFL) at 703-894-2900.

The New First Grade: Too Much Too Soon?

Kids as young as 6 are tested, and tested again, to ensure they're making sufficient progress. Then there's homework, more workbooks and tutoring.

PEG TYRE

Brian and Tiffany Aske of Oakland, Calif., desperately want their daughter, Ashlyn, to succeed in first grade. That's why they're moving—to Washington state. When they started Ashlyn in kindergarten last year, they had no reason to worry. A bright child with twinkling eyes, Ashlyn was eager to learn, and the neighborhood school had a great reputation. But by November, Ashlyn, then 5, wasn't measuring up. No matter how many times she was tested, she couldn't read the 130-word list her teacher gave her: words like "our," "house" and "there." She became so exhausted and distraught over homework—including a weekly essay on "my favorite animal" or "my family vacation"—that she would put her head down on the dining-room table and sob. "She would tell me, 'I can't write a story, Mama. I just can't do it'," recalls Tiffany, a stay-at-home mom.

The teacher didn't seem to notice that Ashlyn was crumbling, but Tiffany became so concerned that she began to spend time in her daughter's classroom as a volunteer. There she was both disturbed and comforted to see that other kids were struggling, too. "I saw kids falling asleep at their desks at 11 a.m.," she says. At the end of the year, Tiffany asked the teacher what Ashlyn could expect when she moved on to the first grade. The requirements the teacher described, more words and more math at an even faster pace, "were overwhelming. It was just bizarre."

So Tiffany and Brian, a contractor, looked hard at their family finances to see if they could afford to send Ashlyn to private school. Eventually, they called a real-estate agent in a community where school was not as intense.

In the last decade, the earliest years of schooling have become less like a trip to "Mister Rogers' Neighborhood" and more like SAT prep. Thirty years ago first grade was for learning how to read. Now, reading lessons start in kindergarten and kids who don't crack the code by the middle of the first grade get extra help. Instead of story time, finger painting, tracing letters and snacks, first graders are spending hours doing math work sheets and sounding out words in reading groups. In some places,

recess, music, art and even social studies are being replaced by writing exercises and spelling quizzes. Kids as young as 6 are tested, and tested again—some every 10 days or so—to ensure they're making sufficient progress. After school, there's homework, and for some, educational videos, more workbooks and tutoring, to help give them an edge.

Not every school, or every district, embraces this new work ethic, and in those that do, many kids are thriving. But some children are getting their first taste of failure before they learn to tie their shoes. Being held back a grade was once relatively rare: it makes kids feel singled out and, in some cases, humiliated. These days, the number of kids repeating a grade, especially in urban school districts, has jumped. In Buffalo, N.Y., the district sent a group of more than 600 low-performing first graders to mandatory summer school; even so, 42 percent of them have to repeat the grade. Among affluent families, the pressure to succeed at younger and younger ages is an inevitable byproduct of an increasingly competitive world. The same parents who played Mozart to their kids in utero are willing to spend big bucks to make sure their 5-year-olds don't stray off course.

> **"I worry that we are creating school environments that are less friendly to kids who just aren't ready . . . Around third grade, sometimes even the most precocious kids begin to burn out."**
>
> —Holly Hultgren, Principal
> Lafayette Elementary School

Like many of his friends, Robert Cloud, a president of an engineering company in suburban Chicago, had the Ivy League in mind when he enrolled his sons, ages 5 and 8, in a weekly after-school tutoring program. "To get into a good school, you need to have good grades," he says. In Granville, Ohio, a city known for its overachieving high-school and middle-school students, an elementary-school principal has noticed a dramatic shift over the past 10 years. "Kindergarten, which was once very play-based," says William White, "has become the new first grade." This pendulum has been swinging for nearly a century: in some decades, educators have favored a rigid academic curriculum, in others, a more child-friendly classroom style. Lately, some experts have begun to question whether our current emphasis on early learning may be going too far. "There comes a time when prudent people begin to wonder just how high we can raise our expectations for our littlest schoolkids," says Walter Gilliam, a child-development expert at Yale University. Early education, he says, is not just about teaching letters but about turning curious kids into lifelong learners. It's critical that all kids know how to read, but that is only one aspect of a child's education. Are we pushing our children too far, too fast? Could all this pressure be bad for our kids?

Kindergarten and first grade have changed so much because we know so much more about how kids learn. Forty years ago school performance and intelligence were thought to be determined mainly by social conditions—poor kids came from chaotic families and attended badly run schools. If poor children, blacks and Hispanics lagged behind middle-class kids in school, policymakers dismissed the problem as an inevitable byproduct of poverty. Its roots were too deep and complex, and there wasn't the political will to fix it anyway. Since then, scientists have confirmed what some kindergarten teachers had been saying all along—that *all* young children are wired to learn from birth and an enriched environment, one with plenty of books, stories, rhyming and conversation, can help kids from all kinds of backgrounds achieve more. Politicians began taking aim at the achievement gap, pushing schools to reconceive the early years as an opportunity to make sure that all kids got the fundamentals of reading and math. At the same time, politicians began calling for tests that would measure how individual students were doing, and high-stakes testing quickly became the sole metric by which a school was measured.

President George W. Bush's No Child Left Behind Act, which required every principal in the country to make sure the kids in his or her school could read by the third grade, was signed into federal law in 2002. Its aim was both simple and breathtakingly grand: to level the academic playing field by holding schools accountable or risk being shut down.

So if the curriculum at Coronita Elementary School, 60 miles outside Los Angeles, is intense, that's because it has to be. Seventy percent of kids who go there live below the poverty line. Thirty percent don't speak English at home. Even so, No Child Left Behind mandates that Coronita principal Alma Backer and her staff get every student reading proficiently in time for the California state test in the spring of second grade or face stiff penalties: the school could lose its funding and the principal could lose her job. "Our challenges are great," she says. "From day one, our kids are playing catch-up." First grade is like literacy boot camp. Music, dance, art, phys ed—even social studies and science—take a back seat to reading and writing. Kids are tested every eight weeks to see if they are hitting school,

district and statewide benchmarks. If they aren't, they get remedial help, one-on-one tutoring and more instruction. The regular school day starts at 7:45 A.M. and ends at 2:05 P.M.; about a fifth of the students go to an after-school program until 5:30, where they get even more instruction: tutoring, reading group and homework help. Backer says most parents appreciate what the school is trying to do. "Many of them have a high-school diploma or less," says Backer, "but they're still ambitious for their children."

> **"If you push kids too hard, they get frustrated. Those are the kids who act out, and who can look like they have attention-span or behavior problems."**
>
> —Dominic Gullo, Professor
> Queens College, N.Y.

Parents whose kids attend Clemmons Elementary School near Winston-Salem, N.C., are ambitious for their children, too. But the scale of their expectations is different: the upper-middle-class, college-educated parents in this district don't just want their kids to get a good education, they want them to be academic stars. Principal Ron Montaquila says kids of all ages are affected. Last year, says Montaquila, one dad wanted to know how his son stacked up against his classmates. "I told him we didn't do class ranking in kindergarten," recalls Montaquila. But the father persisted. If they did do rankings, the dad asked, would the boy be in the top 10? Like almost all elementary schools, kindergarten and first grade at Clemmons have become more academic—but not because of No Child Left Behind. Unlike poor schools, wealthy schools do not depend on federal money. The kids come to school knowing more than they used to. "Many of our kindergartners come in with four years of preschool on their résumé," says Montaquila. Last year nine children started kindergarten at Clemmons reading chapter books—including one who had already tackled "Little House on the Prairie."

In wealthier communities, where parents can afford an extra year of day care or preschool, they are holding their kids out of kindergarten a year—a practice known in sports circles as red-shirting—so their kids can get a jump on the competition. Clemmons parent Mary DeLucia did it. When her son, Austin, was 5, he was mature, capable, social and ready for school. But the word around the local Starbucks was that kindergarten was a killer. "Other parents said, 'Send him. He'll do just fine'," says DeLucia. "But we didn't want him to do fine, we wanted him to do great!" Austin, now in fourth grade, towers over his classmates, but he's hardly the only older kid in his grade. At Clemmons last year, 40 percent of the kindergartners started when they were 6 instead of 5. Other parents say they understand where the DeLucias are coming from but complain that red-shirting can make it hard for other kids to compete. "We're getting to the point," says Bill White, a Clemmons dad whose kids started on time, where "we're going to have boys who are shaving in elementary school."

Ten Ways to Prepare Your Child for School

For Kindergarten

1. **Read to Them**—Pull out the board books, get cozy and channel Mr. Rogers. Kids love repetition and there's no such thing as reading too much to your child.
2. **Talk to Them**—Sing songs, recite rhymes and narrate your activities as you go about the day. Ask questions and invite them to name objects and describe whatever they're seeing. At night, recap the day's events together out loud.
3. **Take Them on Trips**—No, not Europe. The supermarket, the post office, a museum or the zoo will do. Then, talk about what you see and ask questions.
4. **Write It Down**—Kids love to scribble. Give them paper and plenty of pencils, crayons, paints and markers. Finger paints are colorful and feel squishy, too.
5. **Socialize**—Whether it's a big birthday party or a one-on-one play date, kids benefit from hearing a range of words in a variety of voices. Story hour at the library or a puppet show can be especially good for encountering new sounds and ideas.
6. **Use Your Fingers**—Drawing, cutting and pasting can seem laborious but these activities will help them learn to write more legibly—and result in keepsakes.

For First Grade

7. **Read Some More**—Let them "read" to you, too, by flipping the pages—themselves, thank you very much—and retelling a favorite story in their own words.
8. **Teach Recognition**—Logos on food packages. Names and addresses on the mail. A stop sign. A "walk" signal. The letter B. Give them opportunities to demonstrate that they know what these things mean and then heap on praise.
9. **Do the Math**—Talk about numbers. Count everything out loud. How many grapes do you have on your plate? One more would make how many?
10. **Grow Their Attention Span**—Card games, board games, setting the table, picking photos out of a magazine. Set aside time to focus on a single activity or one task before moving on to active play.

Source: Dominic Gullo, Queens College, N.Y.

Parents are acutely aware of the pressure on their kids, but they're also creating it. Most kids learn to read sometime before the end of first grade. But many parents (and even some teachers and school administrators) believe—mistakenly—that the earlier the kids read independently, write legibly and do arithmetic, the more success they'll have all through school. Taking a cue from the success of the Baby Einstein line of videos and CDs, an entire industry has sprung up to help anxious parents give their kids a jump-start. Educate, Inc., the company that markets the learning-to-read workbooks and CDs called "Hooked on Phonics," just launched a new line of what it calls age-appropriate reading and writing workbooks aimed at 4-year-olds. In the last three years, centers that offer school-tutoring services such as Sylvan Learning Centers and Kumon have opened junior divisions. Gertie Tolentino of Darien, Ill., has been bringing her first grader, Kyle, for Kumon tutoring three times a week since he was 3 years old. "It's paying off," she says. "In kindergarten, he was the only one who could read a book at age 5." Two weeks ago Tiffani Chin, executive director of Edboost, a non-profit tutoring center in Los Angeles, saw her first 3-year-old. His parents wanted to give him a head start, says Chin. "They had heard that kindergarten was brutal" and they wanted to give him a leg up.

All this single-minded focus on achievement leaves principals like Holly Hultgren, who runs Lafayette Elementary School in Boulder County, Colo., in a quandary. In this area of Colorado, parents can shop for schools, and most try to get their kids into the top-performing ones. Two years ago Hultgren

moved to Lafayette from a more affluent school, in part to help raise the tests scores, improve the school's profile and raise attendance. Every day Hultgren has to help her staff strike a balance between the requirements of the state, the expectations of parents—and the very real, highly variable needs of all kinds of 5- and 6-year-olds. She is adamant that her staff won't "teach to the test." Yet, in keeping with her district's requirements, on the day before the first day of kindergarten, students come in for a reading assessment. Sitting one-on-one with her new teacher, a little girl named Jenna wrinkles her nose and in a whispery voice identifies most of the letters in the alphabet and makes their sounds. Naming words that start with each letter is harder for her. Asked to supply a word that starts with B, Jenna scrunches her face and shakes her head.

Hultgren is ambivalent about high-stakes testing. The district reading test, administered three times a year, helps parents see how the school measures up and helps teachers see "exactly what kind of instruction is working and what isn't." But the pressure to improve scores makes it hard for teachers to stay sensitive to the important qualities in children that tests can't measure—diligence, creativity and potential—or to nurture kids who develop more slowly. "I worry," she says, that "we are creating school environments that are less friendly to kids who just aren't ready."

Some scholars and policymakers see clear downsides to all this pressure. Around third grade, Hultgren says, some of the most highly pressured learners sometimes "burn out. They began to resist. They didn't want to go along with the program anymore." In Britain, which adopted high-stakes testing about six years before the United States did, parents and school boards are trying to dial back the pressure. In Wales, standardized testing of young children has been banned. Andrew Hargreaves, an expert on international education reform and professor at Boston College, says middle-class parents there saw that "too much testing too early was sucking the soul and spirit out of their children's early school experiences."

> "When Austin was 5, he was ready for school. Other parents said, "Send him. He'll do just fine." But we didn't want him to do fine, we wanted him to do great!"
>
> —Mary DeLucia, Parent
> Clemmons Elementary School

While most American educators agree that No Child Left Behind is helping poor kids, school administrators say a bigger challenge remains: helping those same kids succeed later on. Until he resigned as Florida's school chancellor last year, Jim Warford says he scoured his budget, taking money from middle- and high-school programs in order to beef up academics in the earliest years. But then he began to notice a troubling trend: in Florida, about 70 percent of fourth graders read proficiently. By middle school, the rate of proficient readers began to drop. "We can't afford to focus on our earliest learners," says Warford, "and then ignore what happens to them later on."

What early-childhood experts know is that for children between the ages of 5 and 7, social and emotional development are every bit as important as learning the ABCs. Testing kids before third grade gives you a snapshot of what they know at that moment but is a poor predictor of how they will perform later on. Not all children learn the same way. Teachers need to

Interview: What Would Big Bird Do?

"Sesame Street" began in 1969 with a revolutionary idea: learning could be fun. The cast of furry Muppets and their inimitable songs became so popular among kids of all backgrounds—and not just the disadvantaged kids the show originally intended to help—that "Sesame Street" spawned an entire industry of DVDs, toys and computer games aimed at teaching ever-younger children. The show, meant for 2- to 4-year-olds, is watched today by kids as young as 9 months. NEWSWEEK's Julie Scelfo asked Rosemarie Truglio, "Sesame Street's" VP of education and research, whether she thinks this is a good idea. Excerpts:

SCELFO: Do You Think There's Too Much Pressure on Young Kids to Learn?

TRUGLIO: People want children to be ready to read in kindergarten, so that pressure is now being passed down to preschool and day-care centers. We're putting a lot of pressure on [teachers] and introducing children to some things that may or may not be age-appropriate. Stress is not conducive to learning. If you're put in a stressful environment, you're not going to learn.

What Should Preschoolers Be Learning?

The majority of kindergarten teachers want children to be able to function in a group setting. To be able to listen and take direction. Be able to get along. To be able to regulate their emotions. A lot of what I'm talking about is social-emotional development of children. If they can't function in a group setting, it will interfere with learning to read.

So Reading Is Important, but It's Not the Only Thing?

Every child learns at their own rate. During the preschool years, children's job is to explore and investigate, and adults need to assist learning and facilitate it. I'm not going to say a child can't read by the age of 5. But developmentally, most children in kindergarten are learning the precursors of

reading skills—they have sounds, they do the alphabet, they have rhyming—but they are not reading.

Then Why Do Parents Feel So Pressured?

One reason may be No Child Left Behind. I don't think the intention was for this kind of hysteria. The idea of accountability is great. But I think it's turned into this testing issue, and there's a lot of pressure about testing and performance which I think might be leading to anxiety.

Is That What Is Spurring Sales of All Those Videos for Infants?

What's happening now is, everything is getting pushed down to a younger and younger age. There's pressure even on babies to begin achieving, so parents are buying these videos to make their infants "smarter." But there's no research that shows exposure to videos increases learning.

But Aren't Kids Watching "Sesame Street" at Younger and Younger Ages?

Yes, and that's not something we can control. "Sesame Street" is a show for 2- to 4-year-olds. If you can get that word out, it would be great. Parents grew up on "Sesame Street" and they know it's a safe, educational viewing experience. They think, Why not have my little ones learn their letters and numbers at an accelerated pace? It makes parents feel proud. There's no harm, but the show's content isn't age-appropriate, so a lot of the learning is going over their heads. Also, they burn out. If you start watching it at 9 months, by the time you're 2 you want something else.

How Is This Affecting Children?

Learning should be fun. It shouldn't feel like they're learning, which is what "Sesame Street" is all about. A child's work is through play. I don't think preschoolers should be doing flashcards.

vary instruction and give kids opportunities to work in small groups and one on one. Children need hands-on experiences so that they can discover things on their own. "If you push kids too hard, they get frustrated," says Dominic Gullo, a professor of early education at Queens College in New York. "Those are the kids who are likely to act out, and who teachers can perceive as having attention-span or behavior problems."

There are signs that some parents and school boards are looking for a gentler, more kid-friendly way. In Chattanooga, Tenn., more than 100 parents camped out on the sidewalk last spring in hopes of getting their kids into one of the 16 coveted spots at the Chattanooga School for Arts and Sciences (CSAS), a K-12 magnet program that champions a slowed-down approach to education. The school, which admits kids from all socioeconomic backgrounds, offers students plenty of skills and drills but also stresses a "whole-child approach." The emphasis is not on passing tests but on hands-on learning. Two weeks ago newly minted kindergartners were spending the day learning about the color red. They wore red shirts, painted with bright red acrylic paint. During instructional time, they learned to spell RED. Every week each class meets for a seminar that encourages critical thinking. Two weeks ago the first graders had been read a book about a girl who was adopted. Then, the class discussed the pros and cons of adoption. One girl said she thought adoption was bad because "a kid isn't with her real mom and dad." A boy said it was good because the character "has a new mom and dad who love her." The children returned to their desks and drew pictures of different kinds of families. At CSAS, students are rarely held back, and in fourth grade—and in 12th grade—more than 90 percent of students passed the state's proficiency tests in reading last year.

Tiffany Aske says she wishes she could have found a school like CSAS in Oakland. Instead, they're pulling up stakes and moving to a suburban community in Washington where the school system seems more stable and has more outdoor space, and where the kids have more choices during the school day. In some ways, they feel as if they're swimming against the current. Most of their friends are scrambling, paying top dollar for houses in high-performing school districts. The Askes say they're looking for something more important than high test scores. "We want flexibility," says Tiffany. Ashlyn is a bright girl, says her mom, "but she's only a child." And childhood takes time.

With Matthew Philips, Julie Scelfo, Catharine Skipp, Nadine Joseph, Paul Tolme and Hilary Shenfeld.

Ten Big Effects of the No Child Left Behind Act on Public Schools

The Center on Education Policy has been carefully monitoring the implementation of NCLB for four years. Now Mr. Jennings and Ms. Rentner consider the comprehensive information that has been gathered and present their conclusions about the law's impact thus far.

JACK JENNINGS AND DIANE STARK RENTNER

Test-driven accountability is now the norm in public schools, a result of the No Child Left Behind (NCLB) Act, which is the culmination of 15 years of standards-based reform. Many state and local officials believe that this reliance on tests is too narrow a measure of educational achievement, but NCLB has directed greater attention to low-achieving students and intensified efforts to improve persistently low-performing schools.

For the past four years, the Center on Education Policy (CEP), an independent nonprofit research and advocacy organization, has been conducting a comprehensive and continuous review of NCLB, producing the annual reports contained in the series *From the Capital to the Classroom* as well as numerous papers on specific issues related to the law.[1] Each year, the CEP gathers information for this review by surveying officials in all the state departments of education, administering a questionnaire to a nationally representative sample of school districts, conducting case studies of individual school districts and schools, and generally monitoring the implementation of this important national policy.

Ten Effects

Ten major effects of NCLB on American education are evident from this multi-year review and analysis. We describe these effects broadly, because our purpose is to assess the overall influence of this policy on public schools. The effects on particular schools and districts may be different.

1. State and district officials report that student achievement on state tests is rising, which is a cause for optimism. It's not clear, however, that students are really gaining as much as rising percentages of proficient scores would suggest. Scores on state tests in reading and mathematics that are used for

NCLB purposes are going up, according to nearly three-fourths of the states and school districts, and the achievement gaps on these same tests are generally narrowing or staying the same. States and districts mostly credit their own policies as important in attaining these results, although they acknowledge that the "adequate yearly progress" (AYP) requirements of NCLB have also contributed. However, under NCLB, student achievement is equated with the proportion of students who are scoring at the proficient level on state tests, and states have adopted various approaches in their testing programs, such as the use of confidence intervals, that result in more test scores being counted as proficient. In addition, some national studies support our survey findings of increased student achievement, while others do not.

2. Schools are spending more time on reading and math, sometimes at the expense of subjects not tested. To find additional time for reading and math, the two subjects that are required to be tested under NCLB and that matter for accountability purposes, 71% of districts are reducing time spent on other subjects in elementary schools—at least to some degree. The subject most affected is social studies, while physical education is least affected. In addition, 60% of districts require a specific amount of time for reading in elementary schools. Ninety-seven percent of high-poverty districts have this requirement, compared to 55%–59% of districts with lower levels of poverty.

3. Schools are paying much more attention to the alignment of curriculum and instruction and are analyzing test score data much more closely. Changes in teaching and learning are occurring in schools that have not made AYP for two years. The most common improvements are greater alignment of curriculum and instruction with standards and assessments, more use of test data to modify instruction, use of research to inform decisions about improvement strategies, improvement in the quality and quantity of professional development for teachers, and the provision of more intensive instruction to low-achieving students.

4. Low-performing schools are undergoing makeovers rather than the most radical kinds of restructuring. More intensive changes are taking place in schools that have not made AYP for five consecutive years and thus must be "restructured" under NCLB. Greater efforts to improve curriculum, staffing, and leadership are the most common changes, but very few of these restructured schools have been taken over by the states, dissolved, or made into charter schools. Though only about 3% of all schools were in restructuring during the 2005–06 school year, the number may increase in the current year. The longer the law is in effect, the more likely it is that some schools will not make AYP for five years.

5. Schools and teachers have made considerable progress in demonstrating that teachers meet the law's academic qualifications—but many educators are skeptical this will really improve the quality of teaching. With regard to teacher quality, 88% of school districts reported that by the end of the 2005–06 school year all their teachers of core academic subjects would have met the NCLB definition of "highly qualified." Problems persist, however, for special education teachers, high school math and science teachers, and teachers in rural areas who teach multiple subjects. Despite this general compliance with NCLB's provisions, most districts expressed skepticism that this requirement will improve the quality of teaching.

6. Students are taking a lot more tests. Students are taking many more tests as a result of NCLB. In 2002, 19 states had annual reading and mathematics tests in grades 3–8 and once in high school; by 2006, every state had such testing. In the 2007–08 school year, testing in science will be required under NCLB (although the results need not be used for NCLB's accountability requirements), leading to a further increase in the number of assessments.

7. Schools are paying much more attention to achievement gaps and the learning needs of particular groups of students. NCLB's requirement that districts and schools be responsible for improving not only the academic achievement of students as a whole but also the achievement of each subgroup of students is directing additional attention to traditionally underperforming groups of students, such as those who are from low-income families or ethnic and racial minorities, those who are learning English, or those who have a disability. States and school districts have consistently praised NCLB's requirement for the disaggregation of test data by subgroups of students, because it has shone a light on the poor performance of students who would have gone unnoticed if only general test data were considered.

For the past three years, though, states and districts have repeatedly identified as NCLB problem areas the law's testing and accountability provisions for students with disabilities and students learning English. State and district officials have voiced frustration with requirements to administer state exams to students with disabilities because, for disabled students with cognitive impairments, the state test may be inappropriate and serve no instructional purpose. Similarly, officials don't see the merit in administering an English/language arts test to students who speak little or no English. The U.S. Department of Education (ED) has made some administrative changes in those areas, but, in the view of state officials and local educators, these modifications have not been enough.

8. The percentage of schools on state "needs improvement" lists has been steady but is not growing. Schools so designated are subject to NCLB sanctions, such as being required to offer students public school choice or tutoring services. Over the past several years, there has been a leveling off in the number of schools not making AYP for at least two years. About 10% of all schools have been labeled as "in need of improvement" for not making AYP, though these are not always the same schools every year. Urban districts, however, report greater proportions of their schools in this category than do suburban and rural districts. Earlier predictions had been that by this time there would be a very large number of U.S. schools not making AYP. A major reason for the overall stabilization in numbers of such schools is that, as already noted, test scores are increasing. Another reason is that ED has permitted states to modify their NCLB accountability systems so that it is easier for schools and districts to make AYP.

In the last four years, about 2% of eligible students each year have moved from a school not making AYP for at least two years to another school, using the "public school choice" option. Approximately 20% of eligible students in each of the last two years have taken advantage of additional tutoring (called "supplemental educational services") that must be offered to students from low-income families in schools not making AYP for at least three consecutive years. Although student participation in tutoring has been stable, the number of providers of supplemental services has grown dramatically in the last two years, with more than half of the providers now being for-profit entities. Lower proportions of urban and suburban school districts report that they are providing these services than in the past. School districts are skeptical that the choice option and tutoring will lead to increases in academic achievement, though they are somewhat less skeptical about tutoring than they are about choice. (This month's *Kappan* includes a Special Section on Supplemental Educational Services, which begins on page 117.)

9. The federal government is playing a bigger role in education. Because of NCLB, the federal government is taking a much more active role in public elementary and secondary education than in the past. For example, ED must approve the testing programs states use to carry out NCLB as well as the accountability plans that determine the rules for how schools make AYP. In CEP surveys for the last three years, the states have judged ED's enforcement of many of the key features of the law as being strict or very strict, even while ED was granting some changes in state accountability plans. More states in 2005 than in 2004 reported that ED was strictly or very strictly enforcing the provisions for AYP, supplemental services, public school choice, and highly qualified teachers.

10. NCLB requirements have meant that state governments and school districts also have expanded roles in school operations, but often without adequate federal funds to carry out their duties. State governments are also taking a much more active role in public education, because they must carry out NCLB provisions that affect all their public schools. These state responsibilities include creating or expanding testing programs for grades 3–8 and one year of high school, setting minimum testing goals that all schools must achieve in general and also for their various groups of students, providing assistance to schools in need of improvement, certifying supplemental service providers and then evaluating the quality of their programs, and establishing criteria to determine whether current teachers meet NCLB's teacher-quality requirements. Most state departments of education do not have the capacity to carry out all these duties. Last year, 36 of the 50 states reported to CEP that they lacked sufficient staff to implement NCLB's requirements.

Local school districts must also assume more duties than before because of NCLB. More tests must be administered to students, more attention must be directed to schools in need of improvement, and judgments must be made about whether teachers of core academic subjects are highly qualified. In carrying out these responsibilities, 80% of districts have reported for two years in a row that they are absorbing costs that federal funds are not covering. Overall, federal funding for NCLB has stagnated for several years. Provisions of the law have resulted in a shift of funds so that, in school year 2005–06, two-thirds of school districts in the country received no increases or lost funds compared to the previous year.

NCLB's Future

NCLB is clearly having a major impact on American public education. There is more testing and more accountability. Greater attention is being paid to what is being taught and how it is being taught. Low-performing schools are also receiving greater attention. The qualifications of teachers are coming under greater scrutiny. Concurrently with NCLB, scores on state reading and mathematics tests have risen.

Yet some provisions of the act and of its administration are causing persistent problems. State and local officials have identified the testing and accountability requirements for students with disabilities and for students learning English as troublesome, and other requirements—such as the one to offer a choice of another public school to students in schools needing improvement—have caused administrative burdens with little evidence that they have raised student achievement.

The lack of capacity of state departments of education could undercut the effective administration of NCLB. ED cannot deal with all school districts in the country and so must rely on state agencies to assist in that task. Yet these agencies are under great strain, with little relief in sight. Local school districts must also carry out additional tasks, and they must dig into their own pockets to do so.

The U.S. Congress has begun hearings on the effects of NCLB to prepare for its reauthorization in the new Congress that will assemble in 2007. The key question is whether the strengths of this legislation can be retained while its weaknesses are addressed.

Note

1. For more information on NCLB, including the four annual reports and special papers, go to www.cep-dc.org, the Web site for the Center on Education Policy.

JACK JENNINGS is president of the Center on Education Policy, Washington, D.C., where **DIANE STARK RENTNER** is director of national programs.

From *Phi Delta Kappan,* October 2006, pp. 110–113. Copyright © 2006 by Phi Delta Kappan. Reprinted by permission of Phi Delta Kappan and Jack Jennings and Diane Stark Rentner.

StrengthsQuest in Application

The Power of Teaching Students Using Strengths

GLORIA HENDERSON

Like Chip Anderson, I was initially taught to use the deficit-remediation model with my students. Even in that negative context, though, and with no exposure at all to strengths-based education, I unconsciously based my early teaching on four of my five Clifton StrengthsFinder signature themes: *Significance* (I wanted to be recognized for having made a difference to each student); *Achiever* (I focused on individual students and tried to energize them to establish and reach their goals); *Restorative* (I was confident that I would create success in even those students who had lost all hope); and *Futuristic* (I developed a vision for my students with the identified deficits reduced or eliminated).

As I learned about strengths-based education after I entered Azusa Pacific University's doctoral program, I came to realize the importance of systematic research and the application of research results in developing the most effective instructors possible. I became determined to use my own strengths consciously and deliberately.

Consciously Applying Strengths to Decide on a Job

I knew I had found my calling when I saw a position posting for a late-term-replacement teacher of at-risk kids in a program structured as a school-within-a-school. The school offers more Advanced Placement, International Baccalaureate, and honors classes than regular classes. The students I would teach composed the "school within." They had covered only a minimal amount of content and had not met the state standards.

Being Restorative, I found it natural to identify and take a constructive approach to the students' deficits in skills and the lack of decorum in the classroom. I looked at each student as an individual to determine areas in which performance was satisfactory and those in which it needed improvement. Being Futuristic, I dreamed big for my new students, and being an Achiever, I developed a plan to make my vision a reality. I conducted research to find lessons, discipline plans, and other resources to assist my students. I also sought advice from other teachers, who brought different strengths to bear. Although I endured many tests from those students, I became a much more effective teacher by consciously using my strengths and encouraging them to use theirs.

Consciously Applying Strengths to Develop Teaching Style

I now teach a sophomore English class for at-risk students at the same school. As an Achiever I set high expectations because I know that if I lower the bar and set expectations that are too easy to reach, the students will meet the expectations yet still not pass the required high school exit exam.

Although I fully intend that every student will pass the exit exam (Significance), I employ a Restorative teaching style that seems to fit my students particularly well. I tease them, cajole them, encourage them, tell them they are better than they think they are, and express my concerns and my hopes for them. I do not focus my efforts on content, but they seem to have a huge impact on how well the students learn the content.

So far the fit between my strengths and my job seems to be working well for the students. I have overheard students telling their friends, "Our English class is fun," "We didn't learn how to do that last year," "Can I take this class next semester?" and "I got a B on a test!" And although it is expected that my at-risk students will not perform as well as the others in the school, they did perform as well, if not better, on recent vocabulary benchmark tests.

After I initiated a video-technology program for the school, my at risk students successfully took on the challenge of learning theory and abstract application with very limited experiential learning. Even though the equipment arrived late, the students completed a number of well done projects—remakes, public service announcements, school- and community-focused films, music videos, instructional videos, independent films, and trailers—in only a few short weeks.

For years my students have been told that they are not the best—or worse than that. Evidently, though, many students simply did not understand what was expected of them or lacked the incentive to perform. By consciously using my own strengths, I have been able to address such specific needs. In return I have found it gratifying to make a real, measurable difference. By consciously matching the challenges I undertake with my strengths, I have been able to enjoy greater initial success than I would have otherwise. I have come to believe that although most people already use their strengths intuitively, any teacher will foster greater student achievement and success by clearly identifying and consciously applying strengths.

GLORIA HENDERSON teaches English, video technology, and psychology at Diamond Bar High School in Diamond Bar, California.

Reprinted with permission of *Educational Horizons,* quarterly journal of Pi Lambda Theta Inc., International Honor Society and Professional Association in Education, P O Box 6626, Bloomington, IN 47401, Spring 2005, pp. 202–204.

A "Perfect" Case Study
Perfectionism in Academically Talented Fourth Graders

Jill L. Adelson

"Perfectionism must be seen as a potent force capable of bringing either intense frustration and paralysis or intense satisfaction and creative contribution, depending on how it is channeled."

—Schuler, 2002, p. 71

The topic of perfectionism is bound to surface when discussing the social and emotional development of gifted children and adolescents (Davis & Rimm, 1994; Greenspon, 1998; Kerr, 1991; Parker & Adkins, 1995; Silverman, 1990, 1993a; Schuler, 2002). Whereas Greenspon (2000) asserts that "perfectionism is a wound; it is never healthy" (p. 208), others in the field assert that children with perfectionistic qualities are faced with a double-edged sword that can manifest itself either in a healthy or unhealthy manner. For instance, Silverman (1999) asserts that healthy expressions of perfectionism can lead to achievement, self-confirmation, high self-esteem, responsibility, and "unparalleled greatness" (p. 216). On the other hand, perfectionistic qualities that are exhibited in an unhealthy way may result in procrastination, avoidance, anxiety, a self-defeated attitude, and underachievement (Hamachek, 1978; Reis, 2002; Schuler, 1997, 2002; Silverman, 1993a, 1999).

As a teacher in a self-contained gifted and talented fourth-grade classroom for several years, I observed many students who exhibited perfectionism in a myriad of unhealthy ways, and several findings emerged from my observations of these children. First, across differing rates of development, both mental and physical manifestations of perfectionism abounded. Regardless of group size (e.g., individual, small group, or whole class) or type of activity (e.g., art, music tryouts, recess, math, language arts, or social studies), at least one child exhibited unhealthy perfectionistic behaviors. My observations of the students across various contexts enabled me to document a range of manifestations of perfectionism, suggesting ways in which perfectionism can affect gifted children in schools. I found that these manifestations could be categorized, and the following case studies represent the different types of unhealthy manifestations of perfectionism that emerged in my observations.

The Academic Achiever— "Must Achieve 110%"

Elena[1] was a student academically accelerated in mathematics. When she was first asked to take a diagnostic test, she would become frustrated and would say, "I can't leave it blank!" She believed she should know how to solve every problem, whether or not she had ever been exposed to the concepts tested. Despite the diagnostic nature of the test, she would struggle with the idea of skipping a problem.

Ivan worked diligently on his math practice. He was not satisfied with anything less than 100% correct. If he missed a single problem, he did not believe he was ready for a test of the material. He would continue to do extra practice, even if he only missed one problem due to a "careless" mistake.

While playing a review game in social studies, Sherman became frustrated. For each question asked, he expected himself to remember every detail about the event, person, or place and would become very frustrated if he could not, even resorting to pounding on his head trying to remember. This attitude also affected Sherman's participation in math games. He expected to solve every puzzle and to solve it immediately, or he would become discouraged and upset with himself.

Cho came to the United States when she was in kindergarten. She was identified for the self-contained gifted and talented class and worked very hard to earn top grades. Math and science came easily to her. Although she was reading above grade level in English, her second language, her language arts average was a low A. She was distraught about "not being good" at reading and did extra work each weekend to try to improve. Her parents also were worried about her reading ability and would request extra assignments for Cho.

The Academic Achievers, students exhibiting negative perfectionism in academic pursuits, had unrealistically high expectations for their own performance and were not satisfied with a score of 100, literally pushing for extra credit on everything they did because a score of 100 was not enough for them. If they did not earn the top grade or could not remember the answer word-for-word on every assessment (formal or informal) in every subject, they became upset with themselves. Due to the extremely high standards they imposed on themselves, they put forth more effort than was required to master the material and achieve at the top level. Typically, these students were high achievers and earned very high grades, but they would become disappointed with themselves when they earned anything less and were never satisfied with the achievements and grades they had earned; they wanted to earn all of the extra credit points and obtain the highest possible score for each assessment. Even though they had high grades in all academic subjects, they often completed extra credit projects and assignments and did so with as much energy and effort as they put into their required work. These students focused heavily on their mistakes, and even when they met the expectations of the task at hand, they rarely were satisfied with their performance. Their focus was on the end product or grade, and they judged themselves on that alone. In some cases, like that of Cho, the students had family pressures, as well as their own pressure for perfection. As Davis and Rimm (1994) noted, gifted students may have pressures that arise from their family, their peers, or themselves for "perfect" work.

As an educator, it is important to become aware of these students. Although it is easy to praise students for high grades, it is much more important to praise them for their efforts. Educators need to put more emphasis on effort and strategies and much less on grades and on "personal traits (like being smart)" (Dweck, 1999, p. 3). Furthermore, these students need guidance in taking pride in the process and in using mistakes as learning experiences. For example, Elena learned to take diagnostic tests with less anxiety because she understood the need to identify areas of strength and weaknesses and learn the material she does not know. I had Ivan correct his mistakes and write "WIMI's" ("why I missed it"), leading to a focus on learning from the mistakes instead of on looking at the grade. Despite his competitive nature and tendency to strive for perfection, Sherman learned to identify his mistakes and weaknesses in the math game, and when he was eliminated from the classroom tournament, he focused on learning from the mistakes he made instead of berating himself for them. Despite the completion of the tournament, he took a box of cards home to practice and to improve his own performance for next year. Cho continued to work on her language arts skills, but she learned to focus on improvement rather than the grade. She needed encouragement to recognize and celebrate her strengths rather than focusing solely on her "weakness" and comparing it to the abilities of her peers.

The Risk Evader—"All or Nothing"

Despite the art teacher's compliments of Kathleen's artistic ability and winning a schoolwide artistic contest, she did not think she could draw. In art class, if the task was to draw, Kathleen did not want to participate and only did so reluctantly.

Brandon wanted a major role in the school musical, and he had the singing ability to earn that role. Unfortunately, shortly before the try-outs, Brandon became ill, leaving him with little voice or energy on audition day. He chose not to try out that day and did not request to audition on a different day.

Risk Evaders are plagued by the impact of asynchronous development or physical limitations on their pursuits, and they will avoid allowing their weaknesses to be exposed. When they encounter a task that requires both their mind and their body, gifted children often are faced with asynchrony—their mind has developed faster than their body—which affects perfectionistic behaviors (Morelock, 1992; Silverman, 1993a, 1993b; Tannenbaum, 1992). Although their mind may see ideals and hold high standards, they cannot always meet those expectations in their performance. Fearing this failure to achieve their standards and ideals, they may decide not to even attempt the task, just as Kathleen did in art. In her mind, she could see the intricate details that a botanist sees in a flower

and even noticed the pollen on the stamen, but she feared that her hands, which had the dexterity and precision of a 9-year-old, could not produce the image from her mind.

As an educator, developing a safe classroom environment that encourages risk-taking is essential. Children who exhibit perfectionism must feel supported within their classroom, so the entire class must make a commitment to this safe environment.

Brandon also faced a situation in which he was afraid his body would not be able to perform to his mind's ideal. Students like Brandon are afraid of failure and cannot stand the idea that they may not meet their own expectations. They do not take delight in the process or in their attempts, and they do not even want to try because they fear they will not succeed at a level that meets their personal standards. This is similar to Adderholdt-Elliott's (1987) paralyzed perfectionist, who rationalizes that if he never performs, then he doesn't have to risk being rejected or criticized.

As an educator, developing a safe classroom environment that encourages risk-taking is essential. Children who exhibit perfectionism must feel supported within their classroom, so the entire class must make a commitment to this safe environment. Without it, students may fear not only their own rejection of their work, but also ridicule from their peers. The focus should continue to be placed on the process and revisions. Students should be encouraged to try new and different experiences that may seem challenging. Challenges should be regarded as adventurous and exciting instead of daunting. Students should be applauded for efforts to tackle something new rather than always being judged for their final products.

The Aggravated Accuracy Assessor—"Exactness and Fixation on 'Redos'"

Carlos worked meticulously during several art classes on his drawing of a Confederate soldier for an art gallery focusing on Virginia. Whenever he was nearly done, he decided to redo the drawing because it was not precise enough. He constantly took the drawing up to the art teacher and to his classroom teacher for reassurance.

When taking notes in class, most students appreciate the opportunity to use shorthand and not have to have everything in final copy form. However, Jodie was not this way. When the class period was over, she still would be copying notes. She painstakingly wrote each letter of each word, taking extra time and effort in making her notes as neat as possible, even rewriting her notes if given the opportunity.

Curtis had been working on a drawing for the art gallery for several weeks. His drawing was almost complete when he decided to throw it away. When questioned about his decision, he replied, "But I colored his hair black!" Because he had envisioned the drawing differently but only had a black marker instead of a brown one available to him at the time, Curtis literally threw away his hard work.

Asynchronous development of the gifted child in areas such as writing or artistic expression can result in two different types of unhealthy perfectionists. Students may become Risk Evaders, like Kathleen, and choose an all-or-nothing approach, or they may become Aggravated Accuracy Assessors, like Carlos and Jodie, and attempt the task but become frustrated with their inability to meet their mind's ideal. Likewise, physical limitations, such as the accessibility (or lack thereof) of materials, can result in a final product that does not meet perfectionists' standards, and they can become very frustrated with their efforts and products. They may choose to redo the same work over and over, may look frantically for ways to "fix" their work or find the necessary materials, or may become disappointed in their own work and give up trying.

The key to helping students like these is to recognize their standards as valuable and acceptable as long-term goals and have faith in their vision and their ability to meet their expectations through effort and revision. These students need help modifying their immediate goals or standards and making their unrealistic ones more realistic by setting them as long-term goals. All students could benefit from reading about and discussing people who revised their works multiple times. For example, Thomas Edison did not invent a successful light bulb until after almost 2 years of failed attempts and more than 6,000 different carbonized plant fibers (Grace Products Corporation, 1998), and two young Detroit scientists did not create their famous kitchen-cleaning formula until their 409th attempt (hence the name Formula 409). Because many students struggle in art, examples of famous artists' works, revisions, their biographies, and their autobiographies that illustrate the amount of time devoted to their masterpieces would be beneficial to share.

Students also should have opportunities to critique one another's work, pointing out aspects that they admire and offering constructive suggestions for improvement. This will help students learn to examine their artwork and writing more critically and identify not only weaknesses, but also strengths.

For students like Jodie whose handwriting slows down their ability to participate in class discussions and activities, some prioritizing may be necessary. Younger students may not recognize when "perfect" handwriting is unnecessary or the difference between "perfect" and "legible," and they may need help distinguishing between those times. These students benefit from being forced to create "sloppy copies" that have a stipulation of no eraser marks allowed—they have to write as they think and cross or scribble out, add above and below lines, and draw arrows instead of erasing. This needs to be followed by opportunities to use their "perfect" handwriting and publish the work.

The Controlling Image Manager— "I Could Have Won if I Wanted To"

Brandon not only decided not to audition for the school musical (even though he "could have" gotten the part if he had tried out), but he also "wanted to" be "It." While playing tag on the playground, Brandon ran and yelled, "You can't catch me!" However, as soon as the person who was It got near him, he jumped out of bounds and declared, "I wanted to be It!"

Misty competed in a classroom tournament with great intensity and skill, and she easily won against her classmates. After competing against older students and winning the schoolwide tournament, she contemplated intentionally getting penalties to disqualify herself from the district tournament.

Controlling Image Managers like Brandon and Misty not only want to be perfect, but they also want others to regard them as perfect. If they are afraid they cannot reach their expectations or others' expectations, instead of choosing to not participate, they may intentionally choose to eliminate themselves. This still gives them the opportunity to think—and to say—that they *could have* won and been perfect.

Other children in the class may get frustrated with these students because they either win or give up. The other children never have a chance to fairly win against these students in competitive situations. Role-playing may help these children to better understand others' feelings in competitive situations. They also benefit from reading and discussing other people's losses in competitive situations or having guest speakers talk about their personal defeats, particularly in the sports arena and other competitive situations.

Controlling Image Managers fail to understand the pleasure of competition and of trying to do one's own personal best because they focus too much on winning and being the best. They should be helped to set personal goals before a competitive event so they can strive for a standard based on their personal performance and not that of others. Using these strategies has a positive impact on students and encourages them to compete. For example, setting personal goals helped Misty to decide to take the tournament game home and practice instead of committing to her plan to disqualify herself.

The Procrastinating Perfectionist—"If It Stays in My Mind, Then I Can't Fail"

The class was given the task of creating a social studies review board game over a period of several weeks. Jade excitedly shared her intricate vision. However, just days before the project was due, Jade still had not started working and did not have a plan to create it.

When the class found out they would be competing in a national vocabulary contest, Micah was very excited and announced that he would earn a perfect score. The day before the contest, Micah admitted that he had not begun studying. When asked why not, he just shrugged his shoulders. That night, he stayed up late studying. After he finished the contest the next day, he announced, "I didn't have enough time to study, so I couldn't get them all right."

When assigned an extensive project, some gifted children, like Jade, will plan elaborate, creative projects. They become excited about the project and about sharing their ideas but are not as excited to get started on the project itself for fear of it not turning out the way they imagine it or because they are intimidated by the formidable tasks ahead. Procrastinating Perfectionists have a perfect vision in their mind, but the fear of their inability to achieve that vision causes them to procrastinate, paralyzing them from taking action. They may think, "If I never complete that project, I don't have to risk getting a bad grade" (Adderholdt-Elliott, 1987, p. 27) or even, "If I never complete that project, I don't have to be disappointed that the final project didn't turn out like I wanted it to."

Some Procrastinating Perfectionists, like Micah, are paralyzed by their fear of failure and not meeting their mind's ideal, and they also use their procrastination as a way to control their image. Like Jade, Micah had a vision of perfection in his mind. However, his fear that he could not achieve it lead him to procrastinate. His procrastination also allowed him to preserve his ego and gave him an excuse for not being perfect. Addressing the fear of failure and the tendency to procrastinate will help alleviate the ego-saving behavior that some students use along with procrastination.

Procrastinating Perfectionists need help prioritizing and breaking down a large task into smaller subtasks. In working with a Procrastinating Perfectionist who has great vision but not the steps to commence work on the project, educators need to recognize the need for assistance. Together, the student and teacher can create a plan to break the larger task into smaller segments and identify goals. The student still can have high standards and expectations for the final product, but now he or she has a process to focus on and standards to meet along the way. This helps the student's focus shift from the product to the process and from the outcome to the effort. In designing a schedule, it is important to build in buffers so that when something does not go as planned, the student does not have to feel that he or she already has failed and that there is no need to continue.

Furthermore, all children need help prioritizing at some point. They may need to examine their schedule and see when other tests and projects are due and determine what is most important to them. If they have an elaborate project or challenging goal in mind, they may not be able to put as much effort and focus on their math or social studies test as they normally do—something has to give. Teachers of gifted and talented students need to help them realize that they cannot be perfect at everything and that when they have too much to accomplish they must sacrifice a little of one thing to do well at something else. When discussing these issues with students, it is important to examine the entire picture and what currently requires their attention.

Take Action in Your Classroom

Although it manifests itself in different ways, perfectionism is a strong trait in many gifted children. In a classroom that has gifted children, instances of perfectionism are exhibited every day and in every context. Educators must help students use perfectionism in a positive manner and transform it for future work. Some specific strategies to help each type of perfectionist accomplish this are illustrated in Table 1.

Table 1   Encouraging Healthy Perfectionism in the Classroom

Type of Perfectionist	Defining Characteristics	Action to Take in the Classroom
Academic Achievers	Hold unrealistically high expectations for their performance in academic pursuits and focus on the final grade and on mistakes made	Praise them for their efforts, emphasizing students' hard work rather than their grades Guide students in taking pride in the process and their efforts and using mistakes as learning experiences
Risk Evaders	Fear failure to achieve their standards and ideals due to asynchronous development or physical limitations, so choose no to attempt the task	Develop a safe environment that encourages risk-taking Emphasize process and revisions rather than end products Encourage students to try experiences that are new, different, and challenging Encourage students to look at challenges as adventurous and exciting rather than daunting Applaud students for their efforts to tackle something new
Aggravated Accuracy Assessors	Attempt the task but become frustrated with their inability to meet their mind's ideal due to asynchronous development or physical limitations May choose to redo the same work over and over to try to make it more like their mind's ideal, may look frantically for ways to fix their work or find the necessary materials, or may become disappointed and give up trying	Recognize their standards as valuable and acceptable Have faith in their vision and ability to meet their expectations through effort and revision Read and discuss stories of people who revised their works multiple times Give students opportunities to critique one another's work Have students create "sloppy copies" and also give them opportunities to revise and produce a finished product
Controlling Image Managers	Want others to regard them as perfect If they fear they are unable to meet expectations in competitive situations, choose to eliminate themselves intentionally and say they could have been perfect	Role-play so children understand others' feelings Read and discuss losses in competitive situations Have students set personal goals based on their own performance before a competition
Procrastinating Perfectionists	Plan an extensive project but fail to start it for fear of their inability to achieve their perfect vision	Help students break larger tasks into smaller segments and goals Have students develop a schedule with buffer time Help students prioritize and recognize that they cannot be perfect at everything at every moment

You Can Make a Difference

Using these strategies with gifted students like Judy can help them to pursue work in a healthy manner, resulting in creative contribution and intense satisfaction. Judy, an academically talented fourth grader, grew up in a large family with older and younger siblings who also had been identified for gifted services. She demonstrated many of the types of unhealthy manifestations of perfectionism. Above all else, she was an Academic Achiever. Prior to fourth grade, she had not been challenged sufficiently in the classroom and had channeled her perfectionism in a way that led to being a Risk Evader and, at times, a Procrastinating Perfectionist. During her time in my classroom, I helped her gradually shift her focus from grades to effort and provided her with increasingly challenging academic opportunities, which helped her begin to take more risks in and out of the classroom. Judy had an interest in writing, and focusing on the writing process and revisions helped her learn from her mistakes, as did diagnostic testing and analyzing the problems she had missed in mathematics. She began swimming competitively and would set personal time goals rather than goals of placing first.

During the second semester, Judy accepted a personal challenge and decided to complete an independent study project. This project involved her reading, taking notes, organizing, prioritizing, and presenting. We frequently met to plan the stages of the project, set intermediary goals, analyze her progress, and adjust the timeline as necessary. After completing her research and creating a final product, Judy presented to multiple groups, giving her the opportunity to learn from her experiences and revise her presentation. Finally, Judy reflected in writing about what she learned from the experience, both academically and personally, and what she will do differently the next time she attempts a similar project.

Judy moved to middle school and has continued to channel her perfectionism in a healthy way. She appears to be satisfied in her pursuits (academically, athletically, and artistically) and is making creative contributions in and out of her classrooms. Despite not having exceptional athletic talent, Judy continues to swim and now plays softball. She frequently e-mails me to tell how she increased in the number of hits she had in a game or had a new personal best time in a swim meet, demonstrating her focus on personal performance goals. Judy continues to love to write. She has learned to focus her writing on her ideas and then to revise for grammar and spelling so that she can concentrate on one aspect of the process at a time. Although she still occasionally finds herself procrastinating on studying challenging material for a test or agonizing over an A- rather than an A, Judy has learned to focus on effort, enjoy the process of learning, and accept new challenges.

The story of Judy is one of many stories of gifted students who exhibit unhealthy perfectionistic behaviors in the classroom. By recognizing these behaviors and using strategies like those listed in Table 1, teachers and parents can make a difference and help these students use perfectionism in a positive manner now and in the future.

Note

1. Student names have been changed.

References

Adderholdt-Elliott, M. (1987). *Perfectionism: What's bad about being too good.* Minneapolis, MN: Free Spirit.

Davis, G. A., & Rimm, S. B. (1994). *Education of the gifted and talented* (3rd ed.). Boston: Allyn & Bacon.

Dweck, C. S. (1999). Caution—Praise can be dangerous. *American Educator, 23*(1), 4–9.

Grace Products Corporation. (1998). *The life of Thomas Edison.* Retrieved November 6, 2006, from http://www.graceproducts.com/edison/life.html

Greenspon, T. S. (1998). The gifted self: Its role in development and emotional health. *Roeper Review, 20,* 162–167.

Greenspon, T. S. (2000). "Healthy perfectionism" is an oxymoron! Reflections on the psychology of perfectionism and the sociology of science. *Journal of Secondary Gifted Education, 11,* 197–208.

Hamachek, D. E. (1978). Psychodynamics of normal and neurotic perfectionism. *Psychology, 15,* 27–33.

Kerr, B. A. (1991). *A handbook for counseling the gifted and talented.* Alexandria, VA: American Association for Counseling and Development.

Morelock, M. J. (1992). Giftedness: The view from within. *Understanding Our Gifted, 4*(3), 1, 11–15.

Parker, W. D., & Adkins, K. K. (1995). Perfectionism and the gifted. *Roeper Review, 17,* 173–176.

Reis, S. M. (2002). Internal barriers, personal issues, and decisions faced by gifted and talented females. *Gifted Child Today, 25*(1), 14–28.

Schuler, P. (2002). Perfectionism in gifted children and adolescents. In M. Neihart, S. M. Reis, N. M. Robinson, & S. M. Moon (Eds.), *The social and emotional development of gifted children: What do we know?* (pp. 71–79). Waco, TX: Prufrock Press.

Schuler, P. A. (1997). *Characteristics and perceptions of perfectionism in gifted adolescents in a rural school environment.* Unpublished doctoral dissertation, University of Connecticut, Storrs.

Silverman, L. K. (1990). Issues in affective development of the gifted. In J. VanTassel–Baska (Ed.), *A practical guide to counseling the gifted in a school setting* (pp. 15–30). Reston, VA: Council for Exceptional Children.

Silverman, L. K. (1993a). A developmental model for counseling the gifted. In L. K. Silverman (Ed.), *Counseling the gifted and talented* (pp. 51–78). Denver, CO: Love.

Silverman, L. K. (1993b). The gifted individual. In L. K. Silverman (Ed.), *Counseling the gifted and talented* (pp. 3–28). Denver, CO: Love.

Silverman, L. K. (1999). Perfectionism. *Gifted Education International, 13,* 216–225.

Tannenbaum, A. J. (1992). Early signs of giftedness: Research and commentary. *Journal for the Education of the Gifted, 13,* 22–36.

UNIT 4

Development During Childhood: Family and Culture

Unit Selections

Key Points to Consider

- Should unconventional children be labeled as having disorders . . . or called what they seem, quirky and unique?

- How can childrearing practices come to terms with genetic potentialities to maximize development?

- Why do American parents find it so difficult to say "no" to their children?

- Which is worse, a parent who torments, a parent who hovers, an uninvolved parent, or are all behaving badly?

- Can bad behavior in children be blamed on bad parenting? Are good behaviors the result of good parenting? What roles do genetic factors play in behaviors?

- Are we raising a generation of prosti-tots who idolize pop culture's bad girls?

- Do our young people have good ideas for reforming their academic and social cultures? Do we listen to them? If not, why not?

Student Web Site
www.mhcls.com

Internet References

Harborview Injury Prevention and Research Center
http://depts.washington.edu/hiprc/
Families and Work Institute
http://www.familiesandwork.org/index.html
Parentsplace.com: Single Parenting
http://www.parentsplace.com/

Most people accept the proposition that families and cultures have substantial effects on child outcomes. How? New interpretations of behavioral genetic research suggest that genetically predetermined child behaviors may have substantial effects on how families parent, how children react, and how cultures evolve. Nature and nurture are very interactive. Is it possible that there is a genetic predisposition toward more warlike, aggressive, and violent behaviors in some children? Do some childrearing practices suppress this genetic trait? Do others aggravate it? Are some children predisposed to care for others? The answers are not yet known.

If parents and societies have a significant impact on child outcomes, is there a set of cardinal family values? Does one culture have more correct answers than another culture? Laypersons often assume that children's behaviors and personalities have a direct correlation with the behaviors and personality of the person or persons who provided their socialization during infancy and childhood. Have Americans become paranoid about the extent of terrorist intentions? Do we try to justify our culture's flaws by claims that other cultures are worse? Do we teach our children this fear? Conversely, do other cultures try to hide their atrocities and war-mongering behaviors behind the screen that Americans are worse, or that they must be stopped first?

Are you a mirror image of the person or persons who raised you? How many of their beliefs, preferences, and virtuous behaviors do you reflect? Did you learn their hatreds and vices as well? Do you model your family, your peers, your culture, all of them, or none of them? If you have a sibling, are you alike because the same person or persons raised you? What accounts for all the differences between people with similar genes, similar parenting, and the same cultural background? These and similar questions are fodder for future research.

During childhood, a person's family values are compared to and tested against the values of schools, community, and culture. Peers, schoolmates, teachers, neighbors, extracurricular activity leaders, religious leaders, and even shopkeepers play increasingly important roles. Culture influences children through holidays, styles of dress, music, television, world events, movies, slang, games, parents' jobs, transportation, exposure to sex, drugs, and violence, and many other variables. The ecological theorist Urie Bronfenbrenner called these cultural variables exosystem and macrosystem influences. The developing personality of a child has multiple interwoven influences: from genetic potentialities through family values and socialization practices to community and cultural pressures for behaviors.

The first article in this unit, "You and Your Quirky Kid," questions the current practice of labeling unconventional behaviors as abnormal. Where should the line be drawn between unique children and psychopathology? Individuality

© Getty Images

can be wonderful—something to be celebrated rather than shaped into a "normal" mold.

The second article in this unit, "The Blank Slate," suggests that family forces and cultural factors (e.g., fast foods full of fats and empty calories, Mozart CDs for babies) always interact with genetic potentialities. Parents and society cannot always be credited or blamed for every outcome in a developing child. Advice on how to raise happy, achieving children, and how to keep children healthy, physically fit, and well-nourished, is slavishly adhered to by many parents and caregivers. However, some children will simply not turn out as prescribed by the formulas. Our younglings cannot be molded like lumps of clay. Steven Pinker suggests that social progress proceeds with the inherent natures (both good and bad) of all humans. Blaming and/or crediting amounts to empty vocalizing. Working with our offsprings' genes makes more sense. Can we decipher what that is?

The third article continues to look at contemporary parents, but in a different light. Nancy Gibbs discusses the arena of parent-school interactions. Teachers want parent involvement in education. However, they sometimes get more than they require. Parents may hover like helicopters and volunteer too much. Other parents may torment them with criticisms and accusations. Teachers and parents need mutually supportive, not adversarial, relationships.

The fourth article cautions that parents are not the only force shaping behavior in children. Many behaviors are inherent in human nature, predetermined by genetic factors. They are found in peoples of every culture, regardless of parenting practices. Parents are important and good parenting is vital to a civilized society. Parents, however, should not be blamed or credited for every action taken by normally behaving members of the human race in their childhoods.

Unit 4, subsection B (Culture), emphasizes our increasing population diversity. It is imperative that time and effort be spent to avoid life-threatening misunderstandings.

The first article, "Girls Gone Bad?" decries the influence of female sex symbols of pop culture who are adored by young teenagers. While parents denounce the behavior of these divas, adolescent girls are infatuated. They want to dress, talk, and act like their heroines. The author, Kathleen Deveny, reminds readers that parents also criticized the sex goddesses of the past (e.g., Marilyn Monroe, Liz Taylor, Madonna), and their daughters turned out well. The difference today is the power and pervasiveness of the media, which reports on celebrity antics 24/7. This essay, and the next one, are effective together in portraying the paradox of social forces on our youth.

The last cultural commentary, "Disrespecting Childhood," presents evidence that America is not a child-loving nation. Our media overwhelmingly sputter about what is wrong with our juveniles ("Girls Gone Bad?"). Our childrearing practices and educational policies are directed more at fixing what is wrong than with reinforcing what is right. The authors report on a project called What Kids Can Do, Inc., which respects and listens to the voices of young Americans and celebrates their strengths. It inspires hope for our future.

You and Your Quirky Kid

**The girl who wears her clothes inside out, the boy who loves plumbing.
What parents and experts say about the children who just don't fit in.**

LORRAINE ALI

At a recent pre-school musical, my son was to stand single file onstage with 13 classmates and perform "Let's All Sing Like the Birdies Sing" while flapping the wings of his bright yellow canary suit. As the other kids sang, fidgeted or stood there, stunned by the audience, he broke ranks and began marching to his own tune. He spun, then stomped, then shimmied his way out of line as if responding to several different styles of music no one else could hear. Seemingly unfazed by the crowd of parents seated before him, he wandered about the stage, shouting his own improvisational lyrics (something about babies and broccoli), which were picked up by a nearby mike and broadcast throughout the auditorium. As the other parents laughed, I vacillated between feelings of pride (my son's such an individual!) and fear (why is he so different?).

Because, even at 4, it's clear my son is different. On the playground, he's bonded far more with one particular tricycle than with any classmate, and during circle time he's the only child who consistently wanders off to inspect the pipes under the sink or play with the push broom. His unconventional behavior may not sound like a big deal—and it wasn't, until some well-meaning educators noticed my son's quirks and asked if he'd ever been diagnosed.

But just how do you determine the difference between a nonconformist kid and a child with more serious issues that may need to be addressed? Previous generations of parents could embrace, or overlook, their child's tics, quirks or eccentric personalities much more freely than the moms and dads of today. If their daughter was reading "Moby Dick" by first grade, she was gifted. If their toddler wasn't talking by 2, he'd likely catch up by kindergarten. Even pediatricians were far less versed in things like attention-deficit/hyperactivity disorder (ADHD) and the autism-spectrum disorders, which didn't start showing up on their radar screens until the '80s and early '90s. But today we know so much more about how the brain functions, what causes some unusual behavior and how a child can really benefit from early intervention, that we're obligated as "good parents" to have our children's peculiarities evaluated. (Of course, there is no mistaking the more severe forms of autism for quirkiness.) It can mean running a toddler through a bevy of experts—pediatric neurologists, speech pathologists, behavioral psychologists, socialization experts—before he's out of training pants. More and more, kids who once would have been considered slightly out of step with their peers are emerging with diagnoses of sensory-integration dysfunction, dyspraxia and pervasive developmental disorder, to name a few. In past decades, autism was thought to occur in about one child in 2,000. Today, the U.S. Centers for Disease Control and Prevention estimates that one in 150 kids has an autism-spectrum disorder. And just last week, a new study found that the number of kids in the United States younger than 20 receiving a diagnosis of bipolar disorder had soared from about 18,000 in 1994 to an estimated 800,000 in 2003.

So what do we do about the eighth grader who alienates peers with his obsessive talk of baroque architecture, or the 6-year-old who'd rather spend recess talking to the hamster than playing dress-up with her classmates? Is it possible we shouldn't do anything? "Of course it is a source of deep sorrow when it is obvious that a youngster can never lead 'a normal life' because of special needs," says Dr. Elizabeth Berger, a child and adolescent psychiatrist whose books include "Raising Kids With Character." "All the same, there is something amiss when every mother is susceptible to fears whether or not this week's fashionable diagnosis applies to her child. There is something unexamined in our thinking when we elevate the need for normalcy to a state of spiritual grace, and live under a constant anxiety that we fail to measure up to its demands."

If we examine ourselves and those around us—the husband who shuns picnics because he can't stand the texture of grass, the co-worker who can't get along without those billion organic remedies on her desk—we have to admit that everyone, to some extent, is odd. The terms "normal" and "abnormal" are subjective—words whose interpretations can be as varied as the people who speak them. So when we worry about our kids' strange behavior, is it because they deviate from our own expectations of what life should be like for a "well-adjusted" 5-, 7- or 12-year-old, or is it because that little person in front of us seems to struggling way more than she should? "Parents need to ask themselves, Is this making him unhappy or just making me unhappy?" says Dr. Perri Klass, pediatrician and coauthor of "Quirky Kids: Understanding and Helping Your Child Who Doesn't Fit In—When to Worry and When *Not* to Worry." "Is he having a perfectly good time in school, but he's not interested in the things the other kids are interested in? Or is he desperately trying to be part of something but doesn't seem to understand how? I'm not talking about a child who's a developmental emergency, I'm talking about the kid who's different."

According to Klass and her coauthor, Dr. Eileen Costello, skewed development, temperamental extremes and social complications are the hallmarks of so-called quirky kids. They define this enigmatic and varied group in their book as children with developmental variations: kids who don't talk on time or, alternately, "talk constantly but never seem to get their point across"; kids who have rigid routines or throw "nuclear tantrums"; toddlers who keep to themselves "while the rest of the playgroup lives up to its name."

Children who fall into these (and other) categories include Sam, 6, who confuses peers with his garbled verbal skills, but makes them laugh when he covers with silly voices and impressions; Parker, 13, whose daily routine includes reading *Consumer Reports* cover to cover, twice, and Jaden, 7, who prefers chatting with his Matchbox cars over talking to classmates. Two of these kids are diagnosed with high-functioning disorders, one is not. But all are at the center of a complicated debate among parents, educators and experts that includes arguments for and against getting a diagnosis (do labels help or stigmatize?) and lengthy discussions of the pros and cons of mainstreaming (should we keep quirky kids in "normal" schools, where they challenge themselves and those around them to think differently, or put them in "special" schools?).

A diagnosis can be a godsend, especially for families struggling to help a child who is clearly unable to function. It can give them some concrete answers, and offer resources where once there were none. But for a high-functioning child who may seem more enigmatic than disabled, the process and outcome is often frustratingly subjective. "We've been told Marcus has everything from autism to ADD to a blanket sensory disorder with such a long name, I can't even remember it," says Tara, the mother of a 7-year-old whose "stupid/smart" behavior has mystified his parents. "We get different answers depending on the specialist, and none of them seem to really fit. It makes you wonder how much of this is really founded and how much is just guesswork."

Klass argues that even though none of these diagnoses carries with them a recipe—i.e., take this pill and you're cured—they do "allow parents to access a certain amount of collective experience that may improve their child's strengths and help them work on areas that are weaker." Diagnoses also offer older kids who know they're different a set of clues as to why, and can essentially give those who never fit in a sense of belonging. But Mary-Dean Barringer, of the nonprofit learning institute All Kinds of Minds, says we put too much emphasis on the labels that others assign to our kids. "We're absolutely appalled by this diagnosis of Asperger's syndrome," says Barringer. (Asperger's is a high-functioning form of autism, marked by obsessive interests and impaired social interaction.) "These are very highly specialized minds, and to put a syndrome on it and treat it as an aberration does damage to kids and families. There are still challenges there on how to manage it, but why not call it a highly specialized mind phenomenon rather than a disorder? That label alone shapes public perception about uniqueness and quirkiness."

School is the most brutal frontier for these kids, and as we all know, anything from a lisp to a bad haircut is grounds for persecution. But there are other options, such as schools that specialize in specific disorders: the Monarch School in Houston is geared toward children on the autism spectrum; Landmark College in Vermont is constructed around the needs of kids with ADHD. Another way to go, experts say: if your son seems to focus only in math class, suggest capitalizing on his strengths by sending him to a school that emphasizes math and science. It will build up his confidence, and may lead to an increased interest in other areas. All Kinds of Minds has created courses (available to schools across the country) for all sorts of quirky kids who struggle with learning. Their advice to educators: take each case on an individual basis and empower kids with grass-roots techniques. "If a quirky kid is trying to talk to his 10-year-old peers about architectural design, I'd wait until they're alone, then say, 'You know, with that group, architecture's not going to work, but here are some topics that might'," suggests Barringer. "You can coach them in verbal pragmatics and even topic selection. They may not be the most popular kids, but it could help them navigate socially through those tough school years."

For parents and siblings, living with a kid who's different is almost always challenging: "It's hard on his two older brothers," says Lisa, the mother of a 6-year-old who's bright yet still can't carry on a coherent conversation with classmates. "They get frustrated and embarrassed that Matt is a little quirky. They don't know what to say to their friends, just like I don't know what to say to mine." But the disproportionate meltdowns at home or awkward public scenes that come with these kids are almost always balanced by equally extreme moments of wonder. Lily, who always wears her clothes inside out because the seams "are just too hurty," swears she can hear spiders walking on the wall two rooms away. Funny thing is, the 9-year-old is often right. "My son has never received a formal diagnosis, but has a handful of delays and quirks," says a parent who prefers to remain anonymous. "He's complicated and wonderful. I see his typical peers in preschool talking to each other, standing in line nicely, sitting in a circle. But they seem so 'flat' to me. I'll never have that issue with my son."

Every child is, of course, unique (quirky children, a little more so) and every individual situation calls for its own set of rules. But the challenges for parents with kids who are different—whatever their glitches and eccentricities may be—are remarkably the same. Can we make the world they're going to grow up in sufficiently kind and welcoming to them and their quirks, and can we provide them with the basic skills they need to navigate in that world? I eventually did consult experts. Some of what they said was helpful, but they offered no great, demystifying insights. I never really did expect anyone to totally peg my son; the fascinating little man changes on a daily basis. One day we call him Space Cookie, the next day Sweet Pea, the next our Tasmanian devil. But he is a whole person, the sum of all his average, stellar and quirky parts, and my job is much like any other parent's—to guide him when necessary, let go when I overdo it and constantly sweep for minefields (even ones I have inadvertently laid in his path) that threaten to obliterate his incredibly unique spirit. I can't wait to see who he becomes, this boy in a bright yellow canary suit, who insists on dancing to his own tune.

The Blank Slate

The long-accepted theory that parents can mold their children like clay has distorted choices faced by adults trying to balance their lives, multiplied the anguish of those whose children haven't turned out as hoped, and mangled the science of human behavior.

STEVEN PINKER

If you read the pundits in newspapers and magazines, you may have come across some remarkable claims about the malleability of the human psyche. Here are a few from my collection of clippings:

- Little boys quarrel and fight because they are encouraged to do so.
- Children enjoy sweets because their parents use them as rewards for eating vegetables.
- Teenagers get the idea to compete in looks and fashion from spelling bees and academic prizes.
- Men think the goal of sex is an orgasm because of the way they were socialized.

If you find these assertions dubious, your skepticism is certainly justified. In all cultures, little boys quarrel, children like sweets, teens compete for status, and men pursue orgasms, without the slightest need of encouragement or socialization. In each case, the writers made their preposterous claims without a shred of evidence—without even a nod to the possibility that they were saying something common sense might call into question.

Intellectual life today is beset with a great divide. On one side is a militant denial of human nature, a conviction that the mind of a child is a blank slate that is subsequently inscribed by parents and society. For much of the past century, psychology has tried to explain all thought, feeling, and behavior with a few simple mechanisms of learning by association. Social scientists have tried to explain all customs and social arrangements as a product of the surrounding culture. A long list of concepts that would seem natural to the human way of thinking—emotions, kinship, the sexes—are said to have been "invented" or "socially constructed."

At the same time, there is a growing realization that human nature won't go away. Anyone who has had more than one child, or been in a heterosexual relationship, or noticed that children learn language but house pets don't, has recognized that people are born with certain talents and temperaments. An acknowledgment that we humans are a species with a timeless and universal psychology pervades the writings of great political thinkers, and without it we cannot explain the recurring themes of literature, religion, and myth. Moreover, the modern sciences of mind, brain, genes, and evolution are showing that there is something to the commonsense idea of human nature. Although no scientist denies that learning and culture are crucial to every aspect of human life, these processes don't happen by magic. There must be complex innate mental faculties that enable human beings to create and learn culture.

Sometimes the contradictory attitudes toward human nature divide people into competing camps. The blank slate camp tends to have greater appeal among those in the social sciences and humanities than it does among biological scientists. And until recently, it was more popular on the political left than it was on the right.

But sometimes both attitudes coexist uneasily inside the mind of a single person. Many academics, for example, publicly deny the existence of intelligence. But privately, academics are *obsessed* with intelligence, discussing it endlessly in admissions, in hiring, and especially in their gossip about one another. And despite their protestations that it is a reactionary concept, they quickly invoke it to oppose executing a murderer with an IQ of 64 or to support laws requiring the removal of lead paint because it may lower a child's IQ by five points. Similarly, those who argue that gender differences are a reversible social construction do not treat them that way in their advice to their daughters, in their dealings with the opposite sex, or in their unguarded gossip, humor, and reflections on their lives.

No good can come from this hypocrisy. The dogma that human nature does not exist, in the face of growing evidence from science and common sense that it does, has led to contempt among many scholars in the humanities for the concepts of evidence and truth. Worse, the doctrine of the blank slate often distorts science itself by making an extreme position— that culture alone determines behavior—seem moderate, and by making the moderate position—that behavior comes from an interaction of biology and culture—seem extreme.

Although how parents treat their children can make a lot of difference in how happy they are, placing a stimulating mobile over a child's crib and playing Mozart CDs will not shape a child's intelligence.

For example, many policies on parenting come from research that finds a correlation between the behavior of parents and of their children. Loving parents have confident children, authoritative parents (neither too permissive nor too punitive) have well-behaved children, parents who talk to their children have children with better language skills, and so on. Thus everyone concludes that parents should be loving, authoritative, and talkative, and if children don't turn out well, it must be the parents' fault.

Those conclusions depend on the belief that children are blank slates. It ignores the fact that parents provide their children with genes, not just an environment. The correlations may be telling us only that the same genes that make adults loving, authoritative, and talkative make their children self-confident, well-behaved, and articulate. Until the studies are redone with adopted children (who get only their environment from their parents), the data are compatible with the possibility that genes make all the difference, that parenting makes all the difference, or anything in between. Yet the extreme position—that parents are everything—is the only one researchers entertain.

The denial of human nature has not just corrupted the world of intellectuals but has harmed ordinary people. The theory that parents can mold their children like clay has inflicted child-rearing regimes on parents that are unnatural and sometimes cruel. It has distorted the choices faced by mothers as they try to balance their lives, and it has multiplied the anguish of parents whose children haven't turned out as hoped. The belief that human tastes are reversible cultural preferences has led social planners to write off people's enjoyment of ornament, natural light, and human scale and forced millions of people to live in drab cement boxes. And the conviction that humanity could be reshaped by massive social engineering projects has led to some of the greatest atrocities in history.

The phrase "blank slate" is a loose translation of the medieval Latin term tabula rasa—scraped tablet. It is often attributed to the 17th-century English philosopher John Locke, who wrote that the mind is "white paper void of all characters." But it became the official doctrine among thinking people only in the first half of the 20th century, as part of a reaction to the widespread belief in the intellectual or moral inferiority of women, Jews, nonwhite races, and non-Western cultures.

Part of the reaction was a moral repulsion from discrimination, lynchings, forced sterilizations, segregation, and the Holocaust. And part of it came from empirical observations.

Waves of immigrants from southern and eastern Europe filled the cities of America and climbed the social ladder. African Americans took advantage of "Negro colleges" and migrated northward, beginning the Harlem Renaissance. The graduates of women's colleges launched the first wave of feminism. To say that women and minority groups were inferior contradicted what people could see with their own eyes.

Academics were swept along by the changing attitudes, but they also helped direct the tide. The prevailing theories of mind were refashioned to make racism and sexism as untenable as possible. The blank slate became sacred scripture. According to the doctrine, any differences we see among races, ethnic groups, sexes, and individuals come not from differences in their innate constitution but from differences in their experiences. Change the experiences—by reforming parenting, education, the media, and social rewards—and you can change the person. Also, if there is no such thing as human nature, society will not be saddled with such nasty traits as aggression, selfishness, and prejudice. In a reformed environment, people can be prevented from learning these habits.

In psychology, behaviorists like John B. Watson and B. F. Skinner simply banned notions of talent and temperament, together with all the other contents of the mind, such as beliefs, desires, and feelings. This set the stage for Watson's famous boast: "Give me a dozen healthy infants, well-formed, and my own specified world to bring them up in, and I'll guarantee to take any one at random and train him to become any type of specialist I might select—doctor, lawyer, artist, merchant-chief, and yes, even beggar-man and thief, regardless of his talents, penchants, tendencies, abilities, vocations, and race of his ancestors."

Watson also wrote an influential child-rearing manual recommending that parents give their children minimum attention and love. If you comfort a crying baby, he wrote, you will reward the baby for crying and thereby increase the frequency of crying behavior.

In anthropology, Franz Boas wrote that differences among human races and ethnic groups come not from their physical constitution but from their *culture*. Though Boas himself did not claim that people were blank slates—he only argued that all ethnic groups are endowed with the same mental abilities—his students, who came to dominate American social science, went further. They insisted not just that *differences* among ethnic groups must be explained in terms of culture (which is reasonable), but that *every aspect* of human existence must be explained in terms of culture (which is not). "Heredity cannot be allowed to have acted any part in history," wrote Alfred Kroeber. "With the exception of the instinctoid reactions in infants to sudden withdrawals of support and to sudden loud noises, the human being is entirely instinctless," wrote Ashley Montagu.

In the second half of the 20th century, the ideals of the social scientists of the first half enjoyed a well-deserved victory. Eugenics, social Darwinism, overt expressions of racism and sexism, and official discrimination against women and minorities were on the wane, or had been eliminated, from the political and intellectual mainstream in Western democracies.

At the same time, the doctrine of the blank slate, which had been blurred with ideals of equality and progress, began to show cracks. As new disciplines such as cognitive science, neuroscience, evolutionary psychology, and behavioral genetics flourished, it became clearer that thinking is a biological process, that the brain is not exempt from the laws of evolution, that the sexes differ above the neck as well as below it, and that people are not psychological clones. Here are some examples of the discoveries.

Hundreds of traits, from romantic love to humorous insults, can be found in every society ever documented.

Natural selection tends to homogenize a species into a standard design by concentrating the effective genes and winnowing out the ineffective ones. This suggests that the human mind evolved with a universal complex design. Beginning in the 1950s, linguist Noam Chomsky of the Massachusetts Institute of Technology argued that a language should be analyzed not in terms of the list of sentences people utter but in terms of the mental computations that enable them to handle an unlimited number of new sentences in the language. These computations have been found to conform to a universal grammar. And if this universal grammar is embodied in the circuitry that guides babies when they listen to speech, it could explain how children learn language so easily.

Similarly, some anthropologists have returned to an ethnographic record that used to trumpet differences among cultures and have found an astonishingly detailed set of aptitudes and tastes that all cultures have in common. This shared way of thinking, feeling, and living makes all of humanity look like a single tribe, which the anthropologist Donald Brown of the University of California at Santa Barbara has called the universal people. Hundreds of traits, from romantic love to humorous insults, from poetry to food taboos, from exchange of goods to mourning the dead, can be found in every society ever documented.

One example of a stubborn universal is the tangle of emotions surrounding the act of love. In all societies, sex is at least somewhat "dirty." It is conducted in private, pondered obsessively, regulated by custom and taboo, the subject of gossip and teasing, and a trigger for jealous rage. Yet sex is the most concentrated source of physical pleasure granted by the nervous system. Why is it so fraught with conflict? For a brief period in the 1960s and 1970s, people dreamed of an erotopia in which men and women could engage in sex without hang-ups and inhibitions. "If you can't be with the one you love, love the one you're with," sang Stephen Stills. "If you love somebody, set them free," sang Sting.

But Sting also sang, "Every move you make, I'll be watching you." Even in a time when, seemingly, anything goes, most people do not partake in sex as casually as they partake in food or conversation. The reasons are as deep as anything in biology. One of the hazards of sex is a baby, and a baby is not just any seven-pound object but, from an evolutionary point of view, our reason for being. Every time a woman has sex with a man, she is taking a chance at sentencing herself to years of motherhood, and she is forgoing the opportunity to use her finite reproductive output with some other man. The man, for his part, may be either implicitly committing his sweat and toil to the incipient child or deceiving his partner about such intentions.

On rational grounds, the volatility of sex is a puzzle, because in an era with reliable contraception, these archaic entanglements should have no claim on our feelings. We should be loving the one we're with, and sex should inspire no more gossip, music, fiction, raunchy humor, or strong emotions than eating or talking does. The fact that people are tormented by the Darwinian economics of babies they are no longer having is testimony to the long reach of human nature.

Although the minds of normal human beings work in pretty much the same way, they are not, of course, identical. Natural selection reduces genetic variability but never eliminates it. As a result, nearly every one of us is genetically unique. And these differences in genes make a difference in mind and behavior, at least quantitatively. The most dramatic demonstrations come from studies of the rare people who *are* genetically identical, identical twins.

Identical twins think and feel in such similar ways that they sometimes suspect they are linked by telepathy. They are similar in verbal and mathematical intelligence, in their degree of life satisfaction, and in personality traits such as introversion, agreeableness, neuroticism, conscientiousness, and openness to experience. They have similar attitudes toward controversial issues such as the death penalty, religion, and modern music. They resemble each other not just in paper-and-pencil tests but in consequential behavior such as gambling, divorcing, committing crimes, getting into accidents, and watching television. And they boast dozens of shared idiosyncrasies such as giggling incessantly, giving interminable answers to simple questions, dipping buttered toast in coffee, and, in the case of Abigail van Buren and the late Ann Landers, writing indistinguishable syndicated advice columns. The crags and valleys of their electroencephalograms (brain waves) are as alike as those of a single person recorded on two occasions, and the wrinkles of their brains and the distribution of gray matter across cortical areas are similar as well.

Identical twins (who share all their genes) are far more similar than fraternal twins (who share just half their genes). This is as true when the twins are separated at birth and raised apart as when they are raised in the same home by the same parents. Moreover, biological siblings, who also share half their genes, are far more similar than adoptive siblings, who share no more genes than strangers. Indeed, adoptive siblings are barely similar at all. These conclusions come from massive studies employing the best instruments known to psychology. Alternative explanations that try to push the effects of the genes to zero have by now been tested and rejected.

People sometimes fear that if the genes affect the mind at all they must determine it in every detail. That is wrong, for two reasons. The first is that most effects of genes are probabilistic. If one identical twin has a trait, there is often no more than an even chance that the other twin will have it, despite having a complete genome in common (and in the case of twins raised together, most of their environment in common as well).

The second reason is that the genes' effects can vary with the environment. Although Woody Allen's fame may depend on genes that enhance a sense of humor, he once pointed out that "we live in a society that puts a big value on jokes. If I had been an Apache Indian, those guys didn't need comedians, so I'd be out of work."

Studies of the brain also show that the mind is not a blank slate. The brain, of course, has a pervasive ability to change the strengths of its connections as the result of learning and experience—if it didn't, we would all be permanent amnesiacs. But that does not mean that the structure of the brain is mostly a product of experience. The study of the brains of twins has shown that much of the variation in the amount of gray matter in the prefrontal lobes is genetically caused. And these variations are not just random differences in anatomy like fingerprints; they correlate significantly with differences in intelligence.

People born with variations in the typical brain plan can vary in the way their minds work. A study of Einstein's brain showed that he had large, unusually shaped inferior parietal lobules, which participate in spatial reasoning and intuitions about numbers. Gay men are likely to have a relatively small nucleus in the anterior hypothalamus, a nucleus known to have a role in sex differences. Convicted murderers and other violent, antisocial people are likely to have a relatively small and inactive prefrontal cortex, the part of the brain that governs decision making and inhibits impulses. These gross features of the brain are almost certainly not sculpted by information coming in from the senses. That, in turn, implies that differences in intelligence, scientific genius, sexual orientation, and impulsive violence are not entirely learned.

The doctrine of the blank slate had been thought to undergird the ideals of equal rights and social improvement, so it is no surprise that the discoveries undermining it have often been met with fear and loathing. Scientists challenging the doctrine have been libeled, picketed, shouted down, and subjected to searing invective.

This is not the first time in history that people have tried to ground moral principles in dubious factual assumptions. People used to ground moral values in the doctrine that Earth lay at the center of the universe, and that God created mankind in his own image in a day. In both cases, informed people eventually reconciled their moral values with the facts, not just because they had to give a nod to reality, but also because the supposed connections between the facts and morals—such as the belief that the arrangement of rock and gas in space has something to do with right and wrong—were spurious to begin with.

We are now living, I think, through a similar transition. The blank slate has been widely embraced as a rationale for morality, but it is under assault from science. Yet just as the supposed foundations of morality shifted in the centuries following Galileo and Darwin, our own moral sensibilities will come to terms with the scientific findings, not just because facts are facts but because the moral credentials of the blank slate are just as spurious. Once you think through the issues, the two greatest fears of an innate human endowment can be defused.

One is the fear of inequality. Blank is blank, so if we are all blank slates, the reasoning goes, we must all be equal. But if the slate of a newborn is not blank, different babies could have different things inscribed on their slates. Individuals, sexes, classes, and races might differ innately in their talents and inclinations. The fear is that if people do turn out to be different, it would open the door to discrimination, oppression, or eugenics.

But none of this follows. For one thing, in many cases the empirical basis of the fear may be misplaced. A universal human nature does not imply that *differences* among groups are innate. Confucius could have been right when he wrote, "Men's natures are alike; it is their habits that carry them far apart."

Regardless of IQ or physical strength, all human beings can be assumed to have certain traits in common.

More important, the case against bigotry is not a factual claim that people are biologically indistinguishable. It is a moral stance that condemns judging an *individual* according to the average traits of certain *groups* to which the individual belongs. Enlightened societies strive to ignore race, sex, and ethnicity in hiring, admissions, and criminal justice because the alternative is morally repugnant. Discriminating against people on the basis of race, sex, or ethnicity would be unfair, penalizing them for traits over which they have no control. It would perpetuate the injustices of the past and could rend society into hostile factions. None of these reasons depends on whether groups of people are or are not genetically indistinguishable.

Far from being conducive to discrimination, a conception of human nature is the reason we oppose it. Regardless of IQ or physical strength or any other trait that might vary among people, all human beings can be assumed to have certain traits in common. No one likes being enslaved. No one likes being humiliated. No one likes being treated unfairly. The revulsion we feel toward discrimination and slavery comes from a conviction that however much people vary on some traits, they do not vary on these.

Parents often discover that their children are immune to their rewards, punishments, and nagging. Over the long run, a child's personality and intellect are largely determined by genes, peer groups, and chance.

A second fear of human nature comes from a reluctance to give up the age-old dream of the perfectibility of man. If we are forever saddled with fatal flaws and deadly sins, according to this fear, social reform would be a waste of time. Why try to make the world a better place if people are rotten to the core and will just foul it up no matter what you do?

But this, too, does not follow. If the mind is a complex system with many faculties, an antisocial desire is just one component among others. Some faculties may endow us with greed or lust or malice, but others may endow us with sympathy, foresight, self-respect, a desire for respect from others, and an ability to learn from experience and history. Social progress can come from pitting some of these faculties against others.

For example, suppose we are endowed with a conscience that treats certain other beings as targets of sympathy and inhibits us from harming or exploiting them. The philosopher Peter Singer of Princeton University has shown that moral improvement has proceeded for millennia because people have expanded the mental dotted line that embraces the entities considered worthy of sympathy. The circle has been poked outward from the family and village to the clan, the tribe, the nation, the race, and most recently to all of humanity. This sweeping change in sensibilities did not require a blank slate. It could have arisen from a moral gadget with a single knob or slider that adjusts the size of the circle embracing the entities whose interests we treat as comparable to our own.

Some people worry that these arguments are too fancy for the dangerous world we live in. Since data in the social sciences are never perfect, shouldn't we err on the side of caution and stick with the null hypothesis that people are blank slates? Some people think that even if we were certain that people differed genetically, or harbored ignoble tendencies, we might still want to promulgate the fiction that they didn't.

This argument is based on the fallacy that the blank slate has nothing but good moral implications and a theory that admits a human nature has nothing but bad ones. In fact, the dangers go both ways. Take the most horrifying example of all, the abuse of biology by the Nazis, with its pseudoscientific nonsense about superior and inferior races. Historians agree that bitter memories of the Holocaust were the main reason that human nature became taboo in intellectual life after the Second World War.

But historians have also documented that Nazism was not the only ideologically inspired holocaust of the 20th century. Many atrocities were committed by Marxist regimes in the name of egalitarianism, targeting people whose success was taken as evidence of their avarice. The kulaks ("bourgeois peasants") were exterminated by Lenin and Stalin in the Soviet Union. Teachers, former landlords, and "rich peasants" were humiliated, tortured, and murdered during China's Cultural Revolution. City dwellers and literate professionals were worked to death or executed during the reign of the Khmer Rouge in Cambodia.

And here is a remarkable fact: Although both Nazi and Marxist ideologies led to industrial-scale killing, *their biological and psychological theories were opposites*. Marxists had no use for the concept of race, were averse to the notion of genetic inheritance, and were hostile to the very idea of a human nature rooted in biology. Marx did not explicitly embrace the blank slate, but he was adamant that human nature has no enduring properties: "All history is nothing but a continuous transformation of human nature," he wrote. Many of his followers did embrace it. "It is on a blank page that the most beautiful poems are written," said Mao. "Only the newborn baby is spotless," ran a Khmer Rouge slogan. This philosophy led to persecution of the successful and of those who produced more crops on their private family plots than on communal farms. And it made these regimes not just dictatorships but totalitarian dictatorships, which tried to control every aspect of life, from art and education to child rearing and sex. After all, if the mind is structureless at birth and shaped by its experience, a society that wants the right kind of minds must control the experience.

None of this is meant to impugn the blank slate as an evil doctrine, any more than a belief in human nature is an evil doctrine. Both are separated by many steps from the evil acts committed under their banners, and they must be evaluated on factual grounds. But the fact that tyranny and genocide can come from an anti-innatist belief system as readily as from an innatist one does upend the common misconception that biological approaches to behavior are uniquely sinister. And the reminder that human nature is the source of our interests and needs as well as our flaws encourages us to examine claims about the mind objectively, without putting a moral thumb on either side of the scale.

Parents Behaving Badly

Inside the new classroom power struggle: what teachers say about pushy moms and dads who drive them crazy.

NANCY GIBBS

If you could walk past the teachers' lounge and listen in, what sorts of stories would you hear?

An Iowa high school counselor gets a call from a parent protesting the C her child received on an assignment. "The parent argued every point in the essay," recalls the counselor, who soon realized why the mother was so upset about the grade. "It became apparent that she'd written it."

A sixth-grade teacher in California tells a girl in her class that she needs to work on her reading at home, not just in school. "Her mom came in the next day," the teacher says, "and started yelling at me that I had emotionally upset her child."

A science teacher in Baltimore, Md., was offering lessons in anatomy when one of the boys in class declared, "There's one less rib in a man than in a woman." The teacher pulled out two skeletons—one male, the other female—and asked the student to count the ribs in each. "The next day," the teacher recalls, "the boy claimed he told his priest what happened and his priest said I was a heretic."

A teacher at a Tennessee elementary school slips on her kid gloves each morning as she contends with parents who insist, in writing, that their children are never to be reprimanded or even corrected. When she started teaching 31 years ago, she says, "I could make objective observations about my kids without parents getting offended. But now we handle parents a lot more delicately. We handle children a lot more delicately. They feel good about themselves for no reason. We've given them this cotton-candy sense of self with no basis in reality. We don't emphasize what's best for the greater good of society or even the classroom."

When our children are born, we study their every eyelash and marvel at the perfection of their toes, and in no time become experts in all that they do. But then the day comes when we are expected to hand them over to a stranger standing at the head of a room full of bright colors and small chairs. Well aware of the difference a great teacher can make—and the damage a bad teacher can do—parents turn over their kids and hope. Please handle with care. Please don't let my children get lost. They're breakable. And precious. Oh, but push them hard and don't let up, and make sure they get into Harvard.

But if parents are searching for the perfect teacher, teachers are looking for the ideal parent, a partner but not a pest, engaged but not obsessed, with a sense of perspective and patience. And somehow just at the moment when the experts all say the parent-teacher alliance is more important than ever, it is also becoming harder to manage. At a time when competition is rising and resources are strained, when battles over testing and accountability force schools to adjust their priorities, when cell phones and e-mail speed up the information flow and all kinds of private ghosts and public quarrels creep into the parent-teacher conference, it's harder for both sides to step back and breathe deeply and look at the goals they share.

> **The parent doesn't know what you're giving and accepts what the child says. Parents are trusting children before they trust us. They have lost faith in teachers.**

Ask teachers about the best part of their job, and most will say how much they love working with kids. Ask them about the most demanding part, and they will say dealing with parents. In fact, a new study finds that of all the challenges they face, new teachers rank handling parents at the top. According to preliminary results from the MetLife Survey of the American Teacher, made available exclusively to TIME, parent management was a bigger struggle than finding enough funding or maintaining discipline or enduring the toils of testing. It's one reason, say the Consortium for Policy Research in Education and the Center for the Study of Teaching and Policy, that 40% to 50% of new teachers leave the profession within five years. Even master teachers who love their work, says Harvard education professor Sara Lawrence-Lightfoot, call this "the most treacherous part of their jobs."

"Everyone says the parent-teacher conference should be pleasant, civilized, a kind of dialogue where parents and teachers build alliances," Lawrence-Lightfoot observes. "But what most teachers feel, and certainly what all parents feel, is anxiety, panic and vulnerability." While teachers worry most about the parents they never see, the ones who show up faithfully pose a whole different set of challenges. Leaving aside the monster parents who seem to have been born to torment the teacher, even "good" parents can have bad days when their virtues exceed their boundaries: the eager parent who pushes too hard, the protective parent who defends the cheater, the homework helper who takes over, the tireless advocate who loses sight of the fact that there are other kids in the class too. "I could summarize in one sentence what teachers hate about parents," says the head of a private school. "We hate it when parents undermine the education and growth of their children. That's it, plain and simple." A taxonomy of parents behaving badly:

You get so angry that you don't care what the school's perspective is. This is my child. And you did something that negatively impacted my child. I don't want to hear that you have 300 kids.

The Hovering Parent

It was a beautiful late morning last May when Richard Hawley, headmaster at University School in Cleveland, Ohio, saw the flock of mothers entering the building, eager and beaming. "I ask what brings them to our halls," he recalls. "They tell me that this is the last day the seniors will be eating lunch together at school and they have come to watch. To watch their boys eat lunch? I ask. Yes, they tell me emphatically. At that moment, a group of lounging seniors spot their mothers coming their way. One of them approaches his mother, his hands forming an approximation of a crucifix. 'No,' he says firmly to his mother. 'You can't do this. You've got to go home.' As his mother draws near, he hisses in embarrassment, 'Mother, you have no life!' His mother's smile broadens. 'You are my life, dear.'"

Parents are passionate, protective creatures when it comes to their children, as nature designed them to be. Teachers strive to be dispassionate, objective professionals, as their training requires them to be. Throw in all the suspicions born of class and race and personal experience, a culture that praises teachers freely but pays them poorly, a generation taught to question authority and a political climate that argues for holding schools ever more accountable for how kids perform, and it is a miracle that parents and teachers get along as well as they do. "There's more parent involvement that's good—and bad," notes Kirk Daddow, a 38-year veteran who teaches Advanced Placement history in Ames, Iowa. "The good kind is the 'Make yourself known to the teacher; ask what you could do.' The bad kind is the 'Wait until something happens, then complain about it and try to get a grade changed.'" Overall, he figures, "we're seeing more of the bad."

Long gone are the days when the school was a fortress, opened a couple of times a year for parents' night and graduation but generally off limits to parents unless their kids got into trouble. Now you can't walk into schools, public or private, without tripping over parents in the halls. They volunteer as library aides and reading coaches and Mentor Moms, supplement the physical-education offerings with yoga and kickboxing, sponsor faculty-appreciation lunches and fund-raising barbecues, supervise field trips and road games and father-daughter service projects. Even the heads of boarding schools report that some parents are moving to live closer to their child's school so that they can be on hand and go to all the games. As budgets shrink and educational demands grow, that extra army of helpers can be a godsend to strapped schools.

In a survey, 90% of new teachers agreed that involving parents in their children's education is a priority at their school, but only 25% described their experience working with parents as "very satisfying." When asked to choose the biggest challenge they face, 31% of them cited involving parents and communicating with them as their top choice. 73% of new teachers said too many parents treat schools and teachers as adversaries.

But parents, it turns out, have a learning curve of their own. Parents who are a welcome presence in elementary school as library helpers need to learn a different role for junior high and another for high school as their children's needs evolve. Teachers talk about "helicopter parents," who hover over the school at all times, waiting to drop in at the least sign of trouble. Given these unsettled times, if parents feel less in control of their own lives, they try to control what they can, which means everything from swooping down at the first bad grade to demanding a good 12 inches of squishy rubber under the jungle gym so that anyone who falls will bounce right back. "The parents are not the bad guys," says Nancy McGill, a teacher in Johnston, Iowa, who learned a lot about handling parents from being one herself. "They're mama grizzly bears. They're going to defend that cub no matter what, and they don't always think rationally. If I can remember that, it defuses the situation. It's not about me. It's not about attacking our system. It's about a parent trying to do the best for their child. That helps keep the personal junk out of the way. I don't get so emotional."

While it's in the nature of parents to want to smooth out the bumps in the road, it's in the nature of teachers to toss in a few more: sometimes kids have to fail in order to learn. As children get older, the parents may need to pull back. "I believe that the umbilical cord needs to be severed when children are at school," argues Eric Paul, a fourth- and fifth-grade teacher at Roosevelt Elementary School in Santa Monica, Calif. He goes to weekend ball games and piano recitals in an effort to bond with families but also tries to show parents that there is a line that shouldn't be crossed. "Kids need to operate on their own at school, advocate on their own and learn from each other. So in my class, parents' involvement is limited," he says.

High schools, meanwhile, find themselves fending off parents who expect instant responses to every e-mail; who request a change of teacher because of "poor chemistry" when the real issue is that the child is getting a poor grade; who seek out a doctor who will proclaim their child "exceptionally bright but with a learning difference" that requires extra time for testing; who insist that their child take five Advanced Placement classes, play three varsity sports, perform in the school orchestra and be in student government—and then complain that kids are stressed out because the school doesn't do enough to prevent scheduling conflicts. Teachers just shake their heads as they see parents so obsessed with getting their child into a good college that they don't ask whether it's the right one for the child's particular interests and needs.

> **They'll misbehave in front of you. You see very little of that 'I don't want to get in trouble' attitude because they know Mom or Dad will come to their defense.**

And what if kids grow so accustomed to these interventions that they miss out on lessons in self-reliance? Mara Sapon-Shevin, an education professor at Syracuse University, has had college students tell her they were late for class because their mothers didn't call to wake them up that morning. She has had students call their parents from the classroom on a cell phone to complain about a low grade and then pass the phone over to her, in the middle of class, because the parent wanted to intervene. And she has had parents say they are paying a lot of money for their child's education and imply that anything but an A is an unacceptable return on their investment.

These parents are not serving their children well, Sapon-Shevin argues. "You want them to learn lessons that are powerful but benign. Your kid gets drunk, they throw up, feel like crap—that's a good lesson. They don't study for an exam, fail it and learn that next time they should study. Or not return the library book and have to pay the fine. But when you have a kid leave their bike out, it gets run over and rusty, and you say, 'O.K., honey, we'll buy you a new one,' they never learn to put their bike away."

The Aggressive Advocate

Marguerite Damata, a mother of two in Silver Spring, Md., wonders whether she is too involved in her 10-year-old son's school life. "Because he's not in the gifted and talented group, he's almost nowhere," she says. "If I stopped paying attention, where would he be?" Every week she spends two hours sitting in his math class, making sure she knows the assignments and the right vocabulary so that she can help him at home. And despite all she sees and all she does, she says, "I feel powerless there."

Parents understandably argue that there is a good reason to keep a close watch if their child is one of 500 kids in a grade

level. Teachers freely admit it's impossible to create individual teaching programs for 30 children in a class. "There aren't enough minutes in the day," says Tom Loveless, who taught in California for nine years and is now director of the Brown Center on Education Policy at the Brookings Institution. "You have to have kids tackling subject matter together as a group. That's a shoe that will pinch for someone." Since the passage of the No Child Left Behind Act, which requires schools to show progress in reading and math test scores in Grades 3 through 8 across all racial and demographic groups, parents are worried that teachers will naturally focus on getting as many students as possible over the base line and not have as much time to spur the strongest kids or save the weakest. Some educators argue that you can agree on the goals of accountability and achievement, but given the inequalities in the system, not all schools have the means to achieve them. "A really cynical person who didn't want to spend any more money on an educational system might get parents and teachers to blame each other and deflect attention away from other imperfect parts of the system," observes Jeannie Oakes, director of the Institute for Democracy, Education and Access at UCLA.

> **With the oldest, I think I micromanaged things. I had to come to a point where I said, These are his projects. They're not my projects. I'm not helping him.**

Families feel they have to work the system. Attentive parents study the faculty like stock tables, looking for the best performer and then lobbying to get their kids into that teacher's class. "You have a lot of mothers who have been in the work force, supervising other people, who have a different sense of empowerment and professionalism about them," notes Amy Stuart Wells, professor of sociology and education at Columbia University's Teachers College. "When they drop out of the work force to raise their kids, they see being part of the school as part of their job." Monica Stutzman, a mother of two in Johnston, Iowa, believes her efforts helped ensure that her daughter wound up with the best teacher in each grade. "We know what's going on. We e-mail, volunteer on a weekly basis. I ask a lot of questions," she says. "I'm not there to push my children into things they're not ready for. The teachers are the experts. We've had such great experiences with the teacher because we create that experience, because we're involved. We don't just get something home and say, 'What's this?'"

> **Most teachers will do what they need to, but there are teachers who are uncomfortable, who turn their backs or close their eyes or ears because they do not want what they perceive might be a confrontation.**

Parents seeking to stay on top of what's happening in class don't have to wait for the report card to arrive. "Now it's so easy for the parents through the Internet to get ahold of us, and they expect an immediate response," notes Michael Schaffer, a classroom veteran who teaches AP courses at Central Academy in Des Moines, Iowa. "This e-mail—'How's my kid doing?'—could fill my day. That's hyperbole. But it's a two-edged sword here, and unfortunately it's cutting to the other side, and parents are making demands on us that are unreasonable. Yeah, they're concerned about their kids. But I'm concerned about 150 kids. I don't have time during the day to let the parent know when the kid got the first B." As more districts make assignments and test scores available online, it may cut down on the "How's he doing" e-mails but increase the "Why did she get a B?" queries.

Beneath the ferocious jostling there is the brutal fact that outside of Lake Wobegon, not all children are above average. Teachers must choose their words carefully. They can't just say, "I'm sorry your child's not as smart as X," and no parent wants to hear that there are five other kids in the class who are a lot smarter than his or hers. Younger teachers especially can be overwhelmed by parents who announce on the first day of school that their child is going to be the smartest in the class and on the second day that he is already bored. Veteran teachers have learned to come back with data in hand to show parents who boast that their child scored in the 99th percentile on some aptitude test that 40 other students in the class did just as well.

It would be nice if parents and teachers could work together to improve the system for everyone, but human nature can get in the way. Both sides know that resources are limited, and all kinds of factors play into how they are allocated—including whose elbows are sharpest. Many schools, fearful of "bright flight," the mass departure of high-achieving kids, feel they have no choice but to appease the most outspoken parents. "I understand, having been a parent, the attitude that 'I don't have time to fix the whole system; I don't have time and energy to get rid of systemic injustice, racism, poverty and violence; I have to get what's right for my kid,'" says Syracuse's Sapon-Shevin. "But then the schools do educational triage. They basically attend to the most vocal, powerful people with more resources. They say, 'Don't get angry. We'll take care of this issue.' And they mean, 'We'll take care of it for your child. We'll get your kid out of the class with the bad teacher and leave the other kids in there.'"

At the deepest level, teachers fear that all this parental anxiety is not always aimed at the stuff that matters. Parents who instantly call about a grade or score seldom ask about what is being taught or how. When a teacher has spent the whole summer brightening and deepening the history curriculum for her ninth-graders, finding new ways to surprise and engage them, it is frustrating to encounter parents whose only focus is on test scores. "If these parents were pushing for richer, more meaningful instruction, you could almost forgive them their obnoxiousness and inattention to the interests of all the other children," says Alfie Kohn, a Boston-based education commentator and author of *Unconditional Parenting.* But "we have pushy parents pushing for the wrong thing." He argues that test scores often measure what matters least—and that even high test scores

should invite parents to wonder what was cut from the curriculum to make room for more test prep.

It's a challenge to be a good parent of a high school student. You want to help our kids without putting too much pressure on.

Kohn knows a college counselor hired by parents to help "package" their child, who had perfect board scores and a wonderful grade-point average. When it was time to work on the college essay, the counselor said, "Let's start with a book you read outside of school that really made a difference in your life." There was a moment of silence. Then the child responded, "Why would I read a book if I didn't have to?" If parents focus only on the transcript—drive out of children their natural curiosity, discourage their trying anything at which they might fail—their definition of success will get a failing grade from any teacher watching.

The Public Defenders

By the time children turn 18, they have spent only 13% of their waking lives in the classroom. Their habits of mind, motivation and muscles have much more to do with that other 87%. But try telling that to an Ivy-educated mom and dad whose kids aren't doing well. It can't be the genes, Mom and Dad conclude, so it must be the school. "It's the bright children who aren't motivated who are most frustrating for parents and teachers," says Nancy McGill, a past president of the Iowa Talented and Gifted Association. "Parents don't know how to fix the kid, to get the kid going. They want us to do it, and discover we can't either." Sometimes bright kids intentionally work just hard enough to get a B because they are trying to make a point about what should be demanded of them, observes Jennifer Loh, a math teacher at Ursuline Academy in Dallas. "It's their way of saying to Mom and Dad, 'I'm not perfect.'" Though the best teachers work hard to inspire even the most alienated kids, they can't carry the full burden of the parents' expectations. In his dreams, admits Daddow, the Iowa history teacher, what he would like to say is "Your son or daughter is very, very lazy." Instead, he shows the parents the student's work and says, "I'm not sure I'm getting Jim's best effort."

When a teacher asks parents to be partners, he or she doesn't necessarily mean Mom or Dad should be camping in the classroom. Research shows that though students benefit modestly from having parents involved at school, what happens at home matters much more. According to research based on the National Education Longitudinal Study, a sample of nearly 25,000 eighth-graders, among four main areas of parental involvement (home discussion, home supervision, school communication and school participation), home discussion was the most strongly related to academic achievement.

Any partnership requires that both sides do their part. Teachers say that here again, parents can have double standards: Push hard, but not too hard; maintain discipline, but don't punish my child. When teachers tell a parent that a child needs to be reprimanded at home, teachers say they often get the response, "I don't reprimand, and don't tell me how to raise my child." Older teachers say they are seeing in children as young as 6 and 7 a level of disdain for adults that was once the reserve of adolescents. Some talk about the "dry-cleaner parents" who drop their rambunctious kids off in the morning and expect them to be returned at the end of the day all clean and proper and practically sealed in plastic.

At the most disturbing extreme are the parents who like to talk about values but routinely undermine them. "You get savvier children who know how to get out of things," says a second-grade teacher in Murfreesboro, Tenn. "Their parents actually teach them to lie to dodge their responsibilities." Didn't get your homework done? That's O.K. Mom will take the fall. Late for class? Blame it on Dad. Parents have sued schools that expelled kids for cheating, on the grounds that teachers had left the exams out on a desk and made them too easy to steal. "Cheating is rampant," says Steve Taylor, a history teacher at Beverly Hills High School in California. "If you're not cheating, then you're not trying. A C means you're a loser." Every principal can tell a story about some ambitious student, Ivy bound, who cheats on an exam. Teacher flunks her. Parents protest: She made a mistake, and you're going to ruin her life. Teachers try to explain that good kids can make bad decisions; the challenge is to make sure the kids learn from them. "I think some parents confuse advocating on behalf of their student with defending everything that the student does," says Scott Peoples, a history teacher at Skyview High School outside Denver.

I called the parents on a discipline issue with their daughter. Her father called me a total jerk. Then he said, 'Well, do you want to meet someplace and take care of this man to man?'

Student-teacher disputes can quickly escalate into legal challenges or the threat of them. The fear of litigation that has given rise to the practice of defensive medicine prompts educators to practice defensive teaching. According to Forrest T. Jones Inc., a large insurer of teachers, the number of teachers buying liability insurance has jumped 25% in the past five years. "A lot of teachers are very fearful and don't want to deal with it," says Roxsana Jaber-Ansari, who teaches sixth grade at Hale Middle School in Woodland Hills, Calif. She has learned that everything must be documented. She does not dare accuse a student of cheating, for instance, without evidence, including eyewitness accounts or a paper trail. When a teacher meets with a student alone, the door always has to be open to avoid any suspicion of inappropriate behavior on the teacher's part. "If you become angry and let it get to you, you will quit your job," says Jaber-Ansari. "You will hate what you do and hate the kids."

Teacher's Pests

Some parents ask too much of the school or too little of their kids

Helicopter Parents

In order to grow, kids need room to fail; the always hovering parent gets in the way of self-reliance

Monster Parents

The lurking moms and dads always looking for reasons to disagree are a teacher's worst nightmare

Dry-cleaner Parents

They drop their rambunctious kids off and want them all cleaned up and proper by the end of the day

---

The Culture Warriors

Teachers in schools with economically and ethnically diverse populations face a different set of challenges in working with parents. In less affluent districts, many parents don't have computers at home, so schools go to some lengths to make contact easier. Even 20 minutes twice a year for a conference can be hard for families if parents are working long hours at multiple jobs or have to take three buses to get to the school. Some teachers visit a parent's workplace on a Saturday or help arrange language classes for parents to help with communication. Particularly since a great goal of education is to level the playing field, teachers are worried that the families that need the most support are least able to ask for it. "The standards about what makes a good parent are always changing," notes Annette Lareau, a professor of sociology at Temple University, who views all the demand for parent involvement as a relatively recent phenomenon. "And it's middle-class parents who keep pace."

Lareau also sees cultural barriers getting in the way of the strong parent-teacher alliance. When parents don't get involved at school, teachers may see it as a sign of indifference, of not valuing education—when it may signal the reverse. Some cultures believe strongly that school and home should be separate spheres; parents would no more interfere with the way a teacher teaches than with the way a surgeon operates. "Working-class and poor families don't have a college education," says Lareau. "They are looking up to teachers; they respect teachers as professionals. Middle-class parents are far less respectful. They're not a teacher, but they could have been a teacher, and often their profession has a higher status than teachers'. So they are much more likely to criticize teachers on professional grounds."

And while she views social class as a major factor in shaping the dynamic, Lareau finds that race continues to play a role. Middle-class black parents, especially those who attended segregated schools, often approach the teacher with caution. Roughly 90% of teachers are white and middle class, and, says Lareau, many black parents are "worried that teachers will have lowered expectations of black children, that black boys will be punished more than white boys. Since teachers want parents to be positive and supportive, when African-American parents express concerns about racial insensitivity, it can create problems in their relationship."

Finally, as church-state arguments boil over and principals agonize over what kids can sing at the Winter Concert, teachers need to be eternally sensitive to religious issues as well. This is an arena where parents are often as concerned about content as grades, as in the debate over creationism vs. evolution vs. intelligent design, for instance. Teachers say they have to become legal scholars to protect themselves in a climate where students have "rights." Jaber-Ansari was challenged for hanging Bible quotes on her classroom walls. But she had studied her legal standing, and when she was confronted, "the principal supported me 100%," she says.

Perhaps the most complicated part of the conversation—beyond all the issues of race and class and culture, the growing pressures to succeed and arguments over how success should be defined—is the problem of memory. When they meet in that conference, parent and teacher bring their own school experiences with them—what went right and wrong, what they missed. They are determined for it to be different for the child they both care about. They go into that first-grade room and sit in the small chairs and can easily be small again themselves. It is so tempting to use the child's prospects to address their own regrets. So teachers learn to choose their words with care and hope that they can build a partnership with parents that works to everyone's advantage and comes at no one's expense. And parents over time may realize that when it comes to their children, they still have much to learn. "I think that we love our children so much that they make us a little loony at times," says Arch Montgomery, head of the Asheville School in North Carolina. He winces at parents who treat their child as a cocktail-party trophy or a vanity sticker for the window of their SUV, but he also understands their behavior. "I think most parents desperately want to do what is right for their kids. This does not bring out the better angels of our natures, but it is understandable, and it is forgivable."

With reporting by Amanda Bower, New York, Melissa August, Washington, Anne Berryman, Athens, Cathy Booth Thomas, Dallas, Rita Healy, Denver, Elizabeth Kauffman, Nashville, Jeanne McDowell, Los Angeles and Betsy Rubiner, Des Moines.

Where Personality Goes Awry

A multifaceted research approach is providing more clues to the origins of personality disorders.

CHARLOTTE HUFF

Over the years, few large-scale prospective studies have targeted the causes of personality disorders (PDs). But recently, a new body of research has begun to explore the potential influences of several factors, from genetics and parenting to peer influences, and even the randomness of life events.

Indeed, says Patricia Hoffman Judd, PhD, clinical professor of psychiatry at the University of California, San Diego, research into the origins of PDs is just beginning to take off. "I think for years people thought, 'It's just personality—you can't do anything about it,'" she explains. "There's also been moralism [that people with such disorders] are evil, that they are lazy," adds Judd, author of "A Developmental Model of Borderline Personality Disorder" (American Psychiatric Publishing, 2003).

But research is helping to turn such misconceptions around. Genetics researchers, for example, are closer to identifying some of the biological underpinnings that may influence PDs. Last year, for example, a team located—and described in *Molecular Psychiatry* (Vol, 8. No. 11)—a malfunctioning gene they believe may be a factor in obsessive-compulsive disorder. Other researchers are investigating genetic links to aggression, anxiety and fear—traits that could be influential in the later development of a personality disorder.

However, genetics don't work in a vacuum. Studies continue to indicate that abuse, even verbal abuse, can amplify the risk of developing a personality disorder.

For some disorders, such as antisocial PD, the evidence suggests that genetic factors play a significant role, while others, such as dependent personality disorder, appear to be more environmentally influenced, says longtime PD researcher Theodore Millon, PhD, DSc, editor of an ongoing book series, "Personality-guided Psychology" (APA).

But regardless of the specific disorder, researchers increasingly observe a back-and-forth interplay between genetic and environmental influences.

"We see a paradigm shift taking place in the field now toward a more interactionist perspective," says Jeffrey G. Johnson, PhD, associate professor of clinical psychology in Columbia University's psychiatry department. "I think the field is getting away from genetics versus environment—it's a major change."

The Genetic/Environmental Convergence

One of the largest efforts to look at PDs, the Collaborative Longitudinal Personality Disorders Study (CLPS), is attempting to gain insight into a cross-section of the disorders' characteristics, stability and progression. The multisite study, funded by the National Institute of Mental Health until 2005, has since 1996 enrolled 668 people with the diagnoses of avoidant, borderline, obsessive-compulsive or schizotypal personality disorders. A summary of the study's aims appeared in the *Journal of Personality Disorders* (Vol. 14. No. 4).

Although the study is not looking directly at causes, it's collecting historical information that may one day provide some insights, says Tracie Shea, PhD, associate professor in the department of psychiatry and human behavior at Brown Medical School and one of CLPS's principal investigators. "I like to think of it as generating hypotheses that can be tested," she says.

Shea co-authored a 2002 study in the *Journal of Nervous and Mental Disease* (Vol. 190, No. 8) that looked at CLPS data and found an association between the severity of specific PDs and the number and type of childhood traumas. In particular, people with borderline PDs reported particularly high rates of childhood sexual trauma—55 percent detailing physically forced, unwanted sexual contact. The researchers note, however, that the type of analysis couldn't determine if the personality adaptations occurred in response to the trauma or whether the individuals' underlying character pathology predisposed them.

Among those exploring the genetic and environmental influences linking normal and abnormal personality is Robert Krueger, PhD, associate professor of psychology at the University of Minnesota. In 2002, Krueger co-authored a study in the *Journal of Personality* (Vol. 70, No. 5) that looked at the personality traits of 128 twin pairs who had been raised apart. The study found that the identical twins were more similar in personality traits than the fraternal twins.

Thus, although both genetics and environment contributed to the association between normal and abnormal personality, genetics appeared to play the greater role overall, Krueger says. "The predominant reason normal and abnormal personality are linked to each other is because they are linked to the same underlying genetic mechanisms," he explains.

With borderline PD, for example, ongoing research indicates that there may be a genetic base for the problems with impulsivity and aggression, says the University of California's Judd. But environmental influences are significant and can extend deep into childhood, even infancy, Judd adds.

"There is a pretty high prevalence of maltreatment by caregivers across all personality disorders," she notes. "One of the key problems appears to be neglect. Probably more of an emotional neglect—more of a lack of attention to a child's emotional needs."

Judd points to several studies by Johnson, including one published in 1999 in the *Archives of General Psychiatry* (Vol. 56, No. 7) that followed 639 New York state families and their children for nearly two decades. Children with documented instances of childhood abuse or neglect were more than four times as likely to develop a PD in early adulthood, according to the research.

Another study, led by Johnson and published in 2001 in *Comprehensive Psychiatry* (Vol. 42, No. 1), came to a similar conclusion when examining maternal verbal abuse in the same New York group of families, involving this time 793 mothers and their children. The prospective study asked mothers a variety of questions, including whether they had screamed at their children in the previous month and whether they had told their child they didn't love them or would send them away. Offspring who experienced verbal abuse in childhood—compared with those who didn't—were more than three times as likely to be diagnosed as adults with borderline, narcissistic, obsessive-compulsive and paranoid PDs.

Shea cautions, though, that at this point research into childhood neglect and abuse, albeit intriguing, has largely been suggestive because prospective studies remain limited.

"It's likely that these childhood abuse factors do play an important role," he explains. "It's hard to say what and how big that role is, more specifically."

The Parent-Blame Problem

The role of abuse is particularly controversial among family members of people with a borderline disorder, who say they are being unfairly blamed—similar to what happened in the early days of schizophrenia research. Emphasizing maltreatment and abuse is misleading and has a devastating effect on families, says Valerie Porr, president of a New York-based nonprofit group, Treatment and Research Advancements National Association for Personality Disorder (www.tara4bpd.org/tara.html).

Porr doesn't deny that parental behavior can play a role in borderline PD. "But it's not like it's the evil mother beating her children," she says. Rather, she explains, the child's "behavior is so off the wall [that] the family's responses are off the wall."

Porr, who has a family member with borderline personality disorder, points to emerging research, including that of Harvard University-based psychologist Jerome Kagan, PhD, identifying the high sensitivity to outside stimuli of some children as significant. Family members of people with borderline PD report unusual responses even in the first months of life, Porr says, noting that, "They say, 'The light bothers them. They are sensitive to noise. Texture bothers them.'"

But Kagan, in a 2002 *Dialogues in Clinical Neuroscience* article (Vol. 4, No. 3), says that the role of high reactivity in infancy is far from clear-cut. It's true, he says, that highly reactive infants are more likely to develop shy, timid or anxious personalities. Still, there are puzzling questions, including the significant gap between the percentage of children—20 percent—who are highly reactive infants and the prevalence—less than 10 percent—of those who develop social phobias.

"This fact suggests that many high reactives find an adaptive niche in their society that allows them to titer unpredictable social encounters," Kagan writes.

In the end, says Johnson, the goal of research into environmental influences is not to blame, but to help parents. "We must understand what parenting behaviors are associated with greater risk to the child," he says. "When we identify those parenting behaviors, we can use them to design intervention."

The Role of Peers

Psychologists' findings also suggest that caregivers, teachers and even peers may play a role in PDs—both in positive as well as negative ways. Even a single strong positive relationship—say a close bond with a grandmother—can offset negative influences in a dysfunctional household.

"The child with a predisposition toward developing a personality disorder doesn't need the perfect teacher or the perfect friends to not develop the disorder," says Judith Beck, PhD, director of the Beck Institute for Cognitive Therapy and Research in suburban Philadelphia. "If the child is in an extreme environment, such as abuse or neglect, that may make the difference in terms of developing a personality disorder."

And life events can help tip the balance, Beck says. For example, a child with obsessive-compulsive tendencies who has alcoholic parents may assume the responsibility of caring for his younger siblings—a move that may amplify his propensities until he meets the diagnosis of a disorder. "It's the fit between your environment and your personality," Beck explains.

Over time, researchers will continue probing that fit and will likely identify more than a few causes even for a single personality disorder, says Millon, dean of the Florida-based Institute for Advanced Studies in Personology and Psychopathology. Narrowing down potential causes will help psychologists more quickly isolate what might be influencing a particular patient, he says.

Millon explains: "Once you identify the one cause that seems most probable and most significant, then you can design your therapy in order to unlearn what seemed most problematic for that individual."

CHARLOTTE HUFF is a freelance writer in Fort Worth, Texas.

Girls Gone Bad?

Paris, Britney, Lindsay & Nicole: They seem to be everywhere and they may not be wearing underwear. Tweens adore them and teens envy them. But are we raising a generation of 'prosti-tots'?

KATHLEEN DEVENY WITH RAINA KELLEY

My 6-year-old daughter loves Lindsay Lohan. Loves, loves, *loves* her. She loves Lindsay's hair; she loves Lindsay's freckles. She's seen "The Parent Trap" at least 10 times. I sometimes catch her humming the movie's theme song, Nat King Cole's "Love." She likes "Herbie Fully Loaded" and now we're cycling through "Freaky Friday." So when my daughter spotted a photo of Lindsay in the New York Post at the breakfast table not long ago, she was psyched. "That's Lindsay Lohan," she said proudly. "What's she doing?"

I couldn't tell her, of course. I didn't want to explain that Lindsay, who, like Paris Hilton and Britney Spears, sometimes parties pantyless, was taking pole-dancing lessons to prepare for a movie role. Or that her two hours of research left her bruised "everywhere." Then again, Lindsay's professional trials are easy to explain compared with Nicole Richie's recent decision to stop her car in the car-pool lane of an L.A. freeway. Or Britney Spears's "collapse" during a New Year's Eve party in Las Vegas. Or the more recent report that Lindsay had checked into rehab after passing out in a hotel hallway, an item that ran on the Post's Page Six opposite a photo of Kate Moss falling down a stairway while dressed in little more than a fur jacket and a pack of cigarettes.

Something's in the air, and I wouldn't call it love. Like never before, our kids are being bombarded by images of oversexed, underdressed celebrities who can't seem to step out of a car without displaying their well-waxed private parts to photographers. Videos like "Girls Gone Wild on Campus Uncensored" bring in an estimated $40 million a year. And if US magazine, which changed the rules of mainstream celebrity journalism, is too slow with the latest dish on "Brit's New Man," kids can catch up 24/7 with hugely popular gossip blogs like perezhilton.com, tmz.com or defamer.com.

Allow us to confirm what every parent knows: kids, born in the new-media petri dish, are well aware of celebrity antics. But while boys are willing to take a peek at anyone showing skin, they're baffled by the feuds, the fashions and faux pas of the Brit Pack. Girls, on the other hand, are their biggest fans. A recent NEWSWEEK Poll found that 77 percent of Americans believe that Britney, Paris and Lindsay have too much influence on young girls. Hardly a day passes when one of them isn't making news. Paris Hilton "was always somewhere, doing something," says Melissa Monaco, an 18-year-old senior at Oldfield's boarding school for girls in Maryland, who describes herself as a recovered Paris Hilton addict. "I loved everything from her outfits to her attitude," she says. And it's not just teenagers. Julie Seborowski, a first-grade teacher at Kumeyaay Elementary School in San Diego, says she sees it in her 7-year-old students: girls using words like "sexy," singing pop songs with suggestive lyrics and flirting with boys.

That's enough to make any parent cringe. But are there really harmful long-term effects of overexposure to Paris Hilton? Are we raising a generation of what one L.A. mom calls "prosti-tots," young girls who dress like tarts, live for Dolce & Gabbana purses and can neither spell nor define such words as "adequate"? Or does the rise of the bad girl signal something more profound, a coarsening of the culture and a devaluation of sex, love and lasting commitment? We're certainly not the first generation of parents to worry about such things, nor will we be the last. Many conservative thinkers view our sex-drenched culture as dangerous; liberals are more prone to wave off fears about the chastity of our daughters as reactionary. One thing is not in doubt: a lot of parents are wondering about the effect our racy popular culture may have on their kids and the women they would like their girls to become. The answers are likely to lie in yet another question: where do our children learn values?

Here's a radical idea—at home, where they always have. Experts say attentive parents, strong teachers and nice friends are an excellent counterbalance to our increasingly sleazy culture. Statistical evidence indicates that our girls are actually doing pretty well, in spite of Paris Hilton and those like her: teen pregnancy, drinking and drug use are all down, and there is no evidence that girls are having intercourse at a younger age. And in many ways it's a great time to be a girl: women are excelling in sports, academics and the job market. It's just that the struggle to impart the right values to our kids is a 24/7 proposition. It can be done, but an ancient rule of warfare applies: first, know thy enemy.

I didn't want to explain to my 6-year-old that Lindsay was taking pole dancing to prepare for a movie role.

"It takes a very strong adolescent to know what's right and what's wrong and not get sucked into all this stuff," says Emily Waring, 40, a paralegal from San Diego and mother of two girls, ages 9 and 2. Waring says her "mom radar" is always on because she believes negative influences, including entertainers like Britney Spears, are everywhere. "Kids can so easily stray," she says.

Nobody wants her bright, innocent girls to grow up believing "hard-partying heiress" is a job title to which they can aspire. But does dressing like Paris or slavishly following the details of Britney's love life make kids more likely to stray? Educators say they don't believe most girls in middle school wear short skirts or midriff shirts to attract the attention of older men, or even boys. (High school is, granted, a different story.) Sixth graders dress to fit in with other girls and for acceptance in social groups. "They dress that way because that's what they see in the media," says Nancy T. Mugele, who works in communications at Roland Park Country School in Baltimore. "They don't want to be different."

Which is not to say that hearing about Lindsay Lohan's, um, "fire crotch" doesn't affect the way kids think about sex. A study published last year in the journal *Pediatrics* concluded that for white teens, repeated exposure to sexual content in television, movies and music increases the likelihood of becoming sexually active at an earlier age. (Black teens appear less influenced by media, and more by their parents' expectations and their friends' sexual behavior; those who had the least exposure to sexual content were also less likely to have intercourse.) Specifically, the study found that 55 percent of teens who were exposed to a lot of sexual material had intercourse by 16, compared with only 6 percent of teens who rarely saw sexual imagery in the media. That jibes with what many Americans fear: 84 percent of adults in the NEWSWEEK Poll said sex plays a bigger role in popular culture than it did 20 or 30 years ago, and 70 percent said that was a bad influence on young people.

Many factors affect kids' sexual behavior, and it may be that kids who are already considering sex are more likely to seek out sexy shows and music. But researchers say one of the strongest predictors of early intercourse is the impression—real or imagined—that everybody else is doing it. For some teens, especially those who aren't getting strong messages about abstinence from their parents, the media can become a sort of "sexual superpeer," according to

Jane D. Brown, a journalism professor at UNC Chapel Hill, and an author of the *Pediatrics* study. The message, says Brown, is that "you can walk around with no clothes on, you can have sex with whoever shows up, you can have a baby and not be married."

Some observers think the real effect of the Brit Pack on our culture is more subtle, but no less negative. Rather than instantly inspiring kids to rush and have sex, out-of-control celebs create a sense of normalcy about behavior—drinking, smoking, casual sex—that is dangerous for teens. Britney, Paris and Lindsay have no shortage of "boyfriends" but seem to have few real relationships. "It creates a general sense that life is about being crazy, being kooky, having fun and not carrying on serious relationships," says Christian Smith, professor of sociology at Notre Dame. But the really insidious consequence is that teenagers often consider themselves immune to these influences. "They don't have enough perspective on how they are being formed by the world around them—and when they don't realize it, it can be more powerful," he says.

Eighty-four percent of adults say sex plays a bigger role in popular culture than it did 20 or 30 years ago.

Still, this seems like a lot to place on the slender shoulders of Nicole Richie and her frenemies. That some girls dress like Paris/Britney/Lindsay is empirically true. But it's difficult to draw a straight line between the behavior of celebrities and the behavior of real girls. "We certainly don't see our girls clamoring to get to downtown Chicago to the clubs," says Mark Kuzniewski, principal of Aptakisic Junior High in Buffalo Grove, Ill. And while girls may admire Britney's clothes and dance moves, her students "can't understand why Britney would wear no underwear," says Michelle Freitag, fifth-grade teacher in suburban Chicago. Their verdict: Britney is a "hootch," which is a polite way of saying "slut."

Our anxiety about girls and sex is growing just as the statistics seem to be telling as different story. Sex surveys are notoriously unreliable, but the best available data show that the average age of first sexual intercourse for girls is 17, according to the Guttmacher Institute, and hasn't changed by more than a few months in 20 years. The overall teenage pregnancy rate in 2002, the most recent available, was down 35 percent from 1990, according to the Centers for Disease Control. And while celebrity idols stumble in and out of rehab, the rates of drinking, smoking and overall drug use among teenage girls have declined in recent years, says the Institute for Social Research at the University of Michigan.

Girls born after 1990 live in a world where they have ready access to organized sports, safe contraception and Ivy League colleges. Yale didn't admit women until 1969; its freshman class is currently half female. In the 2004–2005 school year, women earned 57 percent of all bachelor's degrees awarded and 59 percent of master's degrees. The Congress now has 90 female members—the highest in history—with 16 in the Senate and 74 in the House, including Speaker Nancy Pelosi. Hillary Clinton, our first viable female presidential candidate, has thrown her hat into the ring.

Dan Kindlon, a professor of child psychology at Harvard and author of "Alpha Girls," calls these girls the daughters of the revolution, the first generation that is reaping the full benefit of the women's movement. "Sure, there are plenty of girls with big problems out there," he says. "Like the 'Girls Gone Wild' videos. But what percentage of the college population is that?" There is still plenty of pressure to be beautiful and thin, he adds, but now there are more options. Girls can define themselves as athletes or good students. For better or for worse, it may also be that they now feel entitled to dress as crassly as they choose, date unwisely and fall down drunk, the way men have since the dawn of time.

Plenty of high-school bad girls (us, for instance!) grow up to be successful people with happy home lives.

That's at least how long parents have worried about how their children would turn out. The text on a Sumerian tablet from the village of Ur (located in modern-day Iraq) says: "If the unheard-of actions of today's youth are allowed to continue, then we are doomed." Certainly, queens and noblewomen have long gotten away with behaving badly: in the early 16th century, Anne Boleyn not only had an affair with the King of England, Henry VIII, but helped persuade him to throw the Roman Catholic Church out of the country (although we all know how that ended). Their daughter, Elizabeth I, was the "virgin queen" who slept around.

But for most of history, average women who had sex outside the vows of marriage were subject to banishment, beating or death. When Jesus said, "If any of you is without sin, let him be the first to throw a stone at her," he was protecting a woman caught in adultery. In her book "Promiscuities," Naomi Wolf recalls a searing image she came across in her research: a photo of the mummified remains of a 14-year-old German girl from the first century A.D.: "Her right arm still clutched the garrote that had been used to twist the rope around her neck. Her lips were open in an 'O' of surprise or pain . . ." Historians had concluded that the girl had been blindfolded, strangled and drowned, most likely as retribution for "adultery," or what we would now call premarital sex.

Until after the Civil War, women didn't have enough freedom to create much of a public scandal. By the turn of the century, however, the Industrial Revolution had transformed the lives of adolescent daughters of working-class families. Once confined to home, young white women could now work in offices, stores and factories, where they enjoyed unprecedented social freedoms—much to the chagrin of their parents and social critics. Young African-American women didn't have the same economic opportunities, but did gain new autonomy as they fled farms in the South to live and work in Northern cities.

Meanwhile, improved literacy along with technological advances like the wireless telegraph and radio gave rise to a national media. By 1900, there were more than 16,000 newspapers in the United States; circulation numbers at the biggest topped 1 million. Keeping a dirty little secret had become much, much harder. By the time the 1920s rolled around, bad girls could grow up to become not just the destroyers of men (in the tradition of Salome and Delilah), but also to be rich and famous.

Mae West, best remembered for one-liners like "If you don't like my peaches, why do you shake my tree," may have been the original bad girl of the 20th century. Born in Brooklyn in 1893, she wrote and starred in bawdy theatrical productions, delighting and scandalizing audiences. She went too far, however, when she wrote a play called "Sex," about waterfront hookers and pimps, which became a national hit. In 1927, the New York production was raided and she was arrested, convicted of a performance that "tended to corrupt the morals of youth and others," and sentenced to 10 days in jail, according to *The New York Times.* Seven years later she was featured on the cover of NEWSWEEK for a story titled "The Churches Protest," which called her the "personification of Hollywood's sins."

Gypsy Rose Lee, born in 1914, followed closely on Mae West's spike heels. A burlesque superstar, Lee's shows at Minsky's Winter Garden in New York in the 1930s were a sensation. Before a congressional committee in 1937, Herbert Minsky, who co-owned the theater, called Lee "one of the most highly publicized stars in the country." According to a *Washington Post* account, "A momentary hush fell on the hearings . . . The name of Gypsy Rose Lee had been mentioned." Despite her fame—and $2,000-a-week salary—Lee was arrested numerous times by the NYPD for public indecency, once allegedly protesting, "I wasn't naked. I was completely covered by a blue spotlight."

By the '50s, both Hollywood and the public took a harsh view of female stars' off-screen indiscretions. In 1950, Ingrid Bergman was America's sweetheart, having starred in "The Bells of St. Mary's" and "Notorious." But when Bergman, then married, had an affair with director Roberto Rossellini, who was also married, and gave birth to their child, she was shunned by Hollywood and called "a powerful influence for evil" on the floor of the Senate. (Hollywood "forgave" Bergman a few years later by giving her an Oscar for "Anastasia.") After news broke that Marilyn Monroe would be featured in a nude calendar, Hollywood proclaimed her career DOA. (She was on the cover of Life magazine a month later, and went on to the biggest roles of her career.)

America was scandalized in 1962 when Elizabeth Taylor cheated on Eddie Fisher with Richard Burton during the filming of "Cleopatra." The Vatican denounced her as "a woman of loose morals." When "Dickenliz," as they were known, checked into a Toronto hotel, protesters marched outside with signs that read DRINK NOT THE WINE OF ADULTERY, according to a 1964 NEWSWEEK article. But soon America's priorities shifted. The Vietnam War was on television; the civil-rights movement was in the streets, and the national mood had been sobered by the assassinations of John F. Kennedy, Martin Luther King Jr. and Robert Kennedy. The '60s also brought reliable contraception in the form of the birth-control pill and ushered in the sexual revolution. We no longer needed to look to Hollywood for bad influences; the girl next door, the one with birth-control pills and a couple of joints tucked into her fringed purse, became the new object of our anxiety.

America had become harder to shock—until 1984, that is, when Madonna showed up in a wedding dress at the first MTV Video Music Awards and sang "Like a Virgin" while writhing on the floor. When her "Virgin" tour opened a year later, parents fretted over the hordes of Madonna wannabes who thronged her concerts dressed in tatty lace, spandex and armfuls of black rubber bracelets. The Material Girl went on to outrage both Planned Parenthood and the Catholic Church in 1986 with her single "Papa Don't Preach," about a pregnant teenager. The 1992 coffee-table book called "Sex," which glorified nearly every sexual fetish you can think of, cemented her title as the Queen of Bad Girls. Eleven years later she passed on her crown to Britney with a lingering French kiss on the stage of yet another MTV Video Music Awards ceremony.

And Brit, as we know, has run with it. One-day marriages aside, why wouldn't girls be fascinated by her and her celebrity pals? These 21st-century "bad influences" are young, beautiful and rich, unencumbered by school, curfews or parents. "They've got great clothes and boyfriends. They seem to have a lot of fun," explains Emma Boyce, a 17-year-old junior at Louise S. McGehee School in New Orleans. But fascination and admiration are two very different things. As they get arrested for driving drunk and feuding with their former BFFs, the Brit Pack makes it easy for young women like Boyce, a top student and accomplished equestrian, to feel superior to them. "My friends and I look at them to laugh at them," adds Boyce. "Our lives seem pretty good by comparison. We're not going to rehab like Lindsay."

Boyce says she and her friends have simply outgrown their devotion to celebrities. Twelve- to 14-year-olds are probably the most vulnerable to stars' influence. "Clearly it is at this age for girls that they are trying to find an identity to associate with," says Kuzniewski, the junior-high principal from Buffalo Grove, Ill. "It seems desirable to be Lindsay Lohan." Now that's a legitimate cause for parental concern. But it may very well be fleeting. After all, have you read your junior-high journals lately? Like us, you were probably obsessed with trivial things that had little bearing on the person you became at 24 or 34. Even if your daughter does dress like Paris or behave like Lindsay, that doesn't mean she's doomed to a life on the pole. Plenty of high-school bad girls (us, for instance!) grow up to be successful professionals with happy home lives.

And as much as we hate to admit it, we grown-ups are complicit. We're uncomfortable when kids worship these girls, yet we also love US magazine; we can't get enough of YouTube videos or "E! True Hollywood Stories." So rather than wring our hands over an increase in 17-year-olds getting breast implants,

what if we just said no? They're minors, right? And while we worry that middle-schoolers are dressing like hookers, there are very few 11-year-olds with enough disposable income to keep Forever 21 afloat. The greatest threat posed by these celebrity bad girls may be that they're advertising avatars, dressed by stylists and designers, who seem to live only to consume: clothes, cell phones, dogs and men. But there's good news: that problem is largely under the control of we who hold the purse strings.

And even if our adolescents pick up a few tricks from the Brit Pack, we have a big head start on them. We begin to teach our kids values while they're still in diapers. "Kids learn good morals and values by copying role models who are close to them," says Michele Borba, author of "Teaching Moral Intelligence."

Good Times, Bad Apples

By the 20th century, women had freedom enough to cause public scandals. Social critics have been wringing their hands ever since.

1. Ingrid Bergman — The married star had an affair in 1950 with Roberto Rossellini, who was also married, and Bergman gave birth to their child. She was denounced on the floor of the Senate.

2. Mae West — The vaudeville performer spent 10 days in jail for the 1927 play 'Sex.'

3. Marilyn Monroe — Long before she purred 'Happy Birthday' to JFK, she appeared in a calendar in her birthday suit. Hollywood called her career DOA.

4. Monica Lewinsky — The former intern helped create myriad teaching moments about oral sex after her liaison with President Clinton.

5. Madonna — Parents flipped in '85 when girls showed up at her concerts dressed in spandex and black rubber bracelets.

6. Kate Moss — Photos of her apparently using coke showed up in a British tab in 2005. She went to rehab, and has regained her status as a fashion icon.

7. Liz Taylor — She had an affair with Richard Burton in 1962 during the filming of 'Cleopatra'; the Vatican called her 'a woman of loose morals.'

8. Gypsy Rose Lee — A burlesque superstar in the '30s, she was arrested numerous times for taking it almost all off.

9. Nicole Richie — She was arrested last fall for parking on an L.A. freeway.

Experts say that even the most withdrawn teens scrutinize their parents for cues on how to act. So watch your behavior; don't gossip with your friends in front of the kids and downplay popularity as a lifetime goal. Parents need to understand and talk about the things that interest their kids—even if it's what Paris is wearing—without being judgmental. That makes it easier for kids to open up. "The really subtle thing you have to do is hear where they are coming from, and gently direct them into thinking about it," says Borba. That means these celebrities gone wild and all their tabloid antics can be teachable moments. Lesson No. 1: wear underwear.

With Jamie Reno, in San Diego; Karen Springen in Chicago and Susannah Meadows, Anne Underwood and Julie Scelfo in New York.

Disrespecting Childhood

Although Americans see ours as a child-loving nation, the authors present evidence of policies and practices that are not respectful of children or childhood. They call on us to question the assumptions about our young people that form the basis for our teaching, research, and policies.

CURT DUDLEY-MARLING, JANICE JACKSON, AND LISA PATEL STEVENS

What I discovered in Spain was a culture that held children to be its meringues and eclairs. My own culture . . . tended to regard children as a sort of toxic waste.[1]

I n the popular imagination, Americans are a child-loving people. Across the land, selfless parents take classes, read books, create playgroups, and exchange the latest information about how to ensure safe, contented, and productive childhoods. Thousands of contemporary American families indulge their children materially to a degree that may be unparalleled in the world and in our own history. As a society, we have enacted a range of laws designed to protect children from physical and psychological abuse and economic and sexual exploitation. We have legions of pediatricians specially trained to attend to the physical and mental well-being of our children. Even the presence of metal detectors at the entrances of our schools can be taken as emblematic of our collective desire to protect the nation's children.

The range of public programs and policies benefiting children, directly or indirectly, offers further evidence of the high regard Americans have for their children. Tax credits for children and child care, child nutrition and health-care programs, preschool programs like Head Start, and billions of dollars spent each year to support elementary, secondary, and postsecondary education all demonstrate the desire of federal, state, and local governments to look after the physical, emotional, and intellectual well-being of the young. The prominence we give to educational issues in local, state, and federal elections further supports the assertion that children are indeed a high priority for Americans.

More than 133,000 children are in juvenile or adult correctional facilities on any given day.

While these commonly held beliefs communicate a consistent and shared regard for children, when we dig beneath the platitudes,

we find a far messier and more complex set of assumptions, beliefs, and challenges to this inspiring image of the United States as a child-loving society. Writing over 20 years ago, Letty Pogrebin argued that "America is a nation fundamentally ambivalent about its children, often afraid of its children, and frequently punitive towards its children."[2] Pogrebin cited attacks on the cost of public education and child health and nutrition programs, along with an inclination to pathologize an entire period in children's lives—that is, adolescence—to support her contention that the country was afflicted by what she called "an epidemic of pedophobia."[3]

Novelist Barbara Kingsolver has observed that children have come to hold an increasingly negative position in the economy.[4] Children are spoken of as a responsibility, a legal liability, and an encumbrance[5]—or they are seen in terms of potential profits. Today's children and adolescents, weaned on images of McDonald's and toy companies, are targeted as a ripe segment of the market for building powerful brand loyalty for everything from video games to prescriptions for drugs to treat attention deficit disorders.[6] And, if Pogrebin, writing in the early Reagan years, saw child-focused government programs under attack, then Kingsolver, writing 14 years later, had seen many of these same programs ravaged. Funding for virtually every program that benefits children in this country, Kingsolver writes—from "Sesame Street" to free school lunches—has been cut back in the past decade, in many cases cut to nothing.[7] Indeed, programs that support children in the U.S. are, in Kingsolver's words, the hands-down worst in the industrialized world.[8]

The Kingsolver quote that serves as epigraph to this article is disturbing. After all, it is a rare parent who does not put the needs of his or her children first, and Americans generally do care about *their own* children. But the evidence suggests that Americans are not consistent in caring for other people's children, especially children from marginalized populations. Nearly one in six children in the U.S. lives in poverty, a rate as much as two to three times higher than that in other industrialized nations.[9] The data for children of color are even more distressing, as black (32%) and Hispanic (29%) children are far more likely than white children (14%) to live in poverty. And many of these same children attend deteriorating, underfunded schools.[10] Here are some additional statistics from

The State of America's Children: more than 133,000 children are in juvenile or adult correctional facilities on any given day; children under 18 are increasingly incarcerated in adult facilities (more than 21,000 youths under 18 are being held in adult correctional facilities); in 2003, youth jobless rates for ages 16–19 reached nearly 60%, as compared to the 6% unemployment rate for all ages; in 2002, nearly 9.3 million American children were not covered by health insurance; also in 2003, 2,911 children and teens were killed by gunfire; and in 2002, an estimated three million children in the U.S. were reported as suspected cases of child abuse or neglect.[11] While these statistics arise from a complex set of social and economic circumstances, taken together, they challenge the image of America as a child-loving society.

Additional evidence of America's antipathy toward its youths comes from a Public Agenda survey of the attitudes of adult Americans toward the next generation.[12] Only 23% of the respondents had anything positive to say about children and adolescents, while just 37% of the adults surveyed thought that today's children would grow up to make the world a better place; 61% believed that many young people were failing to learn such values as honesty, respect, and responsibility; and just 12% thought it was common for children and adolescents to treat people with respect. Writing in *The Nation*, Annette Fuentes observed that policies like zero tolerance really mean that "to be young is to be suspect,"[13] and a 1995 U.S. Supreme Court ruling supports the notion that simply being an adolescent is reasonable cause for authorities to suspect drug abuse and demand urine samples.[14] Massachusetts is one of a number of jurisdictions proposing widespread "voluntary" drug testing of high school students.[15] This negative assessment of the nation's youths undoubtedly lies behind the willingness of the American public to support a range of "get tough on kids" policies.

America's ambivalence toward young people manifests itself in the suspicion and fear of adolescents. Although we see children largely as burdens of responsibility, we nonetheless romanticize younger children as pliable potential citizens in need of close adult guidance and care. Various public policies seek to preserve their perceived innocence. Indeed, some have argued that an overly myopic focus on children is an attempt to defer—and potentially avoid—"dealing with" the miscreant tendencies of adolescence.[16]

Children under 18 are increasingly incarcerated in adult facilities (more than 21,000 youths under 18 are being held in adult correctional facilities).

The nation's low opinion of its youths is also apparent in the frequent media campaigns that link young people to a host of social "crises," including youth violence, teen pregnancy, violent and sexually explicit movies and video games, offensive lyrics in popular music, drug and alcohol abuse, smoking, and suicide. Underlying the critiques of the American Decency Association and others who blame popular culture for many of the problems of adolescence are two sets of assumptions. First, young people are assumed to mediate their senses of self through the popular culture of music and films. (Arguably, anyone living in this Information Age engages in that kind of identity work, finding and creating images, sounds, and messages that resonate with a sense of self.) However, the

association between young people and the texts of popular culture all but equates the two. This is a misuse and confusion of the terms and concepts of popular culture, youth subculture, and mass-mediated culture. In truth, the variety, breadth, and seemingly endless choices of mass-mediated texts are pervasive throughout the lives of citizens today.

The second assumption underlying the critiques of popular culture's impact on youths is that young people are so impressionable and shallow that a movie scene, rock lyric, or T-shirt slogan will lead them to violence, promiscuity, or drug addiction. While it is not our purpose here to explore the hotly debated relationships between images, beliefs, and behaviors, we simply note that it is taken for granted that youths in general cannot discriminate, be critical, or add perspectives to these media-based practices. In fact, the disregard of young people has begun to affect even those youths who are largely considered to be fortunate, supported, and well loved: the middle class. As sociologist and journalist Elliott Currie argues, the very culture of middle-class materialism and individualism has all but ensured a context of disconnection and stripped-down communities for young people.[17]

Fear, suspicion, and resentment toward the nation's young have led to the appearance of groups of child-free adults, such as No Kidding!, that challenge "family-friendly" public policies seen to (unfairly) favor people with children.[18] Advocacy groups for childless adults seek the creation of child-free zones in such public spaces as restaurants, supermarkets, and health clubs.[19] If it takes a village to raise a child, many villagers are abdicating their responsibilities.

In the face of such examples, we would do well to reconsider our sense of ourselves as a child-loving people. Examining the policies, discourses, and practices that surround children and adolescents sheds light on our ambivalence toward them, at best, and a profound mistrust and disrespect of our youngest charges, at worst. As educators, we have the responsibility to care for and guide our nation's young people, and so we must be prepared to challenge the policies that frame our work with them. Just as the kind of marketing directed toward adolescents tells us something about how certain economic sectors see them, so does the language of our education policies reveal our societal attitudes. Underlying education reform proposals are sets of assumptions about children and adolescents and about childhood and adolescence as stages of life. Underpinning child-centered and back-to-basics reforms, for example, are fundamentally different beliefs about how children learn and about the nature of childhood. Below, we examine some of the dominant themes underlying two strands of education reform—standards and accountability and safe schools—to see what we can learn about the nation's respect for its young people and for childhood and adolescence as special times of life. Then we briefly discuss an alternative and, we believe, more respectful vision of school reform that seeks to engage students in the process.

Standards and Accountability

Former *New York Times* education columnist Richard Rothstein distinguishes two meanings for standards-based reform:

> Standards-based reform has two contradictory meanings. Some policy makers want minimum standards representing what all students must know for promotion or graduation. Others want high standards as goals toward which all

students should strive but not all may achieve. Schools need both, but one standard cannot do both jobs.[20]

The first of these two strands of standards-based reform, which emphasizes high expectations for all students regardless of who they are or where they live, demonstrates respect for students by assuming that all children can (and should) learn. The second, as Rothstein observes, sets up high expectations by requiring that all students achieve the highest standards in all subjects. We argue below that this version of standards-based reform, which has come to dominate today's landscape of reform, is not respectful of children or of childhood and adolescence.

High stakes. Many education reformers assume that the failures of American education alleged in *A Nation at Risk* can be remedied only by high standards tied to sanctions. Presumably, because they lack the intrinsic motivation to excel in school, students can be motivated by the desire to avoid such sanctions as grade retention, the threat of failing courses, and the withholding of high school diplomas. But the desire to get tough on kids through high-stakes decisions is not supported by research. Neither grade retention nor course failure, for example, appears to be related to improved academic performance; grade retention does, however, increase the chances students will drop out of school.[21] Increased dropout rates may also be one of the principal effects of linking high school diplomas to the results of high-stakes tests.[22]

In 2003, youth jobless rates for ages 16–19 reached nearly 60%, as compared to the 6% unemployment rate for all ages.

Education reformers who demand that *all students* be held accountable to the highest standards often argue that they are motivated by faith in the ability of all children to learn challenging academic material. This logic sits uncomfortably beside the underlying assumption that extrinsic retribution is needed to motivate learning. Furthermore, the evidence indicates that *high standards* enforced through grade retention, failing grades, and high school exit exams are diminishing the life chances of significant numbers of students, especially poor and minority students, who are more likely to be retained or drop out of school.[23]

Intensification of schooling. Working from assumptions about needing extrinsic goals to motivate learners, the education reform of "getting tough on kids" has led to an intensification of schooling. Political platforms of more homework, longer school days, and longer school years imply that children need to be pushed to do more of what they've been asked to do in the past. Former Republican leader of the U.S. House of Representatives Newt Gingrich asserted that "every child . . . should be required to do at least two hours of homework a night, or they're being cheated for the rest of their lives."[24]

School districts across the country have taken up this challenge as elementary and secondary students in the U.S. are doing more homework than ever.[25] In some school districts, even kindergartners are doing up to 30 minutes of homework each night and working toward academic report cards.[26] But using intensified homework as a means of increasing academic achievement, especially for elementary students, is unsupported by research.[27] Nonetheless, for many children the increased homework demands, by extending the reach of schooling into children's homes, have

significantly reduced the time available for leisure and recreational opportunities.[28]

Schooling is also being intensified by cutting back on recess for elementary students, as up to 40% of the nation's school districts have either curtailed or eliminated recess.[29] A former superintendent of the Atlanta Public Schools defended the elimination of recess in his district by arguing that academic performance cannot be improved by having kids hanging on the monkey bars.[30] Similar reasoning has been used to justify cutting such educational "frills" as art and music. Of course, recess, art, and music are far more likely to be cut in urban schools—populated disproportionately by children of color and children living in poverty—than in suburban schools, suggesting that, as a nation, we believe that art, music, and play time are more important for some children than for others.

In 2002, nearly 9.3 million American children were not covered by health insurance.

Standardization. Enforcing standards through high-stakes testing demands standards that are specific, measurable, and uniform across jurisdictions.[31] Arguably, such uniform standards lead to a focus on those aspects of learning that can most easily be standardized and, inevitably, create a one-size-fits-all curriculum in which students are processed like so many widgets. Put in raw material at one end, treat it all in exactly the same way, and there will emerge at the other end a predictable and standardized product.[32]

Relegating students to such a passive role—treating them as objects—reveals a fundamental lack of respect for children and adolescents as rational, thoughtful, varied, and interesting people.[33] The expectation that standardized approaches to education can lead to "predictable and standardized" products assumes that, at some level, children (the raw material) are, essentially, all the same. This view of learning, which renders differences in students' learning opportunities, abilities, development levels, background knowledge, and experience irrelevant and even problematic, respects neither children and adolescents nor the homes, neighborhoods, and cultures from which they come.

Focusing relentlessly on academic achievement, as determined by high-stakes tests,[34] has turned many American classrooms into dreary workplaces where the basics are translated into worksheets while art, music, and recess games are seen as unnecessary distractions. High standards and high stakes are creating high-stress environments that leave little room for the playful and aesthetic pursuits of children—in or out of school. David Elkind's words echo across the decades:

> The concept of childhood, so vital to the traditional American way of life, is threatened with extinction in the society we have created. Today's child has become the unwilling, unintended victim of overwhelming stress—the stress born of rapid, bewildering social change and constantly rising expectations.[35]

Safe Schools

As a society, we love children—when they are under control. We hate children who defy us, children who are independent, quirky, free-thinking, nonconforming, idiosyncratic, precocious, or critical of adults.[36]

Despite evidence of a slight decline in violence in our schools,[37] Americans continue to identify lack of discipline, fighting, violence, and substance abuse as serious problems in our schools.[38] Certainly, official data on the decreasing incidence of violence in schools have not been as readily available to the public as media reports on school shootings, infighting among adolescent females, or violent plots in New Bedford, Massachusetts. Influenced by sensational reports in the media, most Americans would probably agree that the gravity of youth violence has increased dramatically in recent years.[39] Conflicts that used to result in fist fights and end with bloody noses, black eyes, and the occasional chipped tooth are now said to result in the drawing of weapons and to end with life-threatening lacerations and occasional gunshot wounds.

Whatever the actual rate of violence in our schools, no one would dispute that all students are entitled to safe, secure learning environments. There is, however, strong disagreement over the means by which safe schools might be best achieved. Social scientists and professional educators tend to prefer approaches to safe schools that focus on improving the school climate through expanded curricular offerings, decreased school and class size, increased staffing, and teaching the skills of conflict resolution.[40] Underlying these initiatives is an assumption that, given an environment that is respectful of their social, emotional, and intellectual needs, children and adolescents will be generally respectful of the needs of teachers and other students. From this perspective, respect begets respect.

Legislators, media pundits, and some segments of the public, on the other hand, are disposed to embrace politically expedient, get-tough-on-kids policies that play on the nation's generally low opinion and fear of its youths. The surveillance cameras, random locker searches, drug testing, and zero tolerance policies that characterize safe school efforts in many states reinforce the impression of youths as "savage beasts," a provocative phrase used by Lilia Bartolome in 1994 and a sentiment that is still common in contemporary circles.[41] The phrase invokes the image of young people who require nearly constant surveillance and control and justifies denying students any right to privacy or due process.

In the absence of data on the efficacy of various get-tough-on-youth policies, it could easily be concluded that the desire to enact these policies is motivated by a general loathing of youths, especially minority youths. The degree to which such policies predominate in urban schools, which are disproportionately populated by students of color, signals a national fear of minority youths out of control. The desire to control children of color may also underlie the proliferation of heavily scripted learning programs that effectively control the bodies and minds of students in urban schools.[42] Whatever the means, control is a quintessentially disrespectful act.

All children and adolescents are entitled to safe schools and challenging curricula. All too often, however, the impulse to create safe and challenging schools is underpinned by an antipathy toward children and adolescents that has resulted in policies and practices that are fundamentally disrespectful of American youths. While the effectiveness of these policies is debatable, they are rarely evaluated at all on the basis of their underlying regard for children and young people. Indeed, a recent book by two fellows at the conservative American Enterprise Institute ridicules school-based practices that attend to students' emotional well-being because they have no demonstrable link to academic achievement[43]—as if

students' psychological and emotional health are beyond the purview of schooling. Other conservative scholars have challenged the efficacy of health and dental care and hot lunch programs because they don't affect measures of academic achievement.[44] Examining the assumptions about our young people that pervade schooling is one way of taking an important step back to consider matters that are often drowned out by the cacophony of agendas, reforms, and platforms.

Including Student Voices: A Demonstration of Respect

I'm not adult enough to get a job and have my own apartment, but I'm adult enough to make decisions on my own, know right from wrong, have ideas about the world. That's why it's hard to be a teenager—it's like a middle stage. . . . To a certain extent [teachers] have to have a personality that students respond to. But that doesn't mean you have to be our best friend, because that will cause our education to suffer. I hate to admit it, but respect and authority are a part of the job. Kids expect adults to give us directions and boundaries, but it's a balance.[45]

The debate about reforming schools to make them better places to prepare young people to participate fully in the life of the community has been raging at least since the 1996 *Breaking Ranks* report from the National Association of Secondary School Principals. In particular, there has been great attention given to redesigning high schools into places that will improve student learning. There have been two main approaches: a policy-oriented, managerial approach and a student-centered approach.[46] The former advocates the alignment of standards, curriculum, and assessment. The latter advocates a cultural change in schools that creates an environment supportive of students' academic and social/emotional development.

Though there is much conversation about improving the relationships between adults and students, neither approach has advocated for including students' ideas as an essential element in a successful reform strategy. Many policy makers and school personnel believe that students lack the ability to be thoughtful about their own circumstances; therefore, little attention is paid to the knowledge and perspectives that students bring with them to the classroom. The students of What Kids Can Do, Inc. (WKCD) call the adults' mistrust into question. Vance, quoted above, was a member of a project to listen to students' thoughts about high school. Their work culminated in the book *Fires in the Bathroom: Advice for Teachers from High School Students,* from which Vance's words are taken. As this work demonstrates, young people are quite articulate about their experience of schooling, and they could make meaningful contributions to conversations regarding the reform of school culture, school governance, curriculum, and pedagogy.

The inclusion of the student voice could provide insights that would help policy makers and school personnel understand students' disengagement from school and how it leads to an increase in the dropout rate. It could provide adults with better insights into the various youth subcultures and young peoples' varied responses to them. "Meaningful and sustained school reform has at its core the involvement and engagement of students. Student voice can be a powerful mechanism for building school morale, improving school climate, and creating demand for high quality instruction," according to students in the Boston project Student Researchers for High School Renewal.[47]

Another WKCD project was the Students-as-Allies Initiative, which was designed to help students and teachers become allies in solving the problems arising in their school communities. In collaboration with the MetLife Foundation, WKCD selected five cities to participate in the project: Chicago, Houston, Oakland, Philadelphia, and St. Louis. WKCD identified local nonprofit organizations in each city to guide the process. The goals of the initiative were to support student voice, to strengthen the relationships between students and teachers in order to bolster school improvement efforts, to provide opportunities for students to serve as resources to their schools and communities, and to model relationship building. The nonprofit partners set the criteria for the development of teams made up of students and teachers to conduct research about their particular schools, to analyze the data, to engage in dialogue, to make recommendations for action, and, finally, to take action.[48]

One objective was to enlist students who were not usually recognized in their schools as leaders. In Houston, teachers wove the project into their writing classes so that all the students they taught could participate. In St. Louis, teachers recruited students in order to build a team that was representative of the many cliques in the school. In Oakland, students were enrolled in a special class designed to cultivate nontraditional leaders.

The participants decided that surveys would be the best tools for gathering information, and each team designed its own survey after looking at a common core of questions derived from a review of teacher and student surveys that had been conducted by MetLife. The focus was on "areas where knowing the thoughts of students and teachers would help students become actors in improving their schools." The teams were taught principles of survey research and guided through an analysis of the data. They learned to present the data and to host dialogues in their schools and communities.

The final phase of the project is to engage students in making recommendations for solutions and in taking appropriate actions. Each of the partnerships is in the early stages of taking action. Detailed information about the initiative can be found on the website of What Kids Can Do, Inc. (www.whatkidscando.org/index.asp).

The work of this group of students demonstrates that many young people care deeply about their own education and are capable of contributing to the reform of high schools in ways that could make deep and long-lasting changes for themselves and their teachers. These examples are not intended to serve as simplistic recommendations of actions to be taken at all levels and in all contexts. Rather, we offer them as examples of the kinds of initiatives that can be entertained when children and adolescents are treated as thoughtful participants in the enterprise of American education and not as problems to be overcome—in short, if they are treated with respect.

When we look past the naive belief that we treat our children with undying care, we find a disconcerting mix of policies and practices that are not respectful of children or of childhood. Examining these platforms and actions is far from a simple matter. We must move beyond simple quantitative tally sheets of how much money is devoted to education and the care of our young. We must also ask what kind of institutional spaces are created for children, what we expect from them, and what we have assumed about them that may in fact restrict their abilities to thrive.

In reform after reform, the lens has not been widened enough to consider underlying assumptions about children. In the application of NCLB to students, younger and older, a consistent set of mistakes marks the policy territory: a fundamental lack of explicit, evidence-based knowledge and respect for students coupled with an overwhelming emphasis on control and singular measurements. We must learn to question what forms the basis for our teaching, research, and policy. And in reviewing our practices, necessarily a discursive and recursive process, we must also consider the ways in which we represent, understand, and listen to our children and young people.

How then do we begin the considerable work of truly valuing and respecting our nation's young? Education is just one institutional site for the enactment, performance, and mediation of values, but it is a multifaceted one. Thus the efforts to reconfigure our beliefs and practices must affect the daily lives of students, teachers, researchers, and policy makers. All of these groups can take the same first step: examining the assumptions we hold about our young.

Notes

1. Barbara Kingsolver, *High Tide in Tucson: Essays from Now or Never* (New York: HarperPerennial, 1996), p. 100.

2. Letty Cottin Pogrebin, *Family Politics: Love and Power on an Intimate Frontier* (New York: McGraw-Hill, 1983), p. 42.

3. Ibid., p. 46.

4. Kingsolver, p. 102.

5. Ibid.

6. Alissa Quart, *Branded: The Buying and Selling of Teenagers* (Cambridge, Mass.: Perseus, 2003).

7. Kingsolver, p. 102.

8. Kingsolver, p. 101.

9. *The State of America's Children, 2004* (Washington, D.C.: Children's Defense Fund, 2004), p. 3; and "Young Children in Poverty Fact Sheet," National Center for Children in Poverty, 1999, available at www.nccp.org, click on Fact Sheets.

10. Jonathan Kozol, *Savage Inequalities: Children in America's Schools* (New York: Crown, 1991).

11. *The State of America's Children, 2004.*

12. Ann Duffet, Jean Johnson, and Steve Farkas, *Kids These Days: What Americans Really Think About the Next Generation* (Washington, D.C.: Public Agenda, 1999).

13. Annette Fuentes, "The Crackdown on Kids," *The Nation*, 15/22 June 1998, pp. 20–22.

14. Mike A. Males, *The Scapegoat Generation: America's War on Adolescents* (Monroe, Me.: Common Courage Press, 1996).

15. John R. Knight, "An F for School Drug Tests," *Boston Globe*, 13 June 2005, p. 15.

16. Allan Luke and Carmen Luke, "Adolescence Lost and Childhood Regained," *Australian Journal of Language and Literacy*, July 2001, pp. 91–120.

17. Elliott Currie, *The Road to Whatever: Middle-Class Culture and the Crisis of Adolescence* (New York: Henry Holt, 2005).

18. Scott Lehigh, "No Kidding," *Boston Globe*, 21 May 2000, pp. E-1, E-5.

19. Elinor Burkett, *The Baby Boon: How Family-Friendly America Cheats the Childless* (New York: Free Press, 2000).

20. Richard Rothstein, "In Judging Schools, One Standard Doesn't Fit All," *New York Times,* 8 December 1999, p. A-20.

21. See, for example, Eugene R. Johnson et al., "The Effects of Early Grade Retention on the Academic Achievement of Fourth-Grade Students," *Psychology in the Schools,* October 1990, pp. 333–38; William A. Owings and Susan Magliaro, "Grade Retention: A History of Failure," *Educational Leadership,* September 1998, pp. 86–88; Melissa Roderick, "Grade Retention and School Dropout: Investigating the Association," *American Educational Research Journal,* Winter 1994, pp. 729–59; Melissa Roderick and Eric Camburn, "Risk and Recovery from Course Failure in the Early Years of High School," *American Educational Research Journal,* Summer 1999, pp. 303–43; Lorrie A. Shepard and Mary L. Smith, "Synthesis of Research on Grade Retention," *Educational Leadership,* May 1999, pp. 84–88; and C. Kenneth Tanner and F. Edward Combs, "Student Retention Policy: The Gap Between Research and Practice," *Journal of Research in Childhood Education,* Fall/Winter 1993, pp. 69–77.

22. Walt Haney, "The Myth of the Texas Miracle in Education," *Education Policy Analysis Archives,* August 2000, available at http://epaa.asu.edu/epaa/v8n41.

23. Ibid.

24. Joel H. Spring, *Political Agendas for Education: From the Christian Coalition to the Green Party* (Mahwah, N.J.: Erlbaum, 1997), p. 16.

25. Sandra Hofferth, "Healthy Environments, Healthy Children: Children in Families," University of Michigan Institute for Social Research, ERIC ED 426779, 1998.

26. Diane Loupe, "Value of Homework Comes Under Question," *Atlanta Constitution,* 22 April 1999, p. 5JA.

27. Harris Cooper, *Homework* (New York: Longman, 1989).

28. Etta Kralovec and John Buell, *The End of Homework: How Homework Disrupts Families, Overburdens Children, and Limits Learning* (Boston, Mass.: Beacon Press, 2000).

29. Donald B. Gratz, "High Standards for Whom?," *Phi Delta Kappan,* May 2000, pp. 681–87; and Anthony D. Pellegrini and Catherine M. Bohn, "The Role of Recess in Children's Cognitive Performance and School Adjustment," *Educational Researcher,* January/February 2005, pp. 13–19.

30. Susan Ohanian, *One Size Fits Few: The Folly of Educational Standards* (Portsmouth, N.H.: Heinemann, 2000), pp. 13–14.

31. Anne T. Lockwood, *Standards: From Policy to Practice* (Thousand Oaks, Calif.: Corwin, 2000).

32. Frank Smith, *The Book of Learning and Forgetting* (New York: Teachers College Press, 1998).

33. Alfie Kohn, *The Schools Our Children Deserve: Moving Beyond Traditional Classrooms and "Tougher Standards"* (Boston: Houghton Mifflin, 1999).

34. Marc S. Tucker and Judy B. Codding, *Standards for Our Schools: How to Set Them, Measure Them, and Reach Them* (San Francisco, Calif.: Jossey-Bass, 1998).

35. David Elkind, *The Hurried Child: Growing Up Too Fast, Too Soon,* rev. ed. (Reading, Mass.: Addison-Wesley, 1988), p. 3.

36. Pogrebin, op. cit.

37. Michael F. Heaney and Robert J. Michela, "Safe Schools: Hearing Past the Hype," *High School Magazine,* May/June 1999, pp. 14–17.

38. Lowell C. Rose and Alec M. Gallup, "The 37th Annual Phi Delta Kappa/ Gallup Poll of the Public's Attitudes Toward the Public Schools," *Phi Delta Kappan,* September 2005, p. 44.

39. Paul M. Kingery, Mark B. Coggeshall, and Aaron A. Alford, "Weapon Carrying by Youth: Risk Factors and Prevention," *Education and Urban Society,* May 1999, pp. 309–33.

40. James A. Fox and Jack Levin, "The Hard (but Doable) Job of Making Schools Safe," *Boston Globe,* 22 August 1999, pp. F-1, F-3.

41. Lilia I. Bartolome, "Beyond the Methods Fetish: Toward a Humanizing Pedagogy," *Harvard Educational Review,* Summer 1994, pp. 173–94; and Nancy Lesko, *Act Your Age! A Cultural Construction of Adolescence* (New York: Routledge, 2001).

42. Jonathan Kozol, "Confections of Apartheid: A Stick-and-Carrot Pedagogy for the Children of Our Inner-City Poor," *Phi Delta Kappan,* December 2005, pp. 264–75.

43. Christina Hoff Sommers and Sally Satel, *One Nation Under Therapy: How the Helping Culture Is Eroding Self-Reliance* (New York: St. Martin's Press, 2005).

44. Gary L. Adams and Siegfried Engelmann, *Research on Direct Instruction: 25 Years Beyond DISTAR* (Seattle: Educational Achievement Systems, 1996).

45. Kathleen Cushman, *Fires in the Bathroom: Advice for Teachers from High School Students* (New York: New Press, 2003).

46. Lynn Olson, "Report Points Out Lack of Clarity for High School Reforms," *Education Week,* 19 May 2004.

47. *School Climate in Boston's High Schools: What Students Say* (Boston, Mass.: Boston Plan for Excellence, 2004).

48. Students as Allies, *Breaking Ranks: Changing an American Institution* (Reston, Va.: National Association of Secondary School Principals, 1996).

Curt Dudley-Marling is a professor of education at the Lynch School of Education, Boston College, Chestnut Hill, Mass., where **Janice Jackson** and **Lisa Patel Stevens** are assistant professors.

From *Phi Delta Kappan,* June 2006, pp. 748–755. Copyright © 2006 by Phi Delta Kappan. Reprinted by permission of Phi Delta Kappan and Curt Dudley-Marling, Janice Jackson, and Lisa Patel Stevens.

UNIT 5

Development During Adolescence and Young Adulthood

Unit Selections

Key Points to Consider

- What evidence do you see of pop culture's influence on those you contact daily?

- What parental behaviors help ensure a peaceful adolescence?

- What are the effects of sleep deprivation? Why do so many adolescents fail to get enough sleep?

- Should incarcerated adolescents continue their education in jail? What would a jail school teach?

- How do spiritual values impact the American psyche?

- Why is drug addiction viewed as a health issue? Can it be cured?

- How can young adults who take "off-ramps" to care for children find appropriate new "on-ramps" to resume their careers?

- Are men with depression underdiagnosed or misdiagnosed? Will improvement in treating male depression reduce drug abuse and/or suicide?

Student Web Site
www.mhcls.com

Internet References

Alcohol & Drug Addiction Resource Center
http://www.addict-help.com/

ADOL: Adolescent Directory On-Line
http://site.educ.indiana.edu/aboutus/AdolescenceDirectoryonLineADOL/tabid/4785/Default.aspx

AMA—Adolescent Health On-Line
http://www.ama-assn.org/ama/pub/category/1947.html

American Academy of Child and Adolescent Psychiatry
http://www.aacap.org/

Depression
http://www.depression-primarycare.org

The term "adolescence" was coined in 1904 by G. Stanley Hall, one of the world's first psychologists. He saw adolescence as a discrete stage of life that bridges the gap between sexual maturity (puberty) and socioemotional and cognitive maturity. He believed it to be characterized by "storm and stress." At the beginning of the twentieth century, it was typical for young men to begin working in middle childhood (there were no child labor laws), and for young women to become wives and mothers as soon as they were fertile and/or spoken for. At the turn of the twenty-first century, the beginning of adolescence was marked by the desire to be independent of parental control. The end of adolescence, which once coincided with the age of legal maturity (usually 16 or 18, depending on local laws), has now been extended upwards. Although legal maturity is now 18 (voting, enlisting in the armed services, owning property, marrying without permission), the social norm is to consider persons in their late teens as adolescents, not adults. The years between 18 and 21 are often problematic for youth tethered between adult and not-adult status. They can be married, with children, living in homes of their own, running their own businesses, yet not be able to drive their cars in certain places or at certain times. They can go to college and participate in social activities, but they cannot legally drink. Often the twenty-first birthday is viewed as a rite of passage into adulthood in the United States because it signals the legal right to buy and drink alcoholic beverages. "Maturity" is usually reserved for those who have achieved full economic as well as socioemotional independence as adults.

Erik Erikson, the personality theorist, marked the passage from adolescence to young adulthood by a change in the nuclear conflicts of two life stages: identity versus role confusion and intimacy versus isolation. Adolescents struggle to answer the question, "Who am I?" Young adults struggle to find a place within the existing social order where they can feel intimacy rather than isolation. In the 1960s, Erikson wrote that females resolve both their conflicts of identity and intimacy by living vicariously through their husbands, an unacceptable idea to many females today.

As adolescence has been extended, so too has young adulthood. One hundred years ago, life expectancy did not extend too far beyond menopause for women and retirement for men. Young adulthood began when adolescents finished puberty. Parents of teenagers were middle-aged, between 35 and 55. Later marriages and delayed childbearing have redefined the line between young adulthood and middle age. Many people today consider themselves young adults well into their 40s.

Jean Piaget, the cognitive theorist, marked the end of the development of mental processes with the end of adolescence. Once full physical maturity, including brain maturity, was achieved, one reached the acme of his or her abilities to assimilate, accommodate, organize, and adapt to sensations, perceptions, associations, and discriminations. Piaget did not feel cognitive processing of information ceased with adulthood. He

© Banana Stock/Jupiter Images

believed, however, that cognitive judgments would not reach a stage higher than the abstract, hypothetical, logical reasoning of formal operations. Today many cognitive theorists believe postformal operations are possible.

The first article, "Parents or Pop Culture? Children's Heroes and Role Models," explores how parents, families, and minorities are portrayed in the popular culture and how those portrayals affect behaviors.

The second article, "A Peaceful Adolescence," addresses the G. Stanley Hall belief that adolescence was a stage of life marked by "storm and stress." While some teenagers do have conflicts with their parents, new research documents that many teenagers have peaceful passages through adolescence. The authors of this article, Barbara Kantrowitz and Karen Springen, report on what adults do to nurture successful teen years.

The third article, "Homeroom Zombies," discusses the effects of sleep deprivation. Many adolescents fail to get the recommended nine hours per night, desirable for optimal growth and development during puberty. The writers, an M.D., Lawrence Epstein, and his co-author, Steven Mardon, detail a number of consequences of lack of sleep during the growth spurt. They also give many reasons why teens and their parents fail to recognize the importance of good sleep habits.

The fourth selection, "Jail Time Is Learning Time," describes efforts to help jailed youth acquire GED instruction and earn high school equivalency diplomas. The program described also teaches anger management and vocational/job skills. Many adolescents are incarcerated in the Unites States every year. They should not be forgotten.

The first article in the Young Adulthood portion of this unit, "How Spirit Blooms," describes the mid-20's faith journey of a woman raised in the Roman Catholic religion. It gives factual information about many contemporary spiritual belief systems, without being preachy. Readers will be stimulated to discuss many of Suzanne Clores' travel discoveries.

The second article of this unit, "What Addicts Need," discusses the bio-psycho-social-spiritual aspects of drug addiction.

It is an illness. New drugs, and possibly future vaccines, may drastically alter the way persons who abuse drugs are viewed and rehabilitated.

"Getting Back on Track" is an exposition about adults who take time off from their career tracks to care for family. The "off-ramps" are not difficult. However, finding an appropriate "on-ramp" leading to a fulfilling job that utilizes the young adult's talents and education may be very troublesome. Daniel McGinn reports that some business schools are providing assistance. They are offering, or planning to offer, courses that teach about how to job hunt and/or jump-start a second career.

The last article of this unit, "Men and Depression: Facing Darkness," explores the belief that men are in control and do not experience depression. However, the fact is, they do. It often leads to drug abuse (self-medication) or suicide. The author explains how medication and psychotherapy can lift the darkness experienced by depressed men.

Parents or Pop Culture? Children's Heroes and Role Models

What kind of heroes a culture promotes reveals a great deal about that culture's values and desires.

KRISTIN J. ANDERSON AND DONNA CAVALLARO

One of the most important features of childhood and adolescence is the development of an identity. As children shape their behavior and values, they may look to heroes and role models for guidance. They may identify the role models they wish to emulate based on possession of certain skills or attributes. While the child may not want to be exactly like the person, he or she may see *possibilities* in that person. For instance, while Supreme Court Justice Ruth Bader Ginsberg may not necessarily directly influence girls and young women to become lawyers, her presence on the Supreme Court may alter beliefs about who is capable of being a lawyer or judge (Gibson & Cordova, 1999).

Parents and other family members are important role models for children, particularly early on. Other influences may be institutional, such as schools, or cultural, such as the mass media. What kind of heroes a culture promotes reveals a great deal about the culture's values and desires. Educators not only can model important behaviors themselves, but also can teach about values, events, and people that a culture holds dear.

Television, movies, computer games, and other forms of media expose children to an endless variety of cultural messages. Which ones do children heed the most? Whom do children want to be like? Do their role models vary according to children's ethnicity and gender? Finally, what role can educators play in teaching children about role models they may never have considered?

This article examines the impact of the mass media on children's choices of heroes and role models. The authors address the questions posed above in light of results from a survey and focus groups conducted with children ages 8 to 13.

The Menu of Pop Culture Choices
Television and Film for Children

Male characters—cartoon or otherwise—continue to be more prevalent in children's television and film than female characters. Gender-stereotyped behaviors continue to be the norm. For instance, male characters are more commonly portrayed as independent, assertive, athletic, important, attractive, technical, and responsible than female characters. They show more ingenuity, anger, leadership, bravery, and aggression, and they brag, interrupt, make threats, and even laugh more than female characters do. In fact, since male characters appear so much more frequently than female characters, they do more of almost *everything* than female characters. Also, while the behavior of female characters is somewhat less stereotypical than it was 20 years ago, in some ways male characters behave *more* stereotypically than 20 years ago (for instance, males are now in more leadership roles, are more bossy, and are more intelligent) (Thompson & Zerbinos, 1995). These gender-stereotyped images, and the inflexibility of male characters' roles, make for a restricted range of role models.

Parents, educators, and policymakers are also concerned about the aggressive and violent content in children's programs. Gerbner (1993) studied the violent content of children's programs and observed that "despite all the mayhem, only 3.2% of Saturday morning characters suffer any injury"; thus, children do not learn about the likely consequences of aggressive action. In children's shows, bad characters are punished 59 percent of the time. Even more telling, good characters who engage in violence are punished only 18 percent of the time. The characters that might be the most appealing to kids—the heroes and protagonists—rarely feel remorse, nor are they reprimanded or impeded when they engage in violence (National Television Violence Study, 1998). The authors found that 77 percent of the children surveyed watch television every day. Thus, many children may be learning to use violence as a problem-solving tool.

Characters in animated films also tend to follow stereotypes. While some positive changes in the portrayal of ethnic minority and female characters can be noted, both groups often remain narrowly defined in children's animated films. In his discussion of Disney films, Henry Giroux (1997) notes how the villains in the film *Aladdin* are racially stereotyped. The main character, Aladdin, the hero of the film, is drawn with very light skin, European features, and no accent. Yet the villains in the story appear as Middle Eastern caricatures: they have beards, large noses, sinister eyes, heavy accents, and swords. *Pocahontas,* who in real life was a young Native American girl, was portrayed by Disney as a brown-skinned, Barbie-like supermodel with an hourglass figure (Giroux, 1997). Consequently, animated characters, even those based on historical record, are either stereotyped or stripped of any meaningful sign of ethnicity. Fortunately, educators have the power to counter such unrealistic images with more accurate representations of historical characters.

Real-Life Television Characters

While some progress can be seen in the representation of ethnic minorities on television, the late 1990s actually brought a decrease in the number of people of color on prime time programming. In 1998, only 19 percent of Screen Actors Guild roles went to people of color. Roles for African American, Latinos, and Native Americans decreased from 1997 to 1998 (Screen Actors Guild [SAG], 1999). Women make up fewer than 40 percent of the characters in prime time. Female characters tend to be younger than male characters, conveying the message to viewers that women's youthfulness is more highly valued than other qualities. In terms of work roles, however, female characters' occupations are now less stereotyped, while male characters' occupations continue to be stereotyped (Signorielli & Bacue, 1999). This research

suggests that girls' potential role models are somewhat less gender-stereotyped than before, while boy's potential role models are as narrowly defined as ever.

From Comic Book to Playground

Superheroes are the larger-than-life symbols of American values and "maleness." Perhaps the medium in which superheroes are most classically represented is comic books, which date back to the 1930s. The role of the hero is central to the traditional comic book. While female superheroes can be found in comics today (e.g., Marvel Girl, Phoenix, Shadow Cat, Psylocke), they represent only a small proportion—about 24 percent of Marvel Universe superhero trading cards (Young, 1993). Moreover, women and people of color do not fare well in superhero comics. To the extent that female characters exist, they often appear as victims and nuisances. People of color are marginalized as well. African American and Native American characters are more likely to be portrayed as villains, victims, or simply incompetent than as powerful and intelligent (Pecora, 1992).

One indirect way to gauge the impact of role models on children is to examine the nature of superhero play. Superhero play involving imitation of media characters with superhuman powers is more prevalent among boys than girls (Bell & Crosbie, 1996). This might be a function of the mostly male presence of superhero characters in comics and on television, or it may be due to girls receiving more sanctions from parents and teachers against playing aggressively. Children's imitations of superheroes in play concerns many classroom teachers, because it usually involves chasing, wrestling, kicking, and mock battles. Some researchers argue that superhero play may serve an important developmental function by offering children a sense of power in a world dominated by adults, thus giving children a means of coping with their frustrations. Superhero play also may allow children to grapple with ideas of good and evil and encourage them to work through their own anxieties about safety. Such play also may help children safely express anger and aggression (Boyd, 1997).

Other researchers and educators express concern that superhero play may legitimize aggression, endanger participants, and encourage stereotypical male dominance (Bell & Crosbie, 1996). One researcher observed children's superhero play in a school setting and found that boys created more superhero stories than girls did, and that girls often were excluded from such play. When girls were included they were given stereotypical parts, such as helpers or victims waiting to be saved. Even powerful female X-Men characters were made powerless in the boys' adaptations (Dyson, 1994). Thus, without teacher intervention or an abundance of female superheroes, superhero play may only serve to reinforce gender stereotypes.

One way to gauge popular culture's influence on superhero play is to compare the kind of play children engaged in before and after the arrival of television. In one retrospective study (French & Pena, 1991), adults between the ages of 17 and 83 provided information about their favorite childhood play themes, their heroes, and the qualities of those heroes. While certain methodological pitfalls common to retrospective studies were unavoidable, the findings are nevertheless intriguing. People who grew up before television reported engaging in less fantasy hero play and playing more realistically than kids who grew up with television. While media was the main source of heroes for kids who grew up with television, the previous generations found their heroes not only from the media, but also from direct experience, friends/siblings, and parents' occupations (French & Pena, 1991).

Recent Media Forms: Music Television and Video Games

Video games and music television videos are relatively recent forms of media. In a recent poll, girls and boys from various ethnic backgrounds reported that television and music were their favorite forms of media (Children Now, 1999). What messages about race/ethnicity and gender emerge from music videos—the seemingly perfect merger of children's favorite two media? Seidman (1999) found that the majority of characters were white (63 percent) and a majority were male (63 percent). When people of color, especially women of color, appeared in a video, their characters were much less likely to hold white collar jobs. In fact, their occupations were more gender-stereotyped than in real life. Gender role behavior overall was stereotypical. Thus, music television is yet another domain that perpetuates racial and gender stereotypes.

In the survey described below, the authors found that nearly half (48 percent) of the children surveyed played video and computer games every day or almost every day. Boys, however, were much more likely than girls to play these games. Of those who play computer/video games every day or almost every day, 76 percent are boys and only 24 percent are girls. Consequently, girls and boys might be differentially influenced by the images represented in video and computer games.

What *are* the images presented in video and computer games? Dietz's (1998) content analysis of popular video and computer games found that 79 percent of the games included aggression or violence. Only 15 percent of the games showed women as heroes or action characters. Indeed, girls and women generally were *not* portrayed—30 percent of the videos did not include girls or women at all. When female characters were included, 21 percent of the time they were the damsel in distress. Other female characters were portrayed as evil or as obstacles. This research points to at least two implications of these games. First, girls may not be interested in playing these video and computer games, because the implicit message is that girls are not welcome as players, and that girls and women can only hope to be saved, destroyed, or pushed aside (see also Signorielli, 2001). Second, these images of girls and women found in video and computer games may influence boys' perceptions of gender.

In the past few years, a growing number of computer and video games geared toward girls have been made available by companies such as Purple Moon and Girl Games. These games have adventurous content without the violence typical of games geared toward boys. Two of the best-selling computer games for girls, however, have been *Cosmopolitan Virtual Makeover* and *Barbie Fashion Designer*. While these games may encourage creativity, ultimately their focus is on beauty. One columnist addresses the dilemma of creating games that will appeal to girls while fostering creativity and ingenuity:

> A girl given a doll is being told, "Girls play with dolls just like mommies take care of babies." A boy given a computer game is being told, "Boys play with computers just like daddies use them for work." A girl given *Barbie Fashion Designer* is being told, "Girls play with computers just like girls play with dolls." A lucky few might get the message that, as some girls exchange dolls for real babies, others might progress from *Barbie Fashion Designer* to real-life fashion designer, or engineering systems designer, or software designer. But there's a good chance that many will not. (Ivinski, 1997, p. 28)

As more and more educators begin using the Internet, CD-ROMs, and videos as teaching tools (Risko, 1999), they will be faced with the challenge of finding materials that fairly represent a wide range of characters, people, and behavior. Paradoxically, the use of "new" technology, such as CD-ROMs and computer games, implies that a student is going to enjoy a progressive, cutting-edge experience. However, educators must be vigilant about the content, as they should be with any textbook or film. The cutting-edge format of these new technologies does not guarantee nonstereotyped material.

A Survey of Children's Role Models and Heroes

Whom do children actually choose as role models, and why? The authors surveyed children about their heroes and role models, both people they know and famous people or imaginary characters. Survey questions also addressed children's interaction with television, film, computer/video games, books, and comic books. The children talked about their answers in small groups. One hundred and seventy-nine children, ages 8 to 13, were surveyed from five day camp sites in central and southern California. The ethnic breakdown of the survey sample was as follows: 24 African Americans, 31 Asian Americans, 74 Latinos, 1 Middle Eastern American, 2 Native Americans, 45 whites, and 2 "other." Ninety-five girls and 84 boys participated. The samples of ethnic and gender categories were then weighted so that each of these demographic groups, when analyzed, reflects their actual contribution to the total population of children in the United States.

Do Children Admire People They Know or Famous People?

The survey began with the following: "We would like to know whom you look up to and admire. These might be people you know, or they might be famous people or characters. You may want to be like them or you might just think they are cool." More respondents described a person they knew (65 percent) rather than a person they did not know, such as a person or character in the media (35 percent). When asked in focus groups why they picked people they knew instead of famous people, one 10-year-old white girl said, "I didn't put down people I don't know because when nobody's paying attention, they do something bad." Another student said, "Some [media figures] are just not nice. Some famous people act good on TV but they're really horrible." Thus, some children employed a level of skepticism when judging the worthiness of a role model.

Figure 1 represents the percentages of role models the children knew versus media heroes they identified. Similar to the overall sample, 70 percent of the African American and 64 percent of the White children chose people they knew as heroes. In contrast, only 35 percent of the Asian American kids and 49 percent of the Latino kids named people they knew. This latter finding seems paradoxical; Asian American and Latino children

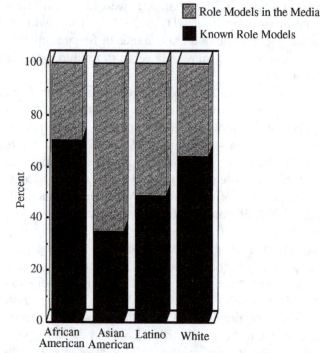

Figure 1   Percentages of Known Role Models and Media Role Models.

would seem more likely to choose people they know as role models because their ethnic groups are represented less frequently in mass media than are African Americans and whites. Perhaps Asian American and Latino children have internalized a message that they should not look up to fellow Asian Americans or Latinos as role models, or it may be a byproduct of assimilation. Obviously, further work in this area is needed.

On average, responses from girls and boys differed. While both girls and boys named people they knew as their heroes, 67 percent of the girls did so as compared with only 58 percent of the boys. Since boys and men are seen more frequently as sports stars, actors, and musicians, girls may have a smaller pool of potential role models from which to choose. Another factor might be that the girls in this study reported watching less television than the boys did, and so they may have known fewer characters. Sixty-seven percent of the girls reported watching television one hour a day or more, while 87 percent of the boys reported watching television this amount.

Do Children Choose Role Models Who Are Similar to Themselves?

One feature of role modeling is that children tend to choose role models whom they find relevant and with whom they can compare themselves (Lockwood & Kunda, 2000).

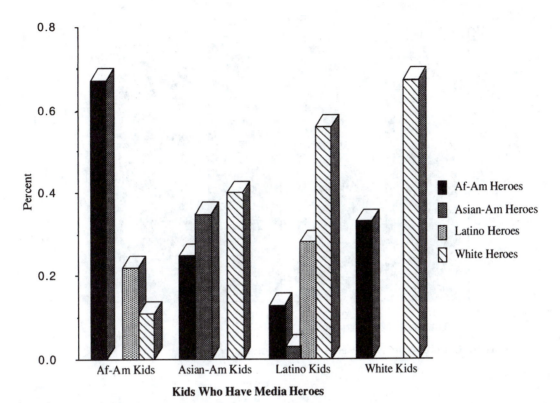

Figure 2   Ethnicity of Media Heroes.

Children who do not "see themselves" in the media may have fewer opportunities to select realistic role models. Two ways to assess similarity is to consider the ethnicity and gender of children's chosen role models. Do children tend to select heroes who are of their same ethnic background? Because data was not available on the ethnic background of the reported role models whom the children knew personally, the authors examined only the heroes from the media, whose backgrounds were known, to explore this question (see Figure 2). African American and white children were more likely to have media heroes of their same ethnicity (67 percent for each). In contrast, Asian American and Latino children chose more white media heroes than other categories (40 percent and 56 percent, respectively). Only 35 percent of the Asian Americans respondents, and 28 percent of the Latino respondents, chose media heroes of their own ethnicity.

How can we explain the fact that African American and white children are more likely to have media heroes of their same ethnicity, compared to Asian American and Latino children? There is no shortage of white characters for white children to identify with in television and film, and African Americans make up about 14 percent of television and theatrical characters (SAG, 2000). While African American characters are represented less frequently than white characters, their representation on television, film, and music television is much higher than for Asian American and Latino characters (e.g., Asians represent 2.2 percent, and Latinos represent 4.4 percent, of television and film characters) (SAG, 2000). Also, fewer famous athletes are Asian American or Latino, compared to African American or white.

Also of interest was whether children choose role models of the same, or other, gender. Overall, children in this study more often chose a same-gender person as someone they look up to and admire. This pattern is consistent across all four ethnic groups, and stronger for boys than girls. Only 6 percent of the boys chose a girl or woman, while 24 percent of the girls named a boy or man. Asian American boys actually picked male heroes exclusively. Asian American girls chose the fewest female role models (55 percent) compared to the other girls (see Figure 3). These findings associated with Asian American children present a particular challenge for educators. Asian Americans, and particularly Asian American women, are seldom presented as heroes in textbooks. This is all the more reason for schools to provide a broader and more diverse range of potential role models.

At the same time, it has been reported that boys will tend to imitate those who are powerful (Gibson & Cordova, 1999). Thus, while boys tend to emulate same-gender models more than girls do, boys may emulate a woman if

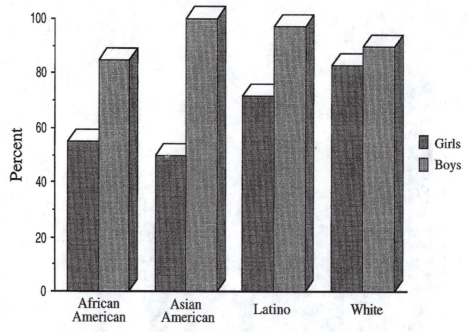

Figure 3   Children Who Have Same-Gender Role Models.

she is high in social power. Therefore, boys may be especially likely to have boys and men as role models because they are more likely to be portrayed in positions of power. It also has been noted that college-age women select men *and* women role models with the same frequency, whereas college-age men still tend to avoid women role models. The fact that young women choose both genders as role models might be a result of the relative scarcity of women in powerful positions to serve as role models (Gibson & Cordova, 1999).

Who Are Children's Role Models and Heroes?

Overall, children most frequently (34 percent) named their parents as role models and heroes. The next highest category (20 percent) was entertainers; in descending order, the other categories were friends (14 percent), professional athletes (11 percent), and acquaintances (8 percent). Authors and historical figures were each chosen by only 1 percent of the children.

Patterns were somewhat different when ethnicity was taken into account. African American and white children chose a parent more frequently (30 percent and 33 percent, respectively). In contrast, Asian Americans and Latinos chose entertainers (musicians, actors, and television personalities) most frequently (39 percent for Asian Americans and 47 percent for Latinos), with parents coming in

second place. When gender was taken into account, both girls and boys most frequently mentioned a parent (girls 29 percent, boys 34 percent), while entertainers came in second place. Figure 4 illustrates these patterns.

When taking both ethnicity and gender into account, the researchers found that Asian American and Latina girls most frequently picked entertainers (50 percent of the Asian American girls and 41 percent of the Latinas), while African American and white girls chose parents (33 percent and 29 percent, respectively). Asian American boys most frequently named a professional athlete (36 percent), African American boys most frequently picked a parent (30 percent), Latino boys most frequently chose entertainers (54 percent), and white boys picked parents (38 percent).

What Qualities About Their Role Models and Heroes Do Children Admire?

When asked why they admired their heroes and role models, the children most commonly replied that the person was nice, helpful, and understanding (38 percent). Parents were appreciated for their generosity, their understanding, and for "being there." For instance, an 11-year-old African American girl who named her mother as her hero told us, "I like that she helps people when they're in a time of need." Parents were also praised for the lessons they teach

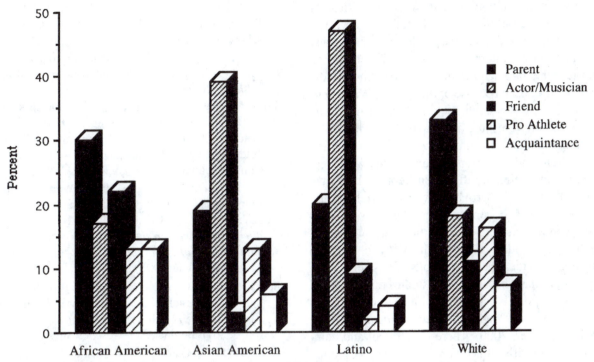

Figure 4   Most Frequently Chosen Role Models By Ethnicity.

their kids. A 9-year-old Asian American boy told us, "I like my dad because he is always nice and he teaches me."

The second most admired feature of kids' role models was skill (27 percent). The skills of athletes and entertainers were most often mentioned. One 12-year-old white boy said he admires Kobe Bryant because "he's a good basketball player and because he makes a good amount of money." A 10-year-old Asian American girl chose Tara Lipinski because "she has a lot of courage and is a great skater." A 9-year-old Latino boy picked Captain America and said, "What I like about Captain America is his cool shield and how he fights the evil red skull." The third most frequently mentioned characteristic was a sense of humor (9 percent), which was most often attributed to entertainers. For instance, a 10-year-old Latino boy picked Will Smith "because he's funny. He makes jokes and he dances funny."

These findings held true for children in all four ethnic groups and across the genders, with two exceptions: boys were more likely than girls to name athletes for their skill, and entertainers for their humor. Given the media attention to the U.S. women's soccer team victory in the World Cup in 1999, and the success of the WNBA (the women's professional basketball league), the researchers expected girls to name women professional athletes as their heroes. However, only four girls in the study did so. Despite recent strides in the visibility of women's sports,

the media continue to construct men's sports as the norm and women's sports as marginal (e.g., references to men's athletics as "sports" and women's athletics as "women's sports").

When children's heroes were media characters, African American and white children were more likely to name media heroes of their same ethnicity. In contrast, Asian American and Latino children tended to name media heroes who were not of their same ethnicity.

Summary and Implications

Whether the children in this study had heroes they knew in real life, or whether they chose famous people or fictional characters, depended, to some extent, on the respondents' ethnicity and gender. Overall, however, the most frequently named role model for kids was a parent. This is good news for parents, who must wonder, given the omnipresence of the media, whether they have any impact at all on their children. Popular culture was a significant source of heroes for children as well. Entertainers were the second most frequently named role models for the children, and the number increases significantly if you add professional athletes to that category. The attributes that children valued depended on whom they chose. For instance, children who named parents named them because they are helpful and understanding. Media characters were chosen because of their skills. When children's heroes were media characters, African American and white children were more likely to name media heroes of their same ethnicity. In contrast, Asian American and Latino children tended to name media heroes who were not of their same ethnicity. Children kept to their own gender when choosing a hero; boys were especially reluctant to choose girls and women as their heroes.

The frequency with which boys in this study named athletes as their role models is noteworthy. Only four girls in the study did the same. The implications of this gender difference are important, because many studies find that girls' participation in sports is associated with a number of positive attributes, such as high self-esteem and self-efficacy (Richman & Shaffer, 2000). Therefore, school and community support of girls' athletic programs and recognition of professional women athletes would go a long way to encourage girls' participation in sports, as well as boys' appreciation of women athletes as potential role models.

The mass media are hindered by a narrow view of gender, and by limited, stereotyped representations of ethnic minorities. Parents and educators must take pains to expose children to a wider variety of potential role models than popular culture does. Historical figures and authors constituted a tiny minority of heroes named by the children surveyed. Educators can play a significant role by exposing students to a wide range of such historical heroes, including people from various professions, people of color, and women of all races.

Finally, educators could capitalize on children's need for guidance to expose them to a greater variety of role models. Doing so affirms for the children that their race and gender are worthy of representation. A variety of potential heroes and role models allows children to appreciate themselves and the diversity in others.

References

Bell, R., & Crosbie, C. (1996, November 13). Superhero play of 3-to 5-year-old children. Available: http://labyrinth.net .au/~cccav/ sept97/superhero.html.

Boyd, B. J. (1997). Teacher response to superhero play: To ban or not to ban. *Childhood Education, 74*, 23–28.

Children Now. (1999, September). *Boys to men: Messages about masculinity*. Oakland, CA: Author.

Dietz, T. L. (1998). An examination of violence and gender role portrayals in video games: Implications for gender socialization. *Sex Roles, 38*, 425–433.

Dyson, A. H. (1994). The ninjas, the X-men, and the ladies: Playing with power and identity in an urban primary school. *Teachers College Record, 96*, 219–239.

French, J., & Pena, S. (1991). Children's hero play of the 20th century: Changes resulting from television's influence. *Child Study Journal, 21*, 79–94.

Gerbner, G. (1993). *Women and minorities on television: A study in casting and fate*. A report to the Screen Actors Guild and the American Federation of Radio and Television Artists, Philadelphia: The Annenberg School of Communication, University of Pennsylvania.

Gibson, D. E., & Cordova, D. I. (1999). Women's and men's role models: The importance of exemplars. In A. J. Murrell, F. J. Crosby, & R. J. Ely (Eds.), *Mentoring dilemmas: Developmental relationships within multicultural organizations* (pp. 121–141). Mahwah, NJ: Lawrence Erlbaum Associates.

Giroux, H. A. (1997). Are Disney movies good for your kids? In S. R. Steinberg & J. L. Kincheloe (Eds.), *Kinderculture: The corporate construction of childhood* (pp. 53–67). Boulder, CO: Westview Press.

Ivinski, P. (1997). Game girls: Girl market in computer games and educational software. *Print, 51*, 24–29.

Lockwood, P., & Kunda, Z. (2000). Outstanding role models: Do they inspire or demoralize us? In A. Tesser, R. B. Felson, et al. (Eds.), *Psychological perspectives on self and identity* (pp. 147–171). Washington, DC: American Psychological Association.

National Television Violence Study. Vol. 3. (1998). Thousand Oaks, CA: Sage.

Pecora, N. (1992). Superman/superboys/supermen: The comic book hero as socializing agent. In S. Craig (Ed.), *Men, masculinity, and the media* (pp. 61–77). Newbury Park, CA: Sage.

Richman, E. L., & Shaffer, D. R. (2000). "If you let me play sports": How might sport participation influence the self-esteem of adolescent females? *Psychology of Women Quarterly, 24*, 189–199.

Risko, V. J. (1999). The power and possibilities of video technology and intermediality. In L. Semali & A. Watts Pailliet (Eds.), *Intermediality: The teachers' handbook of critical media literacy* (pp. 129–140). Boulder, CO: Westview Press.

Screen Actors Guild. (1999, May 3). *New Screen Actors Guild employment figures reveal a decline in roles for Latinos, African American and Native American Indian performers*. Press Release. Available: www.sag.org.

Screen Actors Guild. (2000, December 20). *Screen Actors Guild employment statistics reveal percentage increases in available roles for African Americans and Latinos, but total number of roles to minorities decrease in 1999*. Press Release. Available: www.sag.org.

Seidman, S. A. (1999). Revisiting sex-role stereotyping in MTV videos. *International Journal of Instructional Media, 26*, 11.

Signorielli, N. (2001). Television's gender role images and contribution to stereotyping: Past, present, future. In D. G. Singer & J. L. Singer (Eds.), *Handbook of children and the media* (pp. 341–358). Thousand Oaks, CA: Sage.

Signorielli, N., & Bacue, A. (1999). Recognition and respect: A content analysis of prime-time television characters across three decades. *Sex Roles, 40,* 527–544.

Thompson, T. L., & Zerbinos, E. (1995). Gender roles in animated cartoons: Has the picture changed in 20 years? *Sex Roles, 32,* 651–673.

Young, T. J. (1993). Women as comic book superheroes: The "weaker sex" in the Marvel universe. *Psychology: A Journal of Human Behavior, 30,* 49–50.

KRISTIN J. ANDERSON is Assistant Professor, Psychology and Women's Studies, Antioch College, Yellow Springs, Ohio. DONNA CAVALLARO is graduate student, counseling psychology, Santa Clara University, Santa Clara, California.

Authors' Notes—This project was conducted in conjunction with Mediascope, a not-for-profit media education organization. The terms "hero" and "role model" tend to be used interchangeably in the literature. When a distinction between the terms is made, role models are defined as known persons (e.g., parents, teachers) and heroes are defined as figures who may be less attainable, or larger than life. Both kinds of persons and figures are of interest here; therefore, the terms are used interchangeably, and we specify whether known people or famous figures are being discussed.

A Peaceful Adolescence

The teen years don't have to be a time of family storm and stress. Most kids do just fine and now psychologists are finding out why that is.

BARBARA KANTROWITZ AND KAREN SPRINGEN

At 17, Amanda Hund is a straight-A student who loves competing in horse shows. The high school junior from Willmar, Minn., belongs to her school's band, orchestra and choir. She regularly volunteers through her church and recently spent a week working in an orphanage in Jamaica. Usually, however, she's closer to home, where her family eats dinner together every night. She also has a weekly breakfast date with her father, a doctor, at a local coffee shop. Amanda credits her parents for her relatively easy ride through adolescence. "My parents didn't sweat the small stuff," she says. "They were always very open. You could ask any question."

Is the Hund family for real? Didn't they get the memo that says teens and their parents are supposed to be at odds until . . . well, until forever? Actually, they're very much for real, and according to scientists who study the transition to adulthood, they represent the average family's experience more accurately than all those scary TV movies about out-of-control teens. "Research shows that most young people go through adolescence having good relationships with their parents, adopting attitudes and values consistent with their parents' and end up getting out of the adolescent period and becoming good citizens," says Richard Lerner, Bergstrom chair of applied developmental science at Tufts University. This shouldn't be news—but it is, largely because of widespread misunderstanding of what happens during the teen years. It's a time of transition, just like the first year of parenthood or menopause. And although there are dramatic hormonal and physical changes during this period, catastrophe is certainly not preordained. A lot depends on youngsters' innate natures combined with the emotional and social support they get from the adults around them. In other words, parents do matter.

The roots of misconceptions about teenagers go back to the way psychologists framed the field of adolescent development a century ago. They were primarily looking for explanations of why things went wrong. Before long, the idea that this phase was a period of storm and stress made its way into the popular consciousness. But in the last 15 years, developmental scientists have begun to re-examine these assumptions. Instead of focusing on kids who battle their way through the teen years, they're studying the dynamics of success.

At the head of the pack are Lerner and his colleagues, who are in the midst of a major project that many other researchers are following closely. It's a six-year longitudinal study of exactly what it takes to turn out OK and what adults can do to nurture those behaviors. "Parents and sometimes kids themselves often talk about positive development as the absence of bad," says Lerner. "What we're trying to do is present a different vision and a different vocabulary for young people and parents."

The first conclusions from the 4-H Study of Positive Youth Development, published in the February issue of *The Journal of Early Adolescence,* show that there are quantifiable personality traits possessed by all adolescents who manage to get to adulthood without major problems. Psychologists have labeled these traits "the 5 Cs": competence, confidence, connection, character and caring. These characteristics theoretically lead to a sixth C, contribution (similar to civic engagement). The nomenclature grows out of observations in recent years by a number of clinicians, Lerner says, but his study is the first time researchers have measured how these characteristics influence successful growth.

The 5 Cs are interconnected, not isolated traits, Lerner says. For example, competence refers not just to academic ability but also to social and vocational skills. Confidence includes self-esteem as well as the belief that you can make a difference in the world. The value of the study, Lerner says, is that when it is completed next year, researchers will have a way to quantify these characteristics and eventually determine what specific social and educational programs foster them.

During these years, parents should stay involved as they help kids move on.

In the meantime, parents can learn a lot from this rethinking of the teen years. Don't automatically assume that your kids become alien beings when they leave middle school. They still care what their parents think and they still need love and guidance—although in a different form. Temple University psychology professor Laurence Steinberg, author of "The Ten Basic Principles of Good Parenting," compares raising kids to building a boat that you eventually launch. Parents have to build a strong underpinning so their kids are equipped to face whatever's ahead. In the teen years, that means staying involved as you slowly let go. "One of the things that's natural in adolescence is that kids are going to pull away from their parents as they become increasingly interested in peers," says Steinberg. "It's important for parents to hang in there, for them not to pull back in response to that."

Communication is critical. "Stay in touch with your kids and make sure they feel valued and appreciated," advises Suniya Luthar, professor of clinical and developmental psychology at Columbia University. Even if they roll their eyes when you try to hug them, they still need direct displays of affection, she says. They also need help figuring out goals and limits. Parents should monitor their kids' activities and get to know their friends. Luthar says parents should still be disciplinarians and set standards such as curfews. Then teens need to know that infractions will be met with consistent consequences.

Adolescents are often critical of their parents but they're also watching them closely for clues on how to function in the outside world. Daniel Perkins, associate professor of family and youth resiliency at Penn State, says he and his wife take their twins to the local Ronald McDonald House and serve dinner to say thank you for time the family spent there when the children had health problems after birth. "What we've done already is set up the notion that we were blessed and need to give back, even if it's in a small way." That kind of example sets a standard youngsters remember, even if it seems like they're not paying attention.

Parents should provide opportunities for kids to explore the world and even find a calling. Teens who have a passion for something are more likely to thrive. "They have a sense of purpose beyond day-to-day teenage life," says David Marcus, author of "What It Takes to Pull Me Through." Often, he says,

kids who were enthusiastic about something in middle school lose enthusiasm in high school because the competition gets tougher and they're not as confident. Parents need to step in and help young people find other outlets. The best way to do that is to regularly spend uninterrupted time with teens (no cell phones). Kids also need to feel connected to other adults they trust and to their communities. Teens who get into trouble are "drifting," he says. "They don't have a web of people watching out for them."

Teens should build support webs of friends and adults.

At some point during these years, teen-agers should also be learning to build their own support networks—a skill that will be even more important when they're on their own. Connie Flanagan, a professor of youth civic development at Penn State, examines how kids look out for one another. "What we're interested in is how they help one another avoid harm," she says. In one of her focus groups, some teenage girls mentioned that they decided none would drink from an open can at a party because they wouldn't know for sure what they were drinking. "Even though you are experimenting, you're essentially doing it in a way that you protect one another," Flanagan says. Kids who don't make those kinds of connections are more likely to get in trouble because there's no one their own age or older to stop them from going too far. Like any other stage of life, adolescence can be tough. But teens and families can get through it—as long as they stick together.

With Julie Scelfo

Homeroom Zombies

Teens need at least nine hours of sleep a night, though few get that much and early school start times don't help. Here's what parents can do.

LAWRENCE EPSTEIN, MD AND STEVEN MARDON

As the school year kicks off, parents are once again struggling to cajole and, if need be, drag their exhausted teens out of bed. Later, teachers get a close-up view of sleep deprivation's effects, as bleary students zone out and even doze off in class. "I've learned never to dim the lights, even to show a video," says Lauren Boyle, a history teacher at Waltham High School in Massachusetts. "If I do, there are days when a third of the class falls asleep."

That image may make you laugh, but lack of sleep is no joke. Adolescents who don't get enough rest have more learning, health, behavior and mood problems than students who get at least nine hours a night. In some cases, teens may be incorrectly diagnosed with ADHD when sleep deprivation is actually the source of their symptoms. Perpetual lack of sleep is tied to diabetes, heart disease, obesity, depression and a shortened life span in adults, underscoring the importance of establishing good sleep habits early in life. Lack of sleep can be especially deadly for teens; car accidents are the leading cause of death among adolescents, and safety experts believe drowsy driving is a major factor.

Unfortunately, few adolescents get the sleep they need. In one recent study, researchers at Case Western Reserve University found that more than half of students slept seven hours or less, and almost one in five got less than six hours. In a survey of middle- and high-school students, University of Colorado researchers found that 82 percent said they woke up tired and unrefreshed, and more than half had trouble concentrating during the day at least once a week.

Blame multitasking for some of this. Many students are juggling after-school activities, homework and part-time jobs. Even when they manage to fulfill these obligations by a reasonable hour, television, the Internet, videogames, phone calls and text messages to friends often keep them awake deep into the night. (On average, 12th graders have four major electronic devices in their bedrooms.) Taking caffeinated soda and energy drinks late in the day and going to late-night parties on weekends add to sleep debt.

Biology also works against adolescents' sleep. The body's internal clock, which controls when a person starts to feel tired, shifts after puberty, making it hard for most teens to fall asleep before 11 P.M. Class usually begins before 8:15 A.M., with many high schools starting as early as 7:15 A.M. To get to school on time, most teens have to get up by 6:30 A.M., guaranteeing they'll be sleep-deprived during the week. Teens often sleep much later on weekends to catch up, making it even harder to fall asleep on Sunday night and wake up Monday morning. Playing catch-up on weekends also doesn't help teens stay alert when they need it most: during the week at school.

Since the 1990s, middle and high schools in more than two dozen states have experimented with later school start times. The results have been encouraging: more sleep, increased attendance, better grades and fewer driving accidents. For example, ninth graders' daily attendance rose from 83 percent to 87 percent and overall grades went up slightly when Minneapolis high schools moved the start time from 7:15 to 8:40 A.M. And car crashes involving teen drivers fell 15 percent when high schools in Fayette County, Ky., switched the high-school start time from 7:30 to 8:30 A.M. But most schools still start early, meaning teens have their work cut out for them if they want to get enough sleep.

Despite all these obstacles, parents can play a huge role in helping adolescents get the right amount of sleep. Here are some tips:

Educate your kids about sleep. Teens need to understand that their bodies require at least nine hours of sleep a day in order for them to do their best in school and enjoy their social lives. Explain that even a brief spell of short sleep raises their chances of feeling irritable and anxious, and experiencing minor ills such as headaches and stomach problems.

Keep a regular sleep/wake schedule. This conditions the body to expect to go to bed and get up at the same time every day. Teens should have a regular bedtime on school nights and should avoid staying up more than an hour later on weekends.

Develop a pre-sleep routine. This sets the stage for sleep. Wind down with nonstrenuous activities such as reading, listening to relaxing music or taking a shower. Avoid bright light in the evening, which signals the brain to stay alert. That includes TVs and computer screens.

Haven't Slept a Wink

Teenagers tend to sleep later than preadolescents, and like adults, they don't get enough sleep on the weekdays. How sleep patterns change with age:

Age	Natural bedtime*	Hours of sleep recommended	actual†
0–1 yrs.	7–8 P.M.	14–15 hrs.**	12.8 all days**
1–2	7–8	12–14**	11.8**
3–6	7–8	11–13**	10.3**
7–11	8–9	10–11	9.4
12–17	10:30–11:30	8.5–9.5	7.6 weekdays 8.9 weekends
18–54	10–12	7–8.5	6.8 weekdays 7.4 weekends
55–84	8–10	7–8.5	6.9 weekdays 7.5 weekends

*Refers to bedtime in the natural sleep-wake cycle. Actual bedtimes will vary.
†Based on Natl. Sleep Foundation (NSF) surveys, 2003–2006.
**Includes day and nighttime sleep.
Sources: NSF; Dr. Judith Owens, Hasbro Children's Hospital.

Monitor late-night activities. Keep TV and videogames in the family room, not the bedroom. Teens are less likely to stay up late if these entertainment options are less accessible. Moving these activities out of the bedroom also gives parents a more realistic picture of when their kids really go to sleep.

Limit caffeine intake. Sleep-deprived teens increasingly rely on coffee, soda and caffeinated energy drinks to stay awake during the day. High caffeine intake can make it harder to fall asleep, perpetuating a cycle of bad sleep and daytime fatigue. Adolescents should drink no more than two caffeinated drinks a day and none after 5 P.M. They should also steer clear of stimulant medication as "study aids"; these do not take the place of sleep.

Adopt a healthy lifestyle. Teens who exercise regularly, maintain a healthy diet and avoid alcohol tend to fall asleep faster and stay asleep longer than those who don't. (The same is true for adults.) Teens who smoke or use chewing tobacco should quit for many reasons, but getting better sleep is an additional motivation. Nicotine is a stimulant that can disturb sleep.

Take naps. Buildup of some sleep debt is inevitable—given most schools' yawn-inducing start times and the obstacles to falling asleep at 11. Teens who routinely get much less sleep than they need can make up for some of the difference with a nap after school. To prevent nighttime sleep disruption, teens shouldn't nap longer than 60 minutes or in the evening after dinner.

Set rules. Forbidding teens to drive after 11 P.M. (when they're most likely to nod off) won't win Mom and Dad any popularity contests, but it can save lives.

Be alert for sleep disorders. Teens may suffer from the same disorders that prevent adults from getting a decent night's sleep. These include obstructive sleep apnea (a nighttime breathing disorder), narcolepsy and restless-legs syndrome.

Provide a good example. If parents are staying up late and battling sleep deprivation with gallons of coffee, why should teens follow their advice to get a good night's sleep?

Above all, don't give up. Boyle, the teacher in Massachusetts, talks one-on-one with students who repeatedly fall asleep in class about the importance of sleep and calls parents if the problem continues. "These aren't bad kids," she says. "Often, they're highly motivated, spending hours on homework and also working to save money for college. If you talk to them, you can have a big impact."

LAWRENCE EPSTEIN, MD, former president of the American Academy of Sleep Medicine, is an instructor at Harvard Medical School and the medical director for Sleep HealthCenters in Boston. STEVEN MARDON is a medical writer. They are the authors of "The Harvard Medical School Guide to a Good Night's Sleep" (McGraw Hill, 2006). For more information on sleep, go to health.harvard.edu/newsweek.

Jail Time Is Learning Time

SIGNE NELSON AND LYNN OLCOTT

There is excitement in the large, well-lit classroom. Student work, including history posters and artwork, adorn the walls. A polite shuffling of feet can be heard, as names are called and certificates presented. It is the graduation ceremony at the Onondaga County Justice Center in Syracuse, N.Y. The ceremony is held several times a year, recognizing inmates in the Incarcerated Education Program who have passed the GED exam or completed a 108-hour vocational program. The courses in the Incarcerated Education Program are geared to prepare inmates to transition successfully to several different settings.

The Incarcerated Education Program is a joint effort by the Syracuse City School District and the Onondaga County Sheriff's Office, and is housed inside the nine-story Onondaga County Justice Center in downtown Syracuse. The Justice Center is a 250,000 square-foot maximum-security, nonsentenced facility, completed and opened in 1995. The facility was built to contain 616 beds, but currently houses 745 inmates. Between 13,000 and 14,000 inmates passed through booking during 2004. About 2,500 of them were minors.

The Justice Center

The Justice Center is a state-of-the-art facility, designed for and operating on the direct supervision model. Direct supervision is a method of inmate management developed by the federal government in 1974 for presentenced inmates in the Federal Bureau of Prisons. There are about 140 such facilities operating throughout the United States and a few hundred currently under construction. Direct supervision places a single deputy directly in a "housing pod" with between 32 and 64 inmates. Maximum pod capacity in the Onondaga County Justice Center is 56 inmates. Inmates are given either relative freedom of movement within the pod or confined to their cells based on their behavior.

The program has been providing courses and classes at the Justice Center for 10 years, but this partnership between the school district and the sheriff's office began almost 30 years ago with the provision of GED instruction. The Incarcerated Education Program was originally conceived to ensure education for inmates who are minors. The program has grown tremendously and now has more than 20 offerings in academic, vocational and life management areas.

The Syracuse City School District professional staff includes six full-time and 18 part-time teachers and staff members. The program is unique in that there are three Onondaga County Sheriff's sergeants who hold New York State Adult Education certification and who teach classes in the vocational component. An average of 250 inmates, or about one-third of the Justice Center's incarcerated population, are enrolled in day and/or evening classes. There are about 250 hours of class time in the facility per week.

Varied Educational and Training Opportunities

As in the public education sector, vocational programs have evolved with the times. The Basic Office Skills class now offers two sections, and includes computer repair and office production skills. A course in building maintenance can be complemented by a course in pre-application to pre-apprenticeship plumbing, or in painting and surface preparation, a class that includes furniture refinishing. A baking class and nail technology have been added in the past few years. All vocational courses, before implementation, are approved by the New York State Education Department and are designed to be consistent with New York State Department of Labor employment projections for Onondaga County. No vocational programming is implemented without first identifying whether the occupation is an area of growth in the community.

Additionally, a broadly inclusive advisory board, made up of community representatives who are stakeholders in the local economy and in the quality of life in the Syracuse metropolitan area has been established. The Incarcerated Education Advisory Board meets approximately three times a year to discuss the perceived needs of the community and to address strategies for transitioning students into employment. Ongoing topics of study are issues surrounding employment, continuing education and housing.

Incarcerated Education Program planners are very aware that job skills are ineffective without proper work attitudes. Job Readiness Training addresses work ethic, proper work behavior, communication and critical behavior skills. Vocational classes are voluntary for the nonsentenced population. However, because of their popularity, a waiting list is maintained for several courses. Among these popular courses are Basic Office

Skills and Small Engine Repair. An additional section of Small Engine Repair has been added for female inmates in the class to ensure gender equity in this training opportunity.

New York State law requires that incarcerated minors continue their education while incarcerated. The Incarcerated Education Program enrolls inmates, ages 16 to 21, in Adult Basic Education/GED classes and addresses students with special needs. Other adult inmates attend on a voluntary basis. Inmates are given an initial placement test to determine math and reading skill levels. Because inmates work at a wide range of ability levels, instruction is individualized and materials are geared to independent work. English as a Second Language and English Literacy/Civics are complementary offerings for inmates who are in need of assistance in English language proficiency and knowledge of American culture and history.

The GED exam is given at the Justice Center every 60 days or more often as needed. In the past three years, 225 students have taken the exam. Passing rates fluctuate between 63 percent and 72 percent. The average passing rate for correctional institutions in New York is about 51 percent. The state average passing rate for the general public in community-based courses is fairly stable at 50 percent.[1]

Of course, not everyone will take the GED. Student turnover is high, as inmates are released, bailed out, sent to treatment centers, or sentenced to county, state and federal correctional facilities. Judy Fiorini is a GED teacher who has been with the program for more than 10 years. "Many go back out into our community. We try to teach them something useful for their lives," Fiorini explains.

Transition services form an integral part of the program. The focus is on minors, but help is available for everyone. Two fulltime staff members assist people upon release, with such important tasks as acquiring a driver's license, seeking housing, reenrolling in high school or preparing for job interviews. A very important part of transition services is helping people acquire birth certificates, social security cards and other documents crucial for identification.

Tackling Cognitive Issues

Corrections professionals and educators are aware that it is not enough to improve the skill base of an inmate. There must be cognitive changes as well. The justice center is not a treatment facility, but it has been evolving into a therapeutic community. As the Incarcerated Education Program has grown, there has been the flexibility to add several important courses dealing with life issues, attitude and decision-making. According to data provided by the justice center, about 80 percent of inmates have substance abuse-related issues at the time of their arrest. To support desired cognitive changes, the justice center began establishing "clean and sober" pods in 2002. Currently, there are several clean and sober pods, including pods for adult men, women and youths. There are waiting lists for placement in the clean and sober pods.

The Incarcerated Education Program has been offering anger management groups for several years. Anger management helps group members deal with compulsive behavior and focus on

long-term goals. Other life management offerings include family education, action for personal choice and a course called Parent and Child Together. Most courses of study are developed inhouse by experienced professional faculty. Additionally, the program established gender-specific courses, Men's Issues and Women's Issues, to help inmates become more directly aware of their own responsibilities, separate from the role of a partner or significant other in their lives. The Men's Issues class is led by certified professionals and focuses on actions and their consequences. As in most jails, male inmates significantly outnumber female inmates. Courses and groups continue to be added, though it is sometimes difficult to find space for the abundance of activity in the program.

The program is financially supported, using state and federal funds, via nine carefully coordinated grants. Also significant for the success of the program has been ongoing encouragement and technical assistance from the New York State Education Department, the New York State Association of Incarcerated Education Programs and support from the New York State Sheriffs' Association.[2]

The Incarcerated Education Program continues to encounter challenges. It takes energy and dedication to keep the varied curricula substantial and cohesive, despite high student turnover and complex student needs. With a large civilian staff, the program requires close coordination between security and civilian concerns to help civilian staff work most effectively within the safety and security priorities of the facility. Biweekly meetings facilitate ongoing communication.

Making the Most of Time

Every available square inch of classroom space is in constant use. Classes have exceeded available space and some classes meet in core areas of the justice center as well. Several classes are held in the residence pods, where heavy, white tables are pulled together and portable white-boards are erected to create nomadic classrooms. Overall, the program is succeeding in several ways. Incarcerated minors are directly and meaningfully involved in high school equivalency classes, and inmates older than 21 receive academic and vocational services on a voluntary basis. All inmates are offered the opportunity for life-skills classes and for transitional services upon release. Time served at the Onondaga County Justice Center can also be time used for valuable academic, vocational and life management achievements.

Notes

1. New York State Department of Education maintains statistics for educational activities at correctional facilities in New York state. Patricia Mooney directs the GED Program for the state through the GED Testing Office in the State Department of Education. Greg Bayduss is the State Department of Education coordinator in charge of Incarcerated Education Programs throughout New York state.

2. State Professional Organizations: The New York State Association of Incarcerated Education Programs Inc. is a professional organization for teachers, administrators and security personnel (www.nysaiep.org). Its mission is to

promote excellence in incarcerated education programs in the state, support research in this field and advocate for incarcerated education initiatives through collaboration with other professional organizations. The authors must mention the valuable assistance of the New York State Sheriffs' Association, supporting each county sheriff, as the chief law enforcement officer in his or her county (www.nyssheriffs.org). The association provides valuable information and technical assistance to county sheriffs to help implement programs in their jails.

SIGNE NELSON is the coordinator of the Incarcerated Education Program, and LYNN OLCOTT is a teacher at Auburn Correctional Facility in New York, formerly with the Incarcerated Education Program. The program could not have attained its present strength without the vision and support of law enforcement officials Sheriff Kevin Walsh, Chief Anthony Callisto, and Syracuse City School District administrator Al Wolf. Special thanks to Capt. John Woloszyn, commander of Support Services; Sgt. Joseph Powlina, administrative compliance supervisor; and Deputy Joseph Caruso, photographer. Their assistance in the production of this article was crucial and much appreciated.

How Spirit Blooms

Most people long for spirituality, but what path do you take, and what are its milestones? A writer who tried everything from Buddhism to voodoo describes the four steps to finding a spiritual connection.

Suzanne Clores

O ccasionally, a strange feeling comes over you. You hear a call from inside your heart. A faint, faraway sound you can barely hear amid the office phones, the people who need you, the list of plans for the week, the month, the rest of your life. But when you breathe deeply, the sound is louder and you relax. Finally, one afternoon during your commute home, you hear yourself. You say you need to nurture your soul. But now that you have voiced this need, how do you respond?

I reluctantly began a spiritual search when I was 25. I hated my job—my entire direction—and entered an early midlife panic. Many told me it was just "the age," but I knew it was more. These were the symptoms: A dull sense of separation from my own heart. An uncertainty about what I loved. A feeling that even my family didn't really know me. Doubt that a career path was the only thing worth striving for. Everyone feels that way, said the people I knew. But I felt excluded, apart, even more than usual. I wished I could join the party everyone seemed to be having and wondered how I had become an outsider.

The fact that a recent Gallup poll found that some 84 percent of Americans long for spirituality suggests that many people feel like I did—dissatisfied.

But it's not so easy to suddenly have a relationship with God. There is cynicism, past experiences with organized religion, and the general unhipness of being "religious." There is also our very stressful culture. When the body is confronted by stress, as mine was, it enters a state of fight or flight that drains oxygen from the higher functions of the mind. This makes it difficult to sit still, let alone consider your concerns with God. At the time of my spiritual crisis I was often so stressed about my love life and urban living that spirituality for me was in the same category as TV—something that ate your time and turned your brain to mush. Of course now—like everyone with a meditation or yoga practice—I know better. God is accessible by getting quiet and turning inside. But hindsight is 20/20. And it doesn't account for the pain and suffering that is crucial to acknowledge when stepping onto the spiritual path.

Wicca

Roots: Derived from pre-Christian Celtic religion.
Philosophy/practice: Although many call themselves witches, Wiccans do not practice the evil spells or acts of sorcery commonly associated with the word. They believe in a ubiquitous force, which they refer to as the All or the One, and are guided by the cycles of nature, symbols, and deities of ancient Celtic society.
Modern take: Wicca has grown in popularity since its revival in the United Kingdom in the 1940s. It remains an earth-based religion, with an emphasis on preserving nature and working with natural forces to create harmony and healing.

Yet in the last several years numerous medical studies have linked the benefits of a spiritual practice to improved mental health, particularly coping with depression, anxiety, and long-term illness. Fifty-eight percent of female trauma survivors found that a relationship with God gave them strength to create positive relationships with others. But it takes time, trust, and self-inquiry to have a real spiritual practice. You have to want it. You have to make it happen, and often that means finding support in a strange new world all by yourself.

My trepidation, it turns out, is common. Studies have shown people in physical or psychological crisis often feel left out of their religious or spiritual traditions, even when faith is a priority in their lives. Why is it so hard to believe we belong? Plenty of scientific studies prove that spirituality is inherently part of us. Books like *The God Gene* by Dean Hamer and *The "God" Part of the Brain* by Matthew Alper propose that, like other cognitive functions, our spiritual instincts, cognitions, sensations, and behaviors are generated from a particular cluster of neurons in the brain. We are wired to believe in something larger. Then why do we have so many lapses in faith? Because in the face of extreme distress, we are also wired to forget.

While I could not walk the path of St. Catherine of Siena or St. Francis of Assisi and shun material items, social life, and other worldly things holy people relinquish, I still craved spiritual depth. Six years later, I am finally onto something. It took a three-year search before I finally found yoga, another year before I felt comfortable with meditation, and another two years before landing in a real community. In that time my whole life changed. I moved from New York City to Tucson, Arizona, traded the city for the desert, and became part of a yoga-based spiritual practice called Yoga Oasis, a group of Anusara yogis and meditators who create what senior yoga teacher John Friend calls a "kula," or community of the heart. We devote several hours a week to practicing at the yoga center, creating a safe environment where spiritual exploration is welcome. Finally, I know contentment is possible.

But there was a long time of discontent. And guilt about the discontent. (Why can't I just be happy like other people? Why can't I just be a good Catholic or a resigned atheist?) I doggedly moved from tradition to tradition. Each time I met with joy and astonishment and chaos. My life filled with elation. Then my life fell apart. It sounds dramatic, but I can tell you this: With effort and vigilance, you are safe on the spiritual path though it may mean that your life changes entirely.

From my journey I've distilled four steps. They may help your spirituality blossom.

1. Imagine What You Want

What do I want? It seems like an obvious question. But for a long time, I didn't know what I wanted. It is natural—and easier—to continue feeling dissatisfied with situations before actually articulating to yourself "I want something more." Like everyone, I needed the security of faith, a promise of survival. Think of spring flowers that wait to bloom until the summer sun is warm enough. Or underpaid employees who wait until they have another job before leaving the one they have. Spiritual

seekers are similar. We seek not just the right spiritual perspective but a safe environment in which to explore it.

The overwhelming but wonderful news is that help is available. The quest for calm has made it into our consumer culture, for better or worse. I soon found many organizations, groups, chat sites, books, magazines, and products available to a practitioner of anything. I know what you're thinking; it sounds like a trend seeker on a shopping spree. But not all investments in mala beads and yoga mats lead to materialism. As seekers we use these tools to respond to that inner voice, that inner calling. Once responding to that voice, you will soon meet others doing the same.

I found others at classes offered by spiritual spas and resorts like Omega, Esalen, and Kripalu. On the cliffs of Big Sur, Esalen had been exploring America's consciousness movement since the 1960s. Omega had intoxicating-looking psychospiritual programs for the New York intellectual, and Kripalu welcomed all seekers with restorative weekends in the bosom of the Berkshires in Massachusetts. Eventually I attended all of these centers and learned various teachings that helped create more peace in my life. But at the beginning of my search, even these resorts were too organized—I wanted raw experience.

I went to the right place. Something about the secrecy and female-centrism of paganism (specifically Wicca), called to me. I stepped into this rich, earth-based religion and found tools for acquiring security: The four elements—water, earth, air, and fire—were frequently invoked in bonfire chants and used in ceremonies to unify all life. How did I stave off my Catholic guilt while on a Wicca retreat? Don't laugh, but on some level I believed chanting around a fire at midnight and Drawing Down the Moon (when the Goddess is invoked in the priestess) was similar to drinking the wine and taking Communion. On a bus ride back to Manhattan from an outdoor pagan festival, I marveled at the idea that through nature, I was connected to the divine.

I arrived back in the concrete jungle knowing what I wanted: security; community; philosophical consistency, but not dogma; a connection with the divine that felt rooted and physical, not magical. I also knew that I didn't need ceremonies in the woods

---

Yoga

Roots: India, 4th century B.C.

Philosophy/practice: Yoga, which in Sanskrit means "union," is a practice of unifying with the divine Self, that exists beyond the ego, or small self. Yogis maintain that through physical, psychological, and spiritual practice, we can transcend the small, ego-driven chatter of our minds and enter into a higher consciousness.

Modern take: The physical aspect of yoga has attained an unparalleled following in the United States. A meditative, relaxing practice that also strengthens and tones the body, it appeals to people looking to stretch their spiritual frontiers—and their legs.

Sufism

Roots: First brought to America by Hazrat Inayat Khan in 1910.

Philosophy/practice: Sufism is best known as the mystical movement within the Islamic religion, emphasizing personal union with the divine. Ritual song and dance also play a role in Sufi tradition.

Modern take: *Adab*, a long-standing Sufi tradition that is still practiced, is defined as a "profound courtesy of heart that arises from the deep relationship with the Divine and expresses itself in refined behavior of all kinds with other beings." Today a small yet devoted group of about 500 to 600 Americans are actively associated with Sufi spiritual practice.

to find those things. In quiet moments I consulted with my level of self-connection: Do I feel secure now? When do I feel secure? How can I cultivate more security? I didn't know it at the time, but creating those quiet moments was the first step to creating a space for spiritual experience to exist.

2. Walk around the Temple

Once I began my search, I kept my interests under wraps at first. I said nothing to my family. Not because they were Catholic, and not because they worried about me, but because my trust was brittle. I needed support, not reactions like, "What the heck are you doing?" or "That sounds weird; what's wrong with you?" If you ask around generally, most people claim openness to religious and spiritual freedom. Still, ours is a culture where most people consider non-Christian religion to be outside of the norm.

My whole life I had tried to understand how to be a good Catholic. I was exhausted and badly needed a fresh take on spirituality. Any outside doubts would have fanned the flames of my own doubts. And since doubt and cynicism were default attitudes among my peers, I felt it best to keep quiet.

But that may have been a mistake. It wasn't until my cousin Mary confided to me that she had been part of a Sufi community for 25 years—a secret she had held from the family for just as long—that I could see it was really possible to change my life. My cousin Mary remembers the loneliness in the first few years of her search. "When I first started looking for spiritual solace, I went to churches, synagogues, even Quaker meetings, and found nice people, but not what I was looking for. Eventually I found a spiritual teacher who called that part of the investigative process 'walking around the temple.' It was the time of seeking before I was ready to go inside."

People in crisis often feel left out of their religious or spiritual traditions, even when faith is a priority in their lives.

Carefully, I began talking to people. I mentioned to a friend's mother that I sought a kind of personal spirituality, and she gladly loaned me her dusty Kabbalah books. My Aunt Maureen invited me to a psychic fair featuring Sylvia Browne and John Edward. (She was hoping my grandfather would play one of his famous practical jokes from the beyond. He didn't.) I didn't know whether or how these spiritual events would fulfill my yearning, but I accepted everything people gave me. I regarded them as gifts, tokens from worlds that promised me something fantastic. But what?

It helps to see all spiritual offerings as gifts, even if not exactly fashioned for you. Also, try giving a little yourself. If you know people who are interested in making the world a safer, more sensitive place, talk with them. Sharing spiritual interests with open minds and hearts gives permission to others to do the same. My yoga community grows because people

---

Shamanism

Roots: Origins date back more than 30,000 years.
Philosophy/practice: Based on the belief that medicine men (shamans) in ancient hunter-gatherer societies possessed special healing powers that allowed them to act as mediums between the earth and spirit worlds. With these gifts, they were capable of everything from curing diseases to reviving weak crops.
Modern take: Modern-day medicine people continue to cultivate this subtle relationship. They are mostly found in Native American communities and come to their vocation in various ways. Some receive a calling in a dream state, others embark upon a "vision quest," and others apprentice with a skilled shaman.

---

share their experiences. We commemorate every life event—a war, a marriage, a birth, a death, a holy day—with a special yoga or meditation practice. Plus, there is a danger to keeping it all inside. If you don't share your needs, desires, or experiences with anyone, there is a chance the stress and alienation will cause psychic and bodily harm.

3. Conquer the Fear

So many of us spend time walking around the temple that it almost becomes a spiritual path in and of itself. Though my cousin Mary is now a devoted student of Indian teacher Meher Baba, she maintains that spiritual searching was an important part of finding her true teacher. I took her advice and for many months—years, actually—slowly confronted my spiritual longings. I didn't know what I wanted. So I tried this and that. With as much of my heart as I could, I took shamanic journeys. I attended pagan ceremonies. I sought out voodoo rituals. And while most of the time I had powerful spiritual experiences, there was a major problem: I was scared.

All heroic myths, fairy tales, and spiritual heroes encounter what is called "the dark night of the soul." It is a time when seekers are deeply frightened, lonely, and uncertain about going forward. Yet they are aware that they cannot turn back. Sometimes, I found, it lasts longer than a night. Even after I attended deeply meaningful ceremonies and found a yoga teacher I liked, I kept asking myself, Is this really necessary? Is it sacrilegious? Will I be punished somehow for leaving my old religion and trying to find something as abstract as spirituality? Despite my frustration at not having answers, asking questions was one of the most productive and helpful steps I could take to relieve myself of fear. Asking honest questions leads to hearing honest answers, and honest answers led me to the truth that I needed to surrender to the paths that felt right.

One man I met on the spiritual path encountered his darkest night after he had already been studying with a teacher. It came right after his teacher asked that he make a greater commitment. "I tried everything to bring about a transformation in myself," the man told me. "All of the deep experiences I'd had, all of my

Buddhism

Roots: India, 525 B.C., where Prince Siddhartha received enlightenment under the bodhi tree at the river Neranjara. Thereafter he was known as the Buddha, or Awakened One.

Philosophy/practice: Buddhist religion is based on the theory that life is a continual cycle of birth, death, and rebirth, and that we live in constant suffering. Meditation, persistent self-inquiry, and observance of moral precepts are the way to liberation and freedom from suffering.

Modern take: Buddhism thrives today as the fourth largest religion in the world. Buddhists practicing in the West are drawn to varying sects, including Theravada, Tibetan, Mahayana, and Zen.

Voodoo

Roots: The exact origins of voodoo are unknown, but it's generally believed to have begun in the West African nation of Benin during the slave trade. It's also practiced in Haiti, South America, and New Orleans.

Philosophy/practice: Voodoo practitioners believe in one god, but call upon spirits, the Loa, to heal the sick, help the needy and provide practical solutions to life's problems.

Modern take: Voodoo is a guiding force in communities where it's practiced, and voodoo priests are prominent, respected figures who perform many sacred functions.

understanding of dharma, even my will and perseverance had nothing to do with the kind of radical transformation that lay ahead. I began to experience intense confusion and fear, which grew into even more intense paranoia. I didn't know what to trust."

It took a year for this pilgrim to realize the transformation he needed to make, but he eventually did as a result of staying with it. "Transformation," he told me, "is a process of active surrender. You cannot will your own transformation at the soul level; you can only allow transformation to be enacted by forces greater than yourself."

4. Cross to Safety

There is no guarantee that stepping more deeply onto a spiritual path will solve all your problems. Rather, it demands more empathy and honesty from yourself than a lot of other relationships demand.

I found this can be more complex than comfortable. About two years into my exploration of various spiritual paths, my life had changed dramatically: I had left my long-term relationship, moved in with others on a spiritual path, changed my line of work to do freelance projects with various people. Very little in my life was stable. And yet the space gave my passion room to burn. I felt clear. My resolve was strong that I had made the right choices and let my spiritual vision guide me.

And then everything started collapsing. The couple I lived with were ending their marriage. The people I worked with were terminating our agreement prematurely. I was losing my home and job, and I was angry. What had I done wrong?

I phoned a shamanic practitioner I trusted. After consulting with her own spirit guides, she gave me news I had difficulty swallowing. She said, "The structures you have created for yourself are dissolving of your own doing. You must manifest a new structure for yourself."

I had expected her to say, "You are doing everything right, none of this is your fault. The universe will save you," I answered, with an edge to my voice, "How do I manifest a new life?"

She said seriously; "Get really clear in your mind. Meditate, chant, do whatever you have to do to clear the anxiety. Then dream what you want and need. Write it down very clearly and keep it somewhere."

"Dream?" I asked.

"Yes."

"And write it on a piece of paper?" I asked.

"Yes," she said.

I hung up, annoyed. This advice did not sound concrete. I was losing my home, and she wanted me to dream. But I had spent a year cultivating spiritual awareness and trust. So I sat down and did it. I dreamed a house in a different city than where I lived, with work and people whom I had never met. And within three months I had moved out of town unexpectedly, found the house, community, and work situation I had written on the page, almost exactly.

The spiritual path is not linear. This makes it hard to clear a weekend in October for a "spiritually deep" day. Like love, spiritual life does not work like that. And yet every moment provides an opportunity to begin. Perhaps on the radio, or on the news, a report mentions the word "spirituality," and your heart softens. Or perhaps when you hear somewhere that, post 9/11, attendance at spiritual retreats has increased, and that lay members of churches, synagogues, and mosques have begun to organize nationally, you somehow feel included. You know you are part of this group, these new pilgrims—maybe even the old ones—but how do you respond?

The truth is, to think about it is to begin. You have taken a crucial step. And you are not alone. I can tell you, the most important thing to remember is that you are not alone.

From *Body + Soul,* September 2004, pp. 76, 78–79, 108–110, 113. Copyright © 2004 by *Body + Soul* Magazine. Reprinted by permission.

What Addicts Need

Addiction isn't a weakness; it's an illness. Now vaccines and other new drugs may change the way we treat it.

JENEEN INTERLANDI

Annie Fuller knew she was in trouble a year ago, when in the space of a few hours she managed to drink a male co-worker more than twice her size under the table. Of course, she'd been practicing for a quarter of her life by then; at 47, she was pouring a pint of bourbon, a 12-pack of beer and a couple of bottles of wine into her 115-pound body each day. She had come to prefer alcohol to food, sex or the company of friends and loved ones. Her marriage had ended; she had virtually stopped leaving the house, except to work and to drink. Fuller had tried and failed enough times over the years to know that she would not be able to sober up on her own. The last time she'd stopped drinking her body went into violent seizures, a common and terrifying symptom of alcohol withdrawal. But the single mother and mortgage-company VP refused to sign into rehab. "I live in a small town," she says. "And when you go to a hospital for something like that, everybody knows about it." So when a family doctor told her about Vivitrol, a monthly injection that prevents patients from drinking alcohol by obliterating its ability to intoxicate, Fuller agreed. She took a sabbatical from work, sent her 15-year-old daughter to stay with relatives and hunkered down to weather the painful, frightening blizzard of detoxification in the comfort of her own living room.

What does it mean to be an addict? For a long time the answer was that someone like Fuller "lacked willpower," a tautology that is pretty much useless as a guide to treatment. In the current jargon of the recovery movement, addiction to alcohol, drugs or nicotine is a "bio-psycho-social-spiritual disorder," a phrase that seems to have been invented by the treatment industry to emphasize how complex the problem is and how much more funding it deserves. But the word itself comes from the Latin *addictus*, a debtor who was indentured to work off what he owed; someone addicted to alcohol or drugs is powerless over his or her fate in the same way—except debtors-as-addicts can never fully balance the books. It had been years since the pleasure of drinking outweighed the pain it caused Fuller. Looked at that way, the "social" and "spiritual" aspects of her problem seem insignificant compared with the contribution of biology. If you weigh advances in neuroscience over the last few decades against social and spiritual progress, it's clear which field is more likely to produce the next breakthrough in treatments.

While the roots of addiction remain a dark tangle of factors—most experts agree that addicts trying to quit will always need psychological support—the old white-knuckle wisdom that addicts simply lack resolve passed out of fashion decades ago. The American Medical Association recognized addiction as a disease back in 1956. But only now are we beginning to see treatments that target the underlying biochemistry of that disease.

The emerging paradigm views addiction as a chronic, relapsing brain disorder to be managed with all the tools at medicine's disposal. The addict's brain is malfunctioning, as surely as the pancreas in someone with diabetes. In both cases, "lifestyle choices" may be contributing factors, but no one regards that as a reason to withhold insulin from a diabetic. "We are making unprecedented advances in understanding the biology of addiction," says David Rosenblum, a public-health professor and addiction expert at Boston University. "And that is finally starting to push the thinking from 'moral failing' to 'legitimate illness.'"

In laboratories run and funded by the National Institute on Drug Abuse (NIDA), fMRI and PET scans are forcing that infuriating organ, the addicted brain, to yield up its secrets. Geneticists have found the first few (of what is likely to be many) gene variants that predispose people to addiction, helping explain why only about one person in 10 who tries an addictive drug actually becomes hooked on it. Neuroscientists are mapping the intricate network of triggers and feedback loops that are set in motion by the taste—or, for that matter, the sight or thought—of a beer or a cigarette; they have learned to identify the signal that an alcoholic is about to pour a drink even before he's aware of it himself, and trace the impulse back to its origins in the primitive midbrain. And they are learning to interrupt and control these processes at numerous points along the way. Among more than 200 compounds being developed or tested by NIDA are ones that block the intoxicating effects of drugs, including vaccines that train the body's own immune system to bar them from the brain. Other compounds have the amazing ability to intervene in the cortex in the last milliseconds before the impulse to reach for a glass translates into action. To the extent that "willpower" is a meaningful concept at all, the era of willpower-in-a-pill may be just over the horizon. "The future is clear," says Nora Volkow, the director of NIDA. "In 10 years we will be treating addiction as a disease, and that means with medicine."

Volkow's vision of the future, however, is being greeted warily by big pharmaceutical companies, reluctant to develop products that would associate their brands with drug addicts. It is also facing resistance from some elements in the addiction-treatment community, who are wedded to the 12-Step model pioneered by Alcoholics Anonymous in 1935. Twelve-Step programs traditionally discourage members from using any psychoactive substances, on the ground that addicts will simply trade one dependency for another. That rationale has some unfortunate history on its side; both opium and cocaine were first introduced to the United States as cures for alcoholism in the late 1800s. More recently there is the example of methadone, the synthetic heroin that turned out to be addictive in its own right, and Antabuse, a drug that makes you throw up when you drink alcohol—which suffers from the shortcoming that an alcoholic planning a binge can just skip his dose.

Addictive drugs like cocaine and heroin flood the brain with the neurotransmitter dopamine, a chemical that induces a sensation of pleasure and trains the subconscious to remember everything that preceded that sensation. Together with alcohol, nicotine and amphetamines, these make up the five drugs generally considered the hardest to give up; right now, some 22 million Americans are hooked on at least one of these substances. While each causes a distinct form of intoxication and a different range of side effects and health problems, all five hijack the same pathway, deep within the brain. It's the pathway that conditions us to eat, have sex, form emotional attachments and carry out the other activities essential to our species' survival. But the agents of addiction are far more powerful than any of those natural highs. Just one dose of cocaine, for example, can release two to 10 times the amount of dopamine produced by your favorite meal, person, song or sight. Take a drug like that consistently enough, and your brain and body will come to depend on it—first for euphoria, then for normalcy. Eventually, the pursuit and consumption of drugs will become as instinctive as the pursuit and consumption of food—only far more urgent and destructive.

People vary in their innate sensitivity to dopamine, which may partly explain why addiction runs in families. A gene that codes for a dopamine receptor designated D2 (one of at least five dopamine receptors that have been identified so far) comes in several different versions, and each produces a different concentration of receptors. People with fewer receptors may receive less stimulation from their naturally occurring dopamine, and therefore be more inclined to seek an artificial high from drugs. Unfortunately, tinkering directly with the dopamine system to control addiction hasn't worked out very well. Dopamine is crucial to voluntary movement and interfering with it can cause symptoms resembling Parkinson's.

So far, other neurotransmitters that play a role in addiction have been easier to tackle. Gamma-aminobutyric acid, or GABA, exerts an inhibitory effect on neurons, telling the body to stop instead of go. Addicts' brains are deficient in GABA, so researchers are investigating a drug called Vigabatrin, which stimulates its production. In December, the pill cleared its first double-blind, placebo-controlled trial; 30 percent of patients who took Vigabatrin stayed off cocaine during the nine-week study, compared with just 5 percent in a control group. "It's the best efficacy signal that we've seen in any clinical trial for cocaine treatment," says Frank Vocci, director of the pharmacotherapies division at NIDA. "And it's worked on what many have written off as an intractable population—hard-core, long-term cocaine addicts." A drug called Camparal, which is already on the market as a treatment for alcoholism, works on yet another brain chemical, glutamate. While the early stages of addiction are driven by pleasure-seeking—hence the importance of dopamine—the motive eventually shifts to avoiding the pain of withdrawal; at that point, drug-seeking behavior is fueled by glutamate. By suppressing this neurotransmitter, Camparal has the potential to reduce cravings and help prevent relapses during recovery. Researchers think these drugs hold enormous promise. "The treatment of depression was revolutionized by medications that manipulate serotonin concentrations," says Alan Leshner, former head of NIDA, referring to Prozac and its cousins. "Drugs that act on GABA and glutamate could do the same thing for addiction."

If you're trying to quit drinking, you are advised not to hang out in bars, and if you're trying to kick cigarettes, you probably should avoid French movies from the 1950s. One reason addictions are so hard to break is that the pleasure of taking the drug becomes associated with all the situations and activities around it, which then become cues for a relapse. Researchers at the University of Pennsylvania found that showing cocaine addicts pictures of drugs or crack pipes for just

33 milliseconds—below the threshold of conscious awareness—was enough to trigger cravings. Beverly Dyess, 58, learned this last year when, after six months of sobriety her longest stretch in 15 years—she went into a supermarket and discovered that her favorite brand of Scotch was on sale. She was seeing a therapist daily, but "as soon as I saw the label, everything else went out the window," she says. For the next two months she rode a roller coaster of frenzied drinking and crushing guilt. Some days she would get up early enough to get drunk and then sober up in time for her evening counseling session. Other days she would run to the store, buy a bottle of whisky and then, her resolve mysteriously stiffened, pour it down the sink when she got home. By suppressing the surge of glutamate that directed her to the Scotch aisle in the first place, Camparal helped ease the pain of withdrawal and allowed the counseling and behavioral therapy to work. "I still do the talk therapy," she says. "But Camparal really helps, because everything is still a cue for drinking."

Of course, you can't protect yourself against every encounter with a bottle, or in some environments, heroin, cocaine or amphetamines. So researchers are working on ways to break the association that was Dyess's downfall. A drug called D-cycloserine, or DCS, has the remarkable effect of helping to erase learned fear responses. The classic example, in animals, is the association of a particular place with an electric shock. If you stop giving the shock, the animal eventually "unlearns" the response and is no longer afraid; DCS makes this happen faster. It has been successfully tested in people as a treatment for acrophobia (fear of heights). Now researchers want to see if it can be used to wipe out the association between visual or social cues and the impulse to relapse into addiction. So far, it's been tested only on cocaine, but if it works there it might work for other addictions as well.

Neuroscientists don't talk about "willpower," which is a philosophical concept, but they are starting to get a handle on the parts of the brain involved in self-control, the ability to impose a rational calculus on behavior. They distinguish three kinds of self-control, and, unsurprisingly, addicts score poorly on all of them although it isn't clear whether taking drugs is the cause or consequence of this deficiency, and which of the three types plays the biggest role in addiction has yet to be determined. These are:

- Delayed discounting, the willingness to put off present gratification in the interest of a bigger long-term reward. Addicts always take the immediate reward.

- Reflection impulsivity, a measure of how much information is required to make a decision. Addicts typically act without processing all the available information.

- Intentional action, the ability to consciously stop a behavior that has become automatic. To measure this, NIDA researchers had addicts watch a screen and push one of two buttons, according to whether a light has flashed on the left or right side—except when the light was accompanied by a tone. After several rounds, pushing the button becomes an automatic response that has to be overridden consciously, and addicts were much less able to do this than non-addicts. As scientists have known since the 1980s, the neurons that control movement are activated even before a person is aware of the intention. Now researchers have identified the part of the brain—the fronto-median cortex—that is activated when someone stops himself from executing such automatic behaviors. This is as close as we have got to finding the seat of willpower in the brain. Put an addict in an fMRI machine, and you can observe reduced activity in the fronto-median cortex. But a drug called Provigil, which is ordinarily used to treat narcolepsy, stimulates that part of the brain and is now being tested as a treatment for amphetamine addiction. "The idea that we can restore 'self-control' or 'free will' with medication is a very, very exciting one," says Vocci of NIDA. "It could be paradigm shifting. But we need more studies to see how consistently that impacts recovery."

That is a useful caution; these drugs are new and their mechanisms are still only partially understood. The brain has a way of resisting attempts to tinker with its chemistry. The discovery in 1960 that Parkinsonism was caused by a deficiency of dopamine quickly led to the use of synthetic dopamine precursors, such as L-dopa, which relieved the symptoms at first, but were not the long-term cure patients had hoped for.

A more straightforward approach to treating, or preventing addiction is to block the action of the drug directly. If it doesn't feel good, the thinking goes, you won't do it. Naltrexone, a pill that has been around for a decade, works that way against alcohol, but an addict intent on getting high can just skip his dose. The solution to that problem is Vivitrol, a longer-lasting, injectable form of Naltrexone, which came on the market in 2006. Vivitrol, the drug Annie Fuller took, does not enhance self-control or stop the craving for liquor, but it does block liquor's effects. The day Fuller got her shot, her leg swelled to twice its normal size. The swelling subsided a day or two later, but the next few weeks were a torment of sweating, shaking, vomiting and tears—side effects that came from both Vivitrol and alcohol withdrawal. At times she couldn't walk and needed help to use the bathroom. The only thing that kept her from drinking was the knowledge that she could not get drunk. "The shot just took the relapse option off the table," she says. She got the same injection every month for the rest of the year, suffering a little less each time, and she is now off the medication and sober.

Vaccines that would arm the immune system against addictive drugs and prevent them from making the user high are, potentially, the ultimate weapons against addiction. A cocaine vaccine is poised to enter its first large-scale clinical trial in humans this year, and vaccines against nicotine, heroin and methamphetamine are also in development. In theory, these addiction vaccines work the same way as the traditional vaccines used to treat infectious diseases like measles and meningitis. But instead of targeting bacteria and viruses, the new vaccines zero in on addictive chemicals. Each of the proposed vaccines consists of drug molecules that have been attached to proteins from bacteria; it's the bacterial protein that sets off the immune reaction. Once a person has been vaccinated, the next time the drug is ingested, antibodies will latch onto it and prevent it from crossing from the bloodstream into the brain. Nabi Biopharmaceuticals, a small biotech company in Maryland, has engineered a nicotine vaccine that is in late-stage clinical trials. Earlier studies showed that it was twice as effective as a placebo in helping people quit smoking. The cocaine vaccine, developed by Thomas Kosten of Baylor College of Medicine, could be on the market as early as 2010. It would have to be given three or four times a year, but presumably not for life, says Kosten. While the vaccine is being studied in people who are already addicted to cocaine, it could eventually be used on others. "You could vaccinate high-risk teens until they matured to an age of better decision-making," Kosten says. He acknowledges the obvious civil-liberties issues this raises. "Lawyers certainly want to argue with us on the ethics of it," he says, "but parent groups and pediatricians have been receptive to the idea."

The revolution these new drugs promise will have a huge impact on the addiction-treatment industry (or, as it prefers to think of itself, the "recovery movement"), which runs the gamut from locked psychiatric wards in big-city hospitals to spalike mansions in the Malibu Hills of California. And the reaction there is guarded; the people who run them have seen panaceas come and go over the years, and the same addicts return with the same problems. They also, of course, have a large

investment in their own programs, which typically rely on intensive therapy and counseling based on the 12-Step model. "We need four or five more years to see how [Vivitrol] does," says staff psychiatrist Garrett O'Connor at the Betty Ford Center, in Rancho Mirage, Calif. "And we need to be very cautious, because a failed treatment will set a person back." The Ford Center and the Hazelden Foundation, in Minnesota, use drugs sparingly, and mostly just in the first days or weeks of recovery in the "detox" phase. "Hazelden will never turn its back on pharmaceutical solutions, but a pill all by itself is not the cure," says William Moyers, Hazelden's vice president of external affairs. "We're afraid that people are seeking a medical route that says treatment is the end, not the beginning." As for Alcoholics Anonymous and its imitators, they mostly do not forbid members to use medication but there are strong institutional biases against it. "I'm not judging others, but for myself, using something like Vivitrol or Camparal feels like a crutch," says one longtime AA member, who, following the organization's practice, asked not to be named. "It's not true sobriety."

The competing view is that of Lisa Torres, a New York lawyer who has been in recovery from heroin addiction for nearly 20 years, and continues to take methadone, which she regards as medication for a chronic condition, analogous to blood-pressure or cholesterol-lowering drugs. "It's a paradox that some of addicts' biggest advocates have been the most resistant to new treatments," she says. "But a lot of them come to the field after recovering from their own addictions, and they can be very stubborn about what works and what doesn't." More pointedly, she adds, "Some people feel recovery from addiction should not be easy or convenient."

So for this new paradigm to take hold, a lot of long-held prejudices will have to change. Doctors (and insurance companies) will have to get used to the idea of medicating their addicted patients, rather than handing them a brochure for AA, which a study published in 2005 in The New England Journal of Medicine found was the most common form of "treatment" offered. "If you have hypertension and it flares up, you go to a specialist," says psychologist Thomas McLellan of the University of Pennsylvania. "The specialist doesn't discharge you to a church basement. If he did, we would call it malpractice." Addicts, he adds, are by no means unique in their propensity to relapse. In a study comparing alcoholics and drug addicts to patients with diabetes, asthma and hypertension, McLellan found nearly identical rates of noncompliance and relapse; between 30 and 40 percent of each group failed to follow even half their doctors' guidelines.

Where doctors go, drug companies are likely to follow. Most of the research on addiction treatments has been done by NIDA (total 2007 budget: $994 million) or small pharmaceutical companies. "I have been imploring the bigger companies to work on this," says Volkow. "Their scientists get it, but the business people are tough to persuade." Companies with billion-dollar stakes in selling drugs for osteoporosis or cholesterol don't want their names on a product used by heroin addicts, says Leshner. Even the relatively unknown Nabi, according to CEO Raafat Fahim, decided to focus on a vaccine for nicotine "because it's not illicit and it's not something you can overdose on" (and afterward sue the company that made the drug that didn't stop you from taking it). But Steven Paul, the head of research for Eli Lilly, believes the landscape is changing. There used to be a stigma attached to depression, too, he says, but the development of Prozac put an end to that. "Anything that has a large unmet need," says Paul, "is ultimately going to succeed commercially."

And addicts may need to change their thinking, too. For nearly 75 years, that thinking has been dominated by the principles laid down by Bill W., the founder of Alcoholics Anonymous. The amount of good AA has done in the world is incalculable; most people reading this article probably can think of someone they know who owes his or her life to it. Some readers themselves have surely benefited. But in 1935

And Now, Back in the Real World . . .

A Report from the Front in the Never-Ending War on Drugs.

Seth Norman, a criminal court Judge in Nashville, doesn't know a lot about dopamine receptors or glutamate. A cure for addiction? "I'd love to see it," he says. But Norman is too busy dealing with a docket full of drug addicts—largely meth and crack-cocaine users—to think much about the science behind their behavior.

The judge does believe that drug addiction is a disease, however, and he is adamant about moving nonviolent drug offenders away from prison and into treatment. In 1997 he opened a unique residential addiction program, which has offered intensive rehab instead of incarceration to more than 1,000 men and women. "We got tired of the revolving door, seeing the same person coming through court all the time," says Norman.

Since the United States stepped up efforts to crack down on drugs—with Nixon's war on drugs, declared in 1971, and the creation of the Drug Enforcement Administration two years later—jail cells have been the landing pad for addicts. Between 2000 and 2006, the number of drug offenders in federal prison jumped 26 percent, to 93,751. An additional 250,000 are incarcerated in state facilities and thousands more sit in local jail cells. This year the government has budgeted close to $13 billion for drug control, treatment and prevention. The DEA—whose mission is to stop drug trafficking—is certainly not going soft. But when it comes to the individual user, the addict who just can't quit, law-enforcement officials acknowledge that the old lock-'em-up approach is not only burden-some and expensive, it doesn't solve the problem. Addiction, says John P. Walters, director of the White House's Office of National Drug Control Policy, "Is not fundamentally about a moral falling, it's about something that really changes the way the brain functions."

Laws still treat drug use as a crime, but from Maryland to Hawaii, states are looking for new ways to steer drug offenders away from prison cells and into treatment. In the process, they hope to save millions of taxpayer dollars. The most ambitious program so far is California's Proposition 36, which offers convicted nonviolent drug offenders family counseling and job training in addition to treatment. Since the initiative was approved by voters in 2000, more than 36,000 people have been diverted into treatment every year. Still, Prop 36 advocates have fought to maintain adequate funding and the program has struggled with "very, very high rates of dropout," says Angela Hawken, a UCLA researcher.

One critical question: should addicts be held accountable for sticking with treatment? Judges like Norman believe the criminal Justice system must have the upper hand. In his court and in some 2,000 other drug courts nationwide, drug offenders must appear before a judge to make sure they're complying. If not, says Norman, "I'm going to send you back to Jail."

Drug courts reduce crime rates substantially, says West Huddleston of the National Association of Drug Court Professionals. About one quarter of offenders who go through drug courts are rearrested two years after treatment, compared with two thirds of those who don't. Opponents say drug courts are coercive. But "treatment is rarely truly voluntary," says Peter Reuter, a Drug-policy researcher at the University of Maryland. Be it a spouse, an employer or the criminal Justice system, "some degree of coercion is necessary," he says.

The problem is that even when treatment is provided, it often isn't very good. The key challenge is funding. Even as attitudes shift, the federal government still budgets far more for stopping drug flow and enforcing drug laws ($8.3 billion this year) than it does for treatment and prevention ($4.6 billion). Treatment programs are understaffed. Medications like methadone help some addicts, but harm others. Quitting is a grueling proposition. As a result, less than 10 percent of people who need treatment actually get it. And the proportion of people staying in treatment is "horrendously low," says David Gustafson of the Network for the Improvement of Addiction Treatment. New science may change all that one day. But for now, the battle goes on.

—Claudia Kalb with Tina Peng and Karen Springen

AA was essentially, the only legitimate option. There were "cures" of various sorts, including gold chloride injections, but there was virtually no modern neuroscience or psychopharmacology. Many people are now living in society with mental illnesses like schizophrenia and bipolar disorder that would have required institutionalization back then. Addicts, like the rest of the public, need to recognize the fact that we are entering a new era in addiction treatment. Viewing her condition as a chronic recurring disease that could be treated, was precisely what Dyess needed to return to sobriety. "In the past, when I would relapse," she says, "the thinking from 12-Step or from family was that I had failed. Now I know that if it happens, it happens, and I can pick myself up and move on, instead of assuming it's all over so I might as well keep drinking." The 12 Steps begin with a confession of powerlessness over addiction. But there's hope that science may some day help put that power within the reach of anyone who needs it. And then who would choose not to grasp it, and begin the long war for sobriety—a war without end, but one worth the fighting.

With **RAINA KELLEY**.

Getting Back on Track

Women who take career 'off ramps' to raise children often have trouble finding 'on ramps' when they are ready to work again. Now companies in need of talent are finally addressing the problem.

DANIEL McGINN

It's 4:30 on a weekday afternoon and ordinarily Caterina Bandini would be tracking headlines, tweaking scripts and preparing to take her seat at the anchor desk for the 5 o'clock news at Boston's NBC affiliate. Instead Bandini, 38, sits with her feet up in her Back Bay apartment, idly watching television as her station's broadcast begins. In October, Bandini will deliver twin girls. For most TV newswomen, childbirth brings only a brief maternity leave—Bandini's predecessor took six weeks—but she's made a different choice. In August, she quit her anchor job, intending to be a stay-at-home mom after her daughters are born. "I always thought it'd be important, at least for the first formative years, to spend as much time as I possibly could with my kids," she says. Bandini hopes someday to head back to a newsroom, but realizes there are no guarantees. "It's very difficult to get back into it—I took a huge risk doing this," she says.

A few years ago Bandini might have served as a prime example of the hot workplace trend: high-achieving women who were "opting out," quitting high-paying, sought-after jobs to raise children, care for aging parents or just escape from the chaos that often accompanies dual-income coupledom. Feminists decried the trend as a step backward, while skeptics questioned whether the statistics really showed women to be quitting in vast numbers. But lately, the debate over "Why Women Quit" has taken a subtle turn. The problem may not be that so many women take a break from salaried life; the more troubling issue is why it's so difficult for them to restart their careers when they're ready. Instead of persuading women not to leave their jobs and to stay on track toward leadership positions, lately the talk among work-family advocates has focused on finding ways to support women's "non-linear" career paths—and to build better "on ramps" for women wishing to return to work after career pauses.

For women who hope to make this transition, there are a growing number of highly visible role models. Last week Meredith Vieira, who famously quit "60 Minutes" to spend time with her children, slid into Katie Couric's old seat at NBC's "Today" show after nine years on ABC's "The View." Last year

Brenda Barnes, who quit a top job at PepsiCo in 1998 to reconnect with her kids, ascended to become CEO at Sara Lee. This month actress Calista Flockhart returns to network television after five years at home with her child. Meanwhile, a host of companies—investment banks, consulting firms, law firms—are trying to make it easier for nonfamous women to segue back to work as well. These businesses aren't motivated simply by altruism, but by the recognition that these off-ramped women may be an underutilized source of talent. says, Eliza Shanley, cofounder of the Women@Work Network "There's a general sense among employers that whoever figures this out first wins."

The issue is hardly new, women have been talking about the ideal ways to integrate childbearing and family responsibilities into a high-stress career for decades. The growing focus on the issue—along with the vivid on-ramp/off-ramp metaphor—stem from a research study published last year in the Harvard Business Review. Based on a survey of midcareer women who hold graduate degrees or college degrees with honors, it found that 37 percent had taken extended breaks from work, with the average off-ramper staying home for 2.2 years. Most wanted to return to work, but just 40 percent regained full-time employment. The research put a spotlight on one reason so few women are advancing into corner offices. Says Sylvia Ann Hewlett, president of the Center for Work-Life Policy and the study's lead author, "The old idea was, all you needed to do was fill the pipeline with women and wait around for a couple of decades for them to move through the ranks. [But] there's an enormous amount of leakage from the pipeline—once women off-ramp even for a short while, it's incredibly difficult to get back in."

Since the study appeared, companies have begun rolling out new ways to address the problem. Last November Lehman Bros. invited 75 unemployed women who'd once worked on Wall Street to a back-to-work seminar. Part of the program, called Encore, dealt with technical banking issues, providing a sort of Cliffs Notes version of industry changes they've missed in the past few years. But much of it was focused on nuts-and-bolts concerns like how to talk about your years at home during an interview. Lehman hosted a similar event last spring, and will do another this November. So far, it's hired 16 of the women. Beyond the new hires, the program has helped Lehman portray itself as more family-friendly when visiting college campuses (where interest in Wall Street careers among young woman has been waning). It's also helped managers see beyond the firm's traditional MO of recruiting mostly new college grads, new M.B.A.s and employees of rival firms. Says Anne Erni, Lehman's chief diversity officer: "We've now created this fourth legitimate pool of talent."

The focus lately is on finding ways to support women's 'nonlinear' career paths.

Other firms are launching programs to help women ease back to work at a pace that suits them. At consulting firm Booz Allen Hamilton, more than 100 women who were once full-time employees now work in an "adjunct" program. The firm slices off discrete pieces of work—often research or proposal writing—for its adjuncts, who aren't on the payroll but have kept their Booz Allen e-mail addresses. The adjuncts (who include some men) can not only negotiate pay for each project, but also the terms under which they'll accept it. How many days a week must they work? Can they telecommute? Will it involve travel? Ani Singh, a 1997 Wharton M.B.A. who left the firm in 2002, now works as an adjunct in Virginia. She routinely turns down assignments that won't let her spend enough time with her child, but she never lacks for new opportunities. "I still feel like I'm making progress in my career whether I'm within the formal organization or not," Singh says. And the firm hopes that when she's ready to return to full-time work, she won't bother sending out résumés. "We want them to think only about coming back to us—that's why we put this in place," says senior VP DeAnne Aguirre.

Meanwhile, business schools are recognizing that helping women find on ramps could become a profitable market niche. This year several B-schools—Wharton, Harvard, Babson, Dartmouth, Pepperdine—have begun experimenting with on-ramping courses, ranging from Pepperdine's full-blown M.B.A. geared toward mothers with young children (starting in January), to Dartmouth's 11-day "Back in Business" executive education course, which launches next month. Ronna Reyes Sieh, a mother of three who earned her M.B.A. at Columbia in 1998 before logging three years at Morgan Stanley, will attend the Dartmouth program. She hopes not only to jump-start her job

hunt, but to learn more about managing a fast-paced job without neglecting family responsibilities. "I want to be connected with other women in the same position," she says.

Amid the growing focus on helping women on-ramp, there's some fear that companies may view the issue as a magic bullet. Like diets, work-family programs can be faddish; long after firms showed bursts of enthusiasm for on-site day care or job-sharing, women still don't seem to be advancing in the numbers some advocates would like. "These are catchy phrases that are trying to give a simple explanation for a piece of what's very complex," says Ilene Lang, president of Catalyst, a research and advisory group focused on women in business. She fears that even women who make it back on track will still suffer from the larger problems facing female professionals, such as a lack of high-ranking role models and lack of access to informal networks.

It's also true that while progressive companies are rolling out on-ramping initiatives, most of the onus for successfully navigating this transition remains on the women themselves. Monica Samuels is an off-ramped Houston attorney and coauthor of "Comeback Moms," a book she conceived after meeting so many female law-school classmates who'd quit working and had no idea how to resume careers. She cites unexpected factors that intimidate would-be on-rampers, from the shift to business-casual dress to the never-ending rush of technology ("What's a BlackBerry?"). Some of these women also discover that their husbands grew content having them at home. To help overcome self-imposed hurdles—including lack of confidence—Samuels suggests small steps, like continuing to list "lawyer" or "accountant" (instead of "stay-at-home mom") on the "occupation" line when filling out paperwork at the pediatrician's office. "Sometimes women completely divorce themselves from people who are working and become isolated," she says. "That's not a good thing to do."

For Bandini, the newly unemployed news anchor, all thoughts of returning to work take a distant back seat to her soon-to-arrive babies. Financially, she's comfortable, thanks partly to her husband, who runs an aviation-equipment company. But even as she prepares for motherhood, her agent, Pam Pulner, will be making sure TV execs don't forget about her. Bandini may wait until her children are in school to begin working again, but Pulner says most of the TV women she represents resume their careers more quickly than they expected. "When she wants to come back, there will be a place for her," Pulner says. With luck and over time, more women will be able to find their places, too.

With Robbie Brown and Claudia Adrien.

Men & Depression

Facing Darkness

JULIE SCELFO

For nearly a decade, while serving as an elected official and working as an attorney, Massachusetts state Sen. Bob Antonioni struggled with depression, although he didn't know it. Most days, he attended Senate meetings and appeared on behalf of clients at the courthouse. But privately, he was irritable and short-tempered, ruminating endlessly over his cases and becoming easily frustrated by small things, like deciding which TV show to watch with his girlfriend. After a morning at the state house, he'd be so exhausted by noon that he'd drive home and collapse on the couch, unable to move for the rest of the day.

When his younger brother, who was similarly moody, killed himself in 1999, Antonioni, then 40, decided to seek help. For three years, he clandestinely saw a therapist, paying in cash so there would be no record. He took antidepressants, but had his prescriptions filled at a pharmacy 20 miles away. His depression was his burden, and his secret. He couldn't bear for his image to be any less than what he thought it should be. "I didn't want to sound like I couldn't take care of myself, that I wasn't a man," says Antonioni.

Then, in 2002, his chief of staff discovered him on the floor of his state-house office, unable to stop crying. Antonioni, now 48, decided he had to open up to his friends and family. A few months later, invited to speak at a mental-health vigil, he found the courage to talk publicly about his problem. Soon after, a local reporter wrote about Antonioni's ongoing struggle with the disease. Instead of being greeted with jeers, he was hailed as a hero, and inundated with cards and letters from his constituents. "The response was universally positive. I was astounded."

Six million American men will be diagnosed with depression this year. But millions more suffer silently, unaware that their problem has a name or unwilling to seek treatment. In a confessional culture in which Americans are increasingly obsessed with their health, it may seem cliché—men are from Mars, women from Venus, and all that—to say that men tend not to take care of themselves and are reluctant to own up to mental illness. But the facts suggest that, well, men tend not to take care of themselves and are reluctant to own up to mental illness. Although depression is emotionally crippling and has numerous medical implications—some of them deadly—many men fail to recognize the symptoms. Instead of talking about their feelings, men may mask them with alcohol, drug abuse, gambling, anger or by becoming workaholics. And even when they do realize they have a problem, men often view asking for help as an admission of weakness, a betrayal of their male identities.

The result is a hidden epidemic of despair that is destroying marriages, disrupting careers, filling jail cells, clogging emergency rooms and costing society billions of dollars in lost productivity and medical bills. It is also creating a cohort of children who carry the burden of their fathers' pain for the rest of their lives. The Gary Cooper model of manhood—what Tony Soprano called "the strong, silent type" to his psychiatrist, Dr. Melfi—is so deeply embedded in our social psyche that some men would rather kill themselves than confront the fact that they feel despondent, inadequate or helpless. "Our definition of a successful man in this culture does not include being depressed, down or sad," says Michael Addis, chair of psychology at Clark University in Massachusetts. "In many ways it's the exact

---

Living in His Own 'Prison'

Dr. James Siepmann, 47
Siepmann, a family physician and father of five, gave up his medical practice in 2000 when his depression got so bad he couldn't bring himself to get dressed in the morning. Despite numerous types of treatment, he spends most days at home and can only muster the energy to shave once a week. "It's like the life of Aleksandr Solzhenitsyn," he says. "But instead of a Russian gulag, my prison is depression."

Back in the Game, Helping Others

Philip Burguires, 63
As a wealthy CEO, Burguires lived "the American dream." But twice, depression floored him. Today he is fully recovered and spends 10 hours a week counseling other CEOs. "The way you get to those positions in today's world, you work harder, you have to be a little more obsessive, more driven. Those qualities are things that lead to depression." He's met hundreds of CEOs and boldly estimates as many as half the people running Fortune 500 companies have the disease.

opposite. A successful man is always up, positive, in charge and in control of his emotions."

As awareness of the problem grows—among the public and medical professionals alike—the stigma surrounding male depression is beginning to lift. New tools for diagnosing the disease—which ranges from the chronic inability to feel good, to major depression, to bipolar disorder—and new approaches to treating it, offer hope for millions. And as scientists gain insight into how depression occurs in the brain, their findings are spurring research into an array of new treatments including faster-acting, more-effective drugs that could benefit those who struggle with what Winston Churchill called his "black dog."

For decades, psychologists believed that men experienced depression at only a fraction of the rate of women. But this overly rosy view, doctors now recognize, was due to the fact that men were better at hiding their feelings. Depressed women often weep and talk about feeling bad; depressed men are more likely to get into bar fights, scream at their wives, have affairs or become enraged by small inconveniences like lousy service at a restaurant. "Men's irritability is usually seen as a character flaw," says Harvard Medical School's William Pollack, "not as a sign of depression." In many cases, however, that's exactly what it is: depression.

If modern psychologists were slow to understand how men's emotions affect their behaviors, it's only because their predecessors long ago decided that having a uterus was the main risk factor for mental illness. During the last two centuries, depression was largely viewed as a female problem, an outgrowth of hormonal fluctuations stemming from puberty, childbirth and menopause. Even the most skilled psychologists and psychiatrists missed their male patients' mood disorders, believing that depressed men, like depressed women, would talk openly about feeling blue. "I misdiagnosed male depression for years and years," says psychologist Archibald Hart, author of "Unmasking Male Depression."

Some of the symptoms of depression are so severe, like gambling addiction or alcoholism, they are often mistaken for the problem. David Feherty, the affable CBS golf commentator and former golf pro, began drinking at such a young age it became part of his personality. "I drank a bottle of whisky in order to get ready to start drinking," he jokes. By his 40s, he routinely consumed two bottles of whisky a day, and was in such physical pain, he thought he suffered from "some kind of degenerative muscle disease." During that period, he maintained a jovial front, and kept up a steady stream of on-air wisecracks during golf tournaments. "It was a problem that just, I don't know, ate itself up and got bigger and bigger and then, one day, *bang*, I disappeared." When he finally learned in 2005 that he suffered from depression, he felt a combination of shock and relief. "That was the most stunning thing. I just thought I was a lousy husband and miserable bastard and a drunk," says Feherty, now 48. "A mental illness? Me? I had no idea."

The annual economic impact of adult depression is estimated at $83 billion in lost productivity.

The widespread failure to recognize depression in men has enormous medical and financial consequences. Depression has been linked to heart disease, heart attacks and strokes, problems that affect men at a higher rate and an earlier age than women. Men with depression and heart disease are two or three times more likely

Trying to Be a 'Manly Man'

Stephen Akinduro, 35
Despite a family history of depression (his mother committed suicide when he was 8) and years of "feeling bad and isolated," Akinduro didn't seek help. "In the black community, being a black male, we just don't talk about that kind of thing." Instead, he tried to "be the manly man." He was promiscuous and avoided close friendships. Eventually he took a screening test. Today Akinduro takes part in a support group, gets counseling at his church, and longs to marry and start a family.

Getting Better, Staying Sober

David Feherty, 48
Feherty was watching TV, a near-empty bottle of whiskey in hand, when his 6-year-old daughter changed his life. "She actually climbed up in my lap and said, 'Dad, you need another bottle'." Devastated, he sought help for his drinking, and was quickly diagnosed with depression. It took three tries to find the right therapist. "Half of what makes you feel better is having someone to talk to who doesn't think you're irrevocably broken." Feherty has been sober one year.

to die than men with heart disease who are not depressed. Lost productivity due to adult depression is estimated at $83 billion a year. Over the past 50 years, American men of all ages have killed themselves at four or more times the rate of women, depending on the specific age range.

Over the past 50 years, men of all ages have killed themselves at four or more times the rate of women.

A general practitioner is usually the first—and often, the only—medical professional a depressed man encounters. In 1990, when Mark Totten began sleeping a lot, refusing food and acting sullen, his sister, Julie, suggested he see a doctor, but never for a moment did she think it was life threatening. "I didn't know anything about depression back then," says Julie. In November of that year, Mark, 24, lay down on an Iowa train track and ended his life. Totten learned afterward that her brother had indeed visited his primary-care physician but complained only of stomachaches, headaches and just generally "not feeling so great," she says. The doctor didn't make the connection.

Confronted with a patient making vague medical complaints who is unwilling (or unable) to talk about his feelings, the hurried primary-care physician often finds it difficult if not impossible to assess a patient's emotional state. To help clear that hurdle, researchers developed a simple screening test for doctors to use: *Over the last two weeks, have you been bothered by either of the*

A Common Condition

Men in the midst of depression can often feel they're alone. But researchers estimate that more than 6 million men in the United States are depressed, and the disorder has afflicted numerous well-regarded public figures. Some examples:

Explaining the Gender Gap

Experts think depressed men, who are less likely than women to seek help, may find means other than treatment (such as drinking) to cope, leaving many cases unreported. Rates by gender:

Depression		Alcoholism	
Men	7%	Men	7%
Women	12%	Women	3%

Men Who Have Battled Depression

Abraham Lincoln

U.S. President
Of a famously melancholy temperament, Lincoln suffered bouts of serious depression from childhood through the years of his presidency.

Ernest Hemingway

Writer
In his later years, the Nobel Prize-winning author wrestled increasingly with alcoholism and depression. In 1961, he shot himself in his Idaho home.

Buzz Aldrin

Astronaut
Unprepared for the celebrity that followed his famed moonwalk, Aldrin became despondent and turned to alcohol. Treatment helped him to recover.

Thomas Eagleton

VP Candidate
In 1972 he withdrew as George McGovern's running mate after it came to light that he had a history of depression and had received shock therapy.

Dick Cavett

Talk-Show Host
Cavett's affable persona belied an inner despair that had plagued him off and on since college. Antidepressants allowed him to recuperate.

Terry Bradshaw

TV Commentator
Professional help enabled the four-time Super Bowl winner to rebound after he became severely depressed when his third marriage ended.

Mike Wallace

'60 Minutes'
Host
With antidepressants, Wallace overcame the major depression that resulted from a $120 million libel suit filed against CBS because of one of his reports.

William Styron

Writer Styron
described his descent into near suicidal depression and alcoholism as well as his hard-fought recovery in his book "Darkness Visible."

Kurt Cobain

Musician
Cobain's lyrics often expressed emotional anguish, and the journals published after his 1994 suicide detailed his many struggles with depression.

Drew Carey

Comedian
Before Carey made his name as a comic, he weathered recurrent spells of sometimes debilitating depression and twice attempted to kill himself.

Disparities in Suicide

Though more women than men attempt suicide, more men die from suicide, in part because men tend to use more-lethal methods, such as firearms, and are quicker to act on suicidal thoughts.

Suicide Attempts	Deaths from Suicide, 2004	
For every male attempt, there are 2 to 3 female attempts	Men	25,566
	Women	6,873

following problems: (a) little interest or pleasure in doing things? or (b) feeling down, depressed or hopeless? If a patient responds "yes," seven more questions can be administered, which result in a 0 to 27 rating. Score in hand, many physicians feel more comfortable broaching the subject of depression, and men seem more willing to discuss it. "It's a way of making it more concrete," says Indiana University's Dr. Kurt Kroenke, who helped design the questionnaires. "Patients can see how severe their scores are, just like if you showed them blood-sugar or cholesterol levels."

Depression-screening tests are so effective at early detection and may prevent so many future problems (and expenses) that the U.S.

Army is rolling out a new, enhanced screening program for soldiers returning from Iraq. College health-center Web sites nationwide provide the service to their students, and even the San Francisco Giants organization offers these tests to its employees.

At Clark University in Massachusetts, where Sigmund Freud introduced his theories to America, researchers are developing new clinical strategies to encourage men to seek help. The Men's Coping Project, led by Michael Addis, recruits men for interviews and discussion groups that focus not on depression but on how they deal with "the stresses of living." At a recent staff meeting, the team reviewed the file of a middle-aged local man who described himself as stressed, angry and isolated, but vehemently denied that he was depressed. In a questionnaire, the man indicated that he preferred "to just suck it up" rather than dwell on his problems and that he believed part of being a man was "being in control." Researchers decided that rather than say "you have a problem" or "you need help," they would praise his self-reliance and emotional discipline, and suggest that meeting with a counselor might be the most effective way for him to "take charge of the situation." So far, Addis and his team have met with 50 men, some of whom said they would seek counseling, and they plan to interview another 50 before the program concludes next year.

For decades, scientists believed the main cause of depression was low levels of the neurotransmitters serotonin and norepinephrine. Newer research, however, focuses on the nerve cells themselves and how the brain's circuitry can be permanently damaged by hyperactive stress responses, brought on by genetic predisposition, prolonged exposure to stress or even a single traumatic event. "When the stress responses are stuck in the 'on' position, that has a negative effect on mood regulation overall," says Dr. Michael C. Miller, editor of the Harvard Mental Health Letter. A depressed brain is not necessarily underproducing something, says Dr. Thomas Insel, head of the National Institute of Mental Health—it's doing too much.

These discoveries have opened up broad new possibilities for treatment. Instead of focusing on boosting neurotransmitters (the function of antidepressants in the popular SSRI category such as Prozac and Zoloft), scientists are developing medications that block the production of excess stress chemicals, hoping to reduce damage to otherwise healthy nerve cells. They are also looking at hormones. In a recent study, DHEA, an over-the-counter hormonal therapy, was shown to be effective in treating major and minor midlife-onset depression. And Canadian scientists have had success with deep brain stimulation—a procedure in which two thin electrodes are implanted in the brain to send a continuous electrical current to Area 25, a tiny, almond-shaped node thought to play a role in controlling emotions. In recent trials involving patients who got no relief from other forms of treatment, all the subjects reported mood improvements within six months and, remarkably, most said they were completely cured of depression.

Researchers at the NIMH are also experimenting with the idea of fast-acting antidepressants that would relieve symptoms in a few hours instead of the eight weeks or more needed for most antidepressants to take effect. In clinical trials, scientists found that a single, IV-administered dose of ketamine, an animal tranquilizer, reduced the symptoms of depression in just two to three hours and had long-lasting effects. Because of its hallucinogenic side effects, ketamine can never be used out of controlled environments. But the success of the trial is giving scientists new ideas about drugs and methods of administering them.

One study found that 67% of patients who complete from one to four treatment steps can get better.

The most effective remedy remains a combination of medication and therapy, but finding the right drug and dosage is still more art than science. The nation's largest depression-treatment study, STAR*D, a three-year NIMH-funded project, found that 67 percent

Reaching Out, Finding Relief

Sen. Bob Antonioni, 48
Finding the right medication was a difficult process for Antonioni. "I remember grinding my teeth a lot," he says. But his perseverance paid off. "There is relief. I wish I knew that in 1999." Today he experiences the normal ups and downs of modern life, but no longer feels like everything is a struggle. "Life is too short to be hurting so much." Although speaking publicly about his feelings terrified him at first, strangers responded with words of thanks.

of patients who complete from one to four treatment steps, such as trying a different medication or seeking counseling, can reach remission. The process can be onerous and frustrating, and the potential side effects, including a low libido, can be hard to take—especially for men. Stephen Akinduro, 35, an unemployed phone operator in Georgia whose mother had committed suicide, tried two different drugs over a three-year period, but both resulted in weight gain, fatigue and a diminished sexual performance. "When that happened I was, like, 'What is going on here?'" says Akinduro. Frustrated, he gave up on antidepressants. Today he gets free counseling through his church and a local support group. Twelve years after his diagnosis, he is still struggling.

Often the person who seeks treatment isn't the depressed man, but his fed-up wife. Terrence Real, author of "I Don't Want to Talk About It: Overcoming the Secret Legacy of Male Depression," says most men in counseling are what he calls "wife-mandated referrals." When depression left Phil Aronson unable to get out of bed, feed himself or even pick up the phone, his wife, Emme, the well-known model, physically helped him into the shower, found doctors and therapists, and drove him to appointments, even escorting him inside. At one point, when Phil became suicidal, doctors told Emme it was her job to make sure he continued taking his medication and keep him safe from himself. "It was such an incredibly awesome, all-encompassing responsibility," says Emme, who became the sole caretaker of Toby, their daughter, then 2 years old. Even when the depression began to lift, her husband's moodiness took a toll on their marriage and Emme's career. "I had to be caretaker, I had to be a supportive wife, I had to leave my work. I was developing a new TV show and had to drop it." Today Phil is recovered, and Emme is thrilled to once again have a partner who makes her laugh, contributes to the relationship and helps parent Toby, now 5.

Success and wealth offer no protection from the ravages of depression. At 46, Philip Burguières was running a Fortune 500 company, traveling constantly and meeting with shareholders, when, in the middle of a staff meeting on a Tuesday afternoon, he suddenly collapsed. Doctors diagnosed him with depression and encouraged him to leave his high-stress job. But after a short hospital stay, he was back in the game and by the following year was running Weatherford International, an energy-services company with $3 billion in revenues. The pressure became unbearable, and in 1996 he once again took a medical leave. "The second one was a grade-A, level-10, atomic-bomb depression," he says. In his darkest moments, he was certain the world would be better off without him, but even then, he felt enormous pressure to succeed. "I want out, but

'I Never Knew What to Expect'

Depressed Parents Often Leave Their Children a Legacy of Fear and Anxiety

Tammi Landry, 36, loves movies—but not "Father of the Bride." It reminds her of all the ways her own painful childhood didn't measure up. Five years ago, Landry's father, a police officer in Indiana, killed himself. It was devastating for the mother of two young sons, but not a shock. Even as a little girl, she sensed something was wrong. "I never knew what to expect," says Landry, who lives in suburban Detroit. "One day, I'm at the center of his world, and the next day, he could be distant, uninterested. All hell could break loose because I left a towel on the bathroom floor." Landry realizes now that her father suffered from undiagnosed depression. "He was a man, a cop," she says. "There was never any asking for help."

Depressed parents like Landry's father often leave a legacy of fear and anxiety—emotions forged in childhood that can linger a lifetime. Reflecting on her family history after her brother's suicide, Julie Totten, founder of Families for Depression Awareness, realized that her father had been depressed for years. In one recent study at Columbia University, researchers found that rates of anxiety disorders and depression were three times as high among the adult children of depressed parents as they were among people whose parents were not depressed. Adult children of depressed parents also reported about five times the rate of cardiovascular disease—a sign that emotional disorders affect more than mood. Even kids who manage to succeed socially often struggle at home to care for their parents or younger siblings. "Depression has an entire family dynamic," says Myrna Weissman, the lead researcher in the Columbia study.

A predisposition to mood disorders may be inherited, and researchers still haven't teased out how much of a child's problem can be traced to genes and how much to growing up with an unstable or unresponsive parent. They do know that even the youngest children are vulnerable. Babies of depressed mothers, for example, are particularly at risk because infants learn to communicate through their mothers' responses. An apathetic mother sets up a child for a lifetime of social and emotional problems.

But thanks to new research, an unhappy ending is not inevitable. Weissman's team found that many children improved after their parents were treated. At the beginning of her study of 151 depressed mothers and their children, about half the youngsters had a history of psychiatric disorders and a third were suffering from mental-health problems. The mothers were all put on an antidepressant. (The kids were not treated as part of the study, but a few were under medical care.) The recovery rate for kids with mental-health problems whose mothers' depression lifted was nearly three times that of similar kids whose mothers did not respond to treatment.

It took Landry years to face her past. After her father's suicide, she and her husband divorced. That sent her into therapy, where she finally got help. She currently takes medication for anxiety and is doing well but, aware of genetic susceptibilities, she watches her 4-year-old son closely. "He wants to be good at everything," she says. "He's so hard on himself. I would do whatever it takes to make sure he's OK." She's already doing the most important thing she can do for him: taking care of herself.

—Barbara Kantrowitz with Joan Raymond

---

am stuck because I have never quit anything in my life," he wrote in a hospital diary. Strengthened by counseling and a friendship with a similarly depressed CEO, Burguières attained what he describes as a "full recovery" and stepped down as CEO. He found new work running a family investment company and as vice chairman of the NFL's Houston Texans, positions that permit him to delegate more responsibility and have more fun. He also found that helping other people was the best way for him to get better, and since 1998, he has been privately counseling the numerous depressed CEOs who seek him out. "You get outside yourself; you don't obsess on your own issues," he says.

Fading social stigmas are already making it easier for young men to come forward. Recently, Zach Braff, filmmaker and star of TV's "Scrubs," told a reporter from Parade magazine that he thinks he suffers from "mild depression." At colleges and universities across the nation, health officials are putting mental-health care front and center. At UCLA, the Student Psychological Services moved two years ago from a basement office to a bright building in the center of campus across from Pauley Pavilion. In January, center director Elizabeth Gong-Guy walked through the waiting room and noticed that every person there was male. "It was amazing to me," she says. "I've been doing this for 18 years and that's not something you would have seen even three years ago."

Social attitudes toward depression are changing, thanks in part to men themselves. John Aberle is a sales and marketing consultant, retired Air Force security specialist, part-time radio talk-show host, devoted husband, active father and a 6-foot-4, 250-pound bodybuilder who twice faced a depression so deep, he cried on his knees. He readily tells other men it's their duty to get better. "There's no crime in having a disorder, whatever it is," says Aberle, 38. "The crime is not dealing with it. It's your responsibility to be at the top of your game." Taking care of yourself physically, mentally *and* emotionally—maybe that's the real definition of what it means to be a man.

With Karen Springen in Chicago and Mary Carmichael in Boston.

UNIT 6

Development During Middle and Late Adulthood

Unit Selections

Key Points to Consider

- Does laughter serve biological functions? If so, what are the uses of laughter that are regulated by our primitive instincts?

- How do adults over age 50 view their lives? What changes do they see in themselves?

- Are the middle-adulthood years the best years of one's life? What new research suggests that this is true?

- What do adults with disabilities have to teach us about work?

- Why do adults who could live on their retirement incomes choose to continue to work? Why do some of them embark on entirely new careers?

- How do some people live over 100 years and remain in good health? What are their secrets?

- People with Alzheimer's disease have lost many of their memories. Can new therapies help them rediscover some of their past knowledge?

- What do middle and late adulthood Americans believe about life after death?

- What are the ethics of terminal care? Who should prepare advance-care directives? When?

Student Web Site

www.mhcls.com

Internet References

Alzheimer's Disease Research Center
http://alzheimer.wustl.edu/

American Association of Retired Persons
http://www.aarp.org

Lifestyle Factors Affecting Late Adulthood
http://www.school-for-champions.com/health/lifestyle_elderly.htm

National Aging Information and Referral Support Center
http://www.nausa.org/informationandreferral/index-ir.php

Department of Health and Human Services—Aging
http://www.hhs.gov/aging/index.html

Joseph Campbell, a twentieth-century sage, said that the privilege of a lifetime is being who you are. This ego-confidence often arrives during middle and late adulthood, even as physical confidence declines. There is a gradual slowing of the rate of mitosis of cells of all the organ systems with age. This gradual slowing of mitosis translates into a slowed rate of repair of cells of all organs. By the 40s, signs of aging can be seen in skin, skeleton, vision, hearing, smell, taste, balance, coordination, heart, blood vessels, lungs, liver, kidneys, digestive tract, immune response, endocrine functioning, and ability to reproduce. To some extent, moderate use of any body part (as opposed to disuse or misuse) helps retain its strength, stamina, and repairability. However, by middle and late adulthood persons become increasingly aware of the effects of aging organ systems on their total physical fitness. A loss of height occurs as spinal disks and connective tissues diminish and settle. Demineralization, especially loss of calcium, causes weakening of bones. Muscles atrophy, and the slowing of cardiovascular and respiratory responses creates a loss of stamina for exercise. All of this may seem cruel, but it occurs very gradually and need not adversely affect a person's enjoyment of life.

Healthful aging, at least in part, seems to be genetically preprogrammed. The females of many species, including humans, out live the males. The sex hormones of females may protect them from some early aging effects. Males, in particular, experience earlier declines in their cardiovascular system. Diet and exercise can ward off many of the deleterious effects of aging. A reduction in saturated fat (low density lipid) intake coupled with regular aerobic exercise contributes to less bone demineralization, less plaque in the arteries, stronger muscles (including heart and lung muscles), and a general increase in stamina and vitality. An adequate intake of complex carbohydrates, fibrous foods, fresh fruits, fresh vegetables, unsaturated fats (high density lipids), and water also enhances good health.

Cognitive abilities do not appreciably decline with age in healthy adults. Research suggests that the speed with which the brain carries out problems involving abstract (fluid) reasoning may slow but not cease. Complex problems may simply require more time to solve with age. On the other hand, research suggests that the memory banks of older people may have more crystallized (accumulated and stored) knowledge and more insight. Creativity also frequently spurts after age 50. One's ken (range of knowledge) and practical skills (common sense) grow with age and experience. Older human beings also become expert at the cognitive tasks they frequently do. Many cultures celebrate these abilities as the "wisdom of age."

The first article about middle adulthood speaks of the urge to laugh. New brain research reported in "Emotions and the Brain: Laughter" suggests that laughing is a form of instinctive social bonding. We do not make a conscious decision to laugh. We are often unaware that we are laughing. And laughter is contagious. It makes us healthier by enhancing our immune responsivity and

© Keith Thomas Publications/Brand X Pictures/PictureQuest

reducing our stress hormones. The "wisdom of age" may allow us to be more frivolous, and to take more pleasure in happy friendships within our families and communities. Children laugh freely. Somehow many adults learn to suppress laughter and be more serious. Perhaps some wisdom and maturity is evidenced by not trying to suppress this important biological response.

"Fifty Reasons to Love Being 50+" is a collection of anecdotes from older adults (including B. B. King, Judge Judy, and Martina Navratilova) explaining the joys of seniority. Old age for these respondents represents wisdom, veneration, and autonomy, coupled with new creative outlets and the love of friends and family.

"The Fine Art of Letting Go" addresses the angst of launching adult children into independent lives. The anxiety of leaving offspring at college can be overwhelming. Some parents hover with too many phone calls and/or e-mails, text messages, and so on. Barbara Kantrowitz and Peg Tyre present a short quiz about "helicopter parents" and a list of twelve steps to foster independence in both adult children and their detaching parents.

The next selection, "The Myth of the Midlife Crisis," dismisses midlife as the beginning of a downward spiral toward death. New research evidence is presented that suggests increased creativity, a new sense of self, deeper knowledge, and better judgment in the second half of life. It makes one anticipate aging with hope and joy.

The last middle-adulthood selection, "The Wonder of Work," depicts the meaning of employment to persons with disabilities. Teri Arnold writes, "It is often in the most unexpected places where we find the greatest gifts." The grateful workers explain why their jobs bring them so much joy. Their answers are inspirational.

Erik Erikson suggested that the most important psychological conflict of late adulthood is achieving a sense of ego integrity. This is fostered by self-respect, self-esteem, love of others, and a sense that one's life has order and meaning. The articles in the subsection on late adulthood reflect Erikson's concern with experiencing ego integrity rather than despair.

The first late-adulthood article, "Second Time Around," deliberates opinions about second (or third or fourth) careers begun at the age of retirement. Daniel McGinn offers amicable and constructive judgments and conclusions about the benefits of meaningful work in old age. For many people, retirement is the perfect time to begin a new business adventure. It can be an exciting time to pursue one's dreams, with the fall-back security of a guaranteed retirement income.

In "Secrets of the Centenarians," Maya Pines portrays the lives of several people who are over age 100 but who appear to be in their 70s or early 80s. Researchers have identified genetic markers on the fourth pair of chromosomes that may contribute to longevity and good health. It may be possible in the future to manipulate the single-nucleotide polymorphisms (SNPs) to allow everyone to live as long as the centenarians being studied.

The third late-adulthood selection, "Lost and Found," deals with people with Alzheimer's disease. The author, Barbara Basler, describes new therapeutic methods devised by Cameron Camp, the head of the Myers Research Institute in Ohio. Dr. Camp's methods, deemed valid and reliable by researchers, help draw patients out of their confusion and recapture some of their basic skills and knowledge.

The fourth article deals with life after death. Over 1,000 Americans over age 50 were asked to share their beliefs about God, Heaven, Hell, and/or what they believe happens after death. The author found a surprising lack of fear about death. His results give a fascinating picture of opinions about whether Heaven and Hell are places, or states of being. Many respondents mentioned reincarnation. The author also explains what is known about near-death experiences.

The last article describes end-of-life care. The author, Helen Sorenson, discusses the conflicting opinions that create turmoil for patients, family, friends, and health care professionals when death is imminent. "Navigating Practical Dilemmas in Terminal Care" gives useful information on how to reduce such conflicts. Family conferences should occur well ahead of the end of life to discuss the terms of advance-care directives. Asking questions and communicating openly can prevent misunderstandings.

Emotions and the Brain: Laughter

If evolution comes down to survival of the fittest, then why do we joke around so much? New brain research suggests that the urge to laugh is the lubricant that makes humans higher social beings.

STEVEN JOHNSON

Robert Provine wants me to see his Tickle Me Elmo doll. Wants me to hold it, as a matter of fact. It's not an unusual request for Provine. A professor of psychology and neuroscience at the University of Maryland, he has been engaged for a decade in a wide-ranging intellectual pursuit that has taken him from the panting play of young chimpanzees to the history of American sitcoms—all in search of a scientific understanding of that most unscientific of human customs: laughter.

The Elmo doll happens to incorporate two of his primary obsessions: tickling and contagious laughter. "You ever fiddled with one of these?" Provine says, as he pulls the doll out of a small canvas tote bag. He holds it up, and after a second or two, the doll begins to shriek with laughter. There's something undeniably comic in the scene: a burly, bearded man in his mid-fifties cradling a red Muppet. Provine hands Elmo to me to demonstrate the doll's vibration effect. "It brings up two interesting things," he explains, as I hold Elmo in my arms. "You have a best-selling toy that's a glorified laugh box. And when it shakes, you're getting feedback as if you're tickling."

Provine's relationship to laughter reminds me of the dramatic technique that Bertolt Brecht called the distanciation effect. Radical theater, in Brecht's vision, was supposed to distance us from our too-familiar social structures, make us see those structures with fresh eyes. In his study of laughter, Provine has been up to something comparably enlightening, helping us to recognize the strangeness of one of our most familiar emotional states. Think about that Tickle Me Elmo doll: We take it for granted that tickling causes laughter and that one person's laughter will easily "infect" other people within earshot. Even a child knows these things. (Tickling and contagious laughter are two of the distinguishing characteristics of childhood.) But when you think about them from a distance, they are strange conventions. We can understand readily enough why natural selection would have implanted the fight-or-flight response in us or endowed us with sex drives. But the tendency to laugh when others laugh in our presence or to laugh when someone strokes our belly with a feather—what's the evolutionary advantage of that? And yet a quick glance at the Nielsen ratings or the personal ads will tell you that laughter is one of the most satisfying and sought-after states available to us.

Funnily enough, the closer Provine got to understanding why we laugh, the farther he got from humor. To appreciate the roots of laughter, you have to stop thinking about jokes.

There is a long, semi-illustrious history of scholarly investigation into the nature of humor, from Freud's *Jokes and Their Relation to the Unconscious,* which may well be the least funny book about humor ever written, to a British research group that announced last year that they had determined the World's Funniest Joke. Despite the fact that the researchers said they had sampled a massive international audience in making this discovery, the winning joke revolved around New Jersey residents:

A couple of New Jersey hunters are out in the woods when one of them falls to the ground. He doesn't seem to be breathing; his eyes are rolled back in his head. The other guy whips out his cell phone and calls the emergency services. He gasps to the operator: "My friend is dead! What can I do?"

The operator says: "Take it easy. I can help. First, let's make sure he's dead." There is silence, then a shot is heard. The guy's voice comes back on the line. He says, "OK, now what?"

This joke illustrates that most assessments of humor's underlying structure gravitate to the notion of controlled incongruity: You're expecting x, and you get y. For the joke to work, it has to be readable on both levels. In the hunting joke there are two plausible ways to interpret the 911 operator's instructions—either the hunter checks his friend's pulse or he shoots him. The context sets you up to expect that he'll check his friend's pulse, so the—admittedly dark—humor arrives when he takes the more unlikely path. That incongruity has limits, of course: If the hunter chooses to do something utterly nonsensical—untie his shoelaces or climb a tree—the joke wouldn't be funny.

A number of studies in recent years have looked at brain activity while subjects were chuckling over a good joke—an attempt to locate a neurological funny bone. There is evidence that the frontal lobes are implicated in "getting" the joke while the brain regions associated with motor control execute the physical response of laughter. One 1999 study analyzed patients with damage to the right frontal lobes, an integrative region of the brain where emotional, logical, and perceptual data converge. The brain-damaged patients had far more difficulty than control subjects in choosing the proper punch line to a series of jokes, usually opting for absurdist, slapstick-style endings rather than traditional ones. Humor can often come in coarse,

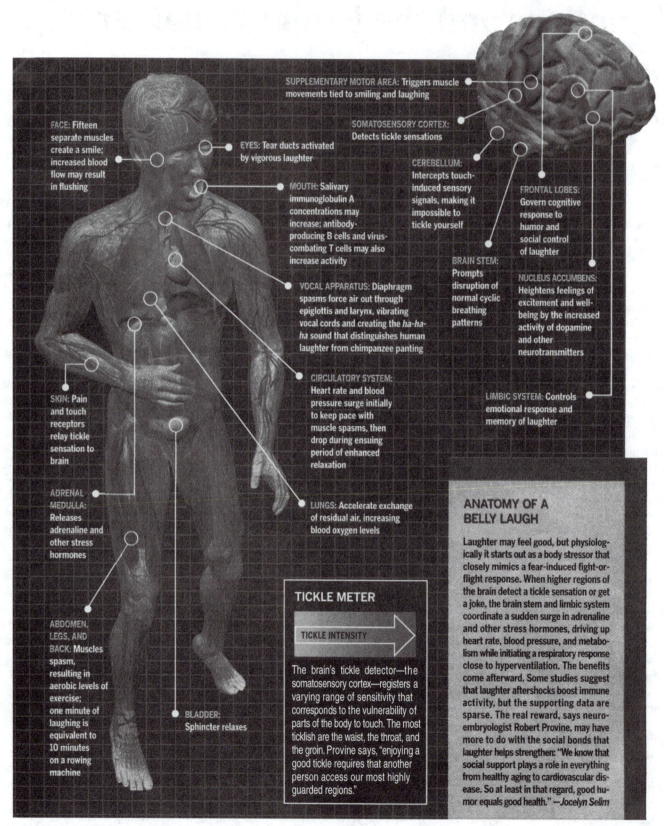

SUPPLEMENTARY MOTOR AREA: Triggers muscle movements tied to smiling and laughing

FACE: Fifteen separate muscles create a smile; increased blood flow may result in flushing

EYES: Tear ducts activated by vigorous laughter

SOMATOSENSORY CORTEX: Detects tickle sensations

MOUTH: Salivary immunoglobulin A concentrations may increase; antibody-producing B cells and virus-combating T cells may also increase activity

CEREBELLUM: Intercepts touch-induced sensory signals, making it impossible to tickle yourself

FRONTAL LOBES: Govern cognitive response to humor and social control of laughter

VOCAL APPARATUS: Diaphragm spasms force air out through epiglottis and larynx, vibrating vocal cords and creating the ha-ha-ha sound that distinguishes human laughter from chimpanzee panting

BRAIN STEM: Prompts disruption of normal cyclic breathing patterns

NUCLEUS ACCUMBENS: Heightens feelings of excitement and well-being by the increased activity of dopamine and other neurotransmitters

SKIN: Pain and touch receptors relay tickle sensation to brain

CIRCULATORY SYSTEM: Heart rate and blood pressure surge initially to keep pace with muscle spasms, then drop during ensuing period of enhanced relaxation

LIMBIC SYSTEM: Controls emotional response and memory of laughter

ADRENAL MEDULLA: Releases adrenaline and other stress hormones

LUNGS: Accelerate exchange of residual air, increasing blood oxygen levels

ABDOMEN, LEGS, AND BACK: Muscles spasm, resulting in aerobic levels of exercise; one minute of laughing is equivalent to 10 minutes on a rowing machine

BLADDER: Sphincter relaxes

ANATOMY OF A BELLY LAUGH

Laughter may feel good, but physiologically it starts out as a body stressor that closely mimics a fear-induced fight-or-flight response. When higher regions of the brain detect a tickle sensation or get a joke, the brain stem and limbic system coordinate a sudden surge in adrenaline and other stress hormones, driving up heart rate, blood pressure, and metabolism while initiating a respiratory response close to hyperventilation. The benefits come afterward. Some studies suggest that laughter aftershocks boost immune activity, but the supporting data are sparse. The real reward, says neuro-embryologist Robert Provine, may have more to do with the social bonds that laughter helps strengthen: "We know that social support plays a role in everything from healthy aging to cardiovascular disease. So at least in that regard, good humor equals good health." —Jocelyn Selim

TICKLE METER

TICKLE INTENSITY →

The brain's tickle detector—the somatosensory cortex—registers a varying range of sensitivity that corresponds to the vulnerability of parts of the body to touch. The most ticklish are the waist, the throat, and the groin. Provine says, "enjoying a good tickle requires that another person access our most highly guarded regions."

Graphics by Don Foley

lowest-common-denominator packages, but actually getting the joke draws upon our higher brain functions.

When Provine set out to study laughter, he imagined that he would approach the problem along the lines of these humor studies: Investigating laughter meant having people listen to jokes and other witticisms and watching what happened. He began by simply observing casual conversations, counting the number of times that people laughed while listening to someone speaking. But very quickly he realized that there was a fundamental flaw in his assumptions about how laughter worked. "I started recording all these conversations," Provine says, "and the numbers I was getting—I didn't believe them when I saw them. The speakers were laughing more than the listeners. Every time that would happen, I would think, 'OK, I have to go back and start over again because that can't be right.'"

Speakers, it turned out, were 46 percent more likely to laugh than listeners—and what they were laughing at, more often than not, wasn't remotely funny. Provine and his team of undergrad students recorded the ostensible "punch lines" that triggered laughter in ordinary conversation. They found that only around 15 percent of the sentences that triggered laughter were traditionally humorous. In his book, *Laughter: A Scientific Investigation*, Provine lists some of the laugh-producing quotes:

I'll see you guys later./Put those cigarettes away./I hope we all do well./It was nice meeting you too./We can handle this./I see your point./I should do that, but I'm too lazy./I try to lead a normal life./I think I'm done./I told you so!

The few studies of laughter to date had assumed that laughing and humor were inextricably linked, but Provine's early research suggested that the connection was only an occasional one. "There's a dark side to laughter that we are too quick to overlook," he says. "The kids at Columbine were laughing as they walked through the school shooting their peers."

As his research progressed, Provine began to suspect that laughter was in fact about something else—not humor or gags or incongruity but our social interactions. He found support for this assumption in a study that had already been conducted, analyzing people's laughing patterns in social and solitary contexts. "You're 30 times more likely to laugh when you're with other people than you are when you're alone—if you don't count simulated social environments like laugh tracks on television," Provine says. "In fact, when you're alone, you're more likely to talk out loud to yourself than you are to laugh out loud. Much more." Think how rarely you'll laugh out loud at a funny passage in a book but how quick you'll be to make a friendly laugh when greeting an old acquaintance. Laughing is not an instinctive physical response to humor, the way a flinch responds to pain or a shiver to cold. It's a form of instinctive social bonding that humor is crafted to exploit.

P rovine's lab at the Baltimore county campus of the University of Maryland looks like the back room at a stereo repair store—long tables cluttered with old equipment, tubes and wires everywhere. The walls are decorated with brightly colored pictures of tangled neurons, most of which were painted by Provine. (Add some Day-Glo typography and they might pass for signs promoting a Dead show at the Fillmore.) Provine's old mentor, the neuroembryologist Viktor Hamburger, glowers down from a picture hung above a battered Silicon Graphics workstation. His expression suggests a sense of concerned bafflement: "I trained you as a scientist, and here you are playing with dolls!"

The more technical parts of Provine's work—exploring the neuromuscular control of laughter and its relationship to the human and chimp respiratory systems—draw on his training at Washington University in St. Louis under Hamburger and Nobel laureate Rita Levi-Montalcini. But the most immediate way to grasp his insights into the evolution of laughter is to watch video footage of his informal fieldwork, which consists of Provine and a cameraman prowling Baltimore's inner harbor, asking people to laugh for the camera. The overall effect is like a color story for the local news, but as Provine and I watch the tapes together in his lab, I find myself looking at the laughters with fresh eyes. Again and again, a pattern repeats on the screen. Provine asks someone to laugh, and they demur, look puzzled for a second, and say something like, "I can't just laugh." Then they turn to their friends or family, and the laughter rolls out of them as though it were as natural as breathing. The pattern stays the same even as the subjects change: a group of high school students on a field trip, a married couple, a pair of college freshmen.

At one point Provine—dressed in a plaid shirt and khakis, looking something like the comedian Robert Klein—stops two waste-disposal workers driving a golf cart loaded up with trash bags. When they fail to guffaw on cue, Provine asks them why they can't muster one up. "Because you're not funny," one of them says. They turn to each other and share a hearty laugh.

"See, you two just made each other laugh," Provine says.

"Yeah, well, we're coworkers," one of them replies.

The insistent focus on laughter patterns has a strange effect on me as Provine runs through the footage. By the time we get to the cluster of high school kids, I've stopped hearing their spoken words at all, just the rhythmic peals of laughter breaking out every 10 seconds or so. Sonically, the laughter dominates the speech; you can barely hear the dialogue underneath the hysterics. If you were an alien encountering humans for the first time, you'd have to assume that the laughing served as the primary communication method, with the spoken words interspersed as afterthoughts. After one particularly loud outbreak, Provine turns to me and says, "Now, do you think they're all individually making a conscious decision to laugh?" He shakes his head dismissively. "Of course not. In fact, we're often not aware that we're even laughing in the first place. We've vastly overrated our conscious control of laughter."

The limits of our voluntary control of laughter are most clearly exposed in studies of stroke victims who suffer from a disturbing condition known as central facial paralysis, which prevents them from voluntarily moving either the left side or the right side of their faces, depending on the location of the neurological damage. When these individuals are asked to smile or laugh on command, they produce lopsided grins: One side of the mouth curls up, the other remains frozen. But when they're told a joke or they're tickled, traditional smiles and laughs animate their entire faces. There is evidence that the physical mechanism of laughter itself is generated in the brain stem, the most ancient region of the nervous system, which is also responsible for fundamental functions like breathing. Sufferers of amyotrophic lateral sclerosis—Lou Gehrig's disease—which targets the brain stem, often experience spontaneous bursts of uncontrollable laughter, without feeling mirth. (They often undergo a comparable experience with crying as well.) Sometimes called the reptilian brain because its basic structure dates back to our reptile ancestors, the brain stem is largely devoted to our most primal instincts, far removed from our complex, higher-brain skills in understanding humor. And yet somehow, in this primitive region of the brain, we find the urge to laugh.

We're accustomed to thinking of common-but-unconscious instincts as being essential adaptations, like the startle reflex or the suckling of newborns. Why would we have an unconscious propensity for something as frivolous as laughter? As I watch them on the screen, Provine's teenagers remind me of an old Carl Sagan riff, which begins with his describing "a species of primate" that likes to gather in packs of 50 or 60 individuals, cram together in a darkened cave, and hyperventilate in unison, to the point of almost passing out. The behavior is described in such a way as to make it sound exotic and somewhat foolish, like salmon swimming furiously upstream to their deaths or butterflies traveling thousands of miles to rendezvous once a year. The joke, of course, is that the primate is *Homo sapiens,* and the group hyperventilation is our fondness for laughing together at comedy clubs or theaters, or with the virtual crowds of television laugh tracks.

I'm thinking about the Sagan quote when another burst of laughter arrives through the TV speakers, and without realizing what I'm doing, I find myself laughing along with the kids on the screen, I can't help it—their laughter is contagious.

We may be the only species on the planet that laughs together in such large groups, but we are not alone in our appetite for laughter. Not surprisingly, our near relatives, the chimpanzees, are also avid laughers, although differences in their vocal apparatus cause the laughter to sound somewhat more like panting. "The chimpanzee's laughter is rapid and breathy, whereas ours is punctuated with glottal stops," says legendary chimp researcher Roger Fouts. "Also, the chimpanzee laughter occurs on the inhale and exhale, while ours is primarily done on our exhales. But other than these small differences, chimpanzee laughter seems to me to be just like ours in most respects."

Chimps don't do stand-up routines, of course, but they do share a laugh-related obsession with humans, one that Provine believes is central to the roots of laughter itself: Chimps love tickling. Back in his lab, Provine shows me video footage of a pair of young chimps named Josh and Lizzie playing with a human caretaker. It's a full-on ticklefest, with the chimps panting away hysterically when their bellies are scratched. "That's chimpanzee laughter you're hearing," Provine says. It's close enough to human laughter that I find myself chuckling along.

Parents will testify that ticklefests are often the first elaborate play routine they engage in with their children and one of the most reliable laugh inducers. According to Fouts, who helped teach sign language to Washoe, perhaps the world's most famous chimpanzee, the practice is just as common, and perhaps more long lived, among the chimps. "Tickling . . . seems to be very important to chimpanzees because it continues throughout their lives," he says. "Even Washoe at the age of 37 still enjoys tickling and being tickled by her adult family members." Among young chimpanzees that have been taught sign language, tickling is a frequent topic of conversation.

Like laughter, tickling is almost by definition a social activity. Like the incongruity theory of humor, tickling relies on a certain element of surprise, which is why it's impossible to tickle yourself. Predictable touch doesn't elicit the laughter and squirming of tickling—it's unpredictable touch that does the trick. A number of tickle-related studies have convincingly shown that tickling exploits the sensorimotor system's awareness of the difference between self and other: If the system orders your hand to move toward your belly, it doesn't register surprise when the nerve endings on your belly report being stroked. But if the touch is being generated by another sensorimotor system, the belly stroking will come as a surprise. The pleasant laughter of tickle is the way the brain responds to that touch. In both human and chimpanzee societies, that touch usually first appears in parent-child interactions and has an essential role in creating those initial bonds. "The reason [tickling and laughter] are so important," Roger Fouts says, "is because they play a role in maintaining the affinitive bonds of friendship within the family and community."

A few years ago, Jared Diamond wrote a short book with the provocative title *Why Is Sex Fun?* These recent studies suggest an evolutionary answer to the question of why tickling is fun: It encourages us to play well with others. Young children are so receptive to the rough-and-tumble play of tickle that even pretend tickling will often send them into peals of laughter. (Fouts reports that the threat of tickle has a similar effect on his chimps.) In his book, Provine suggests that "feigned tickle" can be thought of as the Original Joke, the first deliberate behavior designed to exploit the tickling-laughter circuit. Our comedy clubs and our sitcoms are culturally enhanced versions of those original playful childhood exchanges. Along with the suckling and smiling instincts, the laughter of tickle evolved as a way of cementing the bond between parents and children, laying the foundation for a behavior that then carried over into the social lives of adults. While we once laughed at the surprise touch of a parent or sibling, we now laugh at the surprise twist of a punch line.

Bowling Green State University professor Jaak Panksepp suggests that there is a dedicated "play" circuitry in the brain, equivalent to the more extensively studied fear and love circuits. Panksepp has studied the role of rough-and-tumble play in cementing social connections between juvenile rats. The play instinct is not easily suppressed. Rats that have been denied the opportunity to engage in this kind of play—which has a distinct choreography, as well as a chirping vocalization that may be the rat equivalent of laughter—will nonetheless immediately engage in play behavior given the chance. Panksepp compares it to a bird's instinct for flying. "Probably the most powerful positive emotion of all—once your tummy is full and you don't have bodily needs—is vigorous social engagement among the young," Panksepp says. "The largest amount of human laughter seems to occur in the midst of early childhood—rough-and-tumble play, chasing, all the stuff they love."

Playing is what young mammals do, and in humans and chimpanzees, laughter is the way the brain expresses the pleasure of that play. "Since laughter seems to be ritualized panting, basically what you do in laughing is replicate the sound of rough-and-tumble play," Provine says. "And you know, that's where I think it came from. Tickle is an important part of our primate heritage. Touching and being touched is an important part of what it means to be a mammal."

There is much that we don't know yet about the neurological underpinnings of laughter. We do not yet know precisely why laughing feels so good; one recent study detected evidence that stimulating the nucleus accumbens, one of the brain's pleasure centers, triggered laughter. Panksepp has performed studies that indicate opiate antagonists significantly reduce the urge to play in rats, which implies that the brain's endorphin system may be involved in the pleasure of laughter. Some anecdotal and clinical evidence suggest that laughing makes you healthier by suppressing stress hormones and elevating immune system antibodies. If you think of laughter as a form of behavior that is basically synonymous with the detection of humor, the laughing-makes-you-healthier premise seems bizarre. Why would natural selection make our immune system respond to jokes? Provine's approach helps solve the mystery. Our bodies aren't responding to wisecracks and punch lines; they're responding to social connection.

In this respect, laughter reminds us that our emotional lives are as much outward bound as they are inner directed. We tend to think of emotions as private affairs, feelings that wash over our subjective worlds. But emotions are also social acts, laughter perhaps most of all. It's no accident that we have so many delicately choreographed gestures and facial expressions—many of which appear to be innate to our species—to convey our emotions. Our emotional systems are designed to share our feelings and not just represent them internally—an insight that Darwin first grasped more than a century ago in his book *The Expression of the Emotions in Man and Animals*. "The movements of expression in the face and body, whatever their origin may have been, are in themselves of much importance for our welfare. They serve as the first means of communication between mother and infant; she smiles approval, and thus encourages her child on the right path. . . . The free expression by outward signs of an emotion intensifies it."

And even if we don't yet understand the neurological basis of the pleasure that laughing brings us, it makes sense that we should seek out the connectedness of infectious laughter. We are social animals, after all. And if that laughter often involves some pretty childish behavior, so be it. "I mean, this is why we're not like lizards," Provine says, holding the Tickle Me Elmo doll on his lap. "Lizards don't play, and they're not social the way we are. When you start to see play, you're starting to see mammals. So when we get together and have a good time and laugh, we're going back to our roots. It's ironic in a way: Some of the things that give us the most pleasure in life are really the most ancient."

50 Reasons to Love Being 50+

1 Because you can spoil the grandkids with sweets

It's all about the shamelessness of lots of butter and sugar and eggs. It's about quantity and variety and having things coming warm from the oven when my kids' kids tumble through my kitchen door. It's about gingersnaps and chocolate chips and short-bread. It's about my grandson Ralphie saying, "I want go Nana cookie house."

Twenty-four years ago my first grandchild spackled his mouth with my corn muffins—and two years later, his little brother, when I was showing him a single apple on a tree, held out both hands and said gleefully, "Whole bunch!" I have 12 grandchildren now. They don't all come at the same time, although the two sets of twins born three years ago often show up on the same weekend. Good thing I love to bake.

Living alone, I don't dare bake without kids around. I would never get the cookies into a tin, nor would anything delicious wind up carefully wrapped in the freezer. I'd eat it all. So when the kids come, it is reason for celebration. It's about eating more than is good for you, once in a while.

I was allowed three desserts in a row at my grandmother's house. I like tradition, and I'm passing it on.

ABIGAIL THOMAS writes in *Woodstock*, New York.

2 Gray stripes
(Anthony Bourdain, Edward James Olmos, Jay Leno)

3 Wavy gray
(Emmylou Harris, Linda Evans, Cloris Leachman)

4 Gray beards
(Kofi Annan, Willie Nelson, Sean Connery)

5 Gray bangs
(Olympia Dukakis, Paula Deen, Ruby Dee)

6 Solid gray
(Richard Gere, James Earl Jones, Ted Danson)

7 Faux gray
(Santa Claus, Gandalf, Statler and Waldorf)

8 Because sex gets better with age

Too much of a good thing, Mae West told us, can be wonderful, even at this age. Our hormones aren't as abundant as they used to be, but with a little help from our friends—Viagra, Estrace cream, Astroglide—we can still be as bad as we wanna be. When the spirit is willing but the body isn't, we improvise. We're self-confident enough to say what we want, content enough to swap calisthenics for intimacy. More tenderness and less testosterone can be very sexy indeed.

A female friend of mine says her husband used to want sex so often, she felt "dispensable." These days it feels more like a choice. It's different for men, too. "I'm more concerned with making the other person happy," says a male friend. His wife is happy, too: "Who knew we'd be having so much fun?"

ELIZABETH BENEDICT is a novelist who writes frequently about sex (www.elizabethbenedict.com).

9 Because you're more compassionate

You've always been the rightest person in the room—so why did your boss just fire you? You were certain your parents made terrible mistakes raising you—now your own kids say you made the same errors (and they're forwarding their therapy bills to you). You've led a charmed life—but suddenly you know what it's like to live with depression . . . or cancer . . . or losing a spouse . . . or a sudden turn in fortune that's left you wondering how to pay the bills.

By the time we pass the half-century mark, we've all withstood our share of slights, indignities, or outright suffering. Watched our self-image go up in flames. Played a starring role in our own TV version of *When Bad Things Happen to Good People*.

And maybe it's lucky. Lucky because we've seen enough, felt enough, been self-aware enough to learn from our experiences. What we've learned is that all of us are inherently flawed and very, very vulnerable; that this, in part, is what it means to be human; and that—most important—we really are all in this together. It's the reason we treat our fellow humans with a heavy dose of compassion and respect. Okay, so it's taken a handful of decades and some life upheavals to figure this all out. That still puts us in the catbird seat, compared with people who have never learned it at all.

NANCY WARTIK is a writer based in New York City.

10 Because men can use "midlife crisis" as an excuse for any embarrassing, highly questionable activity

Including body piercings, bad toupees, love-handle surgery, leather pants (or any wardrobe addition that makes you look like David Hasselhoff), and the purchase of a sports car more expensive than your first house.

11 Because you have the guts to change careers

I look up from a phonics lesson to hear screaming in my classroom. Emmanuel, a sad-eyed first grader who joined our class three days earlier, is hurling books, punching any kids who come near. At least ten children are sobbing and hurt. I call the main office: "I need help in 221—*now!*" Emmanuel hits more children in the seconds I'm on the phone. Another teacher runs into the room and ushers him out. I am the lone adult with 24 traumatized children. Now I do the only thing I can think of to calm everyone down: we sing the class favorite, "If I Had a Hammer."

I had brought in some CDs a few weeks earlier, hoping that deciphering song lyrics would improve my students' ability to listen. After a 20-year career as a magazine editor, I'm teaching at-risk first graders in one of the country's poorest neighborhoods. A large percentage of students at this South Bronx school are borderline autistic, have ADD, or suffer from an array of developmental disorders. Some, like Emmanuel, are shuffled from one foster home to another. Many others have parents who are absent, jailed, unemployed, addicted to drugs, or abusive.

Emmanuel returns after a few days' suspension and mumbles "Sorry" after a brief discussion of the earlier events. Juan, a helpful child who loves Spider-Man and sharks, has a suggestion, "Why don't we make Emmanuel the Student of the Day so we can get to know him better?"

I marvel at Juan's maturity. Maybe his live-in-the-moment attitude, however naive, is the best way to cope. I realize how much I can learn from these kids about forgiveness, and the value of starting anew.

EILEEN GARRED

12 Because you get better at crossword puzzles

It's simple. We know words our kids don't. Studies show that 50-plus folks have larger vocabularies than people in their 20s or 30s do, partly because of the younger generation's more video-obsessed lives, but also because we know more obsolete terms (mimeograph, phonograph . . .). What matters is we can kick serious bahookey—an eight-letter word for *buttocks*—at crossword puzzles. Here's a test. Ask your under-30 family members to define these words: **larder, eight-track, analog, Instamatic.** When they can't answer, just smile and return to your puzzle.

13 Because you know money can buy some happiness

Our dog's name is Lucky. The twins named him. They were seven years old and weren't listening when I said naming anything Lucky is tempting fate. I was perfectly willing to go to the shelter for a cute terrier mix named Peanut, but the hypoallergenic hype on Labradoodles—they don't shed!—and the puppy pictures online won the day. The breeder got $900, and we got Lucky.

There were other costs. To fit him into our life, we bought a minivan, slightly used. Of course Lucky needed schooling—a bargain at $10 a week—and I'm sure it helped give him the discipline to chew up just one household object per day for his first two years. From an early age Lucky showed us how to get along with less.

Then there are the four vacuum cleaners, each stronger than the last. I can't fault Lucky for taking after his Labrador mother, but, yes, he does shed, prodigiously. At some point I toted up Lucky-related costs and started calling him our $30,000 dog.

One of my jobs at this magazine is encouraging AARP members to be careful with their money. Really, folks, put away whatever you can. Spend only on necessities. But what is a necessity? Last fall Lucky bolted across the street toward a friend and was hit by a speeding SUV. In 12 days we spent $20,000 to save him.

Yes, there went a semester at college, or a new car, or years off the mortgage. There went the emergency fund. But I have no regrets. We could find the money. In good conscience we couldn't not spend it. Love made that a necessity, just as love prompted family to send unsolicited checks.

And now that Lucky is back to rolling in rabbit poop and eating, let's just say, very widely, he's become my daily reminder of what we really can and can't do without.

GEORGE BLOOSTON

14 Because if Keith Richards can make it into his 60s, there's hope for all of us

1965 Knocked out by electric shock onstage after whacking microphone with guitar

1969 Wrecks his 19-foot Nazi staff car, gets it repaired, then wrecks it down embankment

1973 (Or maybe it was '74 . . .) Falls asleep and crashes into speaker, breaking nose

1974 Falls asleep mid-sentence during live television interview

1980 Declares in interview, "I've been drunk for 27 years"

1981 Doesn't recognize title of new Stones album: "What's this Tattoo You?"

1998 While reaching for book in home library, gets pummeled by avalanche of texts. Suffers three broken ribs and punctured lung

2006 Falls out of coconut tree in Fiji

2007 Claims he snorted Dad's ashes (later denies snorting Dad's ashes)

2008 Gives key to his longevity: "I'm doomed to live"
—Alex Kizer

Because You're Free to Do What You Want!

When we asked readers what they like best about being 50-plus, one answer popped up more than others: freedom.

15 "I do things simply because I want. I can go to a movie or a restaurant alone and not worry whether someone thinks I'm a loser."

GAIL PAUL, Los Angeles, California

16 "No one is shocked if I decide the refrigerator looks nice in the living room."

KAREN EDGAR, Olive Branch, Mississippi

17 "I don't give a flip what other people think. I sing at the top of my lungs in the car with the windows down, even at traffic lights."

BARBARA KEETON, Taylors, South Carolina

18 Because our music rocks!

AARP The Magazine's music critic, Richard Gehr, picks five songs music lovers will still be listening to in 100 years.

Angel-voiced Carl Wilson seeks romantic guidance from above in this gorgeous track from brother Brian's 1966 pop masterpiece, *Pet Sounds.* This one will still be on iPods (or implants) in 2108.

The Queen of Soul unforgettably blends stirring gospel and soaring R&B in her first hit single, written by Ronnie Shannon. She'd soon have bigger hits, but this one gives you chills.

Among the world's most memorable riffs—"Sunshine of Your Love," "Smoke on the Water"—this could be the catchiest, courtesy of the instrumental group that launched a thousand Stax R&B hits.

Motherhood, freight trains, prison, and church. Merle Haggard's autobiographical hit sums up the domestic consolations and outlaw impulses of great American country music. It's an underrated classic.

A cool psychedelic breeze blows through John Lennon's nostalgic memories of his Liverpool childhood. The Beatles rarely sounded more revolutionary than on this dreamy slice of genius.

. . . So tell us your picks for the best songs ever. Go to www.aarpmagazine.org/people.

19 Because you've been embarrassed so much, you're all out of chagrin

When I was in second grade I wet my pants.

It was at a rehearsal of the school play, just before I spoke my lines—well, line. But an important line. For, in our version of *Little Red Riding Hood,* the Big Bad Wolf (yours truly) was transformed from predator ("*Grrr*") to protector ("Leave her alone! *Grrr*").

I didn't grasp that symbolism. I just knew the other parts had gone to sixth graders and that I was one of the few Negro children in the school. Motivated by pride, I spent hours practicing

my snarling. But the script called for the Big Bad Wolf to appear in nearly every scene, and as rehearsals grew longer, eventually, almost inevitably, I experienced . . . a release of dramatic tension.

In the boys' room, waiting for my mother to fetch fresh pants, I *grr*ed at my own stupidity. Big Bad Wolf? Big, bad disgrace. I cringed recalling how, before exiting, dripping, stage left, I'd actually delivered my line. But the next day the director said that showed "stage presence" and told me not to worry; this was not the most embarrassing thing I'd ever do.

Too right. There was that solo I began as a boy soprano and ended sounding like a bullfrog. There was that jump shot at the buzzer that swished through the wrong net. And after I left home in rural Pennsylvania for college, there were all those city customs I never got right.

I practiced public obtuseness, ignoring astonished looks when my savoir fell behind my faire. But privately I was haunted by echoes of my inanities ("A friend of Bill who?" "Aren't you going to cook that?")

As the years passed, I learned to check my facts, and also my fly—better to be caught at that than with my zipper down. But recently, listening to an old friend introduce me with an exaggerated account of one of my Greatest Misses, it struck me, now that I'm fiftysomething, that the most embarrassing thing I'd ever do was probably something I'd already done.

So I checked my fly and I stepped onstage in a state of grace beyond disgrace, beyond chagrin.

DAVID BRADLEY, author of *The Chaneysville Incident,* teaches creative writing at the University of Oregon.

20 Because you *experienced* the Beatles

I was 13 years old when my best friend, Margo, won tickets to see the Beatles in San Francisco in '65. We'd seen girls scream for the Fab Four on television and vowed we would never act so silly. But when the Beatles arrived onstage, we were swept away by the hysteria. We screamed, we jumped, we cried, we shook—we even tried climbing the chainlink fence that surrounded the stage. We were gasping for breath the entire show, slightly lightheaded, tears streaming down our faces. I've been to other concerts, but none were ever like this.

LIBBY GUTHRIE is an AARP member in Redwood Valley, California.

21 Because we know how to fight—literally

In March 2008, Saoul Mamby, age 60, became the oldest boxer to compete in a pro bout, going ten rounds with 32-year-old fighter Anthony Osborne. Okay, Mamby didn't win. So what. The guy is doing what he loves: punching other guys in the face until they drool. Since turning pro in 1969, the Bronx-born fighter has held the World Boxing Council (WBC) junior-welterweight title, amassed 56 wins (plus 11 grandchildren), and fought on the same card as Muhammad Ali. Now he's training in hopes of another bout. "To be successful at boxing—at anything—it has to become a part of you," says Mamby. "You get out of it what you put in—and I put in 100 percent."

NICK KOLAKOWSKI

22 Because love grows deeper over time

In the early days it was all about him. His favorite foods, favorite color, favorite flavor of ice cream, and whether he liked my hair up or down. I loved to make him laugh, and worked hard not to cry in front of him. I cleaned my house before he came over, always wore mascara, always had champagne in the fridge.

Marriage changes that, of course. Artifice goes, as it should. Love deepens, maybe even relaxes a little. And anyway, who has time to set a scene or arrange the canapés when somebody has to be picked up at soccer practice, or the boss has a fit, or the creek rises (literally) into the cellar an hour before the in-laws are to arrive for Easter brunch? When the dog is throwing up, or your mother breaks her hip, who among us can be bothered to murmur, "Darling, I've always loved that color of blue on you."

We've seen each other at our worst, and that's not an exaggeration. Physically ill, emotionally grief-stunned, job-panicked, or angry enough to throw crockery at the wall (and then do it again). Red-faced, blotchy, hoarse from yelling. Our parents grow old, and ill, or nutty; our children make mistakes that drop us to our knees. Through it all, how on earth can he love me, given what a flawed, messy, moody person I am? The artifice is long gone; he sees me. As my oldest friend said when we were girls, "If Prince Charming loves me, he's probably not really Prince Charming."

Well, as it turns out, maybe he is. Okay, so we won't make love on the kitchen table again (there's not enough ibuprofen and, besides, that's why God invented pillow-top mattresses). But lately, when he puts his arm around me in the movie line, or takes my hand as we cross the street, my heart jumps as it did in the beginning. I'm happy to see him in the morning and blessed to sleep beside him at night; there are even days, in a certain light, that he makes me feel all swoony. He *does* see me, which is why he's still here. And I see him, far more clearly than I did—burnished, like my grandmother's sterling silver, and as grounded as the white oak in our front yard. I couldn't have known that's how it would be, back when I was putting on a show.

LARKIN WARREN lives in Connecticut. She is working on her first novel.

23 Because B. B. King proves the pursuit of perfection never ends

I play "The Thrill Is Gone" every night. But I never do exactly what I did last night or the night before. I tell my band to play it as they feel it each night. I like that. It keeps it fresh.

I have a motto: Always do your best. When I was in grade school there was a poem a teacher used to tell us. It went something like "Be the labor great or small, do it well or not at all." I do the best I can each night. Even though a lot of nights my best is nothing as good as I'd like it to be.

Every day I learn something. I have a computer that's my professor. If I don't learn something every day, it's a day lost.

As told to Richard Gehr. B.B. King's new album is *One Kind Favor.*

Because We Can Live Alone and Not Be Lonely

When I used to get home from work, I'd pull up in the driveway and the front door would fly open and out would shoot my three kids, two dogs, and my husband, Vince. They'd all start talking at once as the dogs barked their welcome. "Just let me get in the house," I'd plead. "Then you can tell me what's going on." Flash forward 25 years. Now I come home to an almost empty house. I say almost because my two cats—a fat tabby named Penny Lane and spunky Jenny Jones—are waiting at the front door. No, it's not the same. But those of us who live alone have come to appreciate some simple truths:

24 You can finally hear yourself think

I remember when I'd long for a quiet house. Even after my divorce, there was always someone around. And there was noise. It was the sound-track of my life. Then one day it stopped and my emptying nest was completely empty. And the quiet was almost deafening. It took a long while before I valued hearing my own thoughts. But I never really got used to the silence. To this day I switch on the stereo when I walk in the house.

25 Good neighbors are a godsend

I never realized how true that was until I had to move cross-country for my work. I knew no one. I bought a great house, but even more important, I got a great bunch of neighbors. Over the years they have helped me when I was sick, watched my house, and invited me to their parties. Because of them, I'm never really alone.

26 Single friends are protective friends

I have many friends. But my closest ones are women like me, who live alone. We have an almost natural tendency to look out for one another. Shortly after I moved, a single neighbor came over with a bottle of wine and a welcome. She introduced me to her women friends. We laugh, we cry, we share our deepest secrets. But most important, we understand one another.

27 You cherish new opportunities

I savor being on my own, doing what I want, when I want. But I wouldn't enjoy this freedom half as much if I hadn't experienced a noisy home full of loved ones. Yes, I'm used to living alone, but my door is always open to future possibilities.

KAREN REYES

28 Because . . . Paul Newman

Back in 1961, I was dumb enough to think *The Hustler* was a Jackie Gleason movie. But then came this upstart pool shark with cobalt-blue eyes (yes, *The Hustler* was in black and white, but somehow the blue still showed). He got into The Great One's face and bragged, "I'm the best you ever seen," and there was no arguing the point.

By the time he turned 50 in 1975, Paul Newman could have coasted. But the actor rewrote his career with one breakaway role after another: there he is barreling across the ice in *Slap*

Shot (1977). Then he solemnly offers a summation to the jury in *The Verdict* (1982). Later there's his Oscar-winning return to the role of *The Hustler*'s Fast Eddie Felson in *The Color of Money* (1986).

A new generation knows Newman more as a racecar driver, or as the voice of an old sedan in the animated *Cars,* or as the face on McDonald's salad dressing packets, than for his turn as Butch Cassidy. But for those who grew up with Paul Newman, he's more than a brand, a voice, or a set of blazing peepers. He's proof you can keep chasing that checkered flag even after you've entered the winner's circle.

Read Bill Newcott's Movies for Grownups® reviews at www .aarpmagazine.org.

29 Because your spiritual side grows stronger

The older I get, the more I realize I don't know everything. And that makes me spirituality sensitive to others. I'm less dogmatic, more open to other people's experience of the divine. As we age, we experience things that aren't easily explained—tragedies, failing health—and we become more reflective. There is so much more to learn about the mystery that is the divine, and I've got this thimbleful of knowledge, and I want more. Earlier, a thimbleful was all I could handle. Not anymore. Our spiritual life has a chance to be richer now, with so many more life experiences to reflect upon.

As told to Lynne Meredith Schreiber. Brent Bill is a Quaker minister in Mooresville, Indiana, and the author of *Sacred Compass: The Way of Spiritual Discernment* (Paraclete Press, 2008).

Because We Are Powerful

30
41 percent of American adults are over 50, the highest percentage in U.S. history.

31
80 percent of Congress is over 50.

32
Half of the Americans who voted in the 2006 elections were 50+.

33
People over 55 own 77 percent of all financial assets in the United States.

34
50+ adults account for 45 percent of U.S. consumer spending, or $2.1 trillion per year.

35
By 2011 the American 50+ population will surpass the 100 million mark.

36 Because we're living longer than ever before

Let's get the distressing stats out of the way first: Citizens in 41 countries have longer average life spans than we Americans do. In some parts of the United States—portions of the Deep South, the Midwest—life expectancy has actually declined (the big reasons are smoking, obesity, and high blood pressure). The upbeat stats? If you are 50 today, on average you'll live to be 80.5. If you're 65, you'll live to 83.4. In fact, if you go back to our one-celled ancestors, we're doing way better than humans at any point in history.

Average Years of Life for . . .

Americans today: 78
Americans in 1900: 47.3
Europeans in the Middle Ages: 31.3
Ancient Greeks: 28
Cro-Magnons: 25
Amoebas: 2 to 3 days, tops

37 "When you get older, hopefully you've developed the smarts to know that if you wake up in the morning and you're vertical and your kids are healthy, that's 90 percent of being happy. That's it!"

Judge Judy

38 Because you're secure enough to take as much advice as you dish out

If it's true we are judged by the company we keep, the evidence in my favor is compelling: a bevy of strong, self-sufficient, passionate young women, 30—and more—years younger than I am. Being this far past 50 frees me to wallow in their youthful exuberance without competition or regret. I am both their patient sage and their eager student.

Each appeared at different points in my life and from various spots on the globe, and though we are sometimes separated by months, years, even continents, our links are so elastic that we never lose touch. They are dream catchers, all: the brilliant, book-loving hell-raiser, who at 16 was as skilled with her fists as she was with a pen when we met 18 years ago; the enchanting poet/actress; the fierce lawyer; the self-assured entrepreneur.

Early on, each of them evoked an intense whisper in me—"I know her"—and I recognized they were parts of that girl I used to be. We are "like" attracting "like"—as intensely loyal as we are truthful. So, when I confess to feeling fat, the actress dares me to shut up and flaunt it. In the middle of my tiresome ranting, the businesswoman shames me—lovingly—into clearing my space of ancient hurts and weary narratives. If I am weak, the lawyer argues me back to warrior-woman status. When I get stuck, the hell-raiser—now the college student/wife/mother—leads me out.

I admire all the things they are that I will never be, but because I'm older, my instructions to them rarely change: Trust your gut. Get angry. If it scares you, do it. Don't go with the flow unless you started it. Eat dessert first.

My young friends revel in my steady assurances, even as they rescue me from the tedium of old certainties and instruct me in the protocol of cool. Watching them—and listening—is pure joy and wonder.

BERNESTINE SINGLEY (www.BernestineSingley.com) is a writer and lawyer based in Dallas.

39 Because you've seen the world change in inconceivable ways

At 57 years of age, I am nervous about the future—the economy, the environment, to say nothing of those deepening crow's-feet. But the long view sustains me. My grandfather was born in the 1880s to former slaves. I hung on to the stories he told—about a life before cars, plastics, the Wright brothers, the Panama Canal, even before Jim Crow laws.

My father was born in 1915. Despite five strokes, he is still vibrant and funny. He was a technical editor back in the days of computer mainframes, back when FORTRAN and COBOL were the lingua franca of techno-nerds. He regales my son with tales of automobiles that had to be cranked. He recalls lynchings when he was growing up. The integration of the Army. The battle of Anzio. The etymology of the word *smog*.

My father still types letters on an old sticky-keyed Smith Corona. As I craft my own words on a brand-new MacBook Air, I am grateful for the strength that intergenerational engagement brings. I am a black female law professor, something my grandfather could never have imagined. And I am about to e-mail these words through an invisible cushion of whooshing cyberspace, something my father worked to create but still can't entirely grasp.

Across the table my son is writing a school paper about the oil crisis and looks up with a glint of panic. "How," he asks me, "will humanity continue?"

I am not so fearful. Like my son, I worry about the crossroads at which we stand. But I am old enough to appreciate how quickly the course of events can change—for the worse, to be sure, but also for the better, if only the will is there. If my father can remember the very first U.S. smog alert, then my son might live to see the haze subside and the heavens reemerge. The human spirit is amazingly, unexpectedly resilient. Anything can happen.

PATRICIA WILLIAMS is the James L. Dohr Professor of Law at Columbia University and a columnist for *The Nation*.

40 Because you actually enjoy going to high-school reunions

For the first few decades, high-school reunions are like updated versions of an old cartoon show: the hairstyles and voices are a little different, but, really, Archie and Jughead haven't changed that much. Reunions after age 50 are more like *Return to Mayberry*, where Opie's gone bald and Aunt Bee is dead. This is not a bad thing, because while everyone else looks like a jack-o'-lantern left on the porch too long, you haven't changed a bit. You know this is true, because everybody tells you so. (You tell everybody the same thing, but that's just because you're so nice.) And yet these later reunions are somehow more pleasant than those in years past. The smoldering one-up-manship has

pretty much quenched itself; you've filed away a lot of the old jealousies and insecurities that dogged your younger years. At last you're free to enjoy those fleeting connections with your youth. And if you aren't, that old classmate who's now a psychiatrist will gladly give you his card.

BILL NEWCOTT

Because Older Brains Have New Strengths

41 You're a better judge of character

The proof: In tests at North Carolina State University, older folks outperformed younger participants in determining whether people were honest and intelligent.

42 Your brain is more efficient

The proof: Duke University researchers discovered that older individuals use the brain's right and left hemispheres at the same time (typically the brain uses the left for some tasks, and the right for others). "In effect, the mature brain creates a synergy that helps it think outside the box," says Gene Cohen, MD, PhD, author of *The Mature Mind* (Basic Books, 2005).

43 You're less neurotic than you used to be

The proof: Australian scientists found that neuroticism was less prevalent in subjects ages 50 to 79. Brain scans also revealed a more controlled response to fear. The experts' theory: A growing awareness of mortality and a desire for meaning mellows the mind.

MELISSA GOTTHARDT

44 Because you don't tolerate bad service

For years I went to a hairstylist whose end result never quite worked. A nice person, and so proud of owning her own salon—it was fun to spend time with her every couple of months. The friendship was swell—we went through joy, grief, and menopause together—but the hairdo? Not so much. Yet I couldn't leave her; I didn't want her to feel bad. Then I saw the mother-of-the-groom pictures from my son's wedding. Bad hair. Very bad hair. Anyone with a heart would've handed me a baseball cap.

And so, with shaking hands and a sinking stomach, I took my leave. She cried, I cried, and I soon found someone else, who is better than good; sometimes she's great. Yay me. But, wow, how many hundreds of dollars did I spend over the years for bad hair? What is it that holds us to doctors, mechanics, or electricians who don't or won't do what we need? Why do we cling to friendships that take more than they give, or relationships that drag on our hearts like boat anchors? Is it my mother's fault, for tamping down my big teenage mouth with "Be polite; don't make a scene"? Is it my father's, for instructing me to appreciate other people's efforts? "She's doing the best she can," he said about the piano teacher whose breath melted paint. So I dutifully played my scales, never told a waitress that I'd wanted milk, not orange juice, and grew up to gnash my teeth in my sleep.

Finally, the freedom of a fully flowered adulthood dropped the hammer on this Go Along to Get Along baloney. Bad hairstylist? Gone. The plumber who didn't fix the mess under the kitchen sink and charged me anyway? Gone. The old friend who in a three-week period canceled a lunch date four times, then scolded me for arriving ten minutes late? Well, not gone, exactly, but definitely on my pay-no-mind list. The car dealer who tried to muscle me 20 minutes into our first conversation? Summarily exchanged for the nice, slow-moving guy at the dealership down the road. From him, we'll buy two.

No matter how many birthdays we get, the salient lesson remains the same: Life is short. There's never enough time for the people and activities we love, so why allot time (or sleepless nights, or money) to those we don't? Being nice doesn't equal suffering fools; being compassionate does not translate as "take a hosing, write the check, and feel like a sucker." I don't want to waste my time anymore; I don't want to waste yours. Can we make a deal that will make us both happy? Otherwise (and I say this with deep respect for how good you are, how hard you work, and how long we've known each other), you're fired.

LARKIN WARREN

45 Because you realize that trauma can lead to enlightenment

When I used to tell friends, half jokingly, that a potentially fatal disease had actually saved my life, they rarely understood what I meant. I wasn't claiming I was glad to have it. I wasn't pretending to be overjoyed by the prospect of an early departure. I was simply confessing an odd bit of truth. Without the threat of mortal loss, I would never have had the fuel to find my way through terrible dread to something stronger than my fear.

Hardship can render us bitter, selfish, defensive, and miserable. It can also be used as the artery of interconnection, a bridge to other people in pain, as blood in the muscles that push us forward. Crisis takes us to the brink of our limits and forces us to keep moving. When people in extremis call it a blessing, this is the paradox they are describing. It's why men sometimes blossom in wartime and why women are changed by childbirth—they come alive as never before on that knife-blade danger and pain. There's vitality in facing life's extremes, including our own extinction.

Adapted from Mark Matousek's new book, *When You're Falling, Dive: Lessons in the Art of Living* (Bloomsbury USA).

46 Because you grew up in an age before video games

When we were kids, we played outside. Our bodies were hard-breathing little rainbows of energy and earth—red cheeks from running, brown hands from mud, green-grass streaks on our pants. We dreamed of grandiose forts that never got built, had sword fights with sticks while riding our bikes (okay, that was more of a boy thing). But we lived, baby. We lived! Unlike so many kids today, whose every micromanaged, remote-control moment is seemingly spent indoors. Oh, how the play times have changed:

Then	Now
Eating wild berries in the woods	Eating Lunchables on a play date
Climbing trees	Allergy tests
Walking with pals along train tracks	Walking with parents on a leash
Stickball	Xbox
"Be home by dark"	"Answer your cell phone when I call"
Summer camp	Fat camp
Doing cannonballs off the high dive	Wearing floaties in the shallow end
Skinned knees	Carpal tunnel
Jumping on a trampoline	What's a trampoline?

47 Because we can be as fit now as we were at 20 (Just ask Martina)

Tennis legend Martina Navratilova is 52, and she has a message: age is no excuse for being flabby. Too often, she says, 50-plus folks are inactive for so long, they think: Why bother? But Martina isn't buying it. "Age is not part of the equation," she says. "Exercise at your own level. Take a walk. Anything. Once I saw a woman with one leg running on crutches. Another time I saw a man with no legs in a wheelchair playing hockey. So, what is your excuse? A headache? You're too tired? Look in the mirror."

Yeah, yeah—like the eternally buff Martina has any idea what it's like to fight fat. Turns out she does. When she first came to the United States in 1973, she began a love affair with pancakes and eggs, and her rock-hard tennis bod became . . . pudgy. In 1981, despite Martina's having dropped down to a svelte 145 pounds, a friend told her she wasn't in great shape and was wasting her talent.

Thus was born a lifelong commitment to fitness. But you don't have to be as fanatical as Martina. "Start with a ten-minute walk," she says. "Then do more. Go gradually, not too intense. You'll feel better each day. It doesn't have to be painful."

PAT JORDAN

48 "Happiness no longer seems like an unobtainable goal—it can reside in a superb cup of coffee."

MAGGIE FRIEDE, Quincy, Massachusetts

49 "Before I turned 50, I was always pushing to do more. Now I'm able to step back mentally and just look around. Was all this beauty here all along?"

JAN LUFF, Milford, Delaware

50 Because you know who your friends are

It's no mystery at this point. Your old friends are the ones who don't desert you, who share a beer or a tear when life is dark, who make you laugh. (Your new friends do the same; they just haven't been on the job as long.) Harvard professor Daniel Gilbert, PhD, who studies happiness, says we tend to tighten our circle of friends as we age—to focus on those who make us happy now. Yet the squabbling Simon and Garfunkel model of friendship—my "partner in arguments," Simon once called his musical other half—should not be tossed aside like Oscar flinging dirty socks at an exasperated Felix. We need the people who fight with us but will also fight for us. Friendship is like shares in a growing company: the investment isn't easy, but the dividends enrich our lives.

KEN BUDD

The Myth of the Midlife Crisis

It's time we stopped dismissing middle age as the beginning of the end. Research suggests that at 40, the brain's best years are still ahead.

GENE COHEN, MD, PhD

I was taken by surprise several years ago when my colleagues started to worry that I was going through some sort of midlife crisis. I was in my late 40s, and after two decades as a gerontologist I was pursuing a new passion: designing games for older adults. My first game, a joint effort with artist Gretchen Raber, was a finalist in an internationally juried show on games as works of art. Though I still had a day job directing George Washington University's Center on Aging, Health & Humanities, I was now working hard on a second game.

"Are you turning right on us?" one friend, a neuroscientist, kidded me. He wasn't talking about politics. He was asking whether I'd scrapped the logical, analytical tendencies of the brain's left hemisphere to embrace the more creative, less disciplined tendencies of the right brain. But I wasn't scrapping anything. As a researcher, I had spent years documenting the psychological benefits of intergenerational play. Now I was using both sides of my brain to create new opportunities for myself. Instead of just measuring and studying the benefits of mental stimulation, I was finding creative ways to put my findings to work. What my friends perceived as a crisis was, in truth, the start of a thrilling new phase of my life.

The mature mind gets better at reconciling thoughts and feelings.

In thinking about this experience, I realized that our view of human development in the second half of life was badly outmoded. We tend to think of aging in purely negative terms, and even experts often define "successful" aging as the effective management of decay and decline. Rubbish. No one can deny that aging brings challenges and losses. But recent discoveries in neuroscience show that the aging brain is more flexible and adaptable than we previously thought. Studies suggest that the brain's left and right hemispheres become better integrated during middle age, making way for greater creativity. Age also seems to dampen some negative emotions. And a great deal of scientific work has confirmed the "use it or lose it" adage, showing that the aging brain grows stronger from use and challenge. In short, midlife is a time of new possibility. Growing old can be filled with positive experiences. The challenge is to recognize our potential—and nurture it.

Until recently, scientists paid little attention to psychological development in the second half of life, and those who did pay attention often drew the wrong conclusions. "About the age of 50," Sigmund Freud wrote in 1907, "the elasticity of the mental processes on which treatment depends is, as a rule, lacking. Old people are no longer educable." Freud—who wrote those words at 51 and produced some of his best work after 65—wasn't the only pioneer to misconstrue the aging process. Jean Piaget, the great developmental psychologist, assumed that cognitive development stopped during young adulthood, with the acquisition of abstract thought. Even Erik Erikson, who delineated eight stages of psychosocial development, devoted only two pages of his classic work "Identity and the Life Cycle" to later life.

My own work picks up where these past giants left off. Through studies involving more than 3,000 older adults, I have identified four distinct developmental phases that unfold in overlapping 20-year periods beginning in a person's early 40s: a midlife re-evaluation (typically encountered between 40 and 65) during which we set new goals and priorities; a liberation phase (55 to 75) that involves shedding past inhibitions to express ourselves more freely; a summing-up phase (65 to 85) when we begin to review our lives and concentrate on giving back, and an encore phase (75 and beyond) that involves finding affirmation and fellowship in the face of adversity and loss. I refer to "phases" instead of "stages" because people vary widely during later life. We don't all march through these phases in lock step, but I've seen thousands of older adults pass through them—each person driven by a unique set of inner drives and ideals.

What sparks this series of changes? Why, after finding our places in the world, do so many of us spend our 40s and 50s re-evaluating our lives? The impulse stems partly from a growing awareness of our own mortality. As decades vanish behind us, and we realize how relatively few we have left, we gain new perspective on who we are and what we really care about. This awakening isn't always easy—it often reveals conflicts between the lives we've built and the ones we want to pursue—but only 10 percent of the people I've studied describe the midlife transition as a crisis. Far more say they're filled with a new sense of quest and personal discovery. "I'm looking forward to pursuing the career I always wanted," one 49-year-old woman told me. "I'm tired of just working on other people's visions, rather than my own, even if I have to start on a smaller scale."

While changing our perspective, age also remodels our brains, leaving us better equipped to fulfill our own dreams. The most important difference between older brains and younger brains is also the easiest to overlook: older brains have learned more than young ones. Throughout life, our brains encode thoughts and memories by forming new connections among neurons. The neurons themselves may lose some processing speed with age, but they become ever more richly intertwined. Magnified tremendously, the brain of a mentally active 50-year-old looks like a dense forest of interlocking branches, and this density reflects both deeper knowledge and better judgment. That's why age is such an advantage in fields like editing, law, medicine, coaching and management. There is no substitute for acquired learning.

Knowledge and wisdom aren't the only fruits of age. New research suggests that as our brains become more densely wired, they also become less rigidly bifurcated. As I mentioned earlier, our brains actually consist of two separate structures—a right brain and a left brain—linked by a row of fibers called the corpus callosum. In most people, the left hemisphere specializes in speech, language and logical reasoning, while the right hemisphere handles more intuitive tasks, such as face recognition and the reading of emotional cues. But as scientists have recently discovered through studies with PET scans and magnetic resonance imaging, this pattern changes as we age. Unlike young adults, who handle most tasks on one side of the brain or the other, older ones tend to use both hemispheres. Duke University neuroscientist Robert Cabeza has dubbed this phenomenon Hemispheric Asymmetry Reduction in Older Adults—HAROLD for short—and his research suggests it is no accident.

I n a 2002 study, Cabeza assigned a set of memory tasks to three groups of people: one composed of young adults, one of low-performing older adults and one of high-performing older adults. Like the young people, the low-performing elders drew mainly on one side of the prefrontal cortex to perform the assigned tasks. It was the high-scoring elders who used both hemispheres. No one knows exactly what this all means, but the finding suggests that healthy brains compensate for the depredations of age by expanding their neural networks across the bilateral divide. My own work suggests that, besides keeping us sharp, this neural integration makes it easier to reconcile our thoughts with our feelings. When you hear someone saying, "My head tells me to do this, but my heart says do that," the person is more likely a 20-year-old than a 50-year-old. One of my

patients, a 51-year-old man, remembers how he agonized over decisions during his 20s, searching in vain for the most logical choice. As he moved through his 40s and into his 50s, he found himself trusting his gut. "My decisions are more subjective," he said during one session, "but I'm more comfortable with many of the choices that follow."

As our aging brains grow wiser and more flexible, they also tend toward greater equanimity. Our emotions are all rooted in a set of neural structures known collectively as the limbic system. Some of our strongest negative emotions originate in the amygdalae, a pair of almond-shaped limbic structures that sit near the center of the brain, screening sensory data for signs of trouble. At the first hint of a threat, the amygdalae fire off impulses that can change our behavior before our conscious, thinking brains have a chance to weigh in. That's why our hearts pound when strangers approach us on dark sidewalks—and why we often overreact to slights and annoyances. But the amygdalae seem to mellow with age. In brain-imaging studies, older adults show less evidence of fear, anger and hatred than young adults. Psychological studies confirm that impression, showing that older adults are less impulsive and less likely to dwell on their negative feelings.

An editor I know at a New York publishing company provides a case in point. He was in his 60s, and contemplating retirement, when he realized that he had finally matured into his job. Despite a sharp intellect and a passion for excellence, this man had spent much of his career alienating people with brusque, critical comments and a lack of sensitivity. Now, he told me over lunch, he was finally beginning to master interpersonal communication. As his emotional development caught up to his intellectual development, he morphed from a brilliant but brittle loner into a mentor and a mediator of conflicts. "I feel like a changed man," he said with a bemused smile. His best work was still ahead of him.

Clearly, the aging brain is more resilient, adaptable and capable than we thought. But that doesn't mean we can sit back and expect good things to happen. Research has identified several types of activity that can, if practiced regularly, help boost the power, clarity and subtlety of the aging brain.

Exercise physically. Numerous studies have linked physical exercise to increased brainpower. This is particularly true when the exercise is aerobic—meaning continuous, rhythmic exercise that uses large muscle groups. The positive effects may stem from increased blood flow to the brain, the production of endorphins, better filtration of waste products from the brain and increased brain-oxygen levels.

Exercise mentally. The brain is like a muscle. Use it and it grows stronger. Let it idle and it will grow flabby. So choose something appealing and challenging—and don't be surprised if, once you start, you want to do more. One of the programs I co-chair, the Creativity Discovery Corps, strives to identify unrecognized, talented older adults in the community. A 93-year-old woman we recently interviewed advised us that she might find scheduling the next interview difficult because she was very busy applying for a PhD program.

Pick challenging leisure activities. Getting a graduate degree isn't the only way to keep your brain fit. An important 2003 study identified five leisure activities that were associated with a lower risk of dementia and cognitive decline. In order of impact (from highest to lowest), the winners were dancing, playing board games, playing musical instruments, doing crossword puzzles and reading. Risk reduction was related to the frequency of participation. For example, older persons who did crossword puzzles four days a week had a risk of dementia 47 percent lower than subjects who did puzzles only once a week.

Achieve mastery. Research on aging has uncovered a key variable in mental health called "sense of control." From middle age onward, people who enjoy a sense of control and mastery stay healthier than those who don't. The possibilities for mastery are unlimited, ranging from playing a musical instrument to learning a new language to taking up painting or embroidery. Besides improving your outlook, the sense of accomplishment may also strengthen the immune system.

Establish strong social networks. Countless studies have linked active social engagement to better mental and physical health and lower death rates. People who maintain social relationships during the second half of life enjoy significantly lower blood pressure, which in turn reduces the risk of stroke and its resulting brain damage. Social relationships also reduce stress and its corrosive effects, including anxiety and depression.

The brain is like the foundation of a building—it provides the physical substrate of our minds, our personalities and our sense of self. As we've seen, our brain hardware is capable of adapting, growing and becoming more complex and integrated with age. As our brains mature and evolve, so do our knowledge, our emotions and our expressive abilities. In turn, what we do with those abilities affects the brain itself, forging the new connections and constellations needed for further psychological growth. This realization should embolden anyone entering the later phases of life. If we can move beyond our stubborn myths about the aging brain, great things are possible. Successful aging is not about managing decline. It's about harnessing the enormous potential that each of us has for growth, love and happiness.

GENE COHEN, MD, PhD is founding director of the Center on Aging, Health & Humanities at George Washington University Medical Center. This article is adapted from "The Mature Mind: The Positive Power of the Aging Brain," published by Basic Books, a member of the Perseus Book Group.

The Wonder of Work

A grumbling and disenchanted workforce can learn a lot about gratitude from those who treasure any job they can get—individuals with mental retardation and other severe developmental disabilities.

Teri S. Arnold

Is your place of business driving you crazy? Do your coworkers get on your nerves? There is no question that being on the job can test your patience by lifting you up, tearing you down, or sometimes completely ignoring your contributions. It can be a place of passion and drive or a place of frustrated and burnt out clock-watchers. Yet, there are many, many people with mental retardation and other severe disabilities who have a refreshingly honest point of view about work and how attitudes on the job can greatly affect happiness and job satisfaction. We all can learn a lot from how they choose to see the world.

Be grateful that you have a job to go to every morning. Some 20,300,000 people with severe developmental disabilities are unemployed in this country, and consequently often suffer mentally and physically, while digressing developmentally. Those who have a job, however, come into work with big smiles on their faces. They want to come to work on the weekends, holidays, and even during inclement weather because they know how it dramatically affects their lives for the better. Regardless of who you are, having a job and a purpose in life is essential to self-esteem, independence, and overall well-being. It might be difficult to drag yourself out of bed on Monday morning, but without a job to go to, your quality of life would suffer immensely.

Each and every job—no matter how small it may appear—is important. Whether you have difficulty communicating, moving, hearing, seeing, or comprehending, every job for a person with a severe disability is important. To someone without a disability, putting a cable into a bag can seem monotonous and boring. It may appear to be just a very minute part of a larger contractual obligation with an outside company but, to the individuals performing the task, it is their one chance to be like everyone else. When they are on the job, they are not people with mental retardation; they are coworkers and an essential part of a team with goals and objectives. Status and titles have no meaning here because everyone is a vital cog in the company's success.

Greet your coworkers with a kind word or smile when you pass them in the hallway or when they enter your workspace. In a world that increasingly is cut off from people and emotions, simple gestures that display kindness and openness are harder and harder to find. Walking onto the work floor is an instant mood-lifter. Everyone who visits is welcomed with open arms and greeted in a positive manner, regardless of who they are or how much money they make. Everybody wants to know how your day is going, shake your hand, and tell you how excited they are to be on the job. Think of how differently your day would go if you treated your coworkers in that manner.

Look for ways to encourage your coworkers to perform better and everyone will reap the rewards. It is not uncommon to see people on the work floor assisting others with their daily tasks or giving an encouraging word. No one is viewed as competition or as somebody to fear, but rather as individuals who all are in the same boat, trying to make the best of some very challenging situations. When someone accomplishes a personal or professional goal, his or her achievements are championed by all. There is a deeper understanding that, when one person wins, everyone wins.

Take breaks and have fun, even if for just a few minutes. Understand the value of balance in your life. Due to physical, mental, and emotional limitations, breaks throughout the day are mandatory for our clients. Because of the unique circumstances, becoming stressed and overwhelmed not only affects one person, but quickly can permeate the entire workforce and wreak havoc for everyone concerned. Knowing when to stop, to give your mind and body a respite, is essential to maintaining a happy and healthy work environment for people with and without disabilities.

Take pride in what you do, regardless of the pay or recognition. "We all want to be known for being the best at what we do. It is human nature to crave recognition and monetary compensation for hard work and dedication. Many of the jobs here are assembly-line, labor intensive, or entry level positions that most people would dread. However, every single person is proud of the work he or she does and is eager to tell everyone they know about it. The work is not glamorous, or that creative or dynamic—and it probably never will be seen as something deserving of high wages or praise. Yet, it serves a very important function in our society. These are jobs that give incredible meaning and value to countless lives.

Life is too short to gossip, back-stab, or criticize. People who have the most compelling reasons to complain about difficult life circumstances choose not to. Life is challenging for everyone. We all deal with the daily frustrations of having to work with people who are not like us. Some individuals communicate differently; some are slower or faster than us; and some do not share our enthusiasm, but we all are required to work together. Conflicts arise on the work floor, but they never last long or become spiteful, catty, or mean. Being focused and grateful on the job leaves little time or energy for negative interactions with coworkers. Positive attitudes give way to positive interactions.

Focus on what you have, instead of what you do not. It is easy to get caught up in keeping up with the Jones'. In a society where it is all about the nicest car, clothes, and house, we miss out on enjoying what we have in the constant search for something bigger and better. Many of the clients with mental retardation, autism, and other severe disabilities have very little in life. Almost all cannot drive, do not own a home, and wear the same clothes year after year. However, that does not change how happy and fulfilled they are. The one thing they want is to feel normal in the here and now. Working gives them that—and as long as they are provided the opportunity, they feel like millionaires.

Enjoy the little things in life. Some of the clients get paid two dollars every two weeks but, to them, it is like getting $2,000. It is not about the monetary value of the check, but the paycheck alone that gives them pride in themselves and what they do. While most people take it for granted, for them, going to the mall and buying something with their own hard-earned money is an indescribable joy. The next time you buy something for yourself, remember how hard you worked to get it. It will make your purchase even more rewarding.

Get excited about going to work. Even if it is raining outside or you are stuck in traffic or are running late, you were hired because of your unique abilities and talents. You specifically were chosen because someone was impressed by what only you can bring to the table. Someone had faith in you and believed in you. Celebrate and enjoy that fact. So many people with severe developmental disabilities never even are considered for employment. All too often they are perceived as not being useful to society, much less on the job. Imagine how it would feel knowing you have a lot to contribute to the world, but no one will give you a chance. As a result, you spend your entire life hoping that someone will come along who will see you for who you really are and give you that opportunity to shine.

People with mental retardation and other severe disabilities are elated to be at work. They often are the first to arrive and most days dread having to leave. Their work ethic is something beyond compare because they know how it feels to be isolated and segregated away from normal life. They appreciate the opportunities they are given and show their gratitude by excelling on the job.

Our motto is, "It's not about the work they produce, but what the work produces in them." That is true for all people in all work environments. In many ways, your work defines who you are and brings to the surface your core values and character. It can make your life enjoyable or completely miserable. It is all in how you choose look at it and how you choose to let it affect you. Take some time to see life from someone else's perspective and learn the important lessons that they are trying to teach you. It often is in the most unexpected places where we find the greatest gifts.

TERI S. ARNOLD is director of public relations, Chesapeake (Va.) Service Systems, a nonprofit organization that provides meaningful work opportunities to people with mental retardation and other severe disabilities.

Second Time Around

**After pink slips and midlife crises, a generation of seekers is beginning
to create Career 2.0. In doing so, they may redefine the idea of retirement.**

DANIEL MCGINN

They were the children of the Organization Men, those gray-flannel-clad climbers whose zeal for corporate life remains a defining image of the 1950s. But by the time the first baby boomers began entering the work force in the late 1960s, times were changing. College degrees had become more prevalent. Women were seeking out careers that were once off-limits. Industrial jobs were giving way to even more office work. And America's postwar fascination with materialism—look, there's another new car in the driveway of another newly built suburban home!—was on the wane. When it came to work, baby boomers wanted something more than steady paychecks, predictable promotions and the gold watch. Many wanted their work to be, above all, meaningful.

That quest continues today. Boomers are a wide demographic: the oldest, at 60, are nearing the age when their parents probably thought about retiring, while the youngest, at 42, are just hitting the sweet spot of their careers. Some are fantastically wealthy; some struggle in poverty. But most have approached their working lives with a self-determination unlike any previous generation—and for many, that means starting a whole new career in midlife. "There are tens of millions of people involved here, [asking], 'What am I going to do with the rest of my life?' " says Richard Fein, author of "The Baby Boomer's Guide to the New Workplace." Every day, a few more boomers blast those "new contact info" e-mails out as they pursue new professional adventures. Some are trading high-paying jobs to move into nonprofits or government positions. Some are starting businesses—or trying to parlay an individual passion (for quilting, say) into a way to make a living. Not all these moves are voluntary: for many people nowadays, the journey toward a new career begins with the pain of a pink slip.

And not everyone will find what they're seeking. Harvard political scientist Russell Muirhead, author of "Just Work," says the notion that one's occupation should deliver something more meaningful than a paycheck began with the 19th-century Romantics, but it's boomers who've truly embraced this ideal. "They expect in some sense that their careers will help them realize their authentic self," he says. Muirhead thinks it's an attitude that's a bit overblown; while many of us whine that

our jobs just don't *excite* us, it's worth recalling how happy our Depression-era grandparents were to have any job that delivered a reliable paycheck. But for a generation that invented the midlife crisis, career changes will no doubt continue.

Many of these job changes are driven by altruism. For 28 years, Bruce Pasternack worked at Booz Allen, a management-consulting firm. He counseled CEOs and wrote two books on management. But in the late 1990s, he began doing pro bono consulting work for the Special Olympics, the charity that encourages athletic competition for mentally impaired individuals. Soon Pasternack was on the Special Olympics board. Last year, as the group began to hunt for a new CEO, he mentioned his potential interest to the then CEO Tim Shriver. "What else could you do with your life in the next few years that would have as great an impact on the world?" Shriver asked him. This week marks Pasternack's first anniversary as CEO. He's taken a big pay cut, endured a heavy travel schedule and posed for hundreds of photos with Special Olympians. But at 59, he's happy. "It's more than met my expectations with respect to the personal satisfaction," he says.

For some career-changers, public-sector jobs are also a way to give back. This fall Waynewright Malcolm, 42, will begin teaching pre-algebra to eighth graders in Pembroke Pines, Fla., earning $38,000 a year. He can afford the meager paycheck because in his last job, as treasurer at the home-building giant Lennar, he made millions in salary and stock options. "A part of me has always wanted to teach—it's been in my heart a long time," he says. "My wife was very supportive when I told her what my plans were, but she challenged me—she wanted to make sure I was doing this for all the right reasons." Looking ahead to the fall, he's confident he is.

Traditionally, making a career change required finding another job. But for the generation that counts iconic company founders like Bill Gates and Michael Dell among its members, there's often a smarter route: creating a job of your own by starting a new business. David Thompson got a taste of start-up life when he was chief marketing officer at WebEx, a hot Web-conferencing firm. In 2000, WebEx was slated to go public—potentially making Thompson and his colleagues rich—but as the tech market softened, the IPO was delayed. "I had this huge emotional reaction," says Thompson, now 44. Reappraising his lifestyle, he saw a guy who ate horribly, slept too little and rarely exercised. So he took a nine-month sabbatical, doing yoga and losing 40 pounds. Soon afterward he launched his own firm, Genius.com, Inc., which develops software to support sales-people. As his own boss, he often works from home and sched-ules time for quiet reflection. "Everybody is so damn busy, no one thinks about what they really want," he says. Now, after years of craziness, he says, "my life finally has some balance."

That serenity is hardly the norm among folks who Inc. them-selves. Many say their transition from having a well-defined job to being master of everything (from fixing the copy machine to balancing the books) adds to their stress, at least initially. Seven months ago, when Larry Spear, the 45-year-old vice president of sales and marketing for a Florida utility, left to create his own telecom start-up, he knew he'd miss his prestigious title and his six-figure salary. But at BFE Telecom (it stands for Black Finan-cial Empowerment), he's launching projects like the Black 411, which lets callers throughout the United States dial a special number to locate black-owned businesses they can patronize. "I feel alive—I feel like what I'm doing matters," he says. "I'd like my kids to think, 'Hey, my dad did something more than make money. He did something very cool'."

Entrepreneur Randy Boudouris has found the fulfillment he lacked in the early years of his career. Boudouris, 50, studied art and music in college and hoped to be a rock star. But soon he was married with kids and needed a real job, so he signed on with a family printing business. He left after a dispute in 1998, and now he heads his own company, inventing products like wafer-thin magnetic coatings. "This is the most fun I've ever had," Boudouris says. "As far as I'm concerned, the second half of my life is the best part . . . You're never too old to change."

For some, career change is driven by the sense that they've been doing the same thing for far too long. Jean Blosser, 59, spent 35 years in academia as a speech-pathology professor and administrator. "I was kind of dying on the vine—I needed something more," she says. One day she read a newspaper story about Progressus Therapy, a speech-therapy firm. "That was that 'aha' event," she says, and she began researching how to apply for a job that didn't necessarily even exist. Convinced that her specialized training and leadership skills made her a perfect fit, she persisted in asking for meetings to explain why the firm needed her. Today she's VP for therapy programs and quality. "We created something that was a perfect fit for me and for the company," she says. "My move was risky, but it was worth it."

Some job changes begin with an ominous summons to a conference room, where an HR executive dispatches workers to the purgatory of unemployment. These corporate executions were rare when boomers' parents ruled the workplace; back then, companies "furloughed" manufacturing workers when times were slow but brought them back when sales picked up. Today, in contrast, many companies slice the white-collar head count in good times and bad. "Over the years, the permanent separation of people from their jobs, abruptly and against their wishes, gradually became a standard management practice," writes *New York Times* economics reporter Louis Uchitelle in

Boomer Jobs Starting Fresh

For many boomers, retirement will be the perfect time to begin a second career. Some of the most popular fields, according to a recent survey:

Consultant	27%
Teacher or professor	20%
Customer greeter	15%
Tour guide	13%
Retail-sales clerk	13%
Bookkeeper or auditing clerk	10%
Home handyman	10%
B&B owner or manager	9%
Security screener	8%
Real-estate agent	7%

Source: 2006 Merrill Lynch New Retirement Study.

his new book, "The Disposable American: Layoffs and Their Consequences." Since the 1980s, he figures, more than 30 million workers have been downsized—the majority of them baby boomers.

For some of these folks, the new gigs they land don't quite get them back to even. Bob Dew, 52, was laid off as a welder at a Fortune 500 company in Cleveland in 2002. After 30 years there, he draws a $1,300-a-month pension, but to supplement that income he works as a $7-an-hour shift supervisor at a drug-store; during baseball season he works a second job as an usher at a minor-league park. "It's actually a lot of fun," he says, and since neither job is physically demanding, he can probably do both into old age. But he now eschews name-brand products for generic and has put off his hopes to travel. His retirement plans are "dramatically different" since his layoff, he says. "Every-thing fell apart, and now I'm very guarded with cash."

Some boomers deal with a layoff by trying to turn their pas-sions into careers. Ellen Satter, 44, spent more than 18 years as a computer programmer for NASDAQ before being laid off on April 25. "I could see the writing on the wall," she says, describ-ing how her team had been cut back over time, with more work piled on survivors like her. To prepare for the inevitable, Sat-ter took night classes to earn an M.B.A. Now, with a generous severance package as a cushion, she's set out to create Career 2.0. "I realized I could do anything," she says. "I'm thrilled." She is about to lease a storefront space, and in October she'll open a scrapbooking store. "I can't see how I can get bored with scrapbooking," she says.

Most of the newbie entrepreneurs who are making these leaps say they have no illusions about the economics involved. Yes, there's more upside if a new business flourishes, but the trade-off is less financial security. Russ Klettke, 47, escaped a job as a corporate-communications executive to become a certified fit-ness trainer and research assistant at Northwestern University. On any given day he may be studying how strength training affects hardening of the arteries, or teaching a spin class, training clients one-on-one or working on a follow-up to his 2004 men's diet book. "Being split up between different gigs is exciting," he says. Financially, his new life feels more precarious, "but I wake up every morning and a list pops into my head of all the things I have to do that day, and I like that."

Of course, the people who make these career segues aren't the only ones affected—many have spouses and families who share the joys, pains and risks. Jay and Kendra Jeffcoat have been married for 38 years, but for the past two they've had a commuter marriage so that Jay, a 60-year-old lawyer, can stay in San Diego and work for the Sidney Kimmel Cancer Center, while Kendra works two hours east as a VP of academic affairs at Imperial Valley College. They see each other on weekends and have one "date night" each week midway between their homes. "She supports me and I support her," says Jay, who's looking forward to Kendra's full-time return to San Diego in July. For Tina Thompson, her husband's job transfer from Los Angeles to northern California in 2002 gave her the chance to ditch her teaching career to open an organic-kosher-vegetarian bakery in Pacific Grove. Now her goal is to "make others happy with my cooking," she says.

With life expectancies rising and traditional pension plans evaporating, these folks may need to keep their new careers going for years to come. Most experts predict baby boomers will work longer than their parents, and not just for financial necessity, but also to prevent boredom. According to a report called "The Future of Retirement" by the HSBC bank, "later life is increasingly seen as a time of opportunity and reinvention, rather than of rest and relaxation." The AARP says close to 70 percent of Americans plan to work at least part time during their "retirement" years—for money as well as a sense of purpose. Among human-resource pros, there are countless task forces studying ways that companies can better accommodate seniors.

The AARP even gives annual awards to the Best Employers for Workers Over 50; last year's winners included Volkswagen, Michelin and Whirlpool.

Aside from targeting firms with a senior-friendly track record, there are other steps aspiring career-changers can take. Fein says that just as college students routinely do internships to explore careers, older adults should test-drive new jobs, too. "It's important for people who are thinking about doing something new to try it out in a low-cost, low-risk environment," he says, which often means keeping your day job in the meantime. Sometimes the results will surprise you. Fein recalls a woman intent on opening her own greeting-card store. After working weekends in a similar shop, she realized she didn't really like dealing with customers. Fein says the happiest career changers are those who are jumping *toward* a new job, rather than trying to escape an existing one.

Embracing this advice has helped Janice Stein as she's moved through more careers than she ever expected to have. Stein, 47, has worked as an engineer for Northrop, then as a marketer with several Silicon Valley companies and a Norwegian videoconferencing firm. Two years ago, tired of nonstop travel and her constantly ringing cell phone, she quit to start a business finishing quilts that hobbyists had sewn. "At some point, you have to step back and decide to have a life," she says. She's enjoyed that self-created gig, but now she wants health benefits and more security, so she's going back to school to become certified in medical imaging. She'll be using technology that didn't exist when she came out of college a generation ago—just the kind of adventure these self-determined boomers have grown to welcome.

With Karen Springen, in Chicago, Joan Raymond, in Cleveland and Jamie Reno, in San Diego.

Secrets of the Centenarians

In certain families, small genetic variations bring good health and long life. Can researchers apply this knowledge to benefit us all?

MAYA PINES

I s there a formula for living to the age of 100 or beyond? HHMI investigator Louis M. Kunkel believes there is, and he's working hard to define it.

Besides a healthy dose of good luck (Kunkel says it helps to not be killed in a war or a traffic accident), one key to longevity is a highly unusual combination of gene variants that protects against the customary diseases of old age. Several research teams are now in the process of uncovering these genes.

Kunkel, director of the Genomics Program at Children's Hospital in Boston, and his associates recently identified a genetic variant that is particularly prominent among sibling pairs in the New England Centenarian Study, perhaps the world's largest pool of centenarians. They are seeking additional genetic variants that might retard—or perhaps even prevent—many of the diseases that debilitate the old. "People with this rare combination of genes clearly age more slowly," Kunkel says. "When they reach 90, they don't look any older than 70."

Hundreds of centenarians around the world are now contributing their blood and medical histories to the search for these precious genes. They have become a key resource for researchers who hope that as these genes are revealed, their good effects may be reproduced in other people with the help of new drugs.

Clustered in Families

Kunkel was drawn to the hunt for longevity genes about six years ago, through a chance encounter with Thomas T. Perls, a Boston University Medical School geriatrician who had enrolled a large group of centenarians for his New England Centenarian Study. Kunkel's own research was focused on a deadly genetic disorder called Duchenne muscular dystrophy, which affects mostly boys. In 1986, he discovered a mutation that causes this muscle-wasting disease, and he is still working on a therapy for it (see Cures for Muscle Diseases?). But he could not resist the opportunity to also apply his knowledge of genetics to what he heard from Perls.

The two men were acquainted through Perls's wife, Leslie Smoot, who happened to be a postdoc in Kunkel's lab. When they met on a street in Cambridge, Massachusetts, in 1997 and started talking about their work, "Tom told me that many of the centenarians whose lineage he was examining were clustered in families," Kunkel recalls. "I realized that's just got to be genetics. We soon started a collaboration."

For his part, Perls remembers that at the beginning of his study he thought the centenarians had little in common except for their age. But he soon realized that many of them had an unusually large number of equally aged relatives. "We had a 108-year-old man who blew out his birthday candles next to his 102-year-old sister," Perls recalls. "They told us they had another sibling who was 103, and yet another who was only 99. Two other siblings—also centenarians—had passed away. Four siblings had died in childhood. So here was an incredible clustering, 5 or maybe 6 siblings out of 10! We've since found about 7 families like that." This implied that all these families carried especially protective genes. Shortly after the two scientists met, a new postdoc arrived in Kunkel's lab—Annibale A. Puca, a young Italian neurologist who wanted to work in genetics—and Kunkel suggested he take on this new project. "I warned him it was going to be a lot of work and high risk, but he said okay," Kunkel says, "and he spearheaded the whole program."

Puca and Perls rapidly expanded the group of centenarians, recruiting them through alumni associations, newspaper clippings, and state census lists. After taking samples of the centenarians' blood, the researchers extracted DNA from it and started looking for genetic markers—specific stretches of DNA that might occur more frequently among these extremely old men and women than among a group of younger people who were the study's controls. Most scientists believed that human longevity is far too complicated a trait to be influenced by only a few genes. There are so many independent mechanisms of aging that "the chance that only a few major genes control longevity in man is highly unlikely," wrote a self-styled "pessimist" on this issue, George M. Martin of the University of Washington in Seattle, in the journal *Mechanisms of Ageing and Development* in 2002. But Kunkel's lab took a different view. "In lower organisms, such as nematodes, fruit flies, and yeast, there are only a few genes that need to be altered to give a longer life span," Kunkel says. "My feeling was that there were

Who Are These Centenarians?

"Centenarians tend to be independent, assertive, funny, and gregarious," says Boston University Medical School geriatrician Thomas T. Perls, who at 43 has probably met more people over the age of 100 than anybody else. "They also seem to manage stress very well, which makes sense, since we know that not handling stress predisposes you to cardiovascular disease and high blood pressure."

During a fellowship in geriatrics at Harvard Medical School in the early 1990s, Perls took care of 40 patients at Boston's Hebrew Rehabilitation Center for the Aged. Two of his healthiest patients, who looked as if they were in their seventies, were actually over 100 years old. "They were in really terrific shape," he says. "It was so different from what I expected! This sparked my interest."

As a result, Perls founded the New England Centenarian Study in 1994, becoming one of only a few researchers studying the very old at that time. He started out by looking for people over 100 in eight towns around Boston, using census records, voter registration files, and the media. Later, he expanded the study by adding centenarians from all over the United States. Now it includes 1,600 centenarians and 500 of their children. About 20 percent of the centenarian women in his study had given birth after the age of 40, Perls found, compared to a national average of only 3 percent of mothers. "It showed that these women were aging very slowly," he says.

He also studied the centenarians' siblings and concluded that their chances of living to their early nineties were four times greater than average. More recently, Perls examined the centenarians' children. At the age of 70, he found, they had a 24 percent reduction in mortality compared to the general population, as well as about a 60 percent reduction in the risk of heart disease, hypertension, and diabetes.

More than 90 percent of the centenarians had been in good health and completely independent until their early to mid-90s, Perls says. "They lived the vast majority of their lives with good function," he emphasizes. "So it's not a matter of 'the older you get, the sicker you get' but rather 'the older you get, the healthier you've been.' This is a different way of thinking about aging."

By the time people reach the century mark, however, the healthy ones are in the minority. "We found that 25 percent of the centenarians were doing well, but the remaining 75 percent had mild to severe impairment," Perls reports. "In the end, they die of cardiovascular disease or something that's related to frailty, such as pneumonia."

This fits in well with the theories of Leonard Hayflick, of the University of California, San Francisco, who showed in 1961 that there are limits to the number of times a normal human cell can divide. Even under the most favorable conditions, he said, noncancerous human cells die after about 50 cell divisions (this is now called the "Hayflick limit"). Eliminating the leading causes of death in old age—cardiovascular diseases, stroke, and cancer—"will only result in an increase of about 15 years in human life expectancy," Hayflick declared in the November 9, 2000, issue of *Nature*. Although these 15 years would be a great gift, assuming that people remained healthy during that time, nothing could stop "the inevitable increase in errors and disorders in the cells of vital organs" that results from age, he pointed out. Even the cells' repair processes would become disordered, leading to extreme vulnerability and death.

Then would it be a good thing for more people to live to 100? "Absolutely," says Perls. "Centenarians are sentinels of the health of older people. Our goal is not to get a bunch of individuals to be 120 or 130, but to discover which genes are most protective and then use this information to get a majority of people living almost all their lives in good health, as centenarians generally do."

---

only a few genes, perhaps four to six, in humans that would do the same."

The team proceeded to examine genetic markers for the entire genomes of 308 people, selected because they belonged to 137 sibships (sets of siblings) in which at least one member was over 98 and the others were over 90. "From early on, we saw a blip of a peak on chromosome 4," says Kunkel. "Eventually, in 2001, we found a linkage between one region of this chromosome and longevity."

Search for a SNP

It was "phenomenal" to get a real linkage from such a slight hint in the original data, Kunkel declares. But that didn't mean further research would be easy. This stretch of DNA was so large—12 million DNA base pairs long—that it seemed it could contain as many as 200 genes. Furthermore, the researchers knew that within these genes they would have to look for variations in single bases of DNA—"single-nucleotide polymorphisms," or SNPs (pronounced "snips"). "SNPs really represent the

difference between individuals," Kunkel explains. "Everybody's DNA is 99.9 percent identical—it's the SNPs that make us unique and allow certain people to live longer. Even though most of our DNA is alike, the 0.1 percent variation means that we have more than 10 million SNPs across the genome. And we're on the verge of being able to map them." For Kunkel, the critical question was "how would we find the one SNP in a single gene that might help a person to live much longer than average?"

The groundbreaking work of the Human Genome Project had not yet been completed at that time, and Kunkel realized that finding this particular SNP would be both expensive and time-consuming. It would also be quite different from zeroing in on a missing or severely garbled gene, as had been done for cystic fibrosis, muscular dystrophy, and other single-gene disorders. The widespread diseases of aging—heart disease, stroke, diabetes, cancer, and Alzheimer's disease—are much more complex and are triggered by subtle gene variations that produce only slightly altered proteins, Kunkel says. These proteins may either work a little better or be less active than those in the

Cures for Muscle Diseases?

Ever since Louis M. Kunkel discovered the cause of Duchenne muscular dystrophy (DMD) in 1986, he has been laboring to find a cure for this muscle-wasting disease. DMD—the result of an error in a single gene—attacks 1 out of every 4,000 newborn boys, progressively crippling and then killing them at an early age.

Kunkel saw that patients with DMD lacked a protein, dystrophin, which this gene would have produced if it were functioning normally. So he knew he had to replace the protein somehow. He and others tried many methods—gene therapy to deliver a normal gene to the defective muscle cell, drugs to help restore the mission protein, and cell therapy to inject normal cells into muscle or blood—but despite some partial successes in animals, nothing really worked.

Kunkels lab worked mostly with *mdx* mice, a naturally mutant strain that lack dystrophin. When he and his colleagues attempted to cure these crippled mice with injections of muscle stem cells from normal mice, "some of the donor cells did go into the damaged muscles." he recalls, "but we never got more then 1 to 2 percent of the muscles repaired. Part of the problem was that when you inject cells into a mouses tail vein, which is the most accessible part of its circulation, the donor cells go through all the organs—the lungs, liver, heart, and so on—and out through the arterial system. Most of the cells get filtered and lost, and don't contribute to the therapy."

Today, however, Kunkel feels he is on the verge of success. The big breakthrough came last summer when a team of Italian scientists headed by Giulio Cossu of Milan's Stem Cell Research Institute announced it had found a new route for the injection of stem cells into dystrophic mice directly into an artery. The cells seemed to lodge within the capillary system near the injection site. From there, about 30 percent of them migrated to the diseased muscles. Not only did the cells get there, he says, but at later time points, you could see a larger number of donor cells than at the earliest point, as if they were trying to divide.

"Can we improve on this?" asks Kunkel with a glint in his eye. "If we can get the stem cells into 50 percent of the dystrophic muscles, that's basically a cure."

They had trouble at first because "the mouse artery was 10 times smaller than our smallest injection needles—it was like trying to hit it with a hammer!" Kunkel says. Though a tail vein is even smaller than an artery, it can be hit much more easily because it is right under the surface of the skin and can be made to swell up by warming it. In the new system, the mouse had to be anesthetized and opened up to expose its artery, which was lifted out—a complex procedure.

"It wasn't until we started collaborating with some vascular surgeons who had been doing heart transplants in mice that we were able to get the stem cells into the mouse arteries efficiently," he says. In humans, of course, reaching an artery would not be a problem given that human arteries are so much larger.

Getting the stem cells into the muscles was just the first step. Unless these cells supplied enough dystrophin, the diseased muscles would not be repaired. So Kunkel also tried to find different stem cells that could do the job more effectively. In 1999 his lab and that of his colleague Richard Mulligan announced they could restore some of the missing dystrophin in mdx mice with the aid of a new kind of stem cells called "side population" (SP) cells, which seemed to work much better. These SP cells had to be taken from muscle tissue, however. Last year Kunkel's lab succeeded in deriving similar SP cells from adult skin, which is easier to obtain. Since they originate in adult tissue, both kinds of SP cells will be much less controversial then embryonic stem cells.

"It's my belief that you can do a lot of therapeutic intervention with adult-derived cells," says Kunkel. He notes that the new stem cells seem ready to differentiate into every type of muscle tissue, which implies that they have the potential to treat many forms of muscle disease.

The combination of new cell type and a new delivery system "may revolutionize how one does therapy for muscle diseases," Kunkel suggests. "When we get it perfected in mice, we'll go to humans." He thinks this might happen in a couple of years.

---

normal population, and several of them may work in concert. Searching for a single SNP would require doing thousands of genetic analyses on each of his subjects (now numbering 653) and comparing the results with the control group. "We estimated it would cost at least $5 million," Kunkel said. "It finally cost $8 million and took one-and-a-half years."

Ultimately, all that painstaking work paid off. The paper announcing the discovery of a SNP that contributes to longevity was published in the November 25, 2003, issue of the *Proceedings of the National Academy of Sciences*.

Now for the Others

The long-sought SNP turned out to lie within the gene for microsomal transfer protein, or MTP, which had been known since the mid-1980s to be involved in cholesterol metabolism.

"It's quite clear that to live to be 100, you've got to maintain your cholesterol at a healthy level," says Kunkel. "It makes perfect sense. We know that increased LDL (the 'bad' cholesterol) and lowered HDL (the 'good' cholesterol) raise your cardiovascular risk and that cardiovascular diseases account for a large percentage of human mortality. So variations in the genes involved in cholesterol packaging will influence your life span. It's as if these centenarians had been on Lipitor [a cholesterol-lowering drug] from birth!"

This discovery might lead to drugs that are tailored to intervene in the cholesterol pathway. Because the MTP gene was already in the public domain, however, it could not be patented, much to the disappointment of the former Centagenetix Corporation (founded by Puca, Perls, and Kunkel and now a part of Elixir Pharmaceuticals of Cambridge, Massachusetts), which had bankrolled most of the study.

In any event, this SNP "cannot be the whole story," Kunkel declares. "There must be other gene variations that enable people to avoid age-related diseases. Some of our original families did not show linkages to chromosome 4." Nor did a group of centenarians who were tested in France.

Determined to find some of the other SNPs that produce longevity, Kunkel says he's going back to his sample and will redo the whole study. "We now have 310 sibships," he says. "Our genetic markers are much denser. I believe we can get 10 times the power in our next screen than we had in the first."

Moreover, the work can be done much more rapidly and inexpensively than last time, he notes, given the giant strides that have been made recently in human genetics. Not only has the entire human genome been sequenced, but many of the errors in the original draft have been corrected. Equally important, all the known genes in the genome are now available on a single Affymetrix DNA chip, allowing researchers to promptly identify which genes are activated and which are damped down in any given situation. In addition, as many as 10,000 different human SNPs have been placed on a single chip.

Similar tools have already turned up new gene variants in yeast, worms, and flies. But Kunkel will use the chips to analyze the DNA of humans. Once his lab gets started on the new longevity project, he believes, it will not take very long to get some definitive answers. He hopes these will lead to drugs that could mimic the protective effects of the centenarians' genes.

Gold Standard

In fact, these studies foreshadow a far-reaching attack on all complex diseases—not just those of the aged but others, such as autism and hypertension. None of these ills could be tackled efficiently in the past. "The centenarians are the ideal control group for such research," Kunkel says. "To reach 100, you must have good alleles [versions of the genes] at all points. So if one wants to find the genes that are connected with hypertension, for instance, one can look across the genome for genes that are highly active in the hypertensive population but down-regulated in centenarians. Ultimately, that's what the centenarians' genes will be used for."

He believes that in the future, "every person who comes to our genetic clinic—or goes through any type of care system—with what appears to be a complex disease should be analyzed in detail. I mean that we should gather all the information we can about each patient's symptoms, the family history of these symptoms, any environmental insults the patient suffered, any learning disability—anything that would allow us to categorize the patient and [the patient's] family into subtypes of the disease which could be more related to one another and thus more likely to involve the same gene." To make this happen, Kunkel has just appointed a director of phenotyping (the Greek roots of this word mean "classifying phenomena into specific types") who will collect, categorize, and catalogue such patient information.

"We will also analyze the patients' genes but only in the context of the category of symptoms they exhibit," he says. "The samples we collect—under appropriate protocols—will be available to the national groups of patients and researchers that are organizing to find the underlying genetic bases of specific diseases." Eventually, he hopes, many complex disorders such as heart disease, diabetes, and autism will be broken down into more specific categories, which in turn may lead to more precise treatments or ways of preventing the disorder. Kunkel expects this process to accelerate in the near future as more patients' genes are compared with those of the gold standard for humans—the centenarians.

From *HHMI Bulletin*, Spring 2004. Copyright © 2004 by Howard Hughes Medical Institute. Reprinted by permission.

Lost and Found

Promising therapy for Alzheimer's draws out the person inside the patient.

BARBARA BASLER

The woman wore a plain housedress and a big apron, its pockets stuffed with plastic checkers. Head down, eyes blank, she shuffled aimlessly around the activity room. Cameron Camp, a research psychologist who was visiting this assisted living home in Kentucky, watched the 70-year-old woman for a moment. Then, he recalls, "I went up to her and gave her one of our books—the one on Gene Kelly, the dancer—and asked her to please read a page."

He pauses, remembering the woman and the skeptical staff—and the very next moment.

"She took the book and read aloud—clear as a bell," Camp says with a smile. "A shocked staffer turned to me and said, 'I didn't even know she could speak. That's a miracle.'"

Camp heads the Myers Research Institute in Beachwood, Ohio, and his cutting-edge work with patients in all stages of Alzheimer's has left him improbably upbeat—because he sees miracles like this day after day.

His research is part of a sea of change in the care of Alzheimer's patients who are in the later stages of the disease: "Ten to 15 years ago these people were institutionalized, and their care involved physical or chemical restraints," says Kathleen O'Brien, vice president of program and community services for the Chicago-based Alzheimer's Association, which, with the National Institutes of Health, has helped fund Camp's work.

Psychologist Cameron Camp says patients live in the moment. "Our job is to give them as many good moments as we can."

"Today," she says, "more than 70 percent of those with Alzheimer's are cared for in the family home, and we talk about controlling the disease and enhancing daily life for those who have it."

Alzheimer's, the most common form of dementia in people over the age of 65, affects 4.5 million Americans. An irreversible brain disorder, the disease robs people of their memory and eventually impairs most of their mental and physical functions.

While research typically focuses on preventing Alzheimer's or delaying its progress in the early stages, some medical specialists and long-term care professionals are investigating activities that will help patients in the later stages.

"We can't stop cell death from Alzheimer's," Camp explains. "But at any stage of dementia there is a range of capability. If you give people a reason to get out of bed, activities that engage them and allow them to feel successful, they will be at the top of their game, whatever it is."

Camp, 53, began his research 10 years ago when he looked at the activities developed for young children by the educator Maria Montessori, whose "method" is followed today in Montessori schools around the world. There, children learn by manipulating everyday objects like balls, seashells and measuring spoons in highly structured activities that engage children but rarely allow them to fail.

Camp adapted these kinds of exercises for older people with dementia, tailoring them to the individual's background and interests, and found he could draw out the person inside the patient.

"Suddenly, they just wake up, come alive for the moment," he says.

That happened to Mary Anne Duffy's husband when they took part in Camp's research. James Duffy, 77, has Parkinson's disease and dementia and is confined to a wheelchair in a nursing home in Mentor, Ohio.

"James loved woodworking," Duffy says, "and he liked fixing things, so the researcher brought him a small box to paint, nuts and bolts to put together, puzzles." Before her husband began the activities, she says, he "just sat there, nodding off."

But when he was working a puzzle or painting a box, "James actually smiled—something I hadn't seen for a long time," Duffy says. "And he would talk. That was amazing."

People with Alzheimer's "live in the moment, and our job is to give them as many good moments as we can," Camp says. "We need to be thinking about these people in a new way. Instead of focusing on their problems and deficits, we need to ask what strengths and abilities remain."

People had assumed, for instance, that the woman with the checkers in her apron pockets was too impaired to read. But studies have found that reading is one of the very last skills to fade away. "It's automatic, almost a reflex," Camp says.

"If the print is right," he says as he flips through one of his specially designed books with big, bold letters, many Alzheimer's patients can read.

One goal of Camp's work has been to turn his research into practical how-to guides for professional and family caregivers. Published by the Myers Research Institute, the guides have been translated into Chinese, Japanese and Spanish.

While long-term care residences may have some activities for dementia patients—like coloring in a picture or listening to a story—often they don't have activities "that are meaningful, that call on an adult's past," Camp says. "And even people with Alzheimer's are bored if an activity isn't challenging or interesting."

Much of Camp's research is with residents at Menorah Park Center for Senior Living in Beachwood, which is affiliated with Myers Research. After Alzheimer's patients were given the large-print books that he and his colleagues developed, many could read aloud and discuss the books.

A brief biography of Leonardo da Vinci, for instance, talks about some of his wildly imaginative inventions, like a machine that would let soldiers breathe underwater so they could march underneath enemy ships, drill holes in their hulls and sink them.

"It's a wonderful, wacky idea," Camp says. "Dementia patients react to it just as we do. They love it. They laugh, they shake their heads. They talk about it."

Education Director Lisa P. Gwyther of the Bryan Alzheimer's Disease Research Center at Duke University Medical Center recalls visiting a facility where she saw Alzheimer's patients themselves teaching some of the simple activities they had learned to preschool children. "I was so impressed with the dignity and the purpose and the fun that was observable between the older person and younger child," she says. Camp's work has been rigorously studied in a number of small pilot projects, she adds, "which means this is a reliable, valid method."

At Menorah Park, Camp and his team look at what basic skills remain in those with dementia: Can the person read, sort, categorize, manipulate objects? Then they customize activities for those skills.

"We had one man who loved baseball," Camp says. "We had him sort pictures of baseball players into American and National leagues. Another man who loved opera sorted titles into operas by Puccini and operas by Verdi."

The activities help patients maintain the motor skills needed to feed themselves or button buttons. They also trigger memories, then conversations that connect the patient and the caregiver.

People with dementia won't consciously remember the activity from one session to the next. But, Camp says, "some part of them does remember, and eventually they will get bored. So you can't have them match the same pictures each time."

It doesn't matter if patients make mistakes, Camp adds. "What's important is that they enjoy the process."

Mike Skrajner, a project manager for Myers Research who monitored an Alzheimer's reading group at Menorah Park, recalls one morning when the group was reading a biography of Gene Kelly and came to the part where Kelly tells his father he is quitting law school—to take ballet lessons. "They stopped right there and had a great conversation about how they would react to that news," he says. "It was a wonderful session, and at the end they all wound up singing 'Singin' in the Rain.'"

Manipulating everyday objects helps patients maintain skills for feeding themselves or brushing their teeth.

Camp's research shows that people who engage in such activities tend to exhibit fewer signs of agitation, depression and anxiety.

George Niederehe, acting chief of the geriatrics research branch of the National Institute of Mental Health, which is funding some of Camp's work, says a large study of patients in long-term care facilities is needed for definitive proof of the effectiveness of Camp's approach. But his method could be as helpful to caregivers as it is to people with Alzheimer's, he says, because it would improve "staff morale, knowing they can do something useful for these patients." And that, he adds, would enhance the overall environment for staff and residents alike.

One vital part of Camp's theory—like Montessori's—is that residents need activities that give them a social role, whether it's contributing at a book club or stirring lemonade for a party.

The Menorah Park staff worked with one patient, a former mailman, who loved folding pieces of paper stamped with "Have a Nice Day!" He stuffed the notes into envelopes and delivered them to other residents.

"What we try to do," Camp says, "is let the person you remember shine through the disease, even if it's only a few moments a day."

To Learn More

- To download samples of Cameron Camp's activities for dementia patients, go to www.aarp/bulletin/longterm.
- The caregiver's manual "A Different Visit" costs $39.95 plus shipping, and the special large-print books for Alzheimer's patients cost $5.95 each (or six copies for the price of five) plus shipping. To order, go to www.myersresearch.org, or write Myers Research Institute, 27100 Cedar Road, Beachwood, OH 44122.
- For general information, go to the Alzheimer's Association Web site at www.alz.org.

For nine simple habits you can adopt that may delay dementia, see the September-October issue of *AARP The Magazine.*

Life after Death

If life is a journey, what is the destination? We asked people 50 and over to share their most deeply held beliefs. The result is an illuminating glimpse into America's spiritual core.

BILL NEWCOTT

For all the nudging and pushing and jockeying for position among the sweaty tourists who surround me on the floor of the Sistine Chapel this summer morning, it's nothing compared with the cyclone of activity going on up there on the front wall.

In Michelangelo's painting *The Last Judgment* there's little doubt about who's going where. On the left, a swirl of saints and martyrs ascend Heavenward, their faces a mix of rapture and shock. They soar triumphantly, flanking the figure of a Risen Christ. On the right, it's a decidedly downward trend, a slightly more populated mix of eternal unfortunates being dragged, pushed, and hurled into the abyss. I step around behind the altar—a vantage virtually no one else seems interested in—and marvel at the nearly hidden figures of three apelike creatures, seemingly the gatekeepers of a fiery furnace that is glimpsed just beyond.

In appearance and execution *The Last Judgment* is archetypical Mannerist art. But the fact is, the nuts and bolts of Michelangelo's vision are shared by the vast majority of 50-plus Americans.

In an exclusive survey of 1,011 people 50 and over, AARP THE MAGAZINE sought to learn just what Americans in the second half of life think about life after death. Over the years we've seen countless surveys examining Americans' attitudes and beliefs about the afterlife, but we wanted to hear specifically from the AARP generation—those who are more than halfway to the point of finding out, once and for all, precisely how right or wrong they were about life after death.

To begin, we found that people 50 and over tend to be downright conventional in their basic beliefs: nearly three quarters (73 percent) agree with the statement "I believe in life after death." Women are a lot more likely to believe in an afterlife (80 percent) than men (64 percent).

A copyeditor I once knew insisted that you should always capitalize the word *Heaven*. "Heaven," he explained, "is a place. Like Poughkeepsie."

Two thirds of those who believe also told us that their confidence in a life after death has increased as they've gotten older. Among them is 90-year-old Leona Mabrand. Born in North Dakota, she moved to Oregon in her 20s, married—and watched, one by one, as every member of her family passed on before her. "I'm the only one left of my family tree," she says, her voice a mix of pride and sadness.

Turning down her radio to chat one recent afternoon—Paul Harvey is one of her favorite companions these days—she tells me that the longer she lives, the more miracles she sees, and the more that convinces her that what her Christian faith tells her about the hereafter is true.

77% are not frightened by thoughts of what happens after death.

"The Lord has shown me a lot of good miracles happen," she says. "I'm looking forward to seeing my husband and my family and all those who have gone to their rest before me."

Of course, Christians like Leona aren't the only ones with their eye on an afterlife.

"It reflects our multicultural environment," says Barnard College professor of religion Alan F. Segal, author of *Life After Death: A History of the Afterlife in Western Religion* (Doubleday, 2004). "Most Americans believe they will be saved no matter what they are. In the '60s and '70s there was this thought that the boomers were not particularly religious; they were busy finding jobs and setting up house. But as they entered their fourth decade, they returned. I'm not sure it was a religious revival—it may have been they were just returning."

It may also reflect a repudiation of the long-held notion that science is the source of all of life's answers, adds Huston Smith, Syracuse University professor emeritus of religion and author of the 2.5 million-copy-selling *The World's Religions: Our Great Wisdom Traditions* (HarperSanFrancisco, 1991).

"Belief in an afterlife has risen in the last 50 years," he says. "Serious thinkers are beginning to see through the mistake modernity made in thinking that science is the oracle of truth."

Believers show general agreement over the choice of destinations in the afterlife, as well: 86 percent say there's a Heaven, while somewhat fewer (70 percent) believe in Hell.

After that, the groups break down into subsets. While most people 50 and over believe there's life beyond the grave, there's a spectrum of visions regarding just what's ahead.

Location, Location, Location

A copyeditor I once knew insisted that you should always capitalize the word *Heaven*. "Heaven," he explained, "is a place. Like Poughkeepsie." He'd be in the minority among those 50 and over who believe in Heaven. Just 40 percent believe Heaven is "a place," while 47 percent say it's a "state of being." As for the alternate destination, of those who think Hell exists, 43 percent say it's a "state of being"; 42 percent say it's "a place" (although not, presumably, like Poughkeepsie). "Heaven's a place, all right," says Ed Parlin, 56, of Salem, New Hampshire, about Heaven. And he's got some ideas of what to expect. "It's a better place than this is—that's for sure," he says. "And I guess everybody gets along. It's always a beautifully clear day, and sunny, with great landscaping."

86% believe in Heaven.

"Americans see life after death as a very dynamic thing," says Barnard College's Segal. "You don't really hear about angels and wings, sitting on clouds playing melodies. A lot believe there will be sex in the afterlife, that it'll be more pleasurable, less dangerous, and it won't be physical, but spiritual. They talk about humor in the afterlife, continuing education, unifying families—like a retirement with no financial needs."

There's a line in Matthew's Gospel that states: "It is easier for a camel to go through the eye of a needle than for a rich man to enter the kingdom of God." And perhaps not so coincidentally, our survey shows the richer people are, the less likely they are to believe there's a Heaven. Among those with a household income of $75,000 or more per year, 78 percent believe in Heaven—compared with 90 percent of those earning $25,000 or less. Similarly, 77 percent of college-educated people think there's a Heaven, compared with 89 percent of those who have a high school diploma or less.

The Price of Admission

While the overwhelming majority of Americans 50 and over believe in Heaven, there's a lot of splintering when it comes to just what it takes to arrive there. The largest group, 29 percent of those who believe in Heaven, responded that the prerequisite is to "believe in Jesus Christ." Twenty-five percent said people who "are good" get in. Another 10 percent said that people who "believe in one God" are welcomed into Heaven. Likewise, 10 percent took a come-one, come-all philosophy, saying everyone gets into Heaven.

94% believe in God.

And while 88 percent of people believe they'll be in Heaven after they die, they're not so sure about the rest of us. Those responding said 64 percent of all people get to Heaven. And many think the percentage will be a lot smaller than that.

"Fifteen percent," says Ira Merce of Lakeland, Florida. He admitted it's just a guess on his part, but he's still not happy about it. "I'd like to see the percentages turned exactly around, but I can't see it happening. If you read Scripture, it says, 'Broad is the way that leads to destruction, and narrow is the way that leads to eternal life.' "

Among those who told us they believe in Hell, their attitudes about who goes there generally mirrored the poll's results about Heaven. Forty percent of those who believe in Hell said "people who are bad" or "people who have sinned" go there; 17 percent said, "People who do not believe in Jesus Christ" are condemned to spend their afterlife in Hell. And in what has to be the understatement of all eternity, Ed suggests, "It's probably a place where you're gonna do things that you don't like to do."

70% believe in Hell.

Second Time Around?

Twenty-three percent of those responding said they believe in reincarnation—meaning there are a fair number who have an overlapping belief in Heaven and a return trip to Earth. The percentage was highest in the Northeast (31 percent), and boomers were most likely to believe in reincarnation.

"It's controversial here [in the United States], but reincarnation is a mainstay of the Eastern religions—Hinduism, Jainism, and Sikhism," says Ishani Chowdhury, executive director of the Hindu American Foundation. "You see more and more people of the younger generation weighing it at the same level as Western religions and not dismissing it."

Adds Jeffrey Burton Russell, professor emeritus of history at the University of California, Santa Barbara, and author of *A History of Heaven* (Princeton University Press, 1998): "If you took this study 50 years ago, the belief in reincarnation would be down at about one percent. Generally, the traditionally clear Christian vision of Heaven has declined, while the vaguer visions of the continuation of life have taken its place."

One true believer is Linda Abbott of St. Louis. "We have to come back," she tells me. "We come back over and over until we get it right!"

More than half of those responding reported a belief in spirits or ghosts—with more women (60 percent) than men (44 percent) agreeing. Boomers are a lot more likely to believe in ghosts (64 percent) compared with those in their 60s (51 percent) or 70s or older (38 percent). Their belief is not entirely based on hearsay evidence, either. Thirty-eight percent of all those responding to our poll say they have felt a presence, or seen something, that they thought might have been a spirit or a ghost.

"We've had some strange experiences," says Ed, who once lived in a house he suspected might be haunted. "Doors closing that shouldn't close, things falling down when you know they're stable. Kind of like someone on the other side was trying to get our attention."

Still, despite all those great stories about old haunted houses in the Northeast and Deep South, it was respondents from the West (50 percent) who were especially likely to say they'd felt the presence of a spirit or a ghost.

What's With That White Light?

Can you die and live to tell the tale? Some people come awfully close, and a few return with a remarkable story: of euphoria, a bright light (sometimes at the end of a tunnel), encounters with dead relatives, or an out-of-body experience, in which they feel as if they're hovering over their physical body. Scientists call these near-death experiences, or NDEs; polls show 4 to 5 percent of Americans say they've had one.

Some experts dismiss NDEs as nothing more than an altered state of consciousness. "It's very likely that REM [rapid eye movement] sleep and the arousal system of the brain are contributing to NDEs," says Kevin Nelson, M.D., a University of Kentucky neurophysiologist. His research suggests that people with NDEs have a "different brain switch" that blends sleep with wakefulness—which reduces the ordeal of dying to a dreamlike state.

But lots of people believe NDEs are glimpses of the afterlife—and there's some data to indicate there's something happening beyond the realm of physiology.

Some of the most intriguing findings come from Pim van Lommel, a retired cardiologist from the Rijnstate Hospital in Arnhem, Netherlands, who followed 344 survivors of cardiac arrest; 18 percent reported having had NDEs while their brains showed no wave activity. This perplexes van Lommel because, he says, "according to our current medical concepts it's impossible to experience consciousness during a period of clinical death."

"The out-of-body component of the NDE is actually verifiable," says Sam Parnia, M.D., Ph.D., a critical-care physician at New York City's Weill Cornell Medical Center. He says patients who report watching their own resuscitation from above may have had visions—or they may be recollecting false memories. He plans to place markers, visible only from the ceiling, in emergency rooms across the United Kingdom, then quiz patients who report having had NDEs.

"If they correctly identify these targets," says Parnia, "that suggests the experience was real."

—Anne Casselman

No Place to Go

Nearly one quarter of those responding agreed with the statement "I believe that when I die, that's the end." It's not the sort of statement that invites a lot of questions for clarification, but Tom, a friendly, outspoken fellow I chatted with from the Lake Champlain region of upstate New York, took a shot at it.

To the question "Is there life after death?" Tom responds, "Nope. I've always felt that way. Life's short enough without having to worry about something you can't do anything about anyway. It's just reality, you know? I mean, I'm a Catholic."

Tom waits while I lift my jaw from the table. A *Catholic?*

"Sure. They preach life after death, you know? I just say, hey, people preach a lot of stuff. You just gotta make up your own mind about things. I go to Mass. I live my life like there's life after death, but I don't believe there is. If it's true, well, hey, it's a plus. But if it ain't, I didn't lose nothing."

He laughs, and I laugh with him. (He does ask that I not divulge his last name, and I wonder if that's to cover his tracks just in case God picks up this issue of AARP THE MAGAZINE.) Nonetheless, it's interesting that Tom tries to live as if there were an afterlife, even though he doesn't believe in one. It seems to echo what others tell me about how their beliefs in the hereafter—or lack thereof—impact the way they live their lives. Surprisingly, few confess their beliefs have any effect at all. And everyone I talk to agrees we should be living our lives according to a moral code—which many would define as God's code—whether there's a God at all, or a reward awaits.

As 90-year-old Leona puts it, "I just want to be faithful to Jesus every day and do what's right."

The sentiment, I discovered, is echoed across a wide spectrum of belief—and disbelief. "Atheists celebrate life, but we know death is a reality," says Margaret Downey, president of Atheist Alliance International. "We believe the only afterlife that a person can hope to have is the legacy they leave behind—the memory of the people who have been touched by their lives."

No matter what your belief, adds Omid Safi, former cochair for the study of Islam at the American Academy of Religion, "even though we use words like *afterlife,* or the *next life,* the *life beyond,* it is actually a great mirror about how people like to see themselves now, and the way they see God, and the way they see themselves interacting with other people."

For my money, there have been two great books written about the afterlife: Dante's *The Divine Comedy* and C.S. Lewis's *The Great Divorce.* Of course, Lewis's book is funny, and shorter, so it's better: a guy gets on a commuter bus and finds himself on a tour of Heaven and Hell. Still, both writers seem to reach similar conclusions: whether we choose to take any side in the afterlife conversation, the reality is heading relentlessly toward us. We can straddle the line between belief and unbelief all we want, but in a world where we love to split the difference when it comes to spiritual matters, where inclusiveness often means reaching consensus on conceptual matters, the answer to the ultimate question of life after death leaves no room for quibbling. The position you took during your earthly life is either spot on or dead wrong.

The figures on Michelangelo's monumental fresco seem ready to tumble over me, and I figure it's time to make room for some new tourists. At the back of the Sistine Chapel, I notice two doors: a large one to the left and a smaller one to the right. I ask an English-speaking tour guide which way I should go.

"That way"—he points to the right—"is a lovely long staircase. And if you keep going, there's a shortcut to St. Peter's Basilica. That way"—he jerks his head to the left—"you snake through a dozen more galleries and stand on a two-hour line to get into the basilica."

He pauses, then adds, "It's Hell."

Additional reporting by Emily Chau.

Navigating Practical Dilemmas in Terminal Care

HELEN SORENSON, MA, RRT, FAARC

Introduction

It has been stated that one-fourth of a person's life is spent growing up and three-fourths growing old. The aging process is universal, progressive, irreversible and eventually decremental.[1] Cellular death is one marker of aging. When cells are not replaced or replicated at a rate constant enough to maintain tissue or organ function, the eventual result is death of the organism.

Although not an unexpected endpoint for any human being, death unfortunately is often fraught with turmoil and dilemmas. Patients, family, friends, caregivers and health care professionals often get caught up in conflicting opinions regarding how terminal care should be approached. For the patient, the result often is suboptimal symptom management, an increased likelihood of being subjected to painful and often futile therapy and the unnecessary prolonging of death. For the family and friends of the patient, the psychosocial consequences can be devastating. Conflict at the bedside of a dying loved one can result in long-lasting and sometimes permanent rifts in family relationships.

There are some complicated issues surrounding terminal care, such as fear, lack of trust, lack of understanding, lack of communication, and stubbornness on the part of both the physicians and family members. There are moral, ethical, economic, cultural and religious issues that must be considered. Some of the dilemmas in terminal care come up more frequently than others. This paper will discuss some of the more commonly encountered ones. And possible interventions and/or alternate ways of coming to concordance regarding end-of-life care will be presented for consideration by the reader.

Fear/Death Anxiety

A degree of fear is the natural response of most individuals to the unknown. Despite many attempts at conceptualization and rationalization, preparing for death involves coming to terms with a condition unknown in past or present experience. Fear of death has been referred to in the literature as death anxiety. Research indicates that younger people have a higher level of death anxiety than older people.[2] The reasons are not difficult to understand. Younger adults in our society are often shielded from death. Many young adults may not have had close contact with individuals dying from a terminal or chronic disease. When younger people confront death, it is most likely that of a grandparent, a parent, a sibling or a friend. Death is commonly from an acute cause. Grief is intense, with many unanswered questions and psychological ramifications.

Older adults have had more experience with death, from having lost a spouse, colleagues, a friend or relatives over the years. They undoubtedly will have experienced grief and worked through loss at some time in their life. Older adults may be more apt to express the fear of dying alone.

When facing a terminal diagnosis and impending death older adults are more likely to be concerned with "mending fences" and seeking forgiveness for perceived wrongdoing. There is a need on the part of many adults to put their affairs in order and resolve any outstanding financial matters. Some interesting research on death anxiety and religiosity conducted by Thorson & Powell[3] revealed that persons higher in religiosity were lower in death anxiety.

How can the potential dilemma caused by fear be circumscribed? Possibly allowing patients to discuss the issue may ease death anxiety, but patients may be advised not to talk about funeral arrangements, since "they're not going to die." While well intended, the statement may not be helpful. Instead of preventing the patient from discussing "depressing thoughts," encouraging frank discussions about end-of-life issues may ease death anxiety. Asking the patient to verbalize his or her fears may lead to understanding the fears and alleviate the anxiety they cause.

It is important to guard against treating dying patients as though they are no longer human. For example, asking if a person would like to talk to a minister, priest or rabbi does not impinge the religious belief of the patient—it simply allows another avenue to reduce death anxiety.

Issues of Trust

Patients who have been under the care of a personal physician for an extended period of time generally exhibit a high level of trust in the diagnosis, even when the diagnosis is that of a terminal disease. Good end-of-life care requires a measure of continuity among caregivers. The patient who has had the same physician from the onset of a serious illness to the terminal stages of the disease has a substantial advantage.[4]

Planning, family support and social services, coordinated to meet the patient's needs, can be more easily arranged if there is an atmosphere of trust and confidence.

Health care today however, has become increasingly fragmented. A physician unknown to the family and/or patient may be assigned to a case. It is difficult for very sick patients to develop new relationships and establish trust with an on-going stream of care providers.[5] When circumstances are of an immediate and critical nature, issues of trust become paramount. Lack of trust in the physician and/or the health care system can erode into a lack of confidence in a diagnosis, which often results in a conflict between the patient, the family and the health care system.

Navigating this dilemma can be challenging. Recommending that the services of a hospitalist or a palliative care team be requested may be beneficial. Patients and families who are versed in the standard of care for the specific terminal disease may be in a better position to ask questions and make suggestions. Trust is associated with honesty. Conversely, trust can be eroded by what is perceived as the incompetence of or duplicity by health care providers.

An increased, concerted effort to communicate effectively all pertinent information to a patient and family and members of the health care team caring for the patient may not instantly instill confidence, but it may forestall any further erosion of trust. It is a good feeling to think that everyone on the team is pulling in the same direction.

Issues of Communication

Communication, or lack of adequate communication, is problematic. A recent article published in *Critical Care Medicine* stated, "In intensive care settings, suboptimal communication can erode family trust and fuel so called 'futility disputes'."[6] Lack of communication does not imply wrongdoing on the part of the caregivers, nor does it imply lack of comprehension or skills in patients and families. The message is delivered, but not always in language that is readily understandable. While the message may be received, at times it is not comprehended due to the nature of the message or the emotional state of the recipient.

A few years ago, during a conversation about end-of-life care, a nurse shared with the author a situation she had encountered. The patient, an elderly female, had undergone a biopsy of a tumor. The physician, upon receiving the biopsy report, asked the nurse to accompany him to the patient's room to deliver the results. The patient was told "the results of the biopsy indicate that the tumor was not benign, so I am going to refer you to Dr. ***, an oncologist, for further treatment." The physician asked for questions from the patient and, receiving none, left the room. The patient then got on the phone, called her family and stated: "Good news, I don't have cancer." The nurse left the room and called the physician, who expressed surprise that the patient had misunderstood the message. Reluctantly, he returned to the patient's room and in simple terms told her that she did indeed have cancer and that Dr. *** was a cancer specialist who would discuss treatment options with her and her family. Did the physician, on the first visit, tell the patient she had cancer—of course. Did the patient receive the message—unfortunately, no.

Although anecdotal, the case demonstrates a situation in which there was poor communication. Had the nurse not intervened, how long would it have been before the patient was adequately apprised of her condition?

Because quality communication with patients and families is imperative, the dilemma deserves attention. Many articles have been written, discussing optimal times, situations and environments best suited for end-of-life care discussions. Unfortunately, end-of-life does not always arrive on schedule or as planned.

Because of the severity of some illnesses, intensive care units may be the environment where the futility of further care becomes apparent. Intensive care units are busy places, sometimes crowded, and replete with a variety of alarms and mechanical noises on a continual basis. About 50 percent of patients who die in a hospital are cared for in an intensive care unit within three days of their death. Over thirty percent spend at least ten days of final hospitalization in an intensive care unit.[7] This is a particularly sobering reality for patients with chronic lung disease. Many COPD patients have had serious exacerbations, have been admitted to intensive care units, and many have been on mechanical ventilation. Fortunately, the medications, therapeutic interventions, and disease management skills of physicians and therapists often can turn the exacerbation around. Unfortunately, the airway pathology may not be reversible.

How and when and with whom should communication about the gravity of a situation be handled? Ideally, it should occur prior to any crisis; realistically, when it becomes obvious that a patient is unlikely to survive. Regardless of the answer, effective communication is vitally important.

Because few intensive care unit (ICU) patients (less than 5%) are able to communicate with the health care providers caring for them at the time that withholding/withdrawing life support decisions are made,[8] there is a real need to share information with and seek input from the family.

A recent article published as a supplement to *Critical Care Medicine* reviewed the importance of talking with families about end-of-life care. Although few studies provide hard evidence on how best to initiate end-of-life discussions in an ICU environment, Curtis, et al.[9] provides a framework that could serve as a model for clinicians and families alike. The proposed components of the conference would include: preparation prior to the conference, holding the conference, and finishing the conference.[9]

Preparing in Advance of the ICU-Family Conference

It is important for the participating clinician to be informed about the disease process of the patient, including: diagnosis, prognosis, treatment options, and probably outcomes of various treatments. It is important also for the clinician to identify areas of uncertainty or inconsistencies concerning the diagnosis, prognosis, or potential treatments. Any disagreements between sub-specialists involved in the care of the patient should be resolved before the family conference. Additionally, in preparing for the family conference, it is advantageous for the clinician to have some familiarity with the attitudes of the family and the patient toward illness, life-extending therapy, and death. When possible, the determination of who will attend the conference should be done advance of the conference. The location of the conference should also be pre-determined: a quiet private setting with adequate comfortable seating is ideal. Asking all participants to turn off cell phones and pagers is appropriate and will prevent unwanted distraction. (If the patient is able to participate in the conference but is too ill to leave the ICU, then the conference should take place in the patient's room in the ICU.)

Holding the ICU Family-Conference about End-of-Life Care

Assuring that all participants are introduced and understand the reason for the conference will facilitate the process. It is also helpful to discuss conference goals and determine what the patient and his or her family understand about the prognosis. If the patient is unable to participate in the conference, it may be opportune to pose the question: "What would the patient want?" Explaining during the conference that withholding life-sustaining treatment is not withholding care is an important distinction. Another recommended approach to achieve concord in the conference is to tolerate silence. Giving the family time to absorb any information they have just received, and allowing them to formulate questions, will result in better and more goal-oriented discussions.

When families are able to communicate the fears and emotions they may have, they are better able to cope with difficult decisions.

Finishing the Conference

After the patient and/or family have been provided with the facts and have achieved an understanding of the disease and the treatment issues, the clinician should make recommendations regarding treatment options. It is a disservice, for example, to give family members the impression that they are single-handedly making the decision to "pull the plug" on a loved on. Soliciting any follow-up questions, allowing adequate time, and making sure the family knows how to reach you, should end the conference on a positive note.

Understanding Choices

Another commonly encountered dilemma in terminal care is the number of choices involved, as well as the medical terminology that sometimes mystifies the choices. Advanced directives, living wills, health care proxies, durable powers of attorney for health care; what they are, what they mean, how much weight they carry, are they honored, and does everyone who needs them have them? Not long ago during a conversation with a chaplain at a hospital, the advice shared with me—to pass on to others—was to give family members the gift of knowledge. The final gift you give them may be the most important gift of all. Let them know your wishes.

When advanced directives became available in the late 1980s, it was presumed that the document would solve all the problems and that terminal care would adhere to the patient's wishes. The Study to Understand Prognoses and Preferences for Outcomes and Risks of Treatment (SUPPORT), initiated in 1988, however, showed severe shortcomings in end-of-life care.[10]

Advanced directives, as a legal document, have not necessarily lived up to expectations. A viable option is a Durable Power of Attorney for Health Care, in which a trusted individual is designated to make health care decisions when the patient cannot.

Another option is to have advanced planning sessions with family members. If the patient and his or her family can come to consensus about terminal care in advance, and the doctor is in agreement with any decisions, unnecessary suffering probably can be avoided. (When death becomes imminent and the patient's wishes are not followed, waste no time in seeking a meeting with the hospital ethics committee.)

Adaptive Techniques

There is no "recipe" that, if followed precisely, will allow for the successful navigation of all potential dilemmas. There is no way to prepare for each eventuality that accompanies terminal illness and death. Knowledge remains the safest shield against well-meaning advice-givers. Asking questions of caregivers is the best defense against misunderstanding and mismanagement of the patient.

The University of Iowa Research Center is working on an evidence-based protocol for advanced directives, which outlines in a step-by-step fashion assessment criteria that factor in the patient's age, primary language, and mental capacity for making health care treatment decisions. The protocol also provides a check-list format for health care providers, the documentation thereof is easily accessible and in a prominent position in the patient's chart.[11]

Another alternative health care benefit being proposed is called MediCaring, which emphasizes more home-based and supportive health care and discourages hospitalization and use of aggressive treatment.[12] While not specifically aimed at solving end-of-life care issues, there may be parts of MediCaring that mesh well with terminal care of the oldest old.

Whether in a home setting, a community hospital or an intensive care unit, terminal care can result in moral, ethical, economic, religious, cultural and/or personal/family conflict. Even when death is universally accepted as a normal part of the life cycle, there will be emotional dilemmas to navigate around. Additional education and research initiatives, however, may result in increased awareness that this currently is an unsolved problem, for the patient, the family, and the health care providers. Notwithstanding, however, the medical community should continue to persevere in trying to understand patients' and families' fears and needs, the need for quality communication with questions and answers in lay vocabulary. The clinician's task is to balance communication and understanding with medical delivery.

References

1. Thorson JA. *Aging in a Changing Society,* 2000. 2nd Ed. Taylor & Francis, Philadelphia, PA.
2. Thorson JA & Powell FC. Meaning of death and intrinsic religiosity. *Journal of Clinical Psychology.* 1990;46: 379−391.
3. Thorson JA & Powell FC. Elements of death anxiety and meanings of death. *Journal of Clinical Psychology.* 1998;44: 691−701.
4. Lynn J. Serving patients who may die soon and their families. *JAMA.* 2001;285(7): 925−932.
5. Pantilat SZ, Alpers A, Wachter RM. A new doctor in the house: ethical issues in hospitalist systems. *JAMA.* 1999;282: 171−174.
6. Fins JJ & Soloman MZ. Communication in the intensive care setting: The challenge of futility disputes. *Critical Care Medicine.* 2001;29(2) Supplement.
7. Quill TE & Brody H. Physician recommendations and patient autonomy: Finding a balance between physician power and patient choice. *Ann Internal Med.* 1996;25: 763−769.
8. Prendergast TJ & Luce JM. Increasing incidence of withholding and withdrawal of life support from the critically ill. *Am J Respir Crit Care Med.* 1997;155: 15−20.
9. Curtis JR et al. The family conference as a focus to improve communication about end-of-life care in the intensive care unit: Opportunities for improvement. *Critical Care Medicine.* 2001;29(2) Supplement. PN26−N33.
10. Pioneer Programs in Palliative Care: Nine Case Studies (2000). The Robert Wood Johnson Foundation in cooperation with the Milbank Memorial Fund, New York, NY.
11. Evidence-based protocol: Advanced Directives. Iowa City, IA: University of Iowa Gerontological Nursing Interventions Research Center. 1999. Available; [http://www.guideline.gov/index.asp].
12. Lynn. J. et al. MediCaring: development and test marketing of a supportive care benefit for older people. *Journal of the American Geriatric Society.* 1999;47(9) 1058−1064.

HELEN SORENSON, MA, RRT, FAARC Assistant Professor, Department of Respiratory Care, University of Texas Health Science Center at San Antonio in San Antonio, Texas. Ms. Sorenson is also Managing Editor of "Emphysema/COPD: The Journal of Patient Centered Care."

Test-Your-Knowledge Form

We encourage you to photocopy and use this page as a tool to assess how the articles in *Annual Editions* expand on the information in your textbook. By reflecting on the articles you will gain enhanced text information. You can also access this useful form on a product's book support Web site at *http://www.mhcls.com*.

NAME:

DATE:

_____

TITLE AND NUMBER OF ARTICLE:

_____

BRIEFLY STATE THE MAIN IDEA OF THIS ARTICLE:

_____

LIST THREE IMPORTANT FACTS THAT THE AUTHOR USES TO SUPPORT THE MAIN IDEA:

_____

WHAT INFORMATION OR IDEAS DISCUSSED IN THIS ARTICLE ARE ALSO DISCUSSED IN YOUR TEXTBOOK OR OTHER READINGS THAT YOU HAVE DONE? LIST THE TEXTBOOK CHAPTERS AND PAGE NUMBERS:

_____

LIST ANY EXAMPLES OF BIAS OR FAULTY REASONING THAT YOU FOUND IN THE ARTICLE:

_____

LIST ANY NEW TERMS/CONCEPTS THAT WERE DISCUSSED IN THE ARTICLE, AND WRITE A SHORT DEFINITION:

We Want Your Advice

ANNUAL EDITIONS revisions depend on two major opinion sources: one is our Advisory Board, listed in the front of this volume, which works with us in scanning the thousands of articles published in the public press each year; the other is you—the person actually using the book. Please help us and the users of the next edition by completing the prepaid article rating form on this page and returning it to us. Thank you for your help!

ANNUAL EDITIONS: Human Development 09/10 2010 Update

ARTICLE RATING FORM

Here is an opportunity for you to have direct input into the next revision of this volume.
We would like you to rate each of the articles listed below, using the following scale:

1. **Excellent: should definitely be retained**
2. **Above average: should probably be retained**
3. **Below average: should probably be deleted**
4. **Poor: should definitely be deleted**

Your ratings will play a vital part in the next revision.
Please mail this prepaid form to us as soon as possible.
Thanks for your help!

RATING	ARTICLE	RATING	ARTICLE
	1. The Identity Dance		19. The Blank Slate
	2. The Power to Divide		20. Parents Behaving Badly
	3. The Mystery of Fetal Life: Secrets of the Womb		21. Where Personality Goes Awry
	4. Fat, Carbs, and the Science of Conception		22. Girls Gone Bad?
	5. The Hunt for Golden Eggs		23. Disrespecting Childhood
	6. The Curious Lives of Surrogates		24. Parents or Pop Culture? Children's Heroes and Role Models
	7. HHS Toned Down Breast-Feeding Ads: Formula Industry Urged Softer Campaign		25. A Peaceful Adolescence
	8. Reading Your Baby's Mind		26. Homeroom Zombies
	9. 20 Ways to Boost Your Baby's Brain Power		27. Jail Time Is Learning Time
	10. Long-Term Studies of Preschool: Lasting Benefits Far Outweigh Costs		28. How Spirit Blooms
	11. Accountability Comes to Preschool: Can We Make It Work for Young Children?		29. What Addicts Need
	12. Informing the ADHD Debate		30. Getting Back on Track
	13. Why We Need "The Year of Languages"		31. Men & Depression: Facing Darkness
	14. The New First Grade: Too Much Too Soon?		32. Emotions and the Brain: Laughter
	15. Ten Big Effects of the No Child Left Behind Act on Public Schools		33. 50 Reasons to Love Being 50+
	16. The Power of Teaching Students Using Strengths		34. The Myth of the Midlife Crisis
	17. A "Perfect" Case Study: Perfectionism in Academically Talented Fourth Graders		35. The Wonder of Work
			36. Second Time Around
	18. You and Your Quirky Kid		37. Secrets of the Centenarians
			38. Lost and Found
			39. Life after Death
			40. Navigating Practical Dilemmas in Terminal Care

BUSINESS REPLY MAIL
FIRST CLASS MAIL PERMIT NO. 551 DUBUQUE IA

POSTAGE WILL BE PAID BY ADDRESSEE

McGraw-Hill Contemporary Learning Series
501 BELL STREET
DUBUQUE, IA 52001

ABOUT YOU

Name _____   Date _____

Are you a teacher? ☐ A student? ☐
Your school's name
_____

Department
_____

Address _____ City _____ State _____ Zip _____

School telephone # _____

YOUR COMMENTS ARE IMPORTANT TO US!

Please fill in the following information:
For which course did you use this book?
_____

Did you use a text with this ANNUAL EDITION? ☐ yes ☐ no
What was the title of the text?
_____

What are your general reactions to the Annual Editions concept?
_____

Have you read any pertinent articles recently that you think should be included in the next edition? Explain.
_____

Are there any articles that you feel should be replaced in the next edition? Why?
_____

Are there any World Wide Web sites that you feel should be included in the next edition? Please annotate.
_____

May we contact you for editorial input? ☐ yes ☐ no
May we quote your comments? ☐ yes ☐ no